Europe's Backyard War

Also by Mark Almond

Retreat to Moscow: Gorbachev and the East European Revolution
The Rise and Fall of Nicolae and Elena Ceauşescu

£2.50

Yugoslav Republics, 1991

EUROPE'S BACKYARD WAR

The War in the Balkans

MARK ALMOND

The proposition 'Bosnia is Europe's backyard' is more than stupid – it stinks of neo-imperialist arrogance.

Dr Radovan Karadžić

HEINEMANN : LONDON

First published in Great Britain 1994
by William Heinemann Ltd
an imprint of Reed Consumer Books Ltd
Michelin House, 81 Fulham Road, London SW3 6RB
and Auckland, Melbourne and Singapore

A CIP catalogue record for this book
is available at the British Library
ISBN 0 434 00003 5 (hardback)
ISBN 0 434 00105 8 (paperback)

Typeset by Intype, London
Printed in Great Britain by
Clays Ltd, St. Ives PLC

For Mary Walsh

Contents

Part Four: Grim Futures – Some Conclusions

Introduction

> Over there, beyond our frontiers, three or four hundred thousand individuals hanged, impaled or with their throats cut, hardly count.
>
> Metternich[1]

This is a book by an Englishman about a Balkan disaster whose shadow hangs over the rest of Europe and indeed the world. It is a study of criminal folly and blind insensitivity to human suffering, and not just in what was Yugoslavia.[2] What follows is an account of the attitudes of mind which made the destruction of Yugoslavia, in the most savage way, possible. It is a grim story of ambition, pomposity, dishonesty and blind ruthlessness, and not only on the part of people in Yugoslavia.

Anyone daring to step into the disputed minefield of Yugoslav history is likely to face sniping from all sides. Academics in the West show as much fierce proprietorial interest in their subject as any Serb or Croat in his own history. But this book will not only tread on Balkan toes. It is a history of the life and death of Yugoslavia, but it is also an account of the outside world's role in the catastrophe which has gathered pace before our eyes since midsummer 1991. English-speaking readers may wish to know why Yugoslavia descended into the inferno, but self-interest will also dictate that people with no Balkan concerns will want to know what, if any, significance this most savage war after the Cold War holds for them and their peace and security. Any account of the international involvement in the death throes of Yugoslavia and of so many of its people is bound to offend the foreign ministers and diplomats who have laboured, postured and washed their hands of the problem in regular succession.

The 'international community' – that prolix world of organisations hidden behind initials and acronyms – has never before involved itself so much in a conflict with so little result. Some attribute this to the inflexibility of ancient Balkan feuds and exculpate Western statesmen from the consequences of their naive and well-intentioned forays into the region. No one would deny that the basic responsibility for the conflict and crimes which have taken place lies with people (not 'The People') in Yugoslavia, but the significance of the war cannot be understood unless it is no longer treated as simply a noisy and embarrassing squabble in Europe's backyard.

Far from being an isolated throw-back to some primeval state of human conflict – which people struggling to survive in Bosnia may be forgiven for seeing their terrible state of affairs as – the war in Yugoslavia looks set to be a model of the future in many parts of the world, especially in the post-Soviet world. Counsels of despair encourage the West to wash its hands of the Balkan problem and let the ancient fire burn itself out. To think that the problem will go away of its own accord will turn out to be as fatal a mistake for the West as the illusion that in its moment of triumph over Marxism, the European Community or the West as a whole needed only to speak the word of peace in order to bring to heel the unruly Balkan tribes.

Far from marking the 'end of history', the fall of communist regimes has left a poisonous legacy concocted out of a bitter history which has much more in common from Belgrade to Beijing than many narrow specialists and liberal wishful thinkers were prepared to contemplate. Yugoslavia was in many ways the first communist state to break with the Stalinist system. Instead of being peculiarly backward, Yugoslavia under Tito and afterwards was in many ways the most advanced communist country. It had loosened the shackles of control much more, but still it could not avoid implosion. The terrible prospect is that Yugoslavia may yet prove more of a model than an aberration.

The West is unprepared to deal either with the consequences of the Yugoslav debacle or to learn the lessons. In fact, so far it seems anxious to learn from its mistakes in the run-up to war in 1991 only in order to repeat them on a grander scale in the former Soviet Union. The Yugoslav war certainly offers a vision of cataclysm but it could also offer a warning of catastrophe on an apocalyptic scale.

Any history of the Balkans and foreign involvement in the politics of the peninsula cannot avoid depressing the reader. Of course, the paradox is that Balkan history and the crises which the region has produced for the Great Powers since the early nineteenth century are amongst the most fascinating events of modern history. The tragedy has been that the few promising developments have always been snuffed out early in life, usually brutally. Balkan history is rarely dull. It is also ridden with controversy. Sometimes the issues at dispute have been academic, but often they have roused debate among a much wider public.

More than one hundred years ago, British society was split about how to respond to the moral and political dilemma posed by the great revolts against Turkish rule, first in Bosnia and then Bulgaria, and the atrocities with which the Turkish regime tried to master the situation. The historian Freeman, who actively supported Gladstone's famous return to politics on the back of the Bulgarian issue in 1876, remarked that the reaction to the crisis cut across normal party lines: 'I never remember anything equal to the bitterness already dividing family and friends on this question.'[3] British political life was divided between jingoist supporters of the Ottoman Empire as a bulwark of stability and a block to Russian influence, and proponents of the right to self-determination and sceptics of the viability of Turkey as a guarantor of anything, least of all stability, in view of the discontent among her subjects.

The collapse of the Yugoslav state in 1991 and the bloody war which erupted particularly in Bosnia in 1992 raised similar questions and with the re-emergence of Margaret Thatcher on the political stage as an advocate of military assistance to the Bosnian government the situation took on uncanny echoes of Gladstone's comeback. A fundamental difference was, however, that in the 1990s it was the Muslims who were seen as the chief victims and the object of interventionist sympathy rather than the Orthodox Christian Serbs. Furthermore, instead of Britain being an imperial power ruling over millions of Muslims in India and elsewhere, by the 1990s she had become a multi-ethnic offshore island with a significant domestic Muslim population.

In the battle for public sympathy over Bosnia, the question of how to regard British Muslims played a key part. Serbophiles invariably inveighed against the dangers of Islamic fundamentalism from Sarajevo to Salford. Interventionists argued that British indifference to the plight of Muslims in Bosnia could only worsen relations with the Muslim minority at home.

Britain was not the only European country with historic ties both to Yugoslavia and to the Islamic world. France, like Britain, had a large immigrant Muslim population inherited from her North African empire. Domestic French politics were also riven by the debate over integration, assimilation or exclusion. French Muslims were also exposed to the powerful traditional Serbophile lobby in France.

Whereas Britain's deep involvement with Yugoslavia went back to the Second World War and Churchill's option for Tito, France had enjoyed a near cultural hegemony over Serbia for generations before that. Disliking her German-speaking neighbours and rivals, the Habsburgs, to the north, and anxious to escape the legacy of centuries of Ottoman rule, Serbs looked to France as a cultural mentor as well as a political ally. France saw Serbia as a useful counterweight in the south-east of the continent to its powerful eastern neighbour, Germany. Brotherhood-in-arms during the First World War confirmed the relationship. Paris still records its debt of honour to a loyal ally in its 'avenue Pierre-Ier-de-Serbie', while Lyons rejoices in a 'quai de Serbie' and visitors to Cannes can promenade along the 'rue des Serbes'. Belgrade returns the compliment with its 'Francuska'.[4]

Despite self-conscious efforts at Franco-German rapprochement ever since the Second World War, a visceral suspicion of German ambitions haunts France's elite. President Mitterrand's instinctive response to the Serb-Croat war showed how his long memory for France's old allies and past enemies had not been dimmed by his famous holding of hands with Chancellor Kohl at Verdun in 1984. The French president told German newspaper readers in November 1991, as Vukovar was in its death throes, 'Croatia belonged to the Nazi bloc, not Serbia.'[5] (François Mitterrand delicately overlooked the fact that the Croatian president, Franjo Tudjman, never collaborated with the Ustasha regime, instead fighting against it and the Axis powers in the Partisan army, whereas Mitterrand rose rapidly in the civil service of Vichy France before 1943, even receiving a medal from Pétain's regime for his distinguished service, before changing sides when Allied victory was evident to everyone – even future leaders of the Socialist International.)

The European Community remains bedevilled by national rivalries despite all the talk of common policies and a new united identity. The breakdown of Yugoslavia brought out deep-seated Anglo-French suspicions of Germany which were partly shared and partly played on by the Serbian regime. Just as British and French politicians revealed that in their heart of hearts they could not see Germany as anything other than in essence a domineering and aggressive nation, so they remained trapped with an inherited vision of 'plucky little Serbia', the ancient ally against the *Boche*.

Germany's role in the war has been so lambasted by Serb propagandists anxious to divert responsibility from Belgrade, as well as by her partners in the EC determined to shift any blame for the worst crisis in Europe's history since 1945 from their own shoulders, that myth has replaced facts and often even the chronology of events has been wilfully distorted. Certainly, the revelation of anti-German feeling within the EC and also in the United States cannot but have profound implications for the European Community's viability.

It may yet be that just as the assassination in Sarajevo in June 1914 precipitated the war which led to the collapse of the great European Empires – Austria-Hungary, Russia and Germany – so the antagonisms revealed by the Yugoslav war will set in train the decay of the European Community. Already it has revealed a deep division between the Euro-idealists who saw in the Community a mechanism for securing peace and prosperity throughout the continent of Europe, including in its east, and the professional political and bureaucratic elite of the Community who wanted nothing to do with change in the communist countries in the east. In fact, stability and the preservation of the old order in Yugoslavia as elsewhere in the Soviet bloc were the watchwords of the Eurocrats.

If the proponents of European unification were divided in their reaction to the Bosnian crisis, so also were its opponents. Some saw the breakdown of the Yugoslav multinational federation as evidence of the inevitable failure of the project of European political and economic union according to the arbitrary timetable laid down in the Maastricht Treaty. But others simply welcomed the assertion of national sovereignty for its own sake. For the latter, the more the Serbian regime was reproved for not conforming to the standards set by the European Community, the more they approved of it.

Beyond Europe, the two superpowers were involved in the crisis with varying degrees of intensity. The Soviet Union went through its own version of the collapse of a multi-ethnic communist state and at times seemed to leave a residue of chaos which meant that the Kremlin was no longer the headquarters of a superpower. However, as the Yugoslav war progressed the Russian inheritor of the Soviet Union's international rights returned to the international stage as an actor in its own right. Indeed by the midsummer of 1993, Russia was able to act as an arbiter in the disagreements between the USA and its European allies over how to react to the ever-worsening situation in Bosnia.

The old Soviet Union contained all of the ingredients which had made Yugoslavia so explosive. A decaying communist economic and social system intertwined with a babel of linguistic groups. The scattering of 26 million Russians among the other republics of the USSR mirrored the Serb diaspora in Croatia and Bosnia-Hercegovina. The abandonment of communism as a social ideal did not mean in Russia any more than in Serbia that the communists disappeared like the wicked witches of a fairy story. A host of former Party members still lived by their old connections imbued with the Leninist way of doing things even as they had abandoned Lenin's visionary end which had justified the means for so many. This more than the much-invoked Pan-Slavism, 'ancient friendship', or common Orthodox faith, made for a community of interest between ex-*apparatchiks* in former Yugoslavia and the post-Soviet bloc.

Short-sightedness and wishful thinking was by no means monopolised by the West Europeans when confronted by the collapse of Yugoslavia. American policy-makers too could neither understand why little peoples should wish to break out of the Yugoslav strait-jacket nor could they accept the bad example set by the breakdown of a reformed communist state like Yugoslavia for the USSR itself. Modern Metternichs were to be found in European capitals as well as Washington but the power of the United States meant that President Bush's antagonism to what Metternich called the 'dédoublement des états' was most influential. Of course, in the age of television pictures of atrocities, no Western politician could speak in public with the cold-hearted indifference which Metternich used in his secret diplomatic correspondence.[6] Later on, the Americans' continuing Vietnam syndrome (embodied in Bill Clinton) left the self-proclaimed sole surviving superpower impotent in the face of what its government repeatedly denounced as the unacceptable.

Already a host of myths surround the life and death of Yugoslavia and obscure the question of responsibility for its savage end. Understanding the sources of the catastrophe should alert us to other grim warning-lights if the fate of Bosnia is not to be repeated. Even if a sense of foreboding is the result of studying the causes and consequences of Europe's backyard war, it is a better way to face the future than to turn away from the recent horrors and the farcical policy errors in the confident misplaced expectation that it is a one-off disaster.

PART ONE

The Outbreak of War, 1991

The beginning of fighting in Yugoslavia at the end of June 1991 seemed to take the outside world by surprise. The implosion of the Yugoslav Federation challenged the geopolitical assumptions of the day, not least in the West which was just coming to terms with its apparent victory in the Cold War and was still basking in the afterglow of its unexpectedly easy triumph over Iraq in the Gulf War. What was taken for a storm in a Balkan teacup soon revealed deep flaws in the West's ability to master the real challenges of the post-Cold War world.

1

Outbreak of War

> On all sides nations and *would-be nations* are announcing their right to form a state. *Rotted-corpses* are rising from centuries-old graves, filled with new vitality, and '*unhistoric peoples*', who have never yet formed an independent state, feel a powerful urge to establish a state.
>
> Rosa Luxemburg (1918)[1]

There are few more efficacious ways of inciting hatred of the living than to invoke the unquiet graves of the murdered. The ghosts of Yugoslavia's violent past responded all too readily to the call of present political necessity as the 1980s progressed. Every ethnic and linguistic group in the country still mourned countless dead denied a proper funeral and often resting in unknown mass graves. During the Second World War and immediately afterwards, Yugoslavia witnessed some of the most atrocious war crimes of that boundlessly brutal war. The tragic legacy of the murders committed then was that the vast bulk of the victims were killed not by the German or Italian invaders but by one group of their fellow Yugoslavs or another. Forty years on and more, the ghosts of Yugoslavia's killing fields were reawakened and cried out for vengeance. There are many of the living only too happy to perform the ritual of revenge.

Under the long rule of Tito after 1945, an enormous effort went into suppressing the ghosts of the recent past.[2] Rather than exorcising the accumulated guilt and resentment, the heavy hand of censorship simply drove the sentiments of frustrated vendetta underground. So long as Tito lived, and even for a while afterwards, the necessary myth that the Second World War had been a war of liberation against the fascist invader and his handful of local lackeys was kept alive. Just as Tito himself survived for so long on the most expensive life-support systems, so with the full authority of his state behind the insistence on the official heroic version of Yugoslavia's wartime history, it survived in sclerotic form into the 1980s. Throughout the territory of the Federated Socialist Republic of Yugoslavia, concrete monuments, lifeless as the heroes whom they commemorate, were erected across every type of landscape in that most varied of European countries in order to provide each national group with its own shrine to its local partisan martyrs. Sometimes these grotesque sites honoured genuine heroes in their own monolithic spiritless way. In other places, they immortalised imaginary triumphs or fictional atrocities. But everywhere they insisted on the unity of the Yugoslav peoples in their struggle.

The exhumation of the war dead marked the passing of the last Titoite tabu. As early as the mid–1950s, the literary prophet of a Greater Serbia, Dobrica Ćosić, had written 'our cemeteries are young.'[3] At the time it could be taken (by the censor at any rate) as a reference to the general carnage during the Second World War, but as time passed Ćosić's specific Serbian concern became more and more clear. He was the intellectual father of the exhumationists in Serbia. By 1990, it seemed that mass graves were being dug up everywhere in Slovenia, Croatia and Bosnia-Hercegovina. A grisly competition arose between the different populations to find their victims of wartime and postwar violence and to rebury them with as much ceremony and pathos as possible.

These were not ceremonies of atonement or reconciliation. Instead they conjured up the spirits of dormant hatreds afresh. Again and again, the advocates of a 'Greater Serbia' were to insist that Serb territory extended to wherever a Serb lay buried. Šešelj, one of the leading 'Greater Serbs' who appeared on the political scene in the late 1980s, argued that Serbia's territory covered the territory from the 'sanctuaries of the east to the tombs in the west', meaning from the disputed province of Kosovo to the scenes of Croat fascist crimes during the Second World War. This sort of language was deliberately intended to incite Serb and Croat alike.

The dead-weight in the mass graves was revitalised as an uncanny instrument in the current political struggle between

Serb and Croat. The most notorious of the concentration camps run by the Ustasha in the so-called 'Independent State of Croatia' was at Jasenovac. Under Tito the site was the centre of a cult of Yugoslav remembrance, but by 1990 Serb propagandists were inclined to claim its horrors for themselves alone. In the spooky language of the invocation of the Serb victims of fascism, Jasenovac's mass graves became 'the largest underground Serb city'. An initiative was launched to ask the UN to grant it 'extraterritorial status'![4]

Once the fighting began between Serbs and Croats, the war dead from fifty years earlier were explicitly conjured up to incite vengeance. Serb participants from throughout Yugoslavia were bussed in to the sacred sites to be whipped up into a frenzy of blood feud. In August 1991, a Serbian academic from Sarajevo told the congregation at a reburial of 144 victims of the Ustasha in the Hercegovinan village of Prebilovići, 'Today, above the open tombs, we do not hide the desire for revenge in our hearts.' This vengeance was of course to be taken usually on people born long after the massacre which justified it so it was necessary to show that the contemporary Croats were as fascistic as the Ustasha had been half a century earlier, and necessary too to tar all Croats with the same brush. As part of the diabolisation of the contemporary Croats, parts of the Serb media carried stories about current desecrations of the last resting place of the victims of Jasenovac. According to *Duga* in August 1991, it was possible in Zagreb to buy lamps made out of the skulls of the victims of genocide at Jasenovac. They cost between 100 and 300 Deutschmarks.[5]

It was not only victims of the Second World War who found fresh resting places at ceremonies presided over by Orthodox clergy and approved of by the Serbian authorities a decade after Tito's death. The revivalists reached far back into Serbian history. In 1989, they dug up the purported bones of Tsar Lazar who had gone down to gallant defeat and death at the hands of the invading Turks six centuries earlier on the Blackbird Field at Kosovo on 28 June 1389. In an earnest parody of a medieval cult, Lazar's bones were carried around Serbia to summon up the true spirit of Serbdom before being reburied. It was a pageant involving religious fervour and the sinister grotesque in unique combination.[6]

The Serbs were not alone in discovering their dead. However, even if their dead had not died supporting Tito's Partisans, their cult did not pose a direct threat to the communists because they had after all been slaughtered by the enemies of Tito. Much more problematical was the public evocation of the victims of Tito.

If the name of the camp at Jasenovac came to symbolise the 'unique Golgotha of the Serbian people' so the little southern Austrian town of Bleiburg conjured up Tito's revolutionary revenge after the defeat of the Nazis and their allies. A terrible numbers game developed in the late 1980s as Serb, Croat and Slovene estimated their own war dead, sometimes adding noughts to their own casualties while liberally subtracting from the 'other side's' losses.[7]

Serb propagandists seemed to see no inconsistency in celebrating both dead Serb partisans and the supporters of Tito's rival in the resistance, the Chetniks of Draza Mihailović. On the whole Croats and Slovenes, and later Bosnian Muslims, counted those who had died at the hands of the Partisans, and, in the case of Croats and Muslims, the victims of the Serb nationalist Chetniks. Whereas many of the Serb dead had had some official status as victims of the Nazi invader, most of the non-Serbs had been left in limbo because Tito and his historians preferred not to discuss the massacres at the start of his reign. Only after Tito's death did the skeletons escape from the locked cupboard of official memory.

At the end of the war, scores of thousands of the defeated fled as Tito's armies advanced. They were joined by many who had done nothing to support the Occupation but who feared that their social status or religious convictions would make them targets for persecution by the victorious communist forces. Along with a motley band of other collaborators with the Nazis from all over Eastern Europe and the Soviet Union who had ended up in April/May 1945 in Slovenia and Croatia, they fled across the Alps into British-occupied Austria. They all shared the illusion that the capitalist British would not return them to the communist Tito's tender mercies.

As matters turned out, only the big fish of the collaboration, including Ante Pavelić, the puppet dictator of Croatia, were right to entrust their fate to the British Army. Whereas war criminals like Pavelić were allowed to slip away to safety in Latin America with the aid of British and US intelligence, the bulk of his loyalists along with the flotsam and jetsam of displaced Yugoslav persons were returned to Yugoslavia and to death. Some were shot, others thrown into pits and ravines followed by dynamite. The rest were sent on death marches across the length of liberated Yugoslavia.[8]

In 1990, in Slovenia the remains of the Bleiburg massacre were brought to light. Such reawakening of the wartime ghosts was partly spontaneous. For the first time people felt free to discuss the events of 1941–46 in public forums. Western books which did not take the official Titoite line began to be translated and officially published. However, it also played into the hands of the extremists. Nothing could serve Slobodan Milošević's core purpose of cementing his power-base in Serbia more than apparently objective evidence, particularly as reported and glossed by his *apparatchiks* on Belgrade television or in the Serbian press.

Army officers, like JNA chief of staff Blagoje Adzić, or the defence minister, Veljko Kadijević, had lost family members during the war and their personal tragedy was united with the ideological commitment to the myth of the partisan war. Any revelation that the crimes had not all been on the fascist side was an intolerable affront to such men's self-esteem. Worse still it threatened the myth which legitimised their status and that of the institution which was their life, the JNA.

This exhumation of the dead whose spirits cried out for vengeance was the necessary prelude to the savage war which broke out in 1991, and spread across Yugoslavia. But it was not the cause of the war. Other countries have faced the trauma of public discussion and allegations about their wartime past without renewing the civil war between collaborators and resisters. The renewal and evocation of wartime passions was made necessary by the political crisis of communism in Yugoslavia and the search for a new basis of legitimacy for power – especially by the leaders of the Serbian Communists, whose seat was in the federal capital, Belgrade.

Everyone has their own starting date for the war in Yugoslavia. Most Westerners put the opening shots at the end of June 1991. Others who ignored the growing conflict cannot remember any fighting before Germany's recognition of Slovenia and Croatia in December 1991. Most Yugoslavs date the start of the war earlier, often much earlier. Propagandists might like to see it as round two of a Serb-Croat war begun in 1941, or even earlier, but that is to commit the classic historian's mistake of seeking long-term roots for profound and far-reaching crises.

Since June 1991 everyone has become familiar with television graphics explaining that the conflict's roots go back as far as AD 395 when the death of Theodosius divided the Roman Empire along the River Drina which became the rough boundary between Croat and Serb in more modern times. Of course, the whole past leads to the present, but the search for causes into a murky past leads into an infinite regress and confuses the claims of participants in events about what motivates their behaviour with what actually leads them to act as they do. A knowledge of what politicians and their acolytes claim about history is essential but their histories should not be taken seriously as guides to the past. History in Yugoslavia remained as much a political weapon after de-Titoisation began as it had been under the Marshal: it was just that the sharp edge was turned against new targets.

The re-emergence of nationalism came swiftly after Tito's death, but it was not Serb or Croat nationalism which first threatened the tranquillity of Tito's heirs. Discontent among the poverty-stricken Albanian majority in the autonomous province of Kosovo was the first national challenge to Tito's legacy. At first it rallied the other republics to the centre. Each local communist elite was afraid of the dangerous influence of nationalism, since even though they might rejoice in impeccable Serb or Croat or Macedonian ancestry, their support among their own people had not yet been tested.[9]

Martial law and considerable brutality failed to quell the discontent in Kosovo and the province's plight worsened as it became poorer and poorer compared with the north-western republics. The log-jam between heavy-handed federalism and recalcitrant Albanian nationalism was broken not by concessions from the centre nor by a collapse of Albanian discontent. Instead, it was the emergence onto the political scene of Slobodan Milošević which shattered the stand-off in Kosovo and soon undermined the viability of the whole federal structure of Yugoslavia.[10]

The key date in the death of Yugoslavia was 25 April 1987. Just as the West was accustoming itself to the idea that glasnost in Gorbachev's Soviet Union might be for real (and before it began to recognise that nothing could prevent real liberalisation leading to the collapse of the USSR), a contrasting pattern of development got under way in the communist state most analogous to the Soviet Union. Although for a while it was fashionable to see the architect of this decisive shift in Yugoslavia as the local Gorbachev, soon enough it was apparent that Slobodan Milošević had his own agenda for reform.

For Yugoslavs the scene that late April day has been immortalised. It was caught on video, but its myth remains more vivid than the actual pictures. The events which changed the whole atmosphere of Yugoslav politics took place at Kosovo Polje, a suburb of Priština, the capital of Kosovo but also the scene of the Serbs' key historical event, the mythicised Battle of Kosovo in 1389. Any event in Kosovo is abnormal because it is fitted into the legend of the struggle for Serbia's soul which is bound up with the Blackbird Field.

Into this sacred territory came the new Serb Party boss, Milošević, who was paying a working visit of the standard communist kind to his Albanian comrade in Kosovo. A decade of frustration, fear and resentment among the local Serbs, an ever-dwindling minority, welled up. Something – or someone – told them that Milošević would listen to their complaints sympathetically. The local police thought differently and tried to hold the crowd back. The cry went up, 'They're beating us.' An elderly man managed to push through to Milošević to put his petition direct to the boss. Milošević appeared angry at the allegations. He stopped the police action before uttering his famous declaration, 'No one has the right to beat you.' For the first time, a communist leader had sided with the people against the authorities. It was a dramatic moment. Perhaps it was a genuine reaction to the situation, but nothing in Milošević's life suggests a tendency to impulsive behaviour, least of all in politics. Certainly, afterwards Milošević showed that having played the populist card he intended to use it as his trump in the future.

What Milošević learnt was that he had the gift of communication. Unlike other communists (and many local ex-communists for that matter), Milošević could speak in direct and simple terms. He possessed no gift for oratory or even demagogy in the traditional manner, but he knew how to use evocative homespun language to excite an audience and set its nationalist instincts on fire. This gift for arousing popular emotions among Serbs meant that he could use the mass meeting as a key weapon in his struggle with his rivals in the League of Communists. He was the first communist leader who was not afraid of the expression of popular opinion – provided the ground had been suitably prepared. Unlike his rivals Milošević did not rely simply on the factional politics of the Central Committee's smoke-filled rooms – though he was a master of manoeuvre there too. His opponents lacked the charismatic appeal and the self-confidence to challenge Milošević on the streets. They had been used to the politics of musical chairs and rotating chairmanships not passionate politics in the raw. As elsewhere in the waning communist world, the reform communists, the closet social democrats, turned out to have no roots among the people and no way of stimulating their growth. They were chiefs without Indians and no rivals for Milošević when he put on his war-paint.[11]

Milošević unleashed what became in effect a Serbian version of Mao's Cultural Revolution. Although lacking the scenes of massive crowd hysteria which Mao encouraged in China in the late 1960s, Milošević indulged in a similar mixture of socialist renewal and xenophobia. Like Mao, Milošević directed the populist fury at his comrades in the party leadership who stood in the way of his desire for absolute personal power. Unlike the Great Helmsman, he directed the xenophobia inwards at domestic minorities rather than externally against foreign enemies. (However, like Mao, Milošević used the cover of nationalist frenzy at home to hide his pursuit of good relations with both the Soviet bloc and the NATO states, which served him well after June 1991.)

Officially, Milošević's supporters were campaigning against 'stagnation' – the same slogan as Gorbachev was using to promote perestroika in the USSR at the time. In practice, the sinister term 'differentiation' meant purging Milošević's rivals in the Serbian Party elite, especially those who resisted his hard line towards the Albanians in Kosovo. By October 1987 Milošević and his allies were strong enough to move against Dragisa Pavlović, the president of the Belgrade Party Committee, and then against Pavlović's patron, the Prime Minister of Serbia himself, Ivan Stambolić, who had been Milošević's own patron.[12] Newspaper editors and journalists who had defied the new nationalist line of the Serbian Party were equally 'differentiated' and in a triumph of cynicism accused of an 'opportunistic' approach to politics!

Of course, Milošević did not rely on popularity alone or even primarily. He was not the passive recipient of popular praise or the responsive promoter of Serb desires. He deliberately set about stimulating Serbian nationalism, and not only inside Serbia proper and her two less and less autonomous provinces. Using his close contacts with Serbs in the secret police and military intelligence, Milošević set about fostering trouble in the other republics, especially the two most vulnerable ones, Croatia and Bosnia-Hercegovina.

However fertile the soil of Serbian nationalism may have been in the Krajina and Bosnia, the conflagrations which erupted there in the 1990s would not have occurred without the diligent mischief-making of Belgrade. Money, weapons and personnel were already arriving in these republics in the late 1980s. Long before anyone in the West could imagine dealing with independent republics in Yugoslavia and while Western governments were very publicly backing the integrity of the Soviet Union, Milošević's agents were laying the fuse-trails which would ignite the explosion. Some of their activities came to light in Bosnia as early as October 1989, when the government in Sarajevo was still under loyal LYC control. But their loyalty was not sufficient: it was more than doubtful that they could control the reform process and keep it orientated towards a Slobo-dominated Belgrade. On the contrary, the Bosnian LYC was discredited by its loyalty. For Milošević his comrades in Sarajevo were expendable, particularly as their loss of power would help to foster local Serbian fears of Croat and Muslim domination and play into his hands.[13]

The murky role of the KOS is still impossible to disentangle but it is clear that the Yugoslav security services kept close tabs on society like their counterparts elsewhere in the communist world. In addition to its regular agents, the Yugoslav internal security service could call on the assistance of a large number of informers. Judging from experience elsewhere in Eastern Europe, many of these informers would have been people who had fallen foul of the Titoite state for genuine dissident activities. Once in custody they could be worked over, intimidated or bribed to serve the security service. Life in any Yugoslav prison was not easy and even in the late 1980s few people can have anticipated that the system would collapse. If signing an agreement to inform might reduce a sentence or even lead to the dropping of charges, many people who had fallen into the clutches of the security police for their sincerely held opinions or dissident activities gave in to the temptation to cooperate.

However, cooperation between an ex-dissident informer and the security service was not just a one-way traffic. Nationalist emotions had often led an individual into falling foul of the Titoite state, but many of its servants privately shared some of the prejudices of its critics. Despite the fall in 1966 of its sinister Serb boss for twenty years, Alexander Ranković, the Yugoslav security community remained disproportionately Serb at all ranks below the top levels. Many of the everyday secret policemen had little love for their Croat or Muslim colleagues or neighbours. There was a symbiosis between them and some of their dissident targets. In a way, these sorts of Serb secret policemen were just waiting for a Milošević to come along and legitimise their everyday prejudices. Their commitment to communism even in its Titoite variant was much weaker than their deep-seated national affiliation and their desire to be led by a real boss once more.

Although corruption had been as endemic in Tito's state as in any communist country, with the Marshal leading the way in matters of greed as in everything else, it was only in August 1987 that Yugoslavs suddenly had to learn the vocabulary of a capitalist-style financial scandal. The crash of the Bosnian-based concern Agrokomerc was a key symptom of the decay of the would-be reformed communist system in Yugoslavia. Since then throughout the ex-communist world people have become used to the double phenomenon of so-called *nomenklatura* privatisation followed by fraud. All over the Soviet bloc and in China, too, economic reform has produced fabulous financial fantasies. Suddenly, *apparatchiks* become millionaires and equally rapidly they are exposed as fraudsters whose schemes depended for their success less on their entrepreneurial skills than on their connections with the still powerful Party leaders and economic managers.

The key figure in the scandal was a Bihać 'businessman' of Muslim nationality, Fikret Abdić. Even if he had not popped up five years later to play a prominent role in the death throes of the independent Bosnian state, Abdić, the director of Agrokomerc, would have deserved more than a footnote in any study of the demise of communism and the survival of the ex-communist elite in the new order. He was the first of an army of post-communist 'bizinesmen' who have plundered the remaining assets of ex-communist countries.

Abdić's particular scam depended upon the complacency and collusion of the banks in Yugoslavia, where bankers proved as gullible and corruptible as any in the West. Fikret Abdić's scheme was to issue innumerable promissory notes to the value of more than US$400 million without any real security but backed by the local Party barons. In this way, he turned Agrokomerc from a chicken farm into a multi-faceted enterprise employing more than 13,000 people around Velika Kladusa. But the phenomenal growth of Agrokomerc was purchased on unsustainable credit rather than a genuine supplying of the market. This was not least because of money siphoned off into the pockets of the host of official and private enterprise parasites who took their cut. In effect, Fikret Abdić was a Balkan Robert Maxwell (although the influence of Agrokomerc in north-western Bosnia was more like the dominant role of Polly Peck in Northern Cyprus).

When the hollow nature of the Agrokomerc empire was discovered in 1987, suddenly thousands of employees found themselves unpaid. The local banks had empty vaults. The local economy was plunged into ruins. The animals and poultry which provided the only collateral for the enterprise were left to starve or save themselves by cannibalism. Eventually the JNA had to step in and plough the grisly remains into mass graves. The collapse of Agrokomerc was a terrible premonition of the end of Yugoslavia.

Fikret Abdić complained that he was the victim of a plot. Surprisingly, a lot of locals in Bihać province accepted his version of events – though the courts did not. However, he was able to transform himself from post-communist entrepreneur into a victim of political persecution with remarkable ease. Fikret Abdić was to come to prominence again in 1993 when his preferred company name, Agrokomerc, was associated by the Austrian authorities with allegations of a massive fraud with humanitarian aid. Fikret Abdić embodied the maxim: you can't keep a bad man down.

A contemporary observer remarked, 'Fikret Abdić made only one mistake: he overreached himself. Otherwise, Fikret's innovation is not new in the Yugoslav economy as a whole: whenever someone issues a promissory note, the officials of the commune, the republic or the Federation . . . come to his aid and cover the losses.' The problem was not the nature but the scale of the fraud. It was simply too large for the Yugoslav authorities to hush up. No central bank lifeboat could rescue Agrokomerc. 'Abdić [had] inscribed the whole of Yugoslavia on his promissory note. That Agrokomerc was a motley lie was known by all. Those who did not know did not wish to know.'[14]

The scandal seriously undermined the Bosnian Party and helped to set in train the collapse of its authority there. It also served Milošević's purposes because it contributed to the fall of the Federal Premier, Mikulić, and his replacement by a less authoritative figure, Ante Marković. Although there is no reason to think Milošević had anything to do with the Agrokomerc scandal's coming to light, despite his contacts with the banking bureaucrats, it nevertheless helped his popularity by distinguishing his apparently modest lifestyle and concern for the people from corrupt *apparatchiks*. Unlike the decadent Titoites and reform-communists, Milošević was not 'on the make': he preferred amassing power to setting aside a nest-egg. From the point of view of those seeking a quiet life, corrupt politicians have their advantages.[15]

What Fikret Abdić and the other beneficiaries of Agrokomerc did for personal gain, Slobodan Milošević was soon to imitate for his political cause. By the end of 1990, it was clear that the other republics, especially Slovenia and Croatia with their newly-elected non-communist governments, were no longer prepared to subsidise the cost of Serb oppression in Kosovo. Without transfers from other republics, Belgrade would be quickly bankrupt or would have been had Milošević not engaged in his version of creative accounting. In December 1990 the Serb national bank was ordered by Milošević's government to issue the equivalent of almost 2 billion US dollars even though it had no backing. Among other consequences, this inflationary splurge meant that the Federal Premier, Ante Marković's, stabilisation plan for the Yugoslav economy – much admired in the West – was dead.

Milošević needed the money not just for Kosovo. His clients across Serbia and the other republics needed pay and supplies. Already in August 1990 there were violent clashes between Serb and Croat in the region around Knin and south-west towards the Dalmatian coast, where Croatia's valuable tourist trade was concentrated. The election of Franjo Tudjman's Croat Democratic Union (HDZ) in May 1990 had set off alarm bells among the Serbs of Croatia, but the most vigorous ringing was done by propagandists loyal to Milošević.

Tudjman's government acted unwisely but not oppressively when it reintroduced the traditional chequerboard flag of Croatia. This was immediately denounced as if swastikas had been hoisted over war graves. Local HDZ officials instituted an irritating policy of using the Latin alphabet on public notices instead of Cyrillic script in Serb-inhabited areas. This too was vociferously denounced by the Serb media as the prelude to genocide. Given Belgrade's control over the federal foreign service as well as the international public relations operation of Titoite Yugoslavia, it was fairly easy for Milošević's people in the West to create the impression that a racist neo-fascist regime had come to power in Croatia.

Knowing that 'nationalism' was a mortal sin in the eyes of the West, Milošević's agents painted a picture of Tudjman as a bogeyman cut just to the West's favourite measure. Relying on ignorance of Tudjman's wartime service in Tito's Partisans, and using edited snippets of his admittedly turgid writings, Milošević's disinformation service conjured up the frightening thought that a radical anti-Semite, the heir of the Ustasha state, had come to power in Zagreb. Meanwhile, Slobodan Milošević relied on the same degree of Western ignorance and indifference to the facts to have himself portrayed as a Balkan Lincoln, struggling against the obscurantist forces of Balkan nationalism to preserve a multi-ethnic federal Yugoslavia. This impression was for foreign consumption only, of course.[16]

By the end of the 1980s few politicians in Yugoslavia seemed to expect the Federation to survive. Some even acknowledged that in effect it had already disappeared as a political entity. Slobodan Milošević himself said in 1989, that Tito's constitution (1974) had failed to provide a viable framework for Yugoslavia: 'Even before his death, the system did not function, Tito functioned. After his death, nothing has functioned, and nobody has been able to reach an agreement on anything.' In October 1990, Vlado Kambovski, the Federal Secretary for Justice, faced by the question 'Who speaks in the name of Yugoslavia?' put by a French journalist, replied, 'it is impossible for me to give a brief reply to you . . . Yugoslavia is no more than a name. The mechanisms [of power] don't function any more.'[17] What would replace it was less clear.

On one point, Yugoslavs of all stripes were united. The European Community was seen as a better model – even the ideal one – of future development. Many Slovenes or Croats had seen the EC in action and concluded that it worked. *Gastarbeiter* flaunted their hard currency wages and the big German cars which they bought. But the mirage of European union exercised a fascination for all sectors of Yugoslav opinion. Certainly, the Slovenes and Croats put great hopes in an early entry into the EC as a way of liberating their economies from the negative pull of Serbia and the South. Redrawing and liberalising the rules of Yugoslavia was seen as an essential step towards membership of the Community.

'Europe Now!' was one of the most potent slogans in the campaign leading up to the referendum in December 1990. The twelve stars of the Euro-flag fluttered over many buildings in Slovenia alongside the national flag. But this enthusiasm for the EC gripped even the JNA whose newspaper, *Narodna Armija*, carried articles on the need for European integration alongside denunciations of separatism in the republics. Serbian officers and officials were prepared to join the pro-EC chorus along with other much-disliked nationalities. At the beginning the more Yugoslavia struggled with its own disintegration, the more European integration beckoned as a salvation from impending doom. Looking back, this Yugo-Euro-craze was deeply ironic and some of its statements take on a tragi-comic character. One Belgrade businessman's turn of the year 'hope' at the end of 1990 was that the New Year would see 'Yugoslavia . . . able to solve all its political problems by 1992 and that it will be able to enter the Europe of 1992.'[18]

Like so many other East European peoples emerging from communism, the Yugoslavs did not understand that their desperation to join the existing members of the EC was not matched by an equal enthusiasm on the part of the club to let them in. In fact, their aspirations for entry came at the worst possible time. The schedule of the single market had been drawn up in that halcyon age before perestroika when the world stood still and there was little to distract the Twelve from their preoccupation with harmonising the rules and regulations of the West European economy. Now in the run-up to the much-heralded 1992 process and with the Maastricht Conference set for December 1991, the last thing the Twelve wanted was the distraction of a Balkan squabble. Matters became worse after the breakdown of the Soviet Union following the farcical putsch in August 1991. As one Italian diplomat put it, 'Yugoslavia got caught between Maastricht and the Soviet Union.'[19] But these preoccupations were unknown in Yugoslavia.

If even entrepreneurs in Yugoslavia were so blindly optimistic, perhaps Western economic advisers to the federal government can be forgiven for being either oblivious to the tensions within Yugoslavia or for underrating their importance for reform. One leading Western exponent of shock therapy told Ante Marković that if only he could get the Dinar/Deutschmark rate down to 7:1 then the inter-ethnic tensions would subside of their own accord! Marković remarked that 'international experts told me: you need to have an excellent programme and a consensus.' As Marković pointed out, he had such a programme (was he not the author of the 'Yugoslav miracle'?), but a social consensus had to be built from the bottom up. However, his position left him trying to construct it from the top down. To a great extent Marković shared these illusions that prosperity would cure Yugoslavia's nationalist ills. He once asked a group of workers, 'What would you prefer? To be a Croat, Slovene or Serb or to earn 2,000 DM a month?'[20]

Since they were not likely to earn 2,000 DM a month in the foreseeable future, the workers had little reason to renounce their sense of identity. If anything, the knowledge that they were not about to achieve West European standards of affluence reinforced their clinging to the status which belonging to the Serb or Croat nation gave them. Marković's short-lived economic success was one more nail in the coffin of Yugoslavia and of the idea that economic solutions could be found to any political problem.

A flurry of secret diplomacy took place at the start of 1991. On 20 January, Kučan and Tudjman met but it was only on 13 February that the Slovene newspaper *Delo* reported the event. Kučan and Tudjman signed an eight-point pact committing both Slovenia and Croatia to act together in the event of intervention by the JNA against either republic. Furthermore, the two presidents agreed to call their peoples to arms 'to defend their homelands' and to urge their citizens in the JNA to desert in the event of a military clampdown. They also decided to appeal to foreign states to mediate 'if an agreement on the transformation of the Federation into a loose league of sovereign states could not be achieved'.

Unfortunately, Tudjman's political split personality meant that while he steered Croatia in the direction of a modern pluralistic market democracy with one hand, he was open to the blandishments of Milošević, who held out the prospect of achieving a state integrating all Croats, including those in Bosnia-Hercegovina, on the other. Tudjman liked to play the Machiavellian statesman and his secret meetings with Milošević as well as his unguarded musings about the future of Bosnia to the press did not help him or his cause. Not recognising the seriousness of the Serb threat to Croatia's Dalmatian lifeline, which ran a few miles below Knin, Tudjman could even talk about how 'the division of Bosnia-Hercegovina would be the best solution to the crisis', or at least that was the hostage to fortune which *Tanjug* in Belgrade happily sent on the wires.[21]

Although Serb media accused the Croats of plotting to overthrow Yugoslavia by force, even one of Tudjman's fiercest critics, Nora Beloff, admitted that 'Tudjman himself would have liked to achieve independence by negotiation, but when the Slovenes unilaterally seceded from Yugoslavia, he could not afford to be left behind.'[22] In fact, Franjo Tudjman repeatedly showed a tendency to stall the taking of decisions and to try and find a 'deal'. Contrary to the Western image of him as an out-and-out Croat nationalist of uncompromising nature, Tudjman hid his natural bent for compromise and procrastination behind a barrage of (often impenetrable) rhetoric.

By mid-February 1991 the press in Belgrade too was heightening the tension. *Politika Ekspres* reported on 13 February that an Austrian arms manufacturer had made a deal with an intermediary of the Slovene authorities to supply the republic with tanks, helicopters and machine-guns. Klagenfurt was an unlikely source for such a shopping list and the Slovene government immediately denied the report, but of course in the heated atmosphere it served the purpose of stoking up the flames of mutual suspicion further.

At the same time as one section of the Belgrade press warned that the 'fascists' in Croatia were arming themselves for an attack on Serbs there, other newspapers were promoting the idea of 'Greater Serbia'. Whereas Milošević had warned in public at least only that the disappearance of Federal Yugoslavia would raise the question of the future boundaries between the republics, his supporters in the media already had their plans worked out. On 12 February, *Illustrovna Politika* published a map showing the future shape of Serbia. Serbia would have to incorporate the bulk of Bosnia-Hercegovina and a large part of Croatia. According to this map (and there were variations of the theme), Greater Serbia should stretch to within fifty kilometres of Zagreb. It also generously granted the southern part of Dalmatia, including Dubrovnik, to the future Serb-Montenegrin state. The basis for the map was a similar exercise conducted in 1936 and relying on the census figures for 1931. To the authors of this scheme, what they claimed for Serbia sixty years earlier was just as valid in the 1990s. The genocide of the 1940s was blamed for any alteration in the population balance – and, of course, the highest estimates for Serb losses were taken for granted – and the rights of the Croats, Muslims or anyone else in this 'Greater Serbia' dismissed as 'unhistorical'.

Not all of this nationalist propaganda was made by minions of Milošević's Socialist Party. His most vocal opponents, too, had long waved the national banner as their rallying point. In fact, writers like the bearded Vuk Drasković had led the way in the break-up of the monopoly of LYC in Serbia by accusing the communists of betraying Serbian interests in Kosovo and elsewhere in the Federation. Far more than their demands for Western-style democracy, it was their denunciation of the Serbian *nomenklatura* for selling-out their fellow Serbs which rallied the bulk of what support Drasković and his dissident allies could count on. In 1990, Drasković's programme not only included the restoration of the monarchy but also the establishment of a Serbia running to the Adriatic including parts of Croatia and Bosnia. Even Drasković's flamboyant beard was a self-conscious Chetnik attribute.[23]

In the end, Milošević was to prove the Bismarck of Serbian nationalism. Just as Bismarck was a reactionary Prussian Junker who personally felt little of the emotional pull of German nationalism in the mid-nineteenth century and rather disliked the idea of a *Grossdeutschland* uniting all Germans in one Fatherland, but recognised that he had to swim with the nationalist tide if he was not to abandon hope of preserving what he could of Prussian authoritarianism faced with his liberal opposition, so Milošević was hemmed in by his own evocation of national ghosts in the late 1980s and his ambition to manipulate them to save the communist regime. In the 1860s, Bismarck ruthlessly undercut the liberal nationalist camp in Prussia by waging wars to bring about German unification. Bismarck thereby converted a political opposition to his regime into something like treason. By stirring up trouble with the other republics, Milošević ran the risk of handing an issue to his nationalist-liberal opponents, but on the other hand, he could put them in a potentially fatal bind: either they supported violence against non-Serbs and therefore lost their Western allies and paymasters, or they opposed aid to other Serbs and were discredited in the eyes of their fellow citizens. In either case, Milošević could hope to trump any decision by the opposition given his control of the Serbian state's resources.

However, in 1991, the political situation inside Serbia as judged in the capital seemed far from stable. Belgrade's intelligentsia and students seemed as restive as their counterparts elsewhere in East-Central Europe on the eve of the revolutions there. Hostility towards the Serbian Socialist Party's stranglehold over the broadcast media was particularly widespread among them. At the beginning of March 1991, the simmering crisis in Belgrade seemed to explode according to the now classic recipe witnessed from East Berlin to neighbouring Bucharest.

The events of 9 March were a turning point and the mark of Milošević's political mastery or of his opponents' political inanity. By all other Eastern European precedents, Milošević should have fallen in the wake of the mishandling of the mass demonstrations. The JNA leadership clearly wished to distance themselves from him after the killings. Many of his supporters were worried that he was losing his grip. He was forced to agree to the release of Vuk Drasković. The scene seemed set for a classic Velvet Revolution. The bearded Serb Havel would sweep the beleaguered *apparatchik* from power with another display of people power such as had already consigned Milošević's counterparts in Prague and East Berlin to the scrap heap of history. But the crowds went home satisfied by the release of their hero. Everywhere else such a concession had led to the piling on of new demands until the Party conceded power itself, but in Serbia Milošević's tactical retreat gave him a strategic victory over the opposition. The momentum of events over the next few months was to sweep away any chance of ending his rule without bloodshed – that of Serbs and non-Serbs alike.

Milošević did not appeal to class consciousness in his defence of his power-base. Instead of socialist rhetoric, he summoned up the picture of his opponents as the agents of alien powers, 'the anti-Serb coalition' which wanted to reduce Serbia to a 'vassal-state'. In all this the foreigners' plots were helped by the protesters because 'internecine conflict can only help those wanting to subjugate us'.[24] Since the outbreak of war in Yugoslavia, the idea that the Serbs are the victims of a widely spread 'Serbophobia' has been invoked by many Serbs to explain their unpopularity in the world, but Milošević and his supporters had worked hard before hostilities at fostering the notion of Serbia beleaguered in order to cement their hold on society.[25]

Milošević was not satisfied with words alone. He wanted action against his critics. He demanded that the Federal Presidency impose martial law and be prepared to use force against the demonstrators. The motley collection of post-Titoite bureaucrats could not decide what to do. They would not nail their colours to Milošević's mast, but nor would they act against him. Instead they drifted indecisively and left it to the Serbian government to summon army reservists back to the colours and to prepare a clampdown.

Misha Glenny has pointed out how shabbily opportunistic was Milošević's response to the Federal Presidency's failure to back his call for martial law to save his political skin. Overnight he changed from the defender of the necessity of a continuing Yugoslavia to its public gravedigger. He announced 'Yugoslavia has entered into the final phase of its agony. The Presidency of the Socialist Federated Republic of Yugoslavia has not functioned for a long time, and the illusion of the functioning of the Presidency of Yugoslavia and its powers which in reality do not exist, has since last night finally expired.'[26] It was an obituary which few of Milošević's EC partners in 'the peace process' after June 1991, and the Western defenders of Yugoslav integrity, seem to have noticed, since they took at face value the Serbian President's insistence on the legal continuity of the very Yugoslavia which he had buried in March 1991, three months before Slovenia or Croatia declared their independence.

In May, at the same time as some Westerners were still musing about the advantages of a JNA coup to preserve stability in Yugoslavia, the JNA's acting commander-in-chief, Blagoje Adzić, commented that the 'extermination of tens of thousands of Croats would provoke some grumbling around the world but would soon be forgotten'.[27] The idea that the officer corps of the JNA stood above the whirlpool of visceral hatreds resulting from the atrocities during the civil war between 1941–1945 was one of the great illusions of Western opinion. Certainly, the Communist-Partisan commitment to the preservation of the Federated Socialist Republic of Yugoslavia lived on in its ranks, especially at the higher level, but it was irrevocably intertwined with bitter memories, and the tendency of the Serb-dominated, albeit partisan-fathered officer corps, was to make little or no distinction between the mass-murdering Ustasha of two generations ago and any Croat opponent of the FSRY in 1991.

In the winter beforehand, Kadijević had warned that the Army would preserve socialism and the communist state in Yugoslavia. the military hardliners were cheered up by the apparent shift of the Soviet leadership to a more hardline position. The collapse of the East European communist regimes in 1989 was attributed to their lack of native roots. In Yugoslavia as in the Soviet Union and China, there had been an 'autochthonous revolution'. In January 1990, the last guardian of communist orthodoxy, the political administration of the Ministry of Defence in Belgrade, produced a document which claimed that discontent with the communist system was the product of a Western plot and that now Yugoslavia was to be the focus of attention. This idea that the CIA and its junior services were at the heart of a conspiracy which had already toppled Ceauşescu and Honecker and was bent on doing much the same for Tito's heirs flattered both the Western intelligence agencies and the self-importance of the Yugoslav military.

It was symptomatic of the generals' paranoia that they completely misinterpreted the Western attitude to their country. They had lived in a shadow world of conspiracy for so long that they attributed their own mind-set to their (imaginary) enemies. The CIA and US State Department were trying 'to destroy socialism in Yugoslavia, even at the price of the country's destruction' and were determined to prevent the JNA from 'stemming this process'. Even some of the Soviet officials to whom they looked for support found the JNA leaders' tendency to see the hand of the CIA or the Vatican or Bonn behind all of Yugoslavia's travails unreasonable, but could not persuade Kadijević and his comrades to moderate their views.[28]

Already in 1988 the JNA had expressed its concern about the 'counterrevolutionary' developments in Slovenia. The youth paper *Mladina* published a series of articles exposing the role of the Yugoslav military in the arms trade and even more sensationally the JNA high command's apparent preparations for a *coup d'état* in any republic, but especially Slovenia, which threatened to carry reform too far. The Army responded by arresting the journalists and putting them before a military court. To add insult to injury, the court insisted on carrying out its proceedings in Serbo-Croat (i.e. Serb) rather than Slovene, even though the case was heard in Ljubljana. The case awakened Slovene public opinion to the threat of a hardline military coup which might try to reverse the liberalising developments which so far stopped well short of multi-party politics. (They only followed developments in neighbouring Warsaw Pact states like Hungary or the Soviet Union itself.) Demonstrations marked its progress and the sentences in the end were relatively light and to be served in Slovenia. Although at the time this case seemed a setback to democratisation, it actually gave it a decisive shove, because it popularised reformist ideas previously only discussed by intellectuals. It even forced the JNA to recognise the need to supplement its dependence on force and administrative pressures to get its point of view heard in the increasingly pluralistic media of the northern republics.[29]

As their own response to the pluralisation of Yugoslav politics in 1990, the generals set up their own party – to oppose the trend towards democracy, the market and separatism. When the basic communist cells which had existed in all public organisations from factory floor and agricultural collective to the general staff were abolished as a mark of liberalisation in 1990, the generals simply established their own independent communist party, the 'League of Communists – Movement for Yugoslavia' and the former LCY cells joined it *en bloc*. Led by a galaxy of brass hats (with only Slobodan Milošević's wife, Mirjana, offering any feminine flavour) it was doomed to irrelevance at the polls, but that probably worried its leaders little. Their main aim was to establish an organisation which was not federalised, since they blamed the republican-based operation of the old League of Communists for much of the current disintegration. In practice, however, despite the odd Croat admiral or Slovene air-force officer, this new LC-MY was basically a Serb and certainly an anti-Croat nationalist party.

In other words, to Croats it was further confirmation of their suspicion that the organs of power of communist Yugoslavia were little more than instruments of Serb domination. In fact, the LCY was disproportionately Serb. For instance, the city of Belgrade alone had more Party members than the whole of Slovenia. In Croatia itself, the Serb minority provided a disproportionate number of the LCY's members and still more of its key functionaries, the real holders of power. In the 1980s, 7.4 per cent of the total adult population of Croatia belonged to the LCY, but Serbs living in the republic provided almost a quarter of the local Party membership even though they were at most 15 per cent of its population. In practice, this meant that Serbs held a disproportionate share of sensitive jobs in the state, including in the police apparatus, but also in the economy and even in areas of social provision. In any communist society, the state's control of so much of the economy gave to the people who controlled the state a huge power of patronage. In any system such power would be resented but where it lay even patchily in the hands of an ethnic or linguistic minority it was a recipe for deep-seated discontent.[30]

Croat resentment about the power of Serbs in their republic was compounded by what they saw as the Serbs' misuse of the suffering of the Second World War to pillory all Croats as enthusiastic collaborators with the Nazis. Far from improving relations between Serb and Croat, the harping on the Ustasha theme simply alienated even Croats with a partisan past or family history. However, if a Greater Serbia was to be created and access to the sea achieved, Croatia was bound to suffer deleterious effects. By contrast, Serbia's alienation of Slovenia was a rare political stroke.

More than any other nationality, Slovenes had been associated with the 'Yugoslav idea'. Furthermore, little love was lost between them and their Croat neighbours to the south. If Belgrade had acted in concert with Ljubljana, then Zagreb would have been in a very difficult strategic position. Since Slovenia lacked a Serb minority, there was no obvious cause of ethnic tension between the republic and Serbia.

However, in practice Slovenia was the republic which became most antagonised by Milošević's policies after 1987. Slovenes had long resented the size of their transfer payments to fund Serbian development and in effect to subsidise Belgrade's policy towards Kosovo. As Milošević seized power in Belgrade, so Ljubljana became the focus of criticism of official policy towards Kosovo Albanians but also of the waning totalitarian state. A growing Western-orientation rather than a revival of Slovene nationalism – which had never been strong, unlike the reality of the sense of Slovene identity – led the republic into conflict with Serbia.

Slovenia had never had a military past of its own. Like the Croats, the Slovenes had always served in someone else's army at least until 1941. The cult of the JNA was never well entrenched among the Slovenes who regarded themselves as sophisticated Central Europeans and who looked down on the 'backward' Serbs because of their pride in an uneconomic military prowess. The youth culture of Slovenia was soon a focus for anti-military feeling. Conscription into the JNA was resented, particularly because it could involve service in Kosovo. By 1988, the official youth paper, *Mladina*, added to its list of scandalous attacks on the JNA with its revelations about the mixture of corruption and brutality inside the JNA.

The Serb-dominated Yugoslav military establishment did not take kindly to investigative journalism, particularly not from those it regarded as little better than spoilt children. However, the attempt by military prosecutors to arraign journalists from *Mladina* backfired as popular sentiment in Slovenia pushed Kučan's branch of the LYC into supporting open criticism of a federal institution. (In fact, in many ways the JNA was the only federal institution with any power. All the others depended on the republics.)

Janez Janša was the central figure in the *Mladina* affair and was to play a key role in bringing about the independence of Slovenia and the brief war which won it. Even afterwards, he remained Defence Minister and an important political figure in his own right. But despite his rise to political prominence, Janša's role as the journalistic voice of an increasingly anti-Yugoslav youth culture was his key contribution to the development of the crisis.

To Serb generals brought up on a diet of anti-German and Titoite propaganda, the trend in the Alpine republic to look northwards and rediscover Slovenia's Habsburg connections was profoundly distasteful. But worse was to come. Everywhere rock culture postures in ways designed to outrage the older generation, but in Slovenia youth groups began to blaspheme by adopting Germanic names and *kitsch* styles. The rock group Laibach challenged the Titoite tabus by adopting the German name of Ljubljana for themselves and parodying – or in the eyes of officialdom glorifying – fascistic poses. Along with the other multi-media members of the art movement, also christened with an outrageous German name, Neue Slowenische Kunst, Laibach promoted the image abroad of Yugoslavia as a whole as the communist country with the most permissive regime and society. In fact, the very existence of avant-garde movements did as much to foster hardline neo-Stalinist attitudes elsewhere as they did to break down old mind-sets. If anything their existence re-invigorated the anti-modern tendencies, particularly among Serbs and in the military.[31]

Laibach and Neue Slowenische Kunst reflected the influence of Western modernism on some intellectual circles, but it was for all its raucousness a fairly limited and refined influence. Western commercial popular culture penetrated throughout Yugoslavia and influenced young people of all national groups. Any idea that rock music must be an anti-authoritarian or anti-war force was shattered by the Yugoslav experience. Just as in Nazi Germany swing music was widely popular among the soldiers and SS responsible for terrible atrocities, so much of the fighting after June 1991 was done by the disco generation. The influence of Hollywood's contemporary Neanderthals, Stallone and Schwarzenegger, on the style of the *Soldateska* in the Balkans also goes back to the late 1980s when both cinemas and especially home videos flooded the juvenile minds of Yugoslav men of all ages with images of Rambo-style violence to overlay their own traditions.

As Slovenia's parents looked to the EC and their affluent neighbours as a model and their children frequently flaunted a disillusionment with the myths of Yugoslavia, Serbia was moving in a different direction. Already Belgrade had reacted harshly to Slovene criticisms of its policy in Kosovo and had tried to bring Slovenia into line by imposing sanctions, but these only confirmed the Slovene swing against Yugoslavism towards independence. Perhaps over-optimistically, some Slovene enterprises seemed to welcome the breaking of ties with Serbia. Liberated from the convoluted business of dealing with their poorer southern brothers, they hoped to shift their efforts towards trade with the EC. By the end of 1990, Slovenia's population was deeply disenchanted with the seemingly endless drain on its resources to pay for futile projects and oppression in the south of Yugoslavia.

The decay of the Soviet bloc lifted the external pressure from the east to hold Yugoslavia together. Few Slovenes could believe that the West would maintain its commitment to the existing Yugoslavia come what may, particularly if it was challenged from below by popular democratic pressure. In December 1990, after months of futile negotiations designed to confederalise Yugoslavia and limit the capacity of the centrally placed republic, Serbia, to manipulate the federal system to its own advantage, 90 per cent of Slovenes voted to set a six-month limit on further discussions: if no agreement could be reached by 25 June 1991, then Slovenia would declare itself a sovereign independent state.

Given Slovenia's ethnic homogeneity as well as its high level of economic development and proximity to the West, that was an easy decision.[32] However, it placed pressure on Croatia's new democratically elected government to make a similar decisive move. Contrary to his widely disseminated image as an irrational nationalist bent upon achieving Croat independence at any cost and at breakneck speed, Tudjman was remarkably cautious. Despite his nationalist rhetoric and the fact that his supporters engaged in the sort of symbolic changes which antagonised local Serbs (such as putting up Latin alphabet road signs in place of Cyrillic), Tudjman was well aware of the weakness of Croatia vis-à-vis Belgrade. He avoided provoking the JNA.

When the Army decided to bring under its control the weapons depots of the Territorial Defence in the spring of 1991, Tudjman's government cooperated unwillingly and was much less successful at thwarting the Army's effort to disarm its potential future enemy than the Slovenes were. Even when fighting broke out with the JNA in Slovenia in June 1991, Tudjman restrained those Croats who wanted to fight the Army. In fact, unlike the Slovenes, Croat forces were in a much weaker position to confront the JNA. The Croat embryo defence forces had begun to import some weapons from the collapsing Warsaw Pact forces, especially in Hungary, but backdoor imports were still scarce and essentially involved firearms and light weapons, not heavy weapons capable of resisting a massed attack by the JNA's tanks.

Unlike many of his contemporaries, Tudjman was also more sceptical about the likelihood of Western mediation or intervention in the event of a conflict. The Slovenes and many ordinary Croats had not recognised the bitter truth that what mattered was not how much they loved the European Community but how much the EC loved them. Soon after the fighting began, disillusionment with the EC set in, but Tudjman had told *Tanjug* already in December 1990, with more than a hint of regret, that 'the international democratic public does not accept the programme of Yugoslavia's disintegration and the changing of the borders in Europe.'[33]

The political crisis produced by democratisation in Yugoslavia opened the prospect of a military solution. After the victory of Tudjman's Croatian Democratic Community in the general election in Croatia in May 1990, the Federal Presidency finally broke down. Already two of its members – representing Vojvodina and Kosovo – had been replaced by arbitrary Serb action. Milošević controlled three out of eight votes and with Montenegro firmly allied to Belgrade, the Serb bloc could veto any decision. The loss of communist control in Croatia was a red rag to the Serbian bull. Tudjman the ex-partisan turned nationalist was regarded as beyond the Yugoslav pale. His nominee to take Croatia's seat on the presidency was Stipe Mesić. In May 1991, Mesić could normally have expected to be rotated into the position of formal head of state for a year and therefore nominal commander-in-chief of the Yugoslav armed forces. The Serbian block against all precedent refused to elect Mesić and thus left the Yugoslav state rudderless. The Federal Premier, Ante Marković, had no direct authority over the armed forces.

As the crisis deepened, Yugoslavia lacked any clear lines of command. This suited Milošević because it meant Serbia could egg on the federally minded generals without taking any responsibility for their actions. If they succeeded in thwarting the separatists, Serbia's desire for a more centralised and Serb-controlled federation would be achieved. If they failed, Serbia still had the option of breaking away herself.

Without direct political control, but confident of its capacity to clamp down on Slovenia and Croatia if necessary, the high command of the JNA decided that using troops stationed in

Slovenia alone, it would be able to face down any declaration of independence there. Used to intimidating Albanians in Kosovo and inclined to be dismissive of the Slovenes' powers of resistance because of their anti-military press, the generals thought that a decisive demonstration of force would quickly seal the borders of Slovenia and therefore quash its ambitions for independence by isolating the republic from the outside world. In any case, in the days leading up to the Slovene Declaration of Independence, the countries to whom the Slovenes had looked as natural allies made very unfriendly noises designed to deter the Slovenes from their course even at the last moment.

2

Countdown: the West and the Yugoslav Crisis

> Impotence . . . expresses itself in a single proposition: the maintenance of the *status quo*. This general conviction that a state of things resulting from hazard and circumstances must be obstinately maintained is a proof of bankruptcy, a confession by the leading Powers of their complete incapacity to further the cause of progress and civilization.
>
> Karl Marx (1853)[1]

News of the outbreak of fighting in Slovenia coincided with one of the twice yearly summits of the European Community's heads of government. The newsflash of violence on the fringes of the EC seems to have arrived in Luxembourg like a divine portent. The assembled European leaders saw it as their chance to wipe out the embarrassing memory of the Community's unfortunate inability to act as one (or even two) at the start of the Gulf War six months earlier. Now fate itself it seemed had supplied the Community with a crisis on its own doorstep which it could master and thus banish the haunting doubts about its capacity to act as a counterweight to the two Cold War superpowers, the USA and USSR, on the international stage. In their own way, the enthusiastic responses of the Twelve to the sounds of battle in the Balkans were as naive as reaction had been in European capitals to the start of Balkan wars almost eighty years earlier.

The Twelve seemed to feel that a little excursion into international peacemaking would lighten their regular diet of haggling over food subsidies and pay-offs to unprofitable regions. Given the 'Euro–' rhetoric of various Yugoslav parties over recent months, the Twelve took for granted that its emissaries would be received with respect and their advice heeded with alacrity.

Journalists noted that the official off-the-record briefing was that it had been a 'happy summit'.[2]

It was a happy dawn for the new Europe when the *troika* of three European Community foreign ministers set off from Luxembourg for Ljubljana. At their head was one of Europe's longest-serving foreign ministers, Jacques Poos, the Grand Duchy's very own Metternich who still had a few days of his six-month term as President of the European Council to run. Accompanying him were his predecessor, the Italian foreign minister, Gianni di Michelis, and his successor, the Dutchman Hans van den Broek. But it was Poos who set the tone of the venture. According to Poos, the chance to intervene as mediators in the Yugoslav crisis was 'the hour of Europe'. He added, 'If one problem can be solved by the Europeans, it is the Yugoslav problem. This is a European country and it is not up to the Americans. It is not up to anyone else.'[3]

Journalists covering such EC summits usually have to repeat what the anonymous official briefers tell them as if passing their own comments, so enthusiastic comments like those on the Channel 4 News about how the decision to send the *troika* 'illustrates the speed and unity with which as with the Kurdish crisis at Easter the EC is now able to act' should be taken as official interpretations.[4] Europe was about to seize the moment and come of age as a superpower, no longer a collection of little states huddled under a protective US umbrella. As if to emphasise that the Europe of the Twelve was now the *Ordnungsmacht* for the continent as a whole, Gianni di Michelis told journalists that the *troika* would be briefing the Americans on its activities but not consulting them.[5]

Their own summit in Luxembourg was intended to lay the basis for the future European Union envisaged in the Maastricht Treaty signed six months later, so it was psychologically difficult for the Twelve to adjust to the idea of a federal state collapsing before their eyes. The Luxembourgeois premier, Jacques Santer, the President of the EC Council of Ministers, assured reporters, 'We have to try all means to save the Federation at this moment.' Britain's John Major, too, added his voice to the conservative demands for the preservation of the Socialist Federated Republic of Yugoslavia. He assured journalists that 'the great prize is to hold the federation together'.[6]

Unfortunately, Poos was not well-informed about attitudes in Yugoslavia. An ardent devotee of federalism and *habitué* of the bureaucratic world of revolving presidencies, he was intellectually ill-equipped to deal with peoples trying to escape from their own collapsing federation. Poos of course was no hypocrite: he was perfectly willing to renounce his own country's independence and saw no reason to promote that of others. With Grand Ducal authority, Poos inveighed against small countries – albeit many times larger than his own – who dared to question the status quo: 'Anyone who questions the borders of Yugoslavia puts in question the CSCE Charter.' For Poos the CSCE Charter was as sacrosanct as the Holy Alliance had been for Metternich: 'The idea of national self-determination is dangerous as the basis for international order . . . It would release an explosive development.' It does not seem to have occurred to M. Poos that more often than not, it was the opponents of the popular will who set off the explosions in order to frustrate it. Unwittingly, Poos' rhetoric recalled the plangent complaints of the defenders of the stagnant order in 1848 when Frederick William IV of Prussia admitted that 'Against democrats only soldiers are any use.'[7]

There is no reason to suspect that Poos knew the genealogy of his commitment to a world of stability. No one has ever accused him of making a study of diplomatic history. He would not have read the famous Habsburg diplomatic circular from 1853 which celebrated the restoration of order after the failure of the 1848 revolutions and warned against the insanity of accepting the right to self-determination. It could have been drafted by Metternich himself:

> The claim to set up new states according to the limits of nationality is the most dangerous of all schemes. To put forward such a pretension is to break with history; and to carry it into execution in any part of Europe is to shake to its foundations the firmly organized order of states, and to threaten the Continent with subversion and chaos.[8]

Metternich himself had seen clearly the threat posed to the

multi-ethnic empires of Europe by Balkan nationalism. Even Britain would not be immune from the bad example of Greek independence. In 1826, Metternich warned of the consequences of the British Foreign Secretary George Canning's sympathy for the Greek rebels:

> What would be the fate of Europe – that of civilisation – if the doctrine of the *dédoublement des états* were ever admitted . . .? How can a man of sense advance so subversive a contention, or at least permit himself the attempt to advance it? . . . Is England then ready to regard as a Power equal in rights to those of the King [of Great Britain] the first Irish Club which declares itself the Insurgent Government of Ireland?'

Would England accept France in 'the office of mediator by reason of the sole fact that the invitation had been addressed to it by the *Irish Government* [emphasis in the original] . . . Whither does this absurdity lead us?'[9] M. Poos found himself peering into the same abyss in June 1991. As events showed, once confronted by the methods through which Yugoslav unity was likely to be preserved, the humane M. Poos was genuinely shocked, but by then it was a little late to influence events in a less violent direction.

The European Community was not alone in its determination to preserve the Yugoslav Federation. The United States administration, too, was preoccupied with a profoundly conservative approach to the waning of communism. The old regime in Eastern Europe and stretching across the Eurasian land mass to the Pacific found its last enthusiasts not only in the Kremlin or Pyongyang, but also in the White House, the Élysée and Ten Downing Street. Metternich might have abhorred communism but he would have recognised the emotions underlying the reaction of Bush, Baker, Mitterrand or Major to the unravelling of a superpower and its system.

Metternich's advice in 1827 to his sovereign, Francis I, to ignore any outcry about the brutal suppression of the Greek rebels by their enraged Turkish rulers may seem a world away from the morality of the Western statesmen confronted by the implosion of the Soviet Union and the collapse of Yugoslavia in our own time, but Metternich's preference for the Ottoman Empire as 'the best of neighbours' and the public record of what the self-proclaimed victors in the Cold War said in mourning the passing of their defeated rivals after 1989, and especially once fighting began in Yugoslav Federative Socialist Republic in June 1991, show a deep affinity. (Unfortunately, none of the modern Western statesmen had any of Metternich's wit or lack of self-deception.)

The cult of stability and hostility to boundary changes were not just features of post-Napoleonic Europe. In the late twentieth century, Metternich had his disciples too. The Holy Alliance which he helped to forge in 1815 as a rock of stability against change of any kind was the model for the Conference on Security and Cooperation in Europe. But it also shared debilitating features with the state whose decay was to be the first crucial test of the new pan-European League of Nations: like federal Yugoslavia, the CSCE was a welter of rotating chairmanships, rules of precedence (even before it had acted) and above all the obligation to unanimity. Leonid Brezhnev had drafted the Helsinki foundations of the CSCE well in 1975. As matters turned out, even after the collapse of the Soviet Union its impotence was just as planned.

Fear of the break-up of the Soviet Union was as strong in Washington as Moscow. When the peoples of the Baltic States with the Lithuanians in the vanguard reasserted their right to independence after 1988, the alarm bells began to ring even in Gorbachev's Kremlin. Emboldened by the events of past autumn in Eastern Europe, the Lithuanian Communist Party itself declared its independence from the CPSU on 20 December 1989. Gorbachev was not impressed by this attempt on the part of the Lithuanian communists to try to keep up with the popular mood in their republic. On 25 December 1989, he declared, 'The present Party and state leadership will not allow the break-up of the Union state. I want to state this . . . I say this bluntly. The necessary actions to preserve the Union and ensure its unity are a hard necessity. There should be no illusions here regarding the centre's intentions and capabilities.'

When James Baker III visited Soviet Lithuania shortly afterwards in February 1990, he went out of his way not to meet Vytautas Landsbergis, the freely elected chairman of the Lithuanian Parliament. Instead he kept the company of the officials still loyal to Moscow, a dwindling band.[10] The deliberate distancing of the West from its most enthusiastic supporters in the Soviet Union was to be repeated even more authoritatively by President Bush himself eighteen months later in Kiev on 1 August 1991, on the eve of the fateful putsch against Gorbachev by the hardliners.

1 August 1991, was a fateful day though it passed largely unnoticed outside the Soviet Union and Eastern Europe. It was the day on which George Bush gave the green light to the plotters conspiring against Mikhail Gorbachev determined to reverse his timid reforms and preserve the Soviet Union unchanged. As in so much of his foreign policy, the President did not mean his words to the Ukrainian Parliament to be understood as they were. Someone forgot to tell him what sort of people would be listening when he said,

> Americans will not support those who seek independence in order to replace a far-off tyranny with a local despotism. They will not aid those who promote a suicidal nationalism based on ethnic hatred . . . We can see in Yugoslavia how the proud name of nationalism can splinter a country into bloody civil war.[11]

Undeterred by having put his pennyworth of influence behind the pressures promoting the anti-Gorbachev coup on 19 August 1991, on his farewell visit to Moscow as US President in January 1993, George Bush blithely agreed to sign a joint communiqué with the Russian government which condemned Azerbaijan out of hand for its role in the war with Armenia over the enclave of Nagorny-Karabakh. Hardly surprisingly, the Azeri President Elchibey protested vehemently at this interference in his state's affairs without any consultation. Shortly afterwards, the Russians began intensified assistance to the Armenian military and the tide of battle turned. That change of military fortune led to attacks on Elchibey's leadership. Elchibey was by 1993 the only head of a former Soviet republic who had not been a member of the Communist Party. Almost all the others were former leading functionaries of the Soviet Communist Party. In the early summer of 1993, a revolt began among the Azeri military against Elchibey which presaged the return to power of the former Communist Party boss of Azerbaijan in the Brezhnev era, Geidar Aliev.[12]

In retrospect, George Bush will be seen as the last defender of the status quo in the Soviet bloc. Bush was a bourgeois Metternich trying to be a rock of stability in a changing world. Egged on by James Baker and his acolytes at the State Department, Bush was the Canute at the end of the Cold War. Unlike Canute, George Bush does not seem to have intended his strictures against the historical tide to be taken ironically. If the 37th President of the United States aspired to be the author of a foreign policy doctrine which would go down in the history books alongside the Monroe and Truman Doctrines, then his teaching was surely clear-cut. As he showed by his determination to reverse Saddam Hussein's occupation of Kuwait and by his equally stubborn refusal to countenance the overthrow of the Iraqi dictator at the risk of precipitating the collapse of multi-ethnic Iraq, George Bush preached a clear faith: states should neither be destroyed nor created.[13] Stability was his watchword.

The uncanny decision to end the Gulf War without overthrowing Saddam Hussein and leaving his apparatus of terror still largely intact will probably come to be seen as the *locus classicus* of the Bush Doctrine. It marked the stillbirth of the New World Order. Bush's Defense Secretary put the case for Saddam as a bastion of stability and order in the very region in which his rampaging army had been the cause of crisis for more than a decade:

> If we'd gone to Baghdad and got rid of Saddam . . . Then you've got to put a new government in his place and then you're faced with the question of what kind of government are you going to establish in Iraq? Is it going to be a Kurdish government or a Shia government or a Sunni government? How many forces are you going to have to leave there to keep it propped up . . .?[14]

Both President Bush and Prime Minister Major had indulged their hopes for a rebellion against 'Saddam the dictator' in rhetoric (broadcast repeatedly into Iraq) which undoubtedly encouraged his various peoples to expect Allied support for any revolt.

The crushing defeat of the Iraqi forces in February 1991 set off a great *intifada* against Saddam both among the Shiites of southern Iraq and in Kurdistan in the north. The underlying naivety of Bush's thinking was revealed when he said in March 1991, 'It seems unlikely he can survive . . . People are fed up with him. *They see him for the brutal dictator he is* [emphasis added].'[15] As if the terror which Saddam inspired was not the key to his survival in power. After all, had Stalin's power collapsed when Hitler's soldiers could see the Kremlin in their field-glasses or Hitler's own authority disappeared when the Red Army was outside Berlin?

Bush like so many heads of government in the West (perhaps François Mitterrand alone excepted) could not claim to be a philosopher of international relations, let alone a visionary. The role of *éminence grise* to the White House and State Department in 1991 was played by the former Secretary of State, Henry Kissinger. Kissinger's whole career as statesman had been preoccupied with the pursuit of stability and with efforts to introduce a convergence of interests between policy-makers in Washington and the Kremlin. Kissinger never showed much interest in popular opinion and feared popular emotions as disruptive forces which all too easily could overthrow the wisdom of statesmen. It is not by chance that the guru of the US foreign policy elite started life as an academic historian whose major work, *A World Restored*, was a paean to Metternich's policy of re-establishing order throughout Europe after the defeat of Napoleon in 1815. Central to Kissinger's teaching was the eternal nature of Soviet power: as Secretary of State, he told his fellow Americans, 'for the first time in our history we face the stark reality that the [communist] challenge is unending.'[16] Kissinger's vicar on earth, Helmut Sonnenfeldt, enunciated his famous doctrine in 1975, which committed the West to accepting the division of Europe after Yalta but went further in proposing that the West should not only seek not to destabilise the communist world, but ought actively to promote the preservation of the Soviet order.

Kissinger's faith in the status quo had its corollary in contempt for little nations. Small peoples clutter the earth, but in the eyes of Kissingerites that is no reason to give them space on the map. Edward Heath recalls how far Kissinger's preference for a world run by a very few all-powerful states went – it excluded even the West European states:

> I can remember Henry Kissinger saying to me once, 'Why do I have to go round to all these different capitals [e.g. Paris and London]? I just go to Moscow and I settle the whole thing with one chap. When I come here I have to traipse around every little capital.'[17]

Heath agreed, of course, with Kissinger's contempt for the national identities of his own allies, let alone the Warsaw Pact satellites of Moscow. How happy the age of Brezhnev and Kissinger when Warsaw and Prague could be consulted directly in Moscow.[18]

At the outset of the Yugoslav crisis and throughout the death throes of the Soviet Union, Kissinger's disciples and protégés, especially Deputy-Secretary of State, Lawrence Eagleburger, and National Security Adviser, Brent Scowcroft, were central figures in the US foreign policy establishment. Both had also served in Belgrade in the past and spoke Serbo-Croat. They had every qualification therefore to speak as experts on the situation in dying Yugoslavia. Unfortunately, their previous service in Belgrade (as well as Eagleburger's continuing business contacts there) seems to have introduced a strong element of emotional commitment to the Yugoslav cause (as opposed to Western interests, let alone to the West's would-be friends), which blinded them to the real aims of Milošević.

'Lawrence of Serbia' as his less flattering juniors at the State Department called him was a key figure in the day-to-day policy-making of the US response to Yugoslavia's death throes. James Baker III had never shown much interest in the lesser powers and so his visit to Belgrade only days before the Slovenes intended to proclaim their independence was probably prepared by Eagleburger. But it was with the full authority of Secretary of State that Baker spoke when he told the Belgrade leaders and the media there that the US would 'never' recognise an independent Slovenia or Croatia. Whatever impression was intended by the US Secretary of State, after his meeting with Ante Marković, Belgrade took the view that it had been given the green light to take military action to deter or reverse any declaration of independence.[19]

Already at the end of May 1991 the State Department issued a public statement of its policy towards the galloping Yugoslav crisis. Amid the standard clichés about the 'special importance' of human rights and the need to promote a democratic change and the market economy was a repeated emphasis on the US goal of preserving the 'unity' of Yugoslavia. The statement made clear that the United States opposed changing the status of inner borders, i.e. making them international boundaries. On the contrary, the US government supported the 'territorial integrity of Yugoslavia within its present borders' and it declared 'the US shall not encourage or reward secession.'

The statement made clear that the Americans would do nothing to assist secessionists and implied therefore that any violence which occurred would be their own fault and they would have to face the consequences alone. A sinister and threatening forecast concluded the section on the need to preserve Yugoslavia: 'We believe that ethnic heterogeneousness of most of the Yugoslav republics means that any dismantling of Yugoslavia is likely to aggravate rather than solve ethnic tensions.' Unfortunately the author of the statement (identified as Lawrence Eagleburger by the *New York Times*) did not elucidate the roots of those escalating tensions and ask why violence was likely or, most pertinently of all, who would order it.[20]

Influential elements in the Western media supported the US-EC consensus on the need to preserve Yugoslavia. Some opinion-formers were prepared to advocate the use of force. In early May 1991, the *Financial Times* was dismissive of the Croat view that the JNA served essentially Serbian interests. It assured its readers that 'the army's role, however, is more complicated.' In fact, the Pearson Group's flagship paper seemed to share the assessment of the generals in the Belgrade bunker: 'The army now believes the imposition of a state of emergency is one of the few options available . . . The army's role in this agenda should be clear. It should immediately disarm all paramilitary groups [i.e. the Croatian police] . . . Once order has been restored, it should withdraw to the barracks . . .'

Despite token pieties about the need for the preservation of human rights and the market economy (this in a leader hoping against hope that General Kadijević's approach might be adopted!), the key purpose of Western policy was clearly set out: 'The republics should have no illusions about Europe's intentions *vis-à-vis* Yugoslavia. The time has not yet come to place a re-drawing of Yugoslavia's internal boundaries on the agenda.'[21] The *Financial Times* reflected the tone of post-Thatcher Conservative government opinion, having a chorus of pro-Major commentators on everything from ERM to foreign policy. Whether its views influenced or merely reflected government thinking is immaterial.

Even after the fighting in Slovenia had started, the Foreign Office minister with responsibility for the Balkans still saw an active role for the JNA. Mark Lennox-Boyd told the House of Commons[22] that though the government 'would deplore the use of force . . . I must add however that the Yugoslav federal army might have under the constitution a role in restoring order.' Lennox-Boyd went on to add, as the fighter-bombers swooped over Ljubljana and attacked a convoy of commercial vehicles including British trucks, 'we and our Western partners have a clear preference for the continuation of a single Yugoslav political entity – these words are carefully chosen.'[23]

If the official British position continued to offer aid and comfort to the hardliners, in late May President Mitterrand seemed to anticipate events when he assured Ante Marković on his visit to Paris that France endorsed both his economic programme and his commitment to Yugoslav unity: 'We wish the success of your project and we will help you. We cannot be indifferent to what happens in this region of Europe. We will do everything possible to contribute to your success.' Of course, contrary to Mitterrand's words, it was precisely the assumption that France and her European partners would be indifferent to military measures to preserve Yugoslavia which encouraged the Federalists in Belgrade to contemplate using the army against Slovenia. The same French newspapers reported the President's statement and General Kadijević's threat: 'The Yugoslav Army will defend the frontiers of the republics as much as those of the country and will not be agreeable to the departure of Slovenia.' No one could say that they had not been warned.[24]

However, the capacity of the JNA to impose its will even

temporarily as General Jaruzelski had done in Poland a decade earlier was much more doubtful than the armchair advocates of a hard line in Western newspapers like the *Financial Times* seemed to think. Most observers of Yugoslavia and its military thought that the multi-ethnic components of the JNA would prove unreliable if asked to suppress the democratically elected governments of the republics, especially in the name of saving the Socialist system. Even Serb interests were hardly likely to be served in 'ethnically pure' Slovenia for instance, least of all by 'the large numbers of Albanian . . . conscripts who bear no loyalty to their supposed Serb superiors'.[25] (In fact, the JNA's intervention in Slovenia at the end of June failed as much because of its lack of clear and decisive purposes and the general poor leadership which hampered it throughout its operations against otherwise much less well-equipped opponents in the second half of 1991.)

At the end of the European Community's meeting of heads of government in Rome on 28 October 1990 (best remembered as the one at which the Eleven ganged up against Mrs Thatcher and precipitated her fall because she was rude to Signor Andreotti, whose line on everything from subsidising olive oil producers to preserving the Soviet Union at all costs triumphed – and led to disaster), the Twelve announced their preference for the 'preservation of the unity and territorial integrity of Yugoslavia'. Pious phrases about the need to observe human rights in Yugoslavia were included in the declaration, but any observer in Belgrade could be forgiven for taking more notice of Giulio Andreotti's justification of the Soviet hardliners' crackdown in Lithuania a few weeks later and seeing in it the true expression of the then EC Presidency's feelings towards democratic separatism.[26]

In March 1991, aware of the naive enthusiasm for the idea of membership which existed throughout Yugoslavia, the Twelve issued a statement clearly playing on this aspiration: 'According to the views of the Twelve, a *united* and democratic Yugoslavia has the best chance to harmonically integrate into the new Europe.' (Declaration of 26 March 1991)[27] Unfortunately, the EC like the United States overlooked an inconvenient reality: unity and democracy were logically incompatible in Yugoslavia by then. Encouraging unity as a principle inherently discouraged democracy. Only the Italians recognised this reality. Despite signing such a self-contradictory declaration, Gianni di Michelis then told *Borba* in Belgrade on 17 May 1991, 'According to its present constitutional structure, Yugoslavia could be either united but undemocratic, or democratic – but in pieces.' To rub in the point, di Michelis repeatedly noted that no one in Slovenia or Croatia should be under the illusion that entry to the European Community would be eased by secession from Yugoslavia.[28]

Like his boss, Giulio Andreotti, Michelis was more cynical about what sort of measures were needed to keep multi-ethnic states in one piece, but their colleagues in the Community with the exception of Mrs Thatcher and the Danes regarded the preservation of the Soviet Union and Communist Yugoslavia as a necessity.[29]

The feeling among Mrs Thatcher's colleagues that the disappearance of the Soviet Union would be a disaster for them was shared by her Chancellor of the Exchequer and imminent successor, John Major. Two years after the conflict had started, now Prime Minister, Major told the House of Commons: 'The biggest single cause of what has happened in Bosnia is the collapse of the Soviet Union and the disappearance of the discipline that that exerted over ancient hatreds in the former Yugoslavia . . .'

Mr Major is given to nostalgia and his reverie for the good old days of Mr Brezhnev was palpable when he concluded that 'that collapse was by far the greatest [cause]' of the current tragedy.[30]

Of course, the Prime Minister is always carefully briefed for Question Time, not least given his usual advance knowledge of questions from his own side of the House, and so it is clear that the Foreign Office would have provided the text to back up his natural inclination to preserve the status quo at all costs. Metternich remarked in old age that he and his system had been a 'rock of order' in a changing and unpredictable world. It was a title that the British Prime Minister was apparently willing to bestow posthumously on Leonid Brezhnev and the Soviet regime.

In November 1990, the CIA warned the Bush administration: 'The Yugoslav experiment has failed. The country will fall apart. That will probably be accompanied by acts of violence and unrest that could lead to a civil war.' John Newhouse, who had spoken to various CIA and lower-ranking State Department officials, noted that although they were 'ringing bells' at the beginning of 1991, 'they could not get the attention of their principals – their "betters" . . .'[31] Instead Bush and Baker relied on what Eagleburger called 'a well-tested working relationship' with Milošević.[32] In this they were supported by the West Europeans: one US diplomat remembered that on receiving US intelligence warnings, 'The French were altogether dismissive . . . The British and Germans thought we were overreacting. They weren't prepared for what happened. They could not accept that horrors of the sort going on in Somalia and Kurdistan could occur in their own backyard.'[33]

Whatever the CIA may have read in the tea-leaves, the Administration and especially the State Department were unwilling to face up to the prospect of the disintegration of a country into whose stability so much effort and so many tax-dollars had been put. When the US Senate held hearings on 'civil strife in Yugoslavia' in February 1991 (long before any West European Parliament deigned to take note of disquieting developments there) the State Department sent over experts to emphasise that 'United States policy toward Yugoslavia is founded on support for unity, democracy, dialogue, human rights and market reform. The United States has long supported the unity, independence and territorial integrity of Yugoslavia . . .'

Richard Schifter, the Assistant Secretary of State for Human Rights and Humanitarian Affairs, assured the senators that stability in the new post-Cold War Europe was the Bush administration's prime goal. Good relations with Gorbachev's Kremlin had changed the threat to US interests but not its policy aims: 'Today, it is not so much holding the line against the Warsaw Pact as achieving stability. We are interested in Europe. We are interested in that particular region [the Balkans]. We would like to achieve stability there and a breakup of the Yugoslav federation would be a serious setback.'[34]

Another State Department official told a congressional aide concerned with the human rights situation in Yugoslavia on the eve of the Slovene and Croat declarations of independence not to get too worried about what was happening. 'Don't make a big deal about them. The Serbs are trying to hold the country together . . . Don't break up [Yugoslavia] because [people in] the Soviet Union will use it as a model.' The consequences of a Soviet break-up could be 'nuclear'.[35]

The implications of a collapse of Yugoslavia for the Soviet Union were clearly on the minds of Bush's officials. In a peculiar but revealing slip of the tongue, Deputy-Assistant Secretary of State, James Dobbin, remarked to the Senate Committee, 'An outbreak of violent conflict in Yugoslavia, or indeed *anywhere in the Baltics* [emphasis added], would set back our hopes for a new era of peace, stability and cooperation in Europe.'[36] Although Dobbin presumably meant that violence anywhere in the *Balkans* would set back the Administration's policy, his error revealed the close interlinking between US policy towards ostensibly non-aligned Yugoslavia and the Soviet Union. Eight months later, the British Foreign Office minister, Douglas Hogg, revealed Whitehall's equivalent linkage between the desires of Soviet subject peoples for their independence and the breakdown of Yugoslavia, when he grumpily told a BBC interviewer en route to Vilnius to give hypocritical thanks for Lithuania's just-recognised independence: 'I think it is very important for us in the EC to stress that we are not in the business of recognising Slovenia and Croatia.'[37] Clearly, London, too, shared Bush's irritation with small states and little peoples.

What the West wanted was Yalta with a human face. As soon as Gorbachev offered it, they hurried to accept it. Even as the Soviet Union was decaying before our eyes, and the tide of national independence was flowing so strongly that even the communist *apparatchiks* in the individual Soviet republics were jumping ship, West European political leaders came forward to guarantee the USSR's borders. Against whom, apart from its own peoples, the boundaries of Lenin's crumbling legacy were to be guaranteed was never made clear. Perhaps even the Kohls, Mitterrands and Gonzálezes did not know exactly what they meant by the treaties which they signed. (Giulio Andreotti's sinister endorsement of the hardline clampdown in Lithuania in January 1991 suggests that he at least understood the meaning of his signature on the Treaty on Friendship and Cooperation between the USSR and the Italian Republic signed on 18 November 1990.)[38]

Precisely at the moment when the West seemed to have recovered its will to defend its values and if necessary to impose them by force on malefactors during the Gulf War, the Soviet crackdown in the Baltic states, especially in Lithuania on 20 January 1991, signalled the opposite. Giulio Andreotti hurried to assure the Kremlin that Italy accepted its actions. Tanks on the streets aroused 'emotion' according to Andreotti, but the existence of a state – the USSR – should not be challenged. In Belgrade, the generals and Milošević listened.[39] It seemed that there were moments when it was necessary to have tanks on the streets when the state itself was threatened. In August 1991, Andreotti was honoured with an honorary doctorate in civil law from the University of Beijing, no doubt in recognition of his understanding for the role tanks had played on the streets of that city too. (At the time of writing, Mr Andreotti is under investigation by the public prosecutor in Palermo on the suspicion of involvement with the Mafia, including plotting the murder of political critics.)

Andreotti's commitment to the integrity of federal states which had lost whatever popular legitimacy they might once have possessed was also shared by his rotund, disco-dancing foreign minister, Gianni di Michelis (also currently under investigation for corruption). As late as 31 December 1990, Michelis told *Borba* that he saw 'positive prospects' for Yugoslavia provided the 'extremists' in Slovenia and Croatia did not attempt to break away from Belgrade. Michelis warned Ljubljana and Zagreb that only a 'united' Yugoslavia could hope to enter the coming 'united Europe'. Even his Serbian interviewer seemed shocked by such a blasé attitude towards the impending crisis and asked whether he had really been properly informed by the Italian embassy in Belgrade about the situation in Yugoslavia since all that Michelis' comments would do was help to 'stabilise the confusion' in the country rather than to overcome it.[40]

The EEC had always had a powerful tradition urging preservation of the Socialist Commonwealth to the East as the best guarantor of the peace and quiet essential to West European prosperity. In the aftermath of the Warsaw Pact invasion of Czechoslovakia in August 1968, one of the immortals of the European ideal, the Belgian Paul-Henri Spaak, urged readers of *Le Monde* to remember that 'Not only should member states of NATO refrain from embarking on any cause calculated to weaken the Warsaw Pact, but they should firmly declare their support for the present set-up . . . The policy of détente can only be carried through by the two existing blocs.'[41] As late as April 1991 André Louis, the secretary-general of the Christian Democrat International, the alliance of conservative and Christian Democrat parties into which John Major and Chris Patten took the British Tories, told *Le Monde*, 'The destruction of the Soviet Union has never been an objective of the Christian Democratic International. Many arguments speak in favour of its preservation. The future *incontestably* belongs to the great politico-economic *ensembles*.'[42]

When the EC's foreign ministers met in mid-May 1991, in Brussels along with Jacques Delors, they agreed unanimously to the British Foreign Secretary Douglas Hurd's proposal that it should be made clear to the Yugoslav republics that only a 'united Yugoslavia' could hope for admission to the European Community. Not even the German representative at the meeting, Mrs Seiler-Albring, dissented from the Twelve's decision to send an urgent mission to Belgrade to get that point across to the Yugoslavs. Of course, this support for a continued Yugoslavia was expressed alongside a ritual invocation of a peaceful and negotiated reform of the Yugoslav federation's constitution.[43]

A few days later, the European Parliament in Strasbourg, fresh from its tirade of insults against Boris Yeltsin a month earlier, turned to defending the integrity of another communist multinational state. Although it passed a resolution warning the Yugoslav military against seizing power, the Parliament expressed by an overwhelming majority its preference 'for the preservation of a single Yugoslav state'. How this preservation was to be achieved without the use of force against the declared wishes of the vast majority of inhabitants of Slovenia and Croatia, the Strasbourg Parliament did not condescend to explain.

Few of the European Community's political leaders seem to have understood that the simmering crisis in Yugoslav was about to blow the lid. Perhaps Gianni di Michelis understood the explosive potential better than his colleagues since he admitted to his 'deep worries' about the situation there at the same time as the Community's three key institutions – the Council of Ministers, the European Parliament and the Commission – were still invoking the shadow of dying Yugoslavia.

The only Western statesman in office who persistently warned of the dangers of violence in Yugoslavia and the folly of complacency was the Austrian foreign minister, Alois Mock. Unfortunately, his intuition was ignored by the EC's leaders. Austrian foreign policy-makers were not taken seriously any more in the seats of such continuous great power expertise as London and Paris. Mock's warning that the EC should act 'before every bridge was burnt' in Yugoslavia was ignored by the Twelve who seemed to think, rather like the JNA generals, that securing Yugoslavia's external borders would somehow prevent its internal breakdown.[44]

What the EC's leaders could not comprehend was the bad faith of their interlocutors in Belgrade. Either they lacked any real authority for the undertakings which they gave, like Ante Marković, or they simply lied to buy time for their own preparations, like Milošević. That a simple-minded communist soldier like Kadijević meant what he said also seems to have evaded them. Deluded by their own commitment to federalism in affluent Europe, the EC's elite could not see the widening flaws in the Yugoslav edifice nor that their ill-prepared blundering into the Balkans was in fact helping to promote a violent showdown. The Twelve consistently granted Serbia a veto over how it would respond to any dissolution of Yugoslavia.

On 23 June, the foreign ministers of the Twelve met in Luxembourg and decided not to recognise any declaration of independence by Slovenia and Croatia. The Community also decided 'to refuse all high level contacts' with the two republics if they seceded.[45] According to M. Poos, the Twelve had solemnly concluded that 'the process of internal negotiation has still not been exhausted.' (The following years were to show how exhaustive and debilitating the Twelve's idea of a negotiating process could be.) Poos remarked that recognition of independence could only be the 'result of internal negotiations and arrangements'.

On 24 June, the EEC signed an agreement with Federal Yugoslavia to lend it more than 700 million ECUs until 1995! The NATO Supreme Commander, John Galvin, told Belgrade's *Politika* that NATO would not intervene in any Yugoslav civil war. To round off the incentives to military action, the US Secretary of State, James Baker III, insisted that 'the United States continues to recognize and *support* the territorial integrity of Yugoslavia . . .'[46] En route to a rapturous reception by the naive citizens of the Albanian capital, Tirana, Baker made his fatal comment about 'never' recognising secessionist republics.

At the summit of heads of EC governments in Luxembourg on 26 June 1991, Slovene independence day, eleven of the Twelve showed remarkable indifference to the brewing crisis. The purpose of the summit was to discuss European Union, including the framework for a common foreign and security policy. There was little time for what might be happening just over the Community's borders in Slovenia. That would be a distraction from the process of European unity. Only John Major raised the issue of the Yugoslav crisis at the full session.[47]

This silence on the crisis reflected not indifference but consensus. There was no need to waste time discussing what all agreed on. Events the next day were to confirm that point when the various leaders of the Community who spoke in public as the fighting raged in Slovenia took up John Major's line that 'the great prize is to hold the [Yugoslav] federation together'. The Euro-federalists were not about to let down those whom they assumed to be their blood-brothers in the struggle against petty nationalism. Before too long that illusion would shatter on the rock of stubborn Balkan reality. Others had a less sentimental or idealised view of the merits of the SFRY and clearer reasons for wanting it preserved.

The Soviet government took a close interest in Yugoslav developments throughout the countdown to war. Even on his fateful holiday in the Crimea in August 1991, Mikhail Gorbachev expected to receive each evening a detailed report of the developments there from the Soviet ambassador in Belgrade and the foreign ministry in Moscow.[48] But Gorbachev was no longer in sole control of Soviet policy.

Already in March 1991, Gorbachev's increasingly unreliable defence minister, Dmitri Yazov, had consulted with the Yugoslav hardliners and promised his Yugoslav counterpart, Kadijević, support for the preservation of Yugoslavia and the weapons to achieve that goal. In practice, the high performance Mig-29s and other sophisticated weaponry which Yazov offered proved of little value on the battlefields in Croatia, not least because the JNA proved unable to deploy its equipment to full effect, but the knowledge of support from key figures in the Soviet hierarchy gave encouragement to the generals.

The Soviet foreign ministry was preoccupied with the events in Yugoslavia too. No one in the Stalinist skyscraper which housed the Soviet diplomats on Moscow's Smolensk Square needed reminding of the analogy between the Balkan supranational socialist federation and the USSR itself. If one could fall apart, why should not the other collapse too?

The Soviet deputy foreign minister, Julij Kwizinskij, was sent to Belgrade on 6th July 1991 to assure Milošević, Marković and General Kadijević of the 'willingness of the Soviet Union to help Yugoslavia to solve its problems on a democratic basis and without the use of force' but most importantly 'with the preservation of [Yugoslavia's] unity'.

Even a sympathetic Soviet diplomat like Kwizinskij (who was sacked later in August 1991 for serving the anti-Gorbachev putschists) found General Kadijević's attitudes unreal. 'Like many other Yugoslav politicians, behind the events [Kadijević] saw the hand of the recently reunited Germany, which wanted to extend its sphere of influence as far as the Adriatic . . .' Kwizinskij found this sort of talk 'not very convincing'. Why should Germany provoke a crisis leading to civil war in order to open markets which were already open to her and which German industry dominated? 'Kadijević's ideas seemed to me to be far removed from political reality.' The Yugoslav defence minister was not to be persuaded when Kwizinskij tried to reason with him. 'Do you really think that?' he asked his Soviet visitor harshly. 'We will see who is right. The time is coming again, when Germany will also knock at your door.'

How sincerely Kadijević believed such rantings matters little. The authorities in Belgrade succeeded in hammering home fear of a Fourth Reich into millions of heads including receptive brains in the West. (Sir Alfred Sherman told me that he had been to Germany only once and did not much like what he saw.) As events moved on, so the deep-seated anti-German feelings among Chancellor Kohl's colleagues in London and even more in Paris were to come to the surface. Once the fighting spread to

Croatia, the knee-jerk response of the wartime generation still so influential in London and Paris was to see Tudjman's state through Serb eyes as another puppet of Germany.[49]

However, anyone listening to Chancellor Kohl's views about how to resolve the crisis in the Soviet Union which came to a head after the failure of the putsch with which Kwizinskij had cooperated, would have noted a tone more reassuring for the Yugoslav integralists. On 4 September 1991, the German Chancellor called for the preservation of the Soviet Union. Kohl saw hope in continued unity 'not in fragmentation . . . Only in this way can a framework for effective – and extra – Western commitments be set.' He was backed by the opposition SPD in this line.[50]

Contrary to the view that Helmut Kohl and Hans-Dietrich Genscher deliberately set out to foster the collapse of Yugoslavia, all the evidence points to their desire to preserve it. It was German public opinion which forced Bonn out of the consensus followed by the rest of the EC. Upset by pictures of violence in its former holiday haunts, the German public put pressure on the Bonn establishment to support the right to self-determination in Slovenia and Croatia to which their government had only paid lip-service. In all the fateful months leading up to the crisis the German government loyally endorsed every EC communiqué which misread the situation in Yugoslavia.

Later on, after Chancellor Kohl had pushed his reluctant partners into agreeing to recognise Slovenia and Croatia in the run-up to the Maastricht Conference, the British and French began to spread the legend that Germany had provoked the war by recognising the two republics 'too soon', even though it was in fact six months after the fighting started. This was a crude attempt to sweep under the carpet the Anglo-French role in promoting the disastrous and obdurate policy of trying to hold Yugoslavia together at almost any cost. In fact, like most crude propaganda smears, it succeeded remarkably well. However, it may yet prove to have poisoned the amity among the Twelve since comments by both British and French leaders about Germany's ambitions in the Balkans revealed that a visceral anti-German streak lurked close to the surface in both London and Paris despite the professed devotion of John Major and François Mitterrand to Chancellor Kohl's pet project, the Maastricht Treaty on European Union.

Although as late as November 1991 Warren Zimmermann, the US ambassador to Belgrade, insisted that recognition of the two breakaway republics was not on the agenda,[51] American policy began to waver. From taking a stand against secession, Washington now seemed to want to have it both ways: some sort of Yugoslavia should survive, but equally a kind of self-determination should be tolerated too. By the end of August 1991, the USA had shifted its position from a blind commitment to the preservation of Yugoslavia to an equally rhetorical determination to see neither the external nor the internal borders of the disappearing federation changed by force. The State Department's spokesman, Richard Boucher, informed the press on 29 August, that 'actions which seek to redraw by force the external or internal borders of Yugoslavia represent a dramatic affront to the values and principles which underlie the CSCE.' On 25 September, his boss, James Baker III, addressing the UN Security Council, invoked every initial in the alphabet of the international merry-go-round to denounce the resort to arms in Yugoslavia – without, of course, embarrassing anyone by mentioning names:

> The United States, the European Community and the entire CSCE community have sent a clear message to the peoples of Yugoslavia: the use of force to solve political differences or to change external or internal borders in Yugoslavia is simply not acceptable . . . [They were] a grave challenge to the values and principles which underlie the Helsinki Final Act, the Charter of Paris, and the UN Charter.'

The Security Council itself then voted unanimously that 'no territorial gains or changes *within* Yugoslavia brought about by violence are acceptable.'[52] (Emphasis added.)

The EC mediators put these points to Milošević and his counterparts in a typically condescending manner. Even the Dutch mediator, ambassador Henry Wynaendts, who proved less immune to experience on the ground than his superior ministerial colleagues, could still recount grandly, 'I had more than one occasion to remind President Milošević that the Helsinki Final

Act and the Charter of Paris for a new Europe excluded all forcible changes of borders . . .' These were the very same documents which had been involved only a few months earlier to cow the Slovenes and Croats into revoking their independence. Now these pieces of paper were supposed to intimidate Milošević, but he knew that they had been torn to shreds. Nonetheless, Wynaendts insisted on telling the Serb leader that he was anachronistic, out of touch with the new Europe. These were the harshest words known inside the Twelve, but they cut no ice in Belgrade. Milošević knew who understood the way the world was going better.

Wynaendts' little sermon is worth reading for all that it reveals about the power of an abstract Hegelian idea of the future over a supposedly practical man. It also reveals the deep-seated Eurocentrism, not to say supremacist assumptions of the Eurocrat – and Wynaendts was a most subtle and perceptive one. He records that

> I remarked that in Europe [meaning of course among the Twelve] frontiers were becoming less and less important. The Yugoslavs, who so much aspired to become part of the Community one day, should know that. To change frontiers in order to guarantee the existence of a minority was a notion of the past . . . At the end of our discussion I asked if Yugoslavia wanted to do less well than Africa. The Africans had not touched the frontiers inherited from colonialism.

Little wonder that Milošević and his foreign minister 'smiled' after that homily.[53]

By then, several warm weeks had gone by. The *troika* had brokered ceasefires and returned to renew them when they broke down soon after signature, often before the ink was dry. On 7 July, the Slovenes had been persuaded at Brioni to accept a three-month moratorium on their already proclaimed independence. The EC hoped that all its influence could yet put the Yugoslav Humpty-Dumpty together again. But even in EC capitals that hope began to fade. Only a summer ago, M. Poos had denied the Slovenes and Croats the right to independence because that would break the CSCE Charter's ban on the changing of borders without mutual consent. (Only later, as we shall see, did the question of minority rights, of the Krajina Serbs – i.e. realities on the ground – enter into the discussion.) By September 1991, as the European Community's invocation of a treaty, which none of the Slovenes' or Croats' representatives (nor the Serbs' for that matter) had signed, had failed to halt the war, the big diplomatic guns simply fired off another invocation. Instead of a firm 'no' to independence, now there was a plea not to fight over the boundaries between de facto independent states. It was a little as if the Emperor having admitted that he was not very well dressed, hoped that the little boy pointing to his nakedness would compromise by pretending he was in his underwear. The fantasy life of the Balkans is rich and various but it did not extend that far.

The capacity of Western diplomats to rattle off lists of imposing-sounding initials and to recite the names of mysterious processes and mechanisms reached a peak with the Yugoslav crisis. Whereas the EC was a household name (even if its rotating presidencies and inner workings remained obscure), the CSCE, WEU, Council of Europe and even NACC did – and still do – not figure high in public recognition or respect. The Conference on Security and Cooperation in Europe (CSCE) had been one of Leonid Brezhnev's long-cherished schemes. In 1975, the West Europeans plus the United States and Canada had signed the Helsinki Agreement which guaranteed existing borders. It also contained a human rights 'basket', but Brezhnev and his comrades regarded that as so much window-dressing for the West (so too at the time did the Western signatories). By the late 1980s, that much had changed and Gorbachev's Soviet Union had undergone enormous transformations in terms of civil rights, but no one wanted to change boundaries.

With the end of the Cold War, Gorbachev was able to get the West to enshrine the new order in the so-called Charter of Paris (signed in November 1990). Even then, hints of growing instability caused the architects of the new European order to seek means to freeze change. Just days before the fighting began around Slovenia's borders, one of these new diplomatic methods, the 'conflict prevention mechanism' of the CSCE came into effect. As events turned out, the effectiveness of this piece of paper was more than limited.

The CSCE, like the League of Nations established by the Paris Peace Settlement of 1919, depended upon unanimity for its operations. It also required more than lip-service. Even when the 35 member states of the CSCE could agree to a resolution, it did not oblige them to act on their verbal support. In short, the CSCE was a talking-shop. It shared that characteristic, and several others, with the League of Nations. When it came to dealing with conflict, the CSCE rules presumed, like the League's, that every state would agree who was in the wrong at the outbreak of any conflict and that therefore the aggressor would be friendless. As events showed very quickly in the summer of 1991, agreement on who was to blame for the fighting in Yugoslavia was not forthcoming (even among the West European states) and even when Serbia was generally held responsible that did not mean that she had no friends.

In the confident afterglow of the end of East-West tension, the CSCE members agreed to another 'basket' of mechanisms to add to their array of 'confidence-building measures' already established. The buzz-words were 'conflict prevention' and a 'new European security architecture'. They were pronounced with awe by diplomats and experts like the mumbo-jumbo of an ancient religion whose cult survives even after the meaning of its prayers has been forgotten. Simply pronouncing the alphabet soup gave diplomats the power to bring peace. As late as November 1991, the NATO foreign and defence ministers announced, 'We are working towards a new European security architecture in which NATO, the CSCE, the European Community, the WEU and the Council of Europe complement each other.' As conflict spread from Slovenia to Croatia and threatened Bosnia this sort of meaningless bureaucratic substitute for language was churned out. It was as if Ptolemaic astronomers had continued to pontificate after Copernicus had been published. If knowledge depended upon the CSCE rules of unanimity and its mechanisms, no doubt Ptolemy would enjoy a respected hearing as the last word on astronomy to this very day.

In practice of course the CSCE and its 'conflict prevention mechanisms' – a few unarmed men in suits with diplomatic passports and instructions to see all sides of the question – quickly renounced any role. Instead, in the highest tribute that one quango can pay to another, the CSCE effectively passed the parcel containing the time-bomb to the EC. But the symbolic importance of the CSCE for the ever-deepening crisis should not be overlooked. Its mentality and flaws were not its own. On the contrary they were the product of the coming together of the best and brightest in the post-Cold War world. In reality their mental formation was dominated by the experience of the long years of stability before 1989: the advocates of the CSCE process as the cure-all were the pre-Copernicans of peace.

Members of the CSCE are supposed to be equal, but in reality neither the USA nor Russia can be treated on a par with the others. Britain and France as members of the UN Security Council have always presumed a certain distance from the rest, especially the lesser East-Central European 'new democracies'. The denizens of the FCO in King Charles Street have always expressed disdain for little countries ever since the stable map began to break up with the First World War. As Britain's power declined in the twentieth century, the Foreign Office's condescending attitude to new or weak countries grew as the distance in power and prestige separating them from Britain declined. To the mind trained in the Foreign Office, the desire of small nations for independence and their own identity was synonymous with petty and unworthy squabbling. Why couldn't these foreigners be more like the British, or at least their diplomats, who were quite ready to renounce national sovereignty for the greater good?

When he spoke to the House of Commons as the fighting in Slovenia was continuing, Douglas Hurd – a Foreign Office creature man and boy – evinced this well-rehearsed dislike of the ambitions of lesser races to clutter the map by expressing the fear that the acceptance of their right to self-determination must lead to war. He gave vent to a weary worldly-wise expectation of worse to come if the Slovenes and Croats carried on defying the centralising forces of history. As it happens his words were prescient, but only because he was to labour for two years to turn them into a self-fulfilled prophecy of Lebanonisation:

> I am reluctant to imagine that the only future for the peoples of Yugoslavia is as a series of small states quarrelling [with one another] and all depending in one way or another on the West

> for economic support. There must be some relationship – some effective working relationship – between these peoples, but only they can work it out . . . [54]

The Foreign Secretary admitted that it would have to be 'on a quite different basis from the one that is now disintegrating', but failed to note that the very violent nature of the disintegration precluded a return of Slovenia to the Yugoslav Federation and made further collapse inevitable.

PART TWO

Yugoslav History, 1804–1991

The most common explanation of the war in the Balkans is that it is simply the return of an age-old conflict among traditionally warring tribes. In fact, this is wrong. Unlike the relations between the member states of the European Community, Serbs and Croats do not have a long history of almost incessant warfare. Since medieval times it is only in the twentieth century that they have fought each other on their own account. As much cannot be said about Frenchmen and Germans, or the British and many of their Community partners. Despite the recent basis of the conflict, propaganda has argued that its roots lie deep in the past, so without a discussion of the region's history, and the myths and legends built up around it, the peculiarities of the present conflict cannot be understood.

3

The Road to Sarajevo: The Balkans, 1804–1914

> The last thing that a peacekeeper wants to know is the history of the region he is going into. It complicates the task of mediation.
>
> Major-General Lewis Mackenzie[1]

Anyone who has been subject to the claims and counter-claims of the warring groups in Yugoslavia may be inclined to sympathise with the wilful ignorance of the UNPROFOR commander, but reluctance to get involved in the intricacies of mutually incompatible historical claims should not blind the outside observer to the importance of the past. The facts of the past may be in dispute, but the stuff of these controversies is the background to the current conflict.

Although a great deal of ink has been spilled over the question of the medieval origins and right of first possession to various territories of Serbs or Croats or Muslims or Bosnians or Albanians, the modern history of Yugoslavia began with the decay of Turkish rule. The Turkish conquest of the Balkans in the fourteenth and fifteenth centuries eclipsed the medieval Slav and Christian states, submerging some for centuries under Ottoman rule and pushing the north-western peoples, Slovenes and Croats, plus some Serbs firmly into the grip of the Habsburgs. During this period of Ottoman rule, the ethnic and religious map of the Balkans was in flux beneath the apparently static domination of the Sultan. Migrations and conversions changed the distribution of peoples, but it was only with the waning of the Sublime Porte's power around the turn of the eighteenth century that conditions began to emerge for the creation of independent Balkan states.[2]

The late twentieth-century counterpart to the dilemmas created by the withering of the Ottoman Empire in the nineteenth has been the collapse of the Soviet Union. Unlike contemporary Western leaders who have regarded the disappearance of their great rival with undiluted horror, nineteenth-century statesmen were ambiguous in their response to the decay of Turkey. Few were as openly and undilutedly pro-Turk as Metternich. If the emergence of independent Slav states presented a threat to the Habsburgs – for instance, because of their own Slav minorities – it also offered opportunities for further expansion into the territories abandoned by the Sultan. However, the Habsburgs were not alone in viewing the Sultan's lands with interested eyes. The rivalry between the Great Powers about how best to deal with the power vacuum emerging in south-eastern Europe created what they called the 'Eastern Question'.[3]

External influences were vital to the progress of the 'Eastern Question', or what locals in the Balkans characterised as time went by as a national liberation struggle. Throwing off the shackles of Ottoman rule left an historical void of almost five centuries before the newly independent could find something in their own past worthy of emulation and suitable to be regarded as the basis of continuity in the modern age. Unfortunately, it was easier to conjure up a romanticised medieval history (with the help of easily available models already published in nearby Vienna) than to shake off the legacy of the Ottoman past.

While Slovenes and Croats still lived docilely under Habsburg rule beyond the Ottoman boundary, stirrings of discontent were threatening the Sultan's rule in his northern Balkan provinces. Ironically, this restiveness came primarily not from his Christian subjects, but among his Muslim officials and soldiers who ruled the region around Belgrade on his behalf. What made the Ottoman ruling elite turn against the Sultan was his efforts to reform the system which had degenerated from a pyramid of power devolved downwards from Constantinople into de facto provincial autonomy.

Napoleon's invasion of Egypt and the subsequent direct British involvement in the fighting against the French inside the Empire brought home to the Sultan Selim how vulnerable the Ottoman system was to the infidel powers to the West. Only reform to restore the Empire's military prowess could save it from dismemberment by the Europeans. But reform involved challenging the complacency and corruption which several centuries of relative security had bred among the Ottoman elite. The Ottoman Empire found itself in the not unusual situation for declining powers that its greatness could only be saved by sacrificing the privileges of the elite which had mismanaged it. Needless to say, that elite saw little reason to sacrifice itself to save the Empire.

The beginnings of Serb independence lay therefore not in a Christian revolt against the Sultan, but the willingness of Serbs to fight for the Caliph in Constantinople against his rebellious Muslim subjects, the janissaries. By the 1790s the janissaries had little in common with the elite troops of the Sultans who had been so feared by Christian Europe for centuries. The institution, *devshirme*, of a fighting force composed of the sons of Christians taken from their parents and converted to Islam, then bound to celibacy as soldiers of the Sultan, had decayed by the eighteenth century. The janissaries were allowed to marry and, in an effort to reduce their power over the succession when they had acted like the Praetorians of Imperial Rome, they had been dispersed into the provinces, where they could exploit the Christian population without disturbing the Sultan, it was hoped.[4]

The outbreak of war with Austria in 1788 had brought home to Selim what a threat the corrupt and inefficient janissaries could be to his empire even from a distance. The Austrian invasion found support among local people, including a pig-breeder, Kara Djordje Petrović, who joined an irregular force to help the invader against the Turk, which meant of course in practice against the local Muslim pasha and his janissaries. His nickname 'Kara Djordje', from the Turkish word for 'black' stuck and 'Black George' was to leave his name to the dynasty which was to shape Serbian history for almost one hundred and fifty years. But around 1800 that was still an improbable future with no one expecting it. Because Selim had little affection for his subordinates in Belgrade, Kara Djordje had little difficulty resuming life under Ottoman rule.

Defeat by Austria made Selim even more determined to reform his military as Napoleon's adventure in Egypt began. The Sultan's attempts to re-establish his authority pushed many of the Muslims into open revolt and he was forced to call upon his Christian subjects to help him recover control of the Belgrade pashalik.

Violent and daring men like Kara Djordje were useful to Selim in his struggle with insubordinate local officials.

A confused round of fighting involving Selim's attempts to play off fractious Muslim against ostensibly loyal Serb followed. Although he indicated that the Serbs would enjoy self-rule in return for aiding him against their immediate Muslim rulers, Selim had no intention of granting autonomy to either side if he could help it. Later, nationalist myths were to render these dubious quarrels, where allegiance was flexible and even kinsmen and fellow believers expendable, more clear-cut than they were. (This was true throughout the Balkans: the Byronic philhellenes who arrived to aid the Greek struggle for independence were shocked by the inter-Hellene blood-letting that went on during the so-called patriotic struggle.)[5]

Faced by increasing brutality on the part of the *dayis*, the local Turkish rulers, which culminated in a pre-emptive massacre of the leading local Christians in January and February 1804, the Serbs rose in revolt, hoping to rid themselves of their immediate oppressors and to persuade the distant Sultan of their right to self-government. They chose Kara Djordje as their leader. His business as a pig-trader had given him some contact with the world beyond the Sultan's empire and he recognised that the Serbs could only win their battle with the help of the Austrians and the Russians. Both gave some help, but in the end the intervention of loyal Ottoman forces proved decisive in defeating the Sultan's Muslim enemies. It soon became clear that the Sultan would not grant the concessions which the Serbs led by Kara Djordje had expected and they revolted again, encouraged by Russia, which saw Turkey as a de facto ally of the Tsar's enemy, Napoleon.

So long as Russia was strong, the Serbs had the upper hand, but when France attacked Russia in 1812, their position worsened dramatically. The Turks took advantage of Napoleon's march on Moscow to wreak a terrible revenge on the Serbs. When order was restored an amnesty was issued and many prominent Serbs resumed their normal lives and agreed to serve the Sultan. The most important was Miloš Obrenović, who like Kara Djordje was a pig-farmer and local potentate turned rebel but now willing to ingratiate himself again with the Ottomans. As illiterate and brutal as Kara Djordje, Miloš knew how to control his temper better and therefore offended fewer people needlessly. He possessed an oriental ability to dissimulate his true feelings which anybody who wanted to get on in the Ottoman world had to learn, but most of all a Christian with ambitions.

The Ottoman legacy deeply influenced Serbian culture far more than modern Serb nationalists are prepared to admit. Turkish rule certainly was often harsh, sometimes irrationally so. Memorials of savage repression of any defiance of Ottoman authority survived. The most infamous was the pyramid of human skulls at Niš which recalled the defeat of Serb rebels. Lamartine saw it and left a grisly account:

> There could have been fifteen to twenty thousand [skulls]; to some of them hair was still attached and it hung like lichen or fluttered like moss in the wind; the mountain breeze blew lively and fresh, and it rushed through the innumerable cavities in the heads, through the faces and skulls, making plaintive and pitiful wheezing.[6]

The memory of suffering has marked Serbs. Unfortunately, past victimhood does not necessarily make for virtue in subsequent generations. The misfortunes of the ancestors all too easily are called into account to justify their descendants' own acts of injustice and dishonesty. Even imitation of the methods and crimes of the Turk become legitimised as revenge – even when directed at fellow Christians rather than the infidel enemy. The more they insist on the history of Serb resistance to Ottoman rule, the more elements of continuity appear through the rhetoric. It was not just that Serbs and their relatives the Montenegrins dressed in Turkish style wearing fezzes and turbans as appropriate, ate with their fingers and listened to a clearly orientalised folk music. The Ottoman influence on political attitudes and methods went to the heart of their behaviour. The history of political murder in Serbia is a case in point. The Ottomans were ruthless in dispatching not only their enemies through assassination but also in settling the succession within the family by murder. The silken noose disposed of countless unfortunate and inconvenient siblings of the Sultans. Viziers who failed their lord were equally prone to strangulation or the loss of their heads.[7]

Both Kara Djordje's setting out on the road to rule and his eventual downfall were marked by classic acts of murder. The modern history of Serbia began with a murder. According to legend, Kara Djordje's stepfather advised him against arousing the Sultan's wrath by open rebellion and was unwilling to join the young man, preferring that they should throw themselves on the Sultan's mercy. (In fact, Miloš Obrenović, one of Kara Djordje's erstwhile allies, succeeded in doing just that.) Afraid that the old man's doubts would become contagious and infect his band, and probably furious at anyone questioning his wisdom, the son shot him *pour encourager les autres.*

There had been many violent deaths before Kara Djordje killed his stepfather and there were to be more afterwards, but the decision of the ambitious son to shoot his recalcitrant father, who was unwilling to join his revolt against the Ottoman Sultan at the beginning of the nineteenth century, was symbolic. It showed that the revolt against Ottoman rule would be fought with Ottoman methods. Liberation would not involve cultural transformation. It also foretold Kara Djordje's own fate at the hands of a previously loyal ally.

Kara Djordje's uncontrollable temper made rivals into fearful enemies. He would not tolerate any real limitation on his power as leader, while the other influential Serbs wanted a collegiate approach. Miloš Obrenović came from a similar milieu to Kara Djordje but proved more politic in his approach to his fellow local leaders. Although as illiterate as Kara Djordje, Miloš was a more astute diplomat: his double-crossing of erstwhile partners came as a surprise more often. He courted the Sultan as an ally and rejected as a tactic the head-on clash with Ottoman authority. Even under extreme provocation from savage Turkish reprisals against former rebel Serbs between 1813 and 1815, Milos was always careful to proclaim his loyalty to the Sultan. But by 1821, partly with the aid of international pressure from Russia and even Austria-Hungary on Constantinople to quieten the situation in the border regions, Miloš had gained the position of *knez* or local prince under the Sultan and in effect was able to control the administration of Serbia, given the laxity and corruption of the local Turkish pasha, who took his bribes.

Removing rivals for the leadership of the Serbian people, especially those less inclined to compromise with the Sultan, meant that Miloš strengthened his position and curried favour with distant Constantinople. On 13 July 1817, Kara Djordje was murdered (by his godfather) at Miloš Obrenović's command and his severed head sent to the Sultan in Constantinople where it was displayed to the faithful in the Hippodrome. It was the beginning of a vendetta between the two families which continued until the Obrenovićs were exterminated by the heirs of Kara Djordje in 1903.[8]

Through his ownership of estates in Wallachia across the Danube from Serbia, Miloš knew that Kara Djordje had contact with the local Greek minority, which in turn was the centre of a planned anti-Ottoman revolt across the Balkans. Disposing of his rival distanced Miloš from any rebellion which might bring down the rage of the Sultan on himself and the Serbs. In fact, the savagery of the Turkish response to the Greek revolt backfired because unlike the other Balkan subjects of the Sultan, the Greeks enjoyed a high reputation in the powerful West as the direct descendants of the heroes of Ancient Greece.[9]

Gradually, the British and French were drawn into the Greek conflict. Russia too saw the chance of extending her influence back into the territories of the Second Rome, Byzantium, of which Moscow, 'the Third Rome', was the successor. Only Metternich counselled complete indifference to the carnage in the land of Pericles. Foreshadowing the failures of the CSCE 170 years later, the Concert of Europe tried to limit the scope of the conflict by imposing a naval blockade on the Greek peninsula and islands in order to prevent the movement of troops and arms. Anxious to avoid being drawn into the war, the British government directed Admiral Codrington to enforce the blockade without using force! Both sides were bewildered by the impenetrable machinations of Allied policy.[10]

The tragi-comic Battle of Navarino ensued on 20 October 1827 when the combined Anglo-French and Russian fleets made short work of the Turkish fleet. Greek independence was won, but the consequences of Navarino were almost a disaster for the Serbs, not least for Miloš Obrenovič's representatives in Constantinople at the time. The first reaction of the Sultan was to kill them. Fortunately, Russian intervention saved them and the ensuing Russo-Turkish war created conditions for Serbia's autonomy. By 1830, Miloš had been recognised as hereditary prince of Serbia under the (largely notional) sovereignty of the Sultan. Under a ruler who still wore turbans, pantaloons and slippers, who ate with his fingers and sat on a divan, the Serbs could be said to be breaking their bonds with Ottoman rule. A Turkish garrison remained in the Kalmegdan fortress dominating Belgrade until 1867 and the Sultan's flag was flown until full independence in 1878, but in practice after 1830 the Serbs of the principality ruled themselves.

Choosing their own rulers turned out to be far from a smooth matter. The descendants of Kara Djordje lurked waiting for revenge and could rely on anyone offended by the Obrenovićs to turn to them. Until 1839, Miloš was engaged in regular battles with his most powerful former allies who expected their *knez* to share power and its profits with them. The word 'constitution' was bandied about as a fashionable weapon to attack Miloš, but in practice his opponents disliked the greedy prince's unwillingness to share the fruits of office with them. In 1839, Miloš was forced out and replaced by his sickly son, Milan. But this proved only a stop-gap measure. In 1842, Milan was deposed and replaced by Alexander, son of Kara Djordje. A purge of the Obrenović faction followed in what was to become the normal fashion. Meanwhile old Miloš conspired against his enemies from across the Danube in Wallachia.

The new prince's most important adviser was Ilija Garašanin. His significance lasted far beyond the new prince's reign since he was the first author of a conscious pan-Serb political programme. In 1844, Garašanin prepared a memorandum, 'The Blueprint' (Nacertanije) which was to be the model for the Serbian Academy of Science's fateful document in 1986. Garašanin set out the programme of a 'Greater Serbia.' He looked back to the long vanished greatness of medieval Serbia under Dušan five centuries earlier. He wanted Alexander's principality to act as the core of a future Serb state incorporating the Serbs still under Ottoman or Habsburg rule. Garašanin regarded the Croats simply as Catholicised Serbs, but recognised that religion could prove an obstacle to the pan-Serb unity that he sought, so he urged that it should be a secular ideology.

Like other early proponents of Serb unity, Garašanin looked to the greatest Slav power, Russia, as the likely protector and promoter of Greater Serbia. Again and again the Serb pan-Slavists were to be disappointed as tsars and their ministers regarded their Balkan brothers with thinly disguised contempt. Nicholas I's Foreign Minister, Nesselrode, wrote to Alexander Karadjordjević in November 1852, to remind him in no uncertain terms that 'all the privileges which Serbia enjoys today were paid for so to speak with Russian blood, because they were acquired on the basis of treaties concluded at the end of bloody wars conducted by Russia'.

It was not only Serb ministers who had to face up to brutal reminders of Russian indifference to Serbia as anything other than a pawn on the diplomatic chessboard. Leading figures in reawakening Serb culture got the cold shoulder too. Vuk Karadžić,the poet and shaper of so many Serb national myths, recounted his frustrating experience in St Petersburg in 1818. After a fruitless wait for an imperial audience which had lasted several weeks, he was at last received by Count Golovkin, Alexander I's ambassador to Vienna, who told him dismissively that Serbs 'were nothing more than Germans [!], that the Muscovites had never had any interest in us, now had no interest in us and saw no reason to change their opinion'. When Karadžić offered the Count his famous collection of Serbian folk stories, *Norodna srpska pesnarica*, which had delighted Goethe and the Brothers Grimm, he was told in no uncertain terms, 'He could not read Serbian and in any case had no time for reading.'[11]

Karadžić played a vital role in creating modern Serbian identity. The myths and legends which he collected and published had been recited by countless generations, but his work was an essential link in the process of converting them from exciting or tragic stories about a common past into a national myth justifying political action in the future. Whereas even stories about rebels against the Sultan had a timeless quality about them – the Sublime Porte's authority was taken as a given against which a bold man struggled as a bandit (*Hajduk*) rather than as a revolutionary

– it was only in the nineteenth century that folk legends came to be interpreted as part of a struggle for liberation from Ottoman rule. Instead of a perpetual round of brutal oppression, bold rebellion and savage suppression, hope appeared for the first time that the Turk could be expelled.[12]

In this context, the legends of Kosovo came to play a special role. Redemption of that defeat became imaginable. At the same time, the desire to couple contemporary history back onto the continuum of medieval pre-Ottoman life emerged. The new bards of Serbian and Montenegrin life were widely travelled and well aware of the condescending attitude of their Christian neighbours to the north towards the Sultan's erstwhile subjects, whom they regarded as unfortunate bandits and shepherds without history.

It was not only the Serbs who had passed under Ottoman rule who had disappeared to a great extent from the memory of the West. The Slav subjects of the Habsburgs fared little better. The average Englishman in the nineteenth century probably no more associated his 'cravat' with the Croats ('Hvrats') than his late twentieth-century successors. But the Croats were to suffer a worse fate than simply to be forgotten. When they re-emerged onto the historical stage – at least into the line of sight of opinion formers in the West – in 1848, it was to play the role of reactionaries. Worse still for the Croats, their role was immortally damned by the two most influential ideologues of the modern age – Karl Marx and Friedrich Engels.

While Serbia developed towards full independence, Croatia remained part of the Habsburg Empire. Even in 1848, when so many of Franz Josef's people revolted, the Croats remained loyal. That they did so less out of undiluted affection for Habsburg absolutism than because the Hungarians who had lorded it over Croatia for centuries had transformed themselves into the vanguard of revolution made little difference in the eyes of the world. The role of the Croat forces led by Ban Jellaćić in suppressing the liberal revolution in Vienna and then the Hungarian rebels marked them down as a reactionary nation.

Karl Marx and Friedrich Engels damned them as the arch-collaborators with tottering reaction: 'An Austria shaken to its very foundations was kept in being and secured by the enthusiasm of the Slavs for the black and yellow; . . . it was precisely the

Croats, Slovenes, Dalmatians . . .'[13] But the two prophets of Marxism tinged their savage political condemnation of the Croats with a genocidal, albeit 'progressive', racism.

Along with the Czechs and the Russians, whose troops had dealt the death-blow to the revolutionary dreams of 1848, it was the Croats who were excommunicated from the future communist society by Marx and Engels. An anonymous poet in Marx's paper, the *Neue Rheinische Zeitung* could not find abuse enough for them: the Croats were 'That horde of miscreants, rogues and vagabonds . . . riff-raff, abject peasant hirelings, vomit . . .' But it was left to Engels to issue the terrible formal sentence of annihilation on the Croats like other inherently 'counter-revolutionary peoples'. Convinced that he knew where history was going and that it belonged to great homogenising peoples like the Germans and had no room for little nations who got in the way, like the Gaels or Basques as well as Croats, Engels proclaimed that the 'South Slavs are nothing more than the national refuse of a thousand years of immensely confused development'. Anticipating Poos' horror of autonomous development outside his own intellectual tramlines, Engels noted that 'this national refuse . . . sees its salvation solely in a reversal of the entire development of Europe . . .' His conclusion was that a 'war of annihilation and ruthless terrorism' was necessary against 'reactionary' and 'unhistoric' peoples as well as reactionary classes.[14]

Engels remained decidedly unsympathetic to the aspirations of the South Slavs for independence or unity until the end of his days. Even in the 1880s, *after* all the public outrage in Britain about the Bosnian and Bulgarian atrocities, he could still write to Bernstein that the Hercegovinans' 'right to cattle-rustling must be sacrificed *without mercy* to the interests of the European proletariat', which lay in peace at that time.[15] Both Marx and Engels bequeathed to the Left in the twentieth century a powerful tendency to sympathise with large-scale 'progressive' states at the expense of the poor and small.

Whether Croats or Red Indians, not to mention Kazakhs, progress in the eyes of the Marxists demanded their assimilation into the dominant 'progressive' culture or their destruction. Contemporary left-wing sympathy for the underdog and the disappearing tribe is decidedly un-Marxist. For a hundred years, the dominant assumption on the radical left was that big states were modern and therefore part of the progress towards communism. In the Soviet Union, it stood to reason therefore that 'russification' was beneficial. The association of nationalism with rebellion against the Soviet system simply confirmed the prejudice inherited from 1848 that small nations were inherently reactionary. It was hardly surprising therefore that the last true Marxist groups and their organs (like *Living Marxism*) instantly and instinctively took the side of Greater Serbia after 1991.[16]

The Croats earned the badge of the reactionary Cain who had murdered the Abel of revolution despite the fact that, in 1848, the Hungarian radicals were not Gladstonian liberals. The Hungarian Parliament refused even to recognise the Croatian language until the Russian Army was on the march to help Franz Josef. In fact, far from showing any desire to work with the Slav or Romanian population of Hungary, some of the more advanced Hungarian revolutionaries came up with the idea of 'ethnic cleansing'. After his capture, General Görgey claimed that the Hungarian leader, Lajos Kossuth, had planned 'to eradicate root and branch the Serbs of the Banat [north-west of Belgrade] and to settle the land with Honveds [militia]'.[17] (Of course, their victorious enemies also considered displacing the Hungarian population in many places, but in the end Schwarzenberg did not carry through the plan: it was the nineteenth century and he was a gentleman after all.)

Even when it came to the establishment of a South Slav state after the First World War, the British Prime Minister, David Lloyd George, was not terribly concerned for the Croats because of the centralising ambitions of Belgrade. He sympathised with the Italian claims to Istrian and Dalmatian territory despite the clear evidence of demography. 'It was the Croats,' he wrote, 'who had been used by the Habsburgs to crush and keep down Italian liberty, to hunt, imprison and execute Italian patriots.' Lloyd George quoted A. H. Clough on the theme of the Croat as the oppressor of Italy in the cause of Austria which summed up nineteenth-century liberal attitudes (and how they ran on well into this century):

I see the Croat soldier stands,
Upon the grass of your redoubts;
The eagle with his black wings flouts
The breath and beauty of your land.[18]

Decades of the growth of educational self-help and national assertion in classic liberal ways in Croatia in the nineteenth century did nothing to shake off the reactionary image of the Croats in the West. Their subjection to the Habsburgs meant that they played no part in what enlightened opinion saw romantically as the heroic struggle of Serbia to free itself, and then the other South Slavs, from Ottoman rule. For three decades after his fall, Vienna abided by Metternich's doctrine that Austria should resist the temptation to partition Turkey in Europe for fear of destabilising the whole international system.

A generation after the suppression of the 1848 revolutions, Austria-Hungary bordered to her south-east a region with four Christian states, Greece plus Romania, Serbia and Montenegro scattered around the periphery of the Ottoman possessions in the Balkans. Franz Josef's foreign minister, Andrassy, reported to the Crown Council shortly before the neighbouring Ottoman provinces erupted in revolt in 1875:

> Turkey possesses a utility almost providential for Austria-Hungary. For Turkey maintains the *status quo* of the small Balkan states and impedes their national aspirations. If it were not for Turkey all those aspirations would fall on our heads . . . If Bosnia-Hercegovina should go to Serbia or Montenegro, or if a new state should be formed there which we cannot prevent, then we should be ruined and should ourselves assume the role of 'Sick Man'.[19]

A contemporary Serb nationalist, Svetozar Marković made a parallel point:

> The idea of Serb unity is the most revolutionary idea that exists on the Balkan peninsula, from Istanbul to Vienna. The idea already contains within it the need of destroying Turkey and Austria, the end of Serbia and Montenegro as independent principalities and the revolution in the whole political make-

> up of the Serb people. A new Serbian state will rise from portions of these two empires and two principalities – that is the meaning of Serb unification.[20]

Even in 1875 with the outbreak of open revolt in Bosnia-Hercegovina, then in Bulgaria, the Austrian government hoped to pacify the situation in the Balkans through reform, albeit reforms forced on the Sultan by the Great Powers. This meant that the Slovenes and Croats in the Austrian Army played no role in the great crisis except to move into Bosnia-Hercegovina after the Congress of Berlin had awarded it to Austrian administration in 1878. Instead of serving the national cause as imagined by Western liberals, once again the Slav subjects of Franz Josef seemed hopelessly loyal to the monarchy.

Serbia's intervention on the side of the Bosnian rebels resulted in a military fiasco and Belgrade hurried to make peace with the Sultan in March 1877. Milan Obrenović was afraid that Russia's intervention in the war would be to the benefit of Bulgaria, as indeed turned out to be the case, and he seems to have got wind of the Tsar's offer to Vienna to let Bosnia-Hercegovina pass to Habsburg rule if Franz Josef remained neutral in the coming Russo-Turkish War. In fact, Alexander II's sponsorship of a 'Big Bulgaria' covering the Macedonian and Albanian territory which Belgrade coveted was quickly reversed by the Congress of Berlin in 1878, but it revealed how indifferent, if not downright hostile, Russia was towards Serbia's ambitions.[21] Serbia's unsuccessful war against Turkey was soon followed up by an equally disastrous campaign against newly established Bulgaria in 1881. Any hopes that the Ottomans would be quickly expelled from Europe died with this fresh evidence of the military incapacity of Serbia and the ease with which the newly established states fell on each other.

Political life in Serbia had been unstable throughout the period. The rule of Alexander Karadjordjević proved no more lasting than the previous Obrenović rule. Like many post-colonial states in the twentieth century, Serbia found it difficult to establish even a government, let alone constitutional government. What contemporaries in the West sneered at as 'Balkan' intrigues but which the late twentieth century sees as the typical politics of the

Third World too, were not so much the birth pangs of the new order but the death throes of the old.

Alexander Karadjordjević was overthrown in 1858 and the octogenarian, Miloš Obrenović, put back in power by the cabal of clans which decided such matters under the grand name of the Serbian Soviet. A kind of simulated Western style of constitutionalism plus a simulacrum of Western economic progress had been going on in Serbia during the nineteenth century. There was a formal politics around the rivalry of Liberals and Conservatives, but it was hardly the world of Trollope. Pig-farming remained the country's most lucrative activity.

Already in the 1860s the idea that Serbia would do for South Slav unity what Piedmont had done for Italian unification in 1860 – and what Prussia was doing for Germany – excited the followers of Garašanin, who was close to Miloš Obrenović's successor, Michael. Michael was unable to test his newly established army in anything other than skirmishes with the remaining Turkish garrisons who still flew the Sultan's flag, to the irritation of the surrounding Serbs. Under Milan, his cousin and successor, the Serb Army was found wanting.

Michael himself proved wanting in the basic function of a would-be hereditary monarch: he could not provide an heir of his own flesh. His marital arrangements scandalised the Orthodox Serbs without producing the required son. It probably was not Michael's fault but he certainly seems to have shared a fatal genetic flaw in the Obrenović family: a tendency to marry barren women. This reached its climax under the last Obrenović, but the inability of the Obrenović clan to breed bonny boys must have raised the hopes of the exiled Karadjordjevićs that their time might yet come again. However, the brutal murder of Michael in the company of his hated Catholic fiancée and his mother and grandmother in 1868 was only a faint pre-echo of the bloody dénouement of the Obrenovićs in 1903.

Obrenović rule was marked by a simulated Westernisation. Just as centuries of Ottoman autocracy had taught them to feign obedience to the tenets of the Sultan, so now the hope for respectability in the West and the loans and investment which would follow persuaded successive Serbian rulers to promulgate constitutions with impeccable liberal phrases. Miloš Obrenović's successor, Michael, even established a supreme court and a bill of rights. In practice, neither prince nor people expected much from the written law. Anti-Jewish feeling, for instance, had already alarmed Western observers and diplomats before full sovereignty in 1878; and despite assurances that Serbia would treat all its inhabitants as equal citizens it remained so afterwards.

Of course, Serbia was not alone in Europe in witnessing the survival and even the strengthening of anti-Semitism and xenophobic feelings in a complacently liberal age. Everywhere minorities like Jews or gypsies who might welcome equal rights but did not always wish to renounce their own religion and customs as the price of equality found themselves resented. In France and Germany as well as the Balkans, liberalism in the later nineteenth century did not equal pluralism. On the contrary, the liberals were frequently intolerant of any departure from their model of enlightenment. Religious groups were regarded as inherently reactionary by progressive thinkers, none more so than Jews who had not even taken the step to Christianity which was seen as leading to the wisdom of the enlightenment.[22]

In newly established nation-states, whether Serbia or Germany, intellectuals and state propagandists in the education system as well as the media fostered the identity of race and state often without thinking through the consequences for minorities. At the same time the irony of industrial and scientific progress was that it fostered a nostalgia for pre-modern cultural values even among liberals. A naive primitivism went hand in hand with the railways. It was frequently argued that before Christianity, Europeans had lived simpler, more noble and also more 'enlightened' lives. The Church had replaced primitive rationality with obscurantism and oppression.

Rationalist anti-religious feeling and the new science of race in the later nineteenth century combined with the cult of the nation-state as the secular godhead was promoted by the most prestigious societies in Europe. It was hardly surprising that latecomers to the status of nation-states saw the adoption of such ideas as a badge of respectability. In the case of Serbia, another modern trend was also influential.

If the interest of the Russian tsars in the Balkans had proved a mixed blessing, perhaps their enemies were more worthy of imitation. The nihilist terrorists who struck at the Tsarist system with bomb and bullet aroused considerable sympathy among Serb radicals. The revival of the Kosovo myth connected with the admiration for the assassins of Alexander II of Russia in 1881 and their followers afterwards. Of course, Serbia had seen more than her fair share of political murders, but the example of Miloš Obilić in 1389 made regicide a sacrosanct crime. In general, violence remained the key element in the code of honour. As is usually the case, the more emphasis that was laid on the necessity to take violent revenge for injuries or slights, the less honourably people behaved.

By the early twentieth century, radical political groups existed across Europe who used the murder of the representatives of the existing order as their hallmark. Nihilists, anarchists, revolutionaries became the bane of governments. The roll-call of royal victims of the assassins' bullet, bomb or knife was an impressive one from Alexander II of Russia in 1881 to Franz Ferdinand at Sarajevo in 1914. But it was only in Serbia that the terrorist group developed a double nature: on the one hand, revolutionary, but on the other also sponsored by the state. However, that only came about after 1903.[23]

The Obrenovićs were not perhaps the best family for inspiring loyalty, but despite their tendency to greed and petty-mindedness, they got more disloyalty than they deserved. Despite Garašanin's shifting of his loyalty and Michael and Milan's building up of the army, the Obrenović dynasty generally followed a cautious policy of expansion. The disastrous wars of 1876 and 1881 showed the wisdom of not biting off more than the Serbian military could chew. However, by putting Serbia all too obviously under the patronage of Austria-Hungary, after all her snubs and disappointments at the hands of Russia, Milan and then the last Obrenović, Alexander, deeply antagonised the ambitious proponents of the Greater Serbian idea in the Army, with terrible consequences for Alexander.

Ever since 1878, Austria-Hungary had become the greatest stumbling block to the unification of all Serbs on the model of Germany or Italy. To be sure Turkey still controlled Kosovo, southern Serbia and the disputed territories of Macedonia, but Turkey was clearly waning. Franz Josef 's empire was seeking to expand into the Balkans to compensate itself for its losses of territory elsewhere. After 1878, the Emperor ruled over more South Slav land than the Serbian King and the Sultan put together. Yet far from seeking to undermine Habsburg power, Alexander Obrenović acted as a puppet of Vienna, or that was how the Serb nationalists saw his role.

In addition to offending the 'modern-minded' nationalist elements in his country, and especially his army, Alexander like other Obrenović rulers offended the Orthodox Church. Like other Orthodox Churches the Serb Church had seen itself as the spiritual guarantor of the state and legatee of the nation's heritage and identity. Following the Byzantine tradition it happily subordinated itself to the ruler and had no tradition of conflict between Church and State such as convulsed Catholic kingdoms in the past. But the capricious way in which the Obrenovićs treated the Orthodox Church's strictures on marriage and their arbitrary selection of 'unsuitable' spouses alienated the Orthodox clergy.

The identification of Orthodoxy with Serb nationalism was a political decision despite its religious garb. Orthodoxy served as a justifying cloak for political ambition, as a rare Catholic Serb, Lujo Vojnović, noted in 1888: Serb politicians used even 'elevated' Orthodoxy over Croatdom and even Serbdom, but only as a political rallying cry. At that point in the nineteenth century, although the various Croat political activists were overwhelmingly communicant Catholics, they did not identify their church with their national aspirations.[24] It was only later after 1918 and especially under Pavelić's unpopular regime during the Second World War that an all-out effort was made to instil a conscious link between Catholicism and Croat identity – though, of course, the vast majority of Croats had always been Catholics and took the association for granted. Despite its occasional role as the symbol of national identity in troubled times (as in Poland, for instance, under communism), the international nature of the Catholic Church militated against complete subordination to national interests. The Orthodox Church by contrast was inward-looking and lacked initiative in political questions, preferring loyally to support God's annointed ruler, even when he changed with remarkable and brutal speed.

On 15 June 1903, the Belgrade night was disturbed by terrible screams as Alexander Obrenović, his Queen and several of her relatives and his ministers were cut to bits by supporters of the exiled Karadjordjevićs. What made the murders peculiarly loathsome was not just their brutality (though the dénouement of the bloodied bodies of the royal pair being thrown from their bedroom window with fingers hacked off to remove rings excited and horrified newspaper readers in the more placid capitals of Europe), but the treachery of the crime. The key role in facilitating the murders was played by members of the royal guard. One lieutenant in particular, Peter Zivković, was central to deceiving loyalists into ignoring the danger and luring the king and queen to their deaths. He also distinguished himself in the hacking and slashing of their corpses. Zivković and the intellectual author of the plot, Colonel Dragutin Dimitriejević, known as 'Apis', were to play key roles in the murky politics of Serbia afterwards, not least in the scheming which led to the assassinations in Sarajevo eleven years later.[25]

The Karadjordjević dynasty was represented by an elderly exile, Peter, who spent most of his life outside Serbia, largely in France and Russia. Unlike the Obrenovićs, he was pro-Russian and the complacency of Nicholas II's response to the massacre which took place opposite the windows of the Russian Legation in Belgrade suggest that the events of June 1903 were one revolution of which the Tsar approved. Other countries, like Britain, kept the new regime at a distance for several years out of distaste for its method of coming to power. Greater dangers lay in its likely application of similar methods to hold and extend its power.

From the moment Peter's supporters in Belgrade slashed the last Obrenović to pieces, Serbia was set on the road to Sarajevo and direct confrontation with Austria-Hungary. So long as the Obrenovićs ruled in Belgrade, Vienna could control Serbia through a mixture of bribery and flattery. The return of the House of Karadjordjević to the Serbian throne meant a sea-change in relations. Whatever Peter's ministers said to reassure their counterparts in Vienna and Budapest, no one doubted that the new rulers would pursue a nationalist policy and that such a course could only lead to conflict with Habsburg interests. Either Serbia would challenge Vienna indirectly by seeking to expand into the remaining South Slav dominions of the Sultan or she would confront Franz Josef directly by stirring up discontent among his Slav subjects in Croatia, Dalmatia and Bosnia-Hercegovina.

At the centre of Serb policy was Peter's second son, Alexander, who was a cold-hearted, bold and ruthless man. His sense of his own destiny made him immune to humane considerations. He could sacrifice his servants as willingly as rivals who stood in his way. His own elder brother, Djordje, was sacrificed to his ambition in 1909. (Djordje was alleged to be given to uncontrollable violence – unlike his younger brother's calculated use of savage force – and to have kicked a servant to death. While at dinner with Premier Pasić, Djordje was drugged and awoke the next day in a madhouse.[26]) Bloodshed had brought Alexander's family back to the throne and he was determined that it should fulfil a grand design. His father was too wearied by age to carry on his own shoulders his son's plans for a Greater Serbia and to assert the Karadjordjevićs' independence as a dynasty worthy of respect alongside all others.

Having murdered his Obrenović rival, Alexander may have been tempted by the prospect of precipitating a crisis inside Austria-Hungary by removing Franz Ferdinand. After all the Austrian *Thronfolger* was the only Habsburg to hint at the kind of reforming zeal and energy necessary to reconstitute the multinational empire on a viable basis. Franz Ferdinand's inheritance of Franz Josef's sceptre might well foreclose on Alexander's ambitions for Serbian expansion.

The logic of Serbia's position was inescapable. Leaving aside the nationalist ambitions of the men who had brought Peter to power, Austro-Hungarian antagonism threatened Serbia's trading position. Unlike ever other post-Ottoman Balkan state, Serbia lacked a coastline and was dependent on the Habsburg Empire for most of her international communications. As the 'pig war' in 1906 showed, without access to the sea Serbia could be strangled by an Austrian trade embargo. Neither Peter's ministers nor his son felt strong enough to challenge Franz Josef directly, so instead they turned their eyes southwards to the remaining Ottoman province of Macedonia and the great port of Salonika.

In the past the Balkan peoples had expected that the final expulsion of the Turks from Europe could only be achieved with the aid of the Great Powers. Now it was clear that fear of their own rivalry leading to a Great War between the Powers had made it unlikely that Russia or any other Great Power would act as the liberator of the region. This could only be achieved by the local states themselves. Under the impression that he was fostering a barrier to the expansion of Russia's Austrian rival into the Balkans, the Tsar's foreign minister, Sazonov, supported the creation of a Balkan League allying Serbia with Greece, Bulgaria and Montenegro, but the new allies were looking southwards.[27]

The outbreak of the Balkan War in 1912 was of great significance: 'It is the first time in the history of the Eastern Question that the small states have achieved such an independent position from the Great Powers that they felt in the position to act completely without [consulting] them and even to pull them along in their wake', as the French chargé d'affaires in St Petersburg complained to Poincaré at the end of September 1912. The Russians, or rather some of them, were not only better informed but may have encouraged the Serbs and Bulgars to attack Turkey in order to complete the Ottoman collapse and enable Russia to step in and seize the Straits and Constantinople at long last. Certainly when the First World War broke out less than two years later, the Tsar's representatives were not slow to make their demands.[28]

For the rest of the world, the assassination of the heir to the Austro-Hungarian throne, Franz Ferdinand, in Sarajevo on 28 June 1914 was the start of the Great War, but for Serbia it was simply the continuation of the struggles already begun two years earlier, or even long before that. With magnificent disregard for the global consequences of their actions, Crown Prince Alexander's secret cronies who had brought his father to power in 1903 by slaughtering Alexander Obrenović, his wife, her brothers and a few others besides, plotted the death of the Habsburg Archduke, conscious that their success would precipitate a war with Austria-Hungary and therefore in all probability a conflict between the Great Powers.[29] However, for them the impending First World War was simply the Third Balkan War en route to their goal of a greater Serbia.

Despite all the talk of pan-Slav or Orthodox brotherhood at the time of the establishment of the Balkan League, the victorious allies soon turned against each other. The Bulgarians felt badly done by at the peace settlement. For geographical reasons, they had done most of the fighting, but Serbia and Greece ganged up together to deny Bulgaria the prize of Salonika. For Serbia it was better to partition the Turkish province of Macedonia with Greece than to let Bulgaria get too much of it, especially the vital port, which might lead the local Slavs to look more to Sofia than to Belgrade. Since the local Greeks were not popular, it was unlikely that Greece would pose a threat to Serbian control of inland Macedonia. In 1913, the Bulgarians were swiftly routed in a war distinguished by the brutality of the sides towards their fellow Slav or Orthodox brothers.[30]

The maltreatment of the Bulgars but also of the Albanians in Serb-occupied territory aroused an international outcry. The outbreak of world war a year later deadened the impact of the international concern, but the consequences of Serb victory were important for the long term. Although after 1830 autonomous Serbia had chased away the bulk of its small Muslim and Turkish population, destroying their mosques and minarets in the process, after 1913 for the first time the Karadjordjević regime had to rule over non-Serbs and non-Orthodox in large numbers. It was not a happy experiment. It too was forgotten as world war erupted.[31]

Understandably enough, the scale and consequences of the First World War have led the outside world to look away from the Balkan question to deeper causes at work which led to the general conflagration. However, the obsession with German war guilt or the role of the arms race has obscured one essential lesson of the outbreak of the Great War: the role of small powers in producing crises for the Great Powers, of the energetic tail wagging the big dogs, should not be overlooked.

The twentieth century has provided many grounds for Germanophobia but it is not a good guide to study, any more than any other kind of gut response. However, it has carried the day, not least because German historians since 1945 have wanted to distance themselves from any interpretation of events which might read as an endorsement of the Kaiser or worse still of Hitler. In the English-speaking world, A. J. P. Taylor set the tone for generations of Germanophobe historians. A by-product of his hostility to all things German was his loathing of the Habsburg Empire. Taylor had no sympathy with the doomed Archducal pair:

> The visit [to Sarajevo] was meant to provoke nationalist feeling, or rather to challenge it. It was deliberately timed for Serbia's national day, the anniversary of Kossovo. If a British royalty had visited Dublin on St Patrick's day at the height of the Troubles, he, too, might have expected to be shot at.[32]

His *Struggle for Mastery* in Europe became a standard textbook for generations of students and assured them that the Serbian government was not involved in the plot. If anything it had tried to warn Franz Ferdinand not to go ahead with his visit to Sarajevo.

It all depended on what was meant by the Serbian government. Certainly, the official policy of the ministers of Serbia was not to murder neighbouring Archdukes, but anyone familiar with how far even late twentieth-century democratic governments have gone in pursuing secret policies in flagrant contradiction of their declared aims might be inclined to take official denials from any source with a pinch of salt, most of all from the political class installed in power in Belgrade in 1903. For instance, already in the run-up to the First Balkan War, the Serbian foreign minister told the Bulgarian premier, Gueshov, 'If the disintegration of Austria-Hungary could take place at the same time as the liquidation of Turkey, the solution would be greatly simplified.'[33] The idea of precipitating a Habsburg collapse was not alien to Serbian politicians.

Naturally from the point of view of good nationalists they had every reason to feel offended by Austrian occupation of territory to which they aspired. In practice, Vienna proved indecisive in meeting the Serb challenge. For instance, after 1878, Austrian forces had occupied the largely Muslim area separating Serbia from Montenegro, the Sandjak of Novibazar. In 1908 Austria-Hungary had suddenly annexed Bosnia-Hercegovina after thirty years of occupation.[34] The other powers were upset but did nothing, to Serbia's disgust. Although in 1909 the Austrians had evacuated the Sandjak, which they had also occupied since 1878, they insisted that they would not permit Serbia to occupy it in the future. When the test came only four years later, the Austrians dithered and then did nothing, enabling the Serbians to seize the vital territory bridging the gap between themselves and Montenegro. Even more than their gains further south, this thin strip of territory decisively altered the balance of power in the Balkans between Austria and Serbia.[35]

This set of events shows that too much consistency can be read into the Austrian attitude to Serbia. Even if some of his officials were determined to destroy Serbia, Franz Josef was far from ruthless in his attitude to his southern neighbour. At the outbreak of hostilities in 1914, the commander of the Serbian Army, Radomir Putnik, was in Budapest. The hero of the Balkan wars was not interned; instead the Emperor arranged for a special train to conduct him back to Belgrade where Putnik took over the defence of Serbia and humiliated the Austrian invaders.[36] In fact, nationals of enemy powers remained at liberty in the Dual Monarchy until 1917 – small wonder it lost!

Despite Taylor's claim that the Archduke wanted to provoke the Serbs by his visit to Sarajevo, there is no evidence that Franz Ferdinand had any ambitions with regard to Serbia apart from that his inheritance be let alone. In February 1913 he wrote to the chief hawk in Austria-Hungary, Conrad von Hötzendorff, 'I do not want from Serbia a single plum-tree, a single sheep.[37] Even after Serbia's victory in the Second Balkan War against Bulgaria pushed even Franz Josef into accepting the idea of preventive war against Belgrade if the opportunity arose, Franz Ferdinand resisted the militants.[38] Whatever the belligerent mood among the establishment in Vienna and Budapest, Princip's victim did not share it, which was of course why he had to be killed. As Kaiser, Franz Ferdinand would have the initiative and might implement reforms which would stymie any *Anschluss* between Serbia and the Habsburgs' Slavs.

Undoubtedly, the strategists in Vienna and Budapest could not accept any further extension of Serbian power so soon after its triumphs against Turkey and Bulgaria. Equally Serbia was not in a mood to be restrained. Immediately after the defeat of Bulgaria, feelers were put out and bribes made available to persuade Montenegrin politicians of the benefits of uniting the two South Slav kingdoms. Austria-Hungary could not accept such a dramatic worsening of its strategic position along so much of its southern frontier. War, it was hinted, would be the method to discourage the union if the Serbs and Montenegrins pushed on.[39]

The strategic position of the two Central Powers was getting worse all the time. Italy had effectively dropped out of the Triple Alliance by 1914. Neither Germany nor Austria-Hungary showed much interest in consulting her over the crises in 1912–13. A back-channel between Belgrade and Rome existed due to the commercial and banking interests which Italy had developed in the non-Habsburg Balkans by 1914. A number of prominent Italian politicians were involved in these speculative ventures and certainly King Nikola of Montenegro had long recognised the importance of bribing Roman policy-makers to keep them sweet.[40]

The Russian Minister in Belgrade, N. V. Hartwig, played a decisive role. To the frustration of some of his superiors in the Foreign Ministry in St Petersburg, Hartwig went 'native' and became a forceful advocate of Serbian ambitions. Worse still, he did nothing to impress upon his Serbian hosts St Petersburg's official policy of trying to restrain the Orthodox Balkan states from doing anything which might upset the balance of power in the peninsula, particularly by going to war with either the Sultan or the Austrian Emperor.

So close were Hartwig's views to those of the Serbian government that British diplomats regarded his influence as dominant in Belgrade. In 1913, the British minister wrote to the Foreign Office that 'Serbia is, practically speaking, a Russian province' and that he had never known Belgrade to act 'against the directions of the Russian minister'. Ironically, Hartwig's Russian colleagues were less convinced of the value of Hartwig's undoubted influence in Belgrade. They saw him as putting at risk peace with Austria-Hungary because of his 'incurable Austrophobia'. One of them, Savinsky, reported in January 1914, after a visit to Belgrade, 'I have become convinced that Hartwig's thought is to set Serbia on to Austria.' Certainly, Hartwig revelled in Austria's difficulties and openly spoke about the 'next sick man of Europe'. Like many of the Tsar's Russified German subjects, Hartwig was more Slavophile than the Slavs. As his superior, Sazonov, once remarked to the German ambassador, Portalès, 'A man with the name of Hartwig is always more Slavophile than a man with the name of Sazonov.'[41]

Whatever his senior Foreign Ministry colleagues thought of Hartwig's personal diplomacy in Belgrade, he enjoyed the support of the only person in St Petersburg who really mattered. In 1913, Nicholas II awarded him the Order of the White Eagle as a mark of imperial approval. Whether the Tsar had a *secrète du roi* like so many monarchs and was pursuing a back-channel of diplomacy and intrigue behind the backs of many of his formal representatives and in contradiction to Russia's stated policy remains unknown to this day. There are indications that Nicholas II and his cousin, the Grand Duke Nicholas Nicholaievich, the commander-in-chief of the Russian Army and a son-in-law of Nikola of Montenegro, were distinctly more pan-Slav than many of the Foreign Ministry's high personnel. Through his control over all appointments, military and diplomatic (as well as through the discreet offices of the secret police, the *Okhrana*) Nicholas II and his cousin probably encouraged radical pan-Slavs much more than the diplomatic archives suggest. Nicholas II would not have been the first mediocrity at the head of government who mistook intrigue for policy, but then nor was he the last.

Even the more cautious professional diplomats in the Russian capital regarded Austria-Hungary as doomed to internal decay because of the tensions between Franz Josef's multinational subjects. Instead of quarrelling with Bulgaria and incidentally threatening to push her own zone of influence into areas of the south-eastern Balkans which the Russians reserved for themselves in the none too distant future, the Serbs should look north and west for new conquests. The Foreign Minister, Sazonov, wrote to Hartwig on the eve of the Second Balkan War:

> Serbia's Promised Land lies in the territory of present Austria-Hungary, and not where she is now making efforts and where the Bulgarians stand in the way. Under these circumstances it is of vital interest to Serbia to maintain her alliance with Bulgaria on the one hand and on the other to accomplish with steady and patient work the necessary degree of preparedness for the inevitable struggle of the future.

Sazonov probably did not anticipate how soon the death-knell of the Habsburg Empire would sound when he concluded, 'Time works on the side of decay. Explain all this to the Serbs!' His anxiety to rein in the Serbs from premature action was expressed in his unaccustomed flattery of Hartwig: 'I hear from all sides that if any voice can have full effect at Belgrade it is yours.'[42]

Whether Hartwig tried to carry out his instructions or not, Alexander was not listening to his Russian patrons for once. Instead he launched his lightning war against Bulgaria in cynical alliance with Romania, Greece and even Turkey. Against Balkan rivals, Serbia needed little help from Russia or anyone else but when threatened with intervention by the Great Powers then Alexander needed the support of Russia at least, knowing as he did that France could not afford to let Russia down. Alexander may even have been told by the Russians that the French Prime Minister, Poincaré, had been shocked to discover that Russia had sponsored the aggressive Serbo-Bulgarian pact against Turkey, calling it a 'convention of war', but even so France had stuck to her obligations to Russia despite Petersburg's deceit. If it came to the crunch – a war with Vienna and Berlin – France could hardly abandon Russia without submitting to German domination. In fact, Poincaré told the Foreign Minister, Izvolsky, in 1912 that if Austria invaded Serbia, or indeed any Balkan crisis drew Russia into war with the Central Powers, then 'the French government recognises this in advance as a *casus foederis* and will not waver for one moment to fulfil the obligations lying upon it with respect to Russia.' In short, France gave Russia a free hand. Unfortunately, the Russians had given Serbia a free hand too.[43]

In Serbia, the tradition of the guerrilla band, the holy assassin and the political radical had reached its fruition in the 'Black Hand', the secret organisation masterminded by Colonel Apis. Various secret societies had sprung up to promote the union of the South Slavs, by no means on a purely Serb basis, or at least with a tendency to ignore as insignificant the religious and dialect or linguistic differences among the South Slavs as well as their centuries of (artificial) separation under foreign rulers. Apis had begun his career as a conspirator while many of the key figures in the Sarajevo plot were still babes in arms. He was a master of making connections between disparate, often rival groups. He combined admiration of Prussian efficiency and power with Slavophile anti-German feelings. Apparently a royalist he was the murderer of kings and archdukes and consorted with the political radicals of his age.

Apis penetrated his own supporters into the nationalist anti-Habsburg group, 'Young Bosnia' (*Mlada Bosnia*), which was not difficult. It was composed of young men deeply influenced by contemporary nationalism but also drawing on the sense of holy mission which Serb writers like Vuk Karadžić and Njegos had promoted. The tradition of sacred murder was one that Apis knew, believed in and yet manipulated to serve his own ends. He had already created 'Unity of Death' (*Ujedinjenije ili Smrt*) to promote the union of Macedonia, Sandjak, Dalmatia, Croatia and Bosnia-Hercegovina. With the first part achieved he turned to the second.[44]

Against the background of Nicholas II's clear support for his minister's forward policy in Belgrade, Alexander had little reason to rein in Apis and the Black Hand. Certainly, Hartwig's military colleague in Belgrade, the Russian military attaché, also backed Serbian nationalist ambitions. Neither seems to have informed their superiors of the role of the Black Hand, at least not through the usual channels, but both must have been well aware of the general thrust of what Apis was up to if not in fact *au courant* with his decisive master-stroke.

The tragic and yet farcical circumstances surrounding the death of the Austrian heir to the throne and his wife in Sarajevo on 28 June 1914 have been often described. Governor Potiorek's etiolated incompetence, the earlier failed attempt to kill the Archduke with a hand-grenade patted away into the crowd, the failure to inform the chauffeur of the change of itinerary and his fatal turning off at the wrong place, Princip's being there as the car slowly reversed into perfect position for his gun and his taking of the unexpected second opportunity to kill the pair in the back.

The Serb student, Gavrilo Princip, was immortalised by his deed, but the identity of the group of assassins with whom he operated has often been forgotten. Princip's footsteps on the spot from which he fired the starting pistol for the mutual slaughter of eight million people are set in concrete like some morbid parody of Hollywood's glorification of its chosen sons. But the others should not be forgotten, not least because they did not fit the modern stereotype of Serb nationalist as easily as the contemporary admirers of Princip's deed might like to think.

Like any group of terrorists, their motivations seem less noble and more the result of flawed and unhappy personalities and upbringings than legend would like. Also they were far from a purely Serb bunch. They included the indubitably Muslim Mehmed Mehmedbasić, the only member of the group of assassins to escape from Sarajevo after the murder. Another Bosnian Muslim, Mustafa Golubić, played a key role in training the murderers, as he had already had some terrorist experience. (Later on, in exile, he was to be one of the chief accusers of Alexander, claiming that he played the role of puppet-master in the assassination.) Among the assassins of Franz Ferdinand was the seventeen-year-old student Vaso Čubrilović (brother of another plotter, Veljko). Vaso Čubrilović stood trial but survived to go on to become a theoretician of ethnic cleansing. In 1937, he edited and published a proposal for the *Iseljavanje Arnauta*, the expulsion of the Albanians from Kosovo. He bitterly denounced the ineffective attempts to Serbianise the inhabitants of that province.[45]

The immediate reaction of the people of Sarajevo to the assassination was an outbreak of rioting as loyal if disorderly Croats and Muslims set upon Serbs and their property in revenge for the murders. If the conspirators had intended to set a spark to ignite the fire of South Slav unity they signally failed. They did however ignite a much greater conflagration.

If Princip's act provoked the First World War, and even though the Serbian government was not the innocent party which it was soon to be painted by Entente propaganda, once war had broken out even those who see Alexander's regime as promoting a crisis with Austria-Hungary cannot deny that the assassination seemed opportune to the Great Powers, at least to Germany and Russia. It was not only Wilhelm II in Potsdam who thought it was 'now or never'. Needless to say in Vienna and Budapest it was seen as a heaven-sent opportunity to stifle Serb subversion within the Dual Monarchy once and for all. However, the Habsburg officials mismanaged their public as well as their diplomatic relations.

Vienna moved slowly as it prepared an ultimatum for Belgrade.

As time passed, public sympathy for the victims of the crime in Sarajevo waned and the Entente governments were able to assess the implications of the subordination of Serbia to Germany's ally which would result from Belgrade's acceptance of a punitive ultimatum. At the same time, Serbia's public professions of innocence were not countered by any positive proof of official involvement from Vienna.

Due to typical Habsburg bureaucratic incompetence, the evidence gathered by Austrian intelligence which implicated Apis was never sent from the War Ministry in Vienna to the Ballhausplatz where the ultimatum to Serbia was drafted and where the evidence for the charges against Belgrade was supposed to be assembled. Whether proof of a direct link between officers of the Serbian general staff and the murderers of the Archduke would have sufficed to have restrained Russian and French backing for Belgrade may be doubted. But certainly it might have made the British government more hesitant about depicting its entry into the war as a chivalrous defence of plucky little Serbia and raped Belgium rather than as a manoeuvre to reassert the balance of power by force of arms.

Once the Great Powers entered the war, their clash overshadowed the fighting in the Balkans, but that was probably what Alexander had expected. Out of the ruins of such an unprecedented war, Serbia could hope to rise again more powerful than ever on the back of her allies' victory. This turned out to be true, but the war also transpired to be more devastating and revolutionary than even Alexander could have anticipated.

4

1876 and all that

> If only Turkey could be persuaded to stop crumbling to pieces.
>
> Lord Salisbury (14 January 1876)[1]

If they are worried about their own blunderings in the Balkans, then today's Western statesmen may prefer to take some comfort in the fact that they are repeating the errors of more illustrious predecessors. Almost every mistake which marked Western intervention in the Yugoslav crisis after 1991 can find a precedent in the Great Powers' dealings with the Balkans in the nineteenth century. However, unlike the Metternichs and Salisburys, the Christophers and Hurds of the late twentieth century cannot claim to be dealing with an unprecedented situation. It is fashionable now to say that the end of the Cold War has marked a return to history as normal. Unable to learn from history's past mistakes, instead of contributing new ones, the West's best and brightest have rehashed most of the old errors.

Metternich was the apostle of the preservation of the Ottoman Empire as much as Bush hoped to salvage the Soviet Union and Yugoslavia. Of course, at the start of the nineteenth century, it was the Greek aspirations for independence which concerned the Great Powers. Although what in retrospect became stylised as the Serb war of national liberation began in 1804, it was the Greek revolt after 1821 which attracted the civilised world's attention and sympathies. It was easier to romanticise the Greeks as the inheritors of classical civilisation than to find a convenient legend to arouse aesthetic emotions on behalf of the Serbs. Byron might conjure up the vision of a pig-farmer whose sty occupied an ancient ruin in the Peloponnese as the heir of Leonidas, but

Serb pig-farmers had no august ancestry to call upon with which every classically educated West European could sympathise.[2]

The Serb struggle for independence from the Sultan went on away from the Western gaze. This was probably fortunate because the manner of the war and the actions of its heroes left a great deal to be desired from the romantic point of view. Far from being a simplistic struggle between patriots and foreign tyrants, the revolt was marked by treachery and deviousness unusual even in wars of national liberation, but all largely ignored by the West – and Russia for that matter.

It was only in the 1870s that the Balkans erupted into a crisis worthy of the name modern. Instead of concerning a few diplomats and strategists of the great game, for the first time a Balkan crisis became the focus of public opinion as well as politicians' concerns. To a degree, for Britain the Crimean War had been a forerunner with its first news photographs of carnage, shocking reports of the consequences of military incompetence and the unsanitary nature of military hospitals, and therefore all the associated public clamour. However, the improvements in the speed of communications and the distribution of newspapers, combined with the fact that the Balkans were strategically located and yet filled with local colour, meant that the eruption of disorder there was likely to capture the news media and therefore public attention. The presence almost by chance of a group of distinguished correspondents made certain that the events and the controversy they aroused would be widely discussed.

The Victorian public had already showed its propensity for campaigns and public outrage. The combination of rising affluence, more newspapers and an extended franchise had pushed even international politics into the public domain. Disraeli would have preferred foreign policy to have remained a matter decided in Whitehall, but ironically it was his forerunner as a jingoist, Palmerston, who had begun to accustom the public to taking its views on international matters seriously.

By 1875, all the Great Powers had got settled into the routine of regarding the decaying Ottoman Empire as the least worst solution to the balance of power in the Balkans. Austria-Hungary did not want to see Russian influence replace Turkish, nor did Britain or France, who were generally opposed to Russian penetration towards the Mediterranean as they had been at the time of the Crimean War. The rapid spread across the Balkans of the June rebellion among the Christian subjects of the Sultan unleashed an international crisis which threatened a general war between the Great Powers in a way not seen for a generation. It also produced a clash between two strands of political morality in Britain: the jingoist school of Disraeli, which despised moralising on behalf of small peoples and put imperial interests first, and the Gladstonian liberals who had misgivings even about Britain's imperial expansion and the methods required to maintain the Empire, let alone those used by non-Christian Turks.

Although it was the Bulgarian atrocities which most aroused British public opinion, reports by Arthur Evans among others from Hercegovina already alarmed readers of the liberal press long before the Ottoman government unleashed its bashi bazouks on the Bulgarians in 1876. However, if readers of the opposition press were already alarmed by what they read about events in the Balkans, Whitehall remained aloof from such moralising. It was the first of many symptoms which were to be repeated more than a century later.

The historian of the British reaction to the Balkan events of 1875–1878, Richard Shannon, shrewdly analysed the ossification which hampered government understanding both of what was happening in Bulgaria in 1876 and what would be the public response at home to the revelations. Shannon noted:

> Elliot, the Foreign Office, and the government jointly became victims of their psychology of orthodoxy. Such rumours and reports as came out of Bulgaria from official sources were made to fit into a pattern of preconceived attitudes which deprived them of their significance and their warning value. Even when the fact that something extraordinary had indeed happened in Bulgaria could no longer be ignored or brushed aside, Elliot still neglected to send someone to investigate at first hand.[3]

Late twentieth-century readers will recognise the same complacent superiority of modern British ministers and diplomats. *Ex officio* they knew what was really going on and did not need help or guidance from the press, least of all from the man on the spot.

The British consul in Sarajevo, W. J. Holmes, failed to report to his superiors on what was happening in Hercegovina, not least because he was unable to go there and was dependent on information from the Turks themselves. Understandably, they showed little interest in an accurate picture of the mayhem in Hercegovina. Arthur Evans, the *Manchester Guardian*'s correspondent, sardonically tore shreds from the consul's reputation as well as that of his ambassadorial superior, Elliot:

> It was perfectly natural that Sir Henry Elliot should remain in ignorance of the extent and enormity of the Bulgarian massacres, and it is equally unreasonable and ungenerous to blame Mr Holmes because he was not informed by the Turks themselves and their friends of the horrors which have desolated the greater part of Bosnia, and that he was humanely loath to accept the first accounts of impalements and other atrocities, of the real occurrence of which I for one am prepared to supply overwhelming evidence.[4]

In addition to the cruel savagery of Turkish reprisals against Christians, their rape of Christian women was the major cause of British horror. Although it has been the fashion for modern academic historians to sneer at the Victorians' prudish or even prurient disgust at what *The Spectator* called in October 1876, the 'worst of all evils of war – outrages on women', even in the most sexually permissive Western societies in the 1990s, allegations of widespread rape in Bosnia caused a deep emotional reaction.[5]

The under-secretary at the Foreign Office, Robert Bourke, dismissed what was happening as 'brigandage on a large scale which . . . it has pleased Slav sympathisers to call "insurrection".'[6] His belief that the *Guardian*'s reports 'may or may not be true . . . like everything else in this land of lies' anticipated the confusion about the course of events which often befogged the holder of the same office one hundred and twenty-five years later, Douglas Hogg.

Occasionally, the indignant Western diplomats and correspondents went too far in exonerating the rebels of any crimes against the Muslims. The American consul, Schuyler, who described in vivid detail the aftermath of the holocaust of the Christians in Batak, denied that a single Muslim had been harmed. Walter Baring was sent by the Foreign Office from Constantinople to Bosnia where he found one burnt village and a demolished mosque.[7]

The government and Foreign Office were not alone in their dismissive reaction to reports of atrocities coming out of the Balkans. Jingoism then, as one hundred and twenty years later, was very much a metropolitan phenomenon. The upper classes, certain academic hangers-on and a smattering of upwardly mobile journalists tended to back the court and government's approach to the Balkan crisis. Shannon remarked, 'The metropolitan tone was set by three great agencies: the court and attendant society, the press and the "Cockney mob" . . .'[8] This 'mob's' morality was appealed to as evidence of popular sentiment by the jingoists much as 'Essex man's' alleged indifference to Bosnian suffering was invoked in 1993 to stymie calls for intervention then.[9] Gladstone summed up the opposition to the agitation: 'London is the great focus of mischief: through money, rowdyism, & the Daily Telegraph.'[10] Among Disraeli's core supporters it was the tone to express contempt for moralisers alarmed by the savagery of Turkish reprisals.

Although the Turkophile in-crowd in London took the echo in the press of their own babble as evidence of popular opinion and dismissed the significance of the growing number of public meetings and subscriptions, gradually the weight of popular feeling began to dawn on the government. In the House of Commons on 31 July 1876, Disraeli could still dismiss public concern about the Bulgarian atrocities as 'coffee house babble', anticipating the sentiments of John Major's ministers in April 1993.[11] But only a few weeks later in September 1876, Lord Carnarvon wrote to Disraeli expressing his alarm at how out of touch with public opinion the government was becoming:

> I feel satisfied that the public feeling on the subject is very strong, that it exists in classes which we cannot afford to overlook, and that it will grow . . . If indeed it runs its course

> much further, it will, I fear, become ungovernable and will either drive us into some precipitate and undignified course or will end in a serious catastrophe.[12]

Carnarvon spoke with the authentic voice of the Establishment: government policy should be guided by a fundamental desire to avoid embarrassment, most of all among 'classes which we cannot afford to overlook'. But at the same time, the complacent cynicism underlying that approach turned out as so often afterwards to be out of touch with the electorate once roused.

Unlike the Whig grandees, the genuinely liberal wing of the opposition party had long had an anti-Turkish tradition. Even before men like Cobden and Bright opposed the Crimean War, their voices had been raised against Palmerstonian support for the Ottomans. Richard Cobden wrote one of the most lurid accounts of the Turkish propensity to savage mutilation of rebels as far back as 1836 when he described the brutal conquerors wading through their slaughtered victims, culminating in one effete Oriental monster with 'a chin sticking to his slippers, which were fringed with human beard as if they were lined with fur'. Cobden came as close as anyone to expressing pornographic horror of war's cruelties, where no sadistic invention was suppressed in favour of banal if brutal reality.[13]

But it was the emergence of the Grand Old Man of British politics which made all the difference. Until Gladstone's eruption back onto the political scene again with his pamphlet, *The Bulgarian Horrors and the Question of the East*, in September 1876, the criticisms of Disraeli's government had been pin-pricks in its well-upholstered self-satisfaction. A few years before Disraeli had scornfully referred to Gladstone's cabinet as a row of extinct volcanoes. It now turned out that the GOM had merely been dormant. The loss of office had temporarily silenced him, but it had also given him time to recover his enormous energy. Already twenty years earlier, Gladstone had campaigned against brutal misgovernment in Naples, but now his shock at reading about the atrocities in Bulgaria and his indignation over the government's complacent attitude, boiled over into print and then onto the campaign trail.

Gladstone's onslaught against the government's policy had

three prongs: 'to put a stop to anarchical misrule', to forestall 'the recurrence of outrages' and 'to redeem the honour of the British name, which in the deplorable events of the year has been more gravely compromised than I have known it to be at any former period.'[14] By allying the moral theme of action to redress the crimes of the past with the issue of British honour, Gladstone allied patriotism and morality in a most dangerous cocktail so far as the Tories were concerned.

Disraeli had little to set against the rhetorical appeal of the Grand Old Man in full flight. 'Let the Turks now carry off their abuses in the only possible manner, namely by carrying off themselves. Their Zaptiehs and their Mindirs, their Bimbashis and their Yuzbachis, their Kaimakams and their Pashas, one and all, bag and baggage, shall I hope to clear out from the province they have desolated and profaned.' Gladstone's ringing demand – that the Turks be removed 'bag and baggage' from Europe – has often been misread as a call for the expulsion of all Muslims from the Balkans. In fact, the famous list of exotic and frightening titles was intended by Gladstone to indicate that he meant the thorough withdrawal of the Sultan's officials and soldiers from the territories. He always maintained that Muslim civilians living there should enjoy equal rights with their Christian neighbours.[15]

Gladstone's pamphlet then his speech at Blackheath attracted enormous publicity and evoked a growing public clamour which Disraeli tried to meet by denigrating the rebels and accusing them of being at the service of a plot against all Europe. Just as a hundred years later, Tory sympathisers with the Milošević regime evoked the bogey of a sinister 'Islamic fundamentalist' drive through South-Eastern Europe onto the West to justify official inaction or even their own open support for Belgrade, so Disraeli evoked another international conspiracy. Whereas what haunted the fevered imaginations of late twentieth-century Serbophiles was the idea that the pork-eating, smoking and drinking majority of Bosnian Muslims were in fact a fanatical sect set upon sparking a religious war throughout Europe using its Muslim immigrants as a fifth column, the fear of radical subversion was the conspiracy theory to the fore in the 1870s. Disraeli was in thrall to the Metternichian idea that a web of secret societies was in the process of undermining all existing states, starting with the Ottoman Empire. The Prime Minister of Great Britain declared in September 1876:

> Serbia declared war on Turkey, that is to say, the secret societies of Europe declared war on Turkey, societies which have regular agents everywhere, which countenance assassination and which, if necessary, could produce massacre.'[16]

Disraeli was a man ahead of his time, he even anticipated the late twentieth-century canard that the Bosnian Muslims produced massacres of themselves to gain sympathy – though in his age, the sinister agents of self-inflicted wounds were Serbs. (Alan Clark, the former junior defence minister, famous for being 'economic with the actualité', made the claim that the Muslims shot at their own people on 'Panorama'.[17]

Just as Milošević's apologists a century later tried to shuffle onto other smaller Serbian fry responsibility for what suffering among civilians in Bosnia they were prepared to admit, so Layard could combine decrying his Austrian or German colleagues for seeing only Turkish atrocities and then calmly accuse hangers-on of the Porte of being the responsible parties, but not the Turkish authorities who 'owing to the absence of police and troops in the provinces' had left free rein to 'Kurds, Circassians, Tatars and robbers of all kinds'. These 'marauding Circassians' were at fault for crimes which could therefore hardly be blamed on 'the Turks, who are, if left alone, quiet and inoffensive people'.[18]

Ironically, once war had broken out between Russia and Turkey and the Tsar's army had penetrated into Bulgaria, Disraeli's government hurried to produce a Blue Book of more than six hundred documents to justify its policy and to cast the slur of war crimes at the Russians. Ambassador Layard's carefully edited dispatches served the point of defending the Turks by arguing that since the Russians were no better, then the Sultan ought to be protected. Layard claimed that the Russians intended 'to exterminate and drive out the Mohammedan population of Bulgaria'.[19]

The British government regarded the survival of the Ottoman Empire as essential to keeping its Russian rival from the Mediterranean and access to the new route to India via the Suez Canal.

Instead of thinking about why Turkish rule was so unstable, Whitehall hoped that the Ottomans would act vigorously to put down the rebels and was disappointed that even atrocities did not settle the matter. Reflecting on the diplomacy leading up to the Russian attack on Turkey, Richard Seton-Watson detected a sad pattern:

> In each case, London's reserve weakened the prospects of success; in each case London carefully abstained from any constructive proposal. Worse still, it was Disraeli's deliberate abstention [from supporting international action] that . . . was equivalent to advising prompt suppression before the Powers had time to intervene.[20]

This harsh verdict could be rewritten today about a prime minister lacking any of Dizzie's brilliance but sharing all his diplomatic blindness.

Against the background of jingoistic clamours that Britain go to the aid of Turkey – 'We don't want to fight but by jingo if we do, we've got the ships, we've got the men, we've got the money too . . . The Russians shall not have Constantinople' – Disraeli dispatched the fleet to the Straits and brought Indian troops into the Mediterranean. Britain would not accept the Treaty of San Stefano, but nor would Austria-Hungary tolerate the disappearance of Turkish rule in Europe without some compensation to herself. In practice it was Salisbury who rescued Disraeli and Britain from drifting onto the rocks of war with Russia with a bitterly divided public at home.[21] Salisbury's desire for a peaceful settlement chimed in well with the Russians' recognition that they had over-extended themselves in the Balkans and had no desire to fight a re-run of the Crimean War with their army even more exposed to Anglo-Austrian intervention.

The Congress of Berlin gave Disraeli 'peace with honour' and Cyprus, but it did nothing to remove the underlying cause of disorder in the Balkans. Gladstone was right to want the Turks bag and baggage out of Europe. It would have made better sense. Now it was clear that no reform of the Ottoman system was likely to take place and certainly not one to satisfy the Sultan's Slavic subjects. A pre-emptive partition of the Ottoman territories in

Europe by agreement among the Great Powers might have avoided the spontaneous combustion which followed after 1912. Instead, the Berlin Settlement simply stored up further crises – including the apocalyptic one in 1914. An early partition of the Balkans might have pre-empted Austrian penetration and calmed the rivalry with Russia which arose from the revocation of San Stefano and the occupation of Bosnia-Hercegovina by the Dual Monarchy. Instead the ground was laid for decades of intrigue and preparations for war to end Ottoman power in Europe but also to settle old scores between Austria-Hungary and Russia. Each Great Power would seek to bribe or cajole the lesser Balkan states into its camp in anticipation of the breakdown of the Ottoman Empire and/or relations with the other Great Power and its allies.

Recognising that the Ottoman Empire was rapidly losing its viability as a factor for international stability, Disraeli shifted his ground and threw Britain's weight behind Austria-Hungary as the future guarantor of Balkan stability. He could even imagine the Habsburgs ruling in Constantinople. Unfortunately, the Austrian occupation of Bosnia-Hercegovina did not contribute to stability. On the contrary, the infusion of more Slavs into the Dual Monarchy was a slow-acting poison undermining its health.[22]

Disraeli's contempt for the Balkan peoples came out clearly in his justification of the Treaty of Berlin to the House of Lords. He did not hide his preference for their domination by a strong imperial hand. Justifying the transfer of Bosnia-Hercegovina to Austrian control, Disraeli lumped independent Serbia and Romania into the same pot with the former Ottoman provinces:

> No language can describe adequately the condition of that large portion of the Balkan peninsula occupied – Roumania, Serbia, Bosnia, Hercegovina and other provinces – political intrigues, constant rivalries, a total absence of all public spirit . . . and hatred of races, animosities of rival religions and absence of any controlling power . . . to keep order.

In fact he concluded, 'Nothing short of an army of 50,000 of the best troops would produce anything like order in those parts.'[23]

Disraeli's preference for returning to the status quo rather than risking a grand redrawing of the map turned the Congress of Berlin into a delaying action, albeit a long drawn-out one. The British government did not want to envisage the disappearance of Ottoman rule. Except in the triangle of Adrianople, the Dardanelles and Bosphorus into which Turkey was ultimately successfully confined, the British government wanted to reverse San Stefano rather than make Turkey's disappearance from Europe as equitable as possible. Restoring the Sultan's rule in much of the Balkans was a recipe for preserving the causes of the crisis. However, Disraeli was optimistic about the chances of a successful reform of the Ottoman Empire, something which was bound to be unacceptable to Russia and probably Austria-Hungary as well.[23]

The Concert of Europe, according to Disraeli, had reached 'the unanimous conclusion that the best chance for the tranquillity and order of the world is to retain the Sultan as part of the acknowledged political system of Europe.' He assured the Lords that the statesmen assembled at Berlin 'were not there to partition, but so far as possible to re-establish the dominion of the Sultan on a rational basis'.[24]

Salisbury's accompanying Note to the Treaty of Berlin was less sanguine about Turkey's prospects. In effect, the Treaty marked the Sultan's last chance to put his house in order:

> Whether use will be made of this – probably the last opportunity – which has been obtained by Turkey by the [intervention] . . . of England in particular, or whether it is to be thrown away, will depend upon the sincerity with which Turkish statesmen now address themselves to the duties of good government and the task of reform.[25]

However, the sincerity of the British government's approach was not unquestionable. Disinterestedness is rarely a feature of imperial policy. Of course, in practice Britain and Austria-Hungary had colluded together to take the choice pieces of territory – Cyprus and Bosnia-Hercegovina – which they wanted while pushing Russian influence back to an acceptable distance from the Straits. At the same time, they left festering disputes since Serbs, Greeks and especially the Bulgarians were left disappointed by the settlement. The separation of the principality of Bulgaria from Eastern Rumelia left an obvious sore point and Disraeli's predecessor as leader of the Tory Party, Derby, admitted that he had resigned in protest at that aspect of the Treaty of Berlin (among others). Salisbury was stung into defending the partition of the Bulgarians and made the bold statement, 'I venture to say it will be far more permanent than any which has been proposed to supersede it.'[26]

At a celebration of his triumph at the London Guildhall, Disraeli's optimism about the staying power of the Berlin Settlement was even greater. Apart from his famous statement that he had come back from Berlin 'with peace with honour', Disraeli returned to his earlier interpretation of events in the Balkans as the product of a conspiracy and proclaimed that Austria-Hungary's occupation of Bosnia 'permits us to check, I hope for ever, that Panslavist confederacy and conspiracy which has already proved so disadvantageous to the happiness of the world.'[27]

The irony of Disraeli's notion that a hidden and centrally directing hand lay behind the discontents of the Balkans lay in the fact that his belief in the efficacy of conspiracy encouraged the disappointed Serbs to resort to the secret society as the appropriate agency for the pursuit of their dreams. Certainly, conspiratorial groups developed (as we have seen) and played a decisive role in Serbian politics and the origin of international crises in the future. In fact, the late nineteenth century was to see the beginning of an age of assassination across the Continent, but certainly the Balkans were to contribute more than their share both in numbers and significance.

Whereas in the 1990s a kind of altruistic concern for the preservation of existing states dominated the mind-set of Western leaders and diplomats, a century earlier Disraeli and his colleagues recognised that if the claims of Slav nationalism were heeded in the Balkans, the legitimacy of their own imperial rule would be called into question. Whereas in the 1990s it was the cost and risks of garrisoning Ulster which repeatedly surfaced as a reason for not intervening in Bosnia, in the late nineteenth century it was the fundamental issue at the bottom of the Irish Question which bedevilled the British debate about the Balkan crisis. In 1876, a key issue in the debate between jingo and interventionists was whether independence for Balkan tribes would set a bad example to the Celts across the Irish Sea.

The sympathies for the Turkish position in 1875 and afterwards expressed by the British ambassador to Constantinople, Sir Henry Elliot, were partly explained by the fact that he considered their relationship with their Christian subjects in Bosnia-Hercegovina 'not unlike that of the landlords and tenants in Ireland'.[28] It surprised few that Gladstone, who had tampered with the Protestant ascendancy by initiating a few reforms in Ireland during his first premiership, 1868–1874, should encourage the Balkan peasantry against its Muslim masters. During the Bulgarian agitation, the anti-Gladstone camp harped on the theme of the implications for England's empire if the Ottomans lost ground in Europe.

One anti-Gladstonian pamphleteer charged that the GOM was arguing 'that because a vassal state becomes discontented, every absurd demand it makes on the parent country is to be granted'. Dean Merivale in Dublin voiced the sentiments of the pro-Turkish Ascendancy, admitting that whatever could be said against Ottoman rule in the Balkans, 'the Irish have said, and still say, against us; and I don't want to set a precedent for . . . Home Rule for Ireland, and the occupation of Ulster by the Russians and Dublin by the Americans.'[29]

In fact, though he was cautious of playing up the analogy between Ireland and the Balkan states, Gladstone did not entirely shy away from it after he returned to full-time politics and spent the last fifteen years of his active political life seeking a solution to the Irish problem.[30] Gladstone's explosive re-emergence on the political scene after his apparent retirement was unprecedented but it has never lost its fascination for his successors. Most of them, however, must have doubted that the Balkans would ever provide such an emotive issue again.

If Britain was the decisive Western actor in the great crisis after 1875, then Russia was her counterpart. So much has been said about the 'return to history' in the former Soviet Union, and about historic links between Russia and the South Slavs, especially the Serbs, that it is worth recalling the impact of events one hundred and twenty years ago on Russia too.

Unlike in Britain, public opinion in the modern sense hardly existed in Russia at the time of the Crimean War. Defeat in that war went a long way to changing that state of affairs in Russia as it did so much else. However, the stirrings of Pan-Slavism were already apparent in the early 1850s, but they were restricted to a small audience and carried little weight with Nicholas I's regime, which regarded even favourable comment on government policy as an impertinence.

Konstantin Aksakov wrote a memorandum *On the Eastern Question* in February 1854. He stressed the twin foundations of what he hoped would be an ideological war of liberation: they were Slavic ethnicity and Orthodox religion. Nicholas I should promote

> an alliance of all Slavs under the supreme patronage of the Russian Tsar . . . Russia will fulfil her mission of liberating the ethnically homogeneous and largely Orthodox peoples; she will naturally incorporate her former province of Galicia and the whole Slavonic world will breathe more easily under the patronage of Russia once she finally fulfils her Christian and fraternal duty.

Aksakov did not entirely overlook the existence of non-Slavonic and un-Orthodox peoples in the Balkans, such as the Romanians, but they were dismissed as 'peoples without any individual significance [who] ought naturally to be incorporated into Russia'.

Aksakov's better-known brother, Ivan, was more cautious about extending the Tsar's rule over the Western Slavs, partly because he did not wish to get into trouble with the authorities by suggesting a policy to the autocrat, but also because he recognised that 'the Catholicism of Bohemia and Poland constitutes a hostile and alien element' and in any case 'the greater part of these Slavic peoples are already infected by the influence of Western liberalism which is contrary to the spirit of the Russian people and which can never be grafted onto it.'[31]

Almost a century and a half later, the debate between the two Aksakov brothers is still recognisable in Russia today. On the one hand, there is the school of Alexander Solzhenitsyn (himself still secluded in Vermont) which rejoices in the Russian 'soul' but rejects Russian imperialism or pan-Slavic expansionism. But there is also the raucous body of new nationalists, who hardly yesterday denounced Solzhenitsyn as a CIA agent or worse, and who loudly proclaim their affinity with Slobodan Milošević and the Bosnian Serbs, demanding Russian military intervention against the godless and yet Catholic West which conspires against 'Holy Moscow' as much as Belgrade.

Pan-Slavism remained a minority taste in Alexander II's Russia. Although it attracted interest among journalists and academics as well as curious politicians wondering whether it might serve imperial interests abroad or undermine stability at home, even the Slavic Committee founded in 1858 or the high profile Slavic Congress in Moscow in 1867 attracted little more than interest. Cash to support the idea of Pan-Slavism was in short supply. The Slavic Committee made do with 1700 rubles a year even in 1867, at the height of public interest before the war a decade later.[32]

However, the influence of Pan-Slavism on the intellectual elite should not be underrated. Some of the greatest names in Russian literature, with Dostoevsky at their head, took up the cause. The echo of their involvement can still be heard today after the collapse of Soviet power, when the new Russian nationalists who were so often tinged with a red past have started journals and newspapers to propagate the new ideology, often deliberately reviving the same names as old Slavophile papers (e.g. *Den* (Day), the first pan-Slavist journal in Russia, circulating between 1861 and 1865).[33]

Then, as now, the underlying theme of Russian Pan-Slavism was reactionary. It assumed Russian hegemony over the 'little brothers', which they frequently resented. Certainly, Poles and Czechs already showed little inclination to accept Russian predominance, let alone orders. Soon it was to become clear that Serbs and Bulgars were equally recalcitrant about accepting a role as cats-paws of Moscow and subordinating their interests to Moscow's. However, no Russian ruler could imagine putting his interests second to those of the Balkan Slavs.[34]

The 1877 war was the first democratic war. Certainly newspaper stories of the martyrdom of Orthodox Christian folk at the hands of the infidel had a wider impact than ever before. The secret police noted that even members of the largely illiterate lower classes who had no idea where Bosnia or Bulgaria were

were outraged by the sufferings of their fellow Christians there.[35] However, how deep this outrage went is another matter.

For the first time, public opinion in Russia was mobilised through the press. More than 1000 articles about the Bulgarian atrocities appeared in the sixteen most widely disseminated newspapers in just six months in 1876.[36] Some of Alexander II's subjects were already involved in the unprecedented decision to organise a volunteer army to fight alongside their fellow Orthodox Slavs in the Balkans. The Tsarist system had always discouraged spontaneity as a threat to the autocratic nature of the regime – even when it came from supporters. In *Anna Karenina*, Tolstoy illuminated some of the pressure on the Tsarist system. His character Katavasov expressed the sentiments which threatened Alexander II's government before it intervened in the Balkans: '. . . Cases may arise when the Government does not fulfil the will of its citizens and then Society announces its own will.' His colleague, Koznyshev, explains to the pacific and sceptical Levin:

> Our brothers by blood and religion are being killed . . . Among the [Russian] people there live traditions of Orthodox Christians suffering under the yoke of the 'Infidel Mussulman'. The people have heard of their brothers' suffering and have spoken out.[37]

Tolstoy expressed through Levin and the Prince realistic doubts about how far the average Russian peasant – 90 per cent of the Tsar's subjects – was enthusiastic for war or deeply concerned about the fate of his fellow believers beyond the Black Sea. After all, the peasants did not belong to the newspaper-reading public, which was concentrated in the cities.

Dostoevsky was well aware of the scepticism – 'It may be said: "Those are just lost people who had nothing to do at home and who went just to go somewhere – careerists and adventurers" ' – but he insisted it was 'precisely because the Russian people themselves have been oppressed and, over many centuries, . . . they have not forgotten their "Orthodox cause" . . .' Aware of the growing strains in Russian society and the revolutionary threat (much discussed in the West), Dostoevsky welcomed Chernaiev's volunteers because 'the very rumours about the political and military disintegration of Russian society, as a national entity, which have been accumulating in Europe, must . . . become subject to a strong refutation.' Fear of revolutionary turmoil could be deflected then (as now?) by a foreign adventure.[38]

In fact, Dostoevsky's praise of the volunteers and his cult of the 'lofty soul' of Chernaiev proved ill-placed, but the mentality which Dostoevsky promoted never died entirely. Pan-Slavism for him was part of a moral crusade against Western materialism and the immorality of capitalism as well as for the interests of fellow Orthodox Slavs. Dostoevsky's writings created a reusable rallying cry and a set of instantly recognisable themes for any future proponents of Russian rebirth. But that lay in the future at the time of Dostoevsky's death.[39]

It was not just the bulk of Russians who were in the final analysis indifferent to the cause of their fellow Christians and Slavs in the Balkans. Some of Alexander II's advisers were sceptical about the benefits of fighting for Bulgaria. Those who could remember Nicholas I's generous intervention to rescue the Habsburgs from their rebellious Magyar subjects in 1849 when the Russian Army steam-rollered into Hungary and flattened the rebellion there, did not easily forget Franz Josef's response to Russia's plight during the Crimean War. Immediately after the Habsburg regime had been saved by the Tsar in 1849, the Kaiser's chief minister, Schwarzenberg, had remarked that the world would be astonished by Austria's ingratitude to Russia. A generation later, in the middle of the fighting against Turkey in 1877, the Russian diplomat, Jomini, wrote to his boss, Giers, recalling Schwarzenberg's prophecy and applying to the Serbs and Bulgarians to whose rescue the Tsar's armies had marched: 'The emancipated brother Slavs will astonish us with their ingratitude . . . I continue to think that instead of pursuing these Slavic fantasies, we should have done better to take care of our own Christian Slavs . . .' He wished the Tsar could be persuaded to understand that 'a crusade against drunkenness and syphilis was more necessary and profitable to Russia than the ruinous crusade against the Turks for the profit of the Bulgarians!'[40]

Initially, the Tsar himself seems to have shared his advisers' reluctance to get drawn into a Balkan war. Certainly, Alexander II told the German ambassador, Schweinitz, in August 1876, that he was unwilling to risk war with Britain just for 'les beaux yeux des Slaves'. His war minister, Milyutin, was very conscious of how inadequate Russia's military preparations remained and how unwise it would be for her to undertake an aggressive war beyond her borders.[41] However, neither imperial disdain for the Bulgarians nor military caution could be sustained.

Despite the probable indifference of the bulk of his subjects to the plight of the Sultan's Christian subjects, Alexander II's government was not in a position to ignore intellectual and journalistic pressures for intervention with the same haughty lack of concern which Nicholas I had shown to nascent pan-Slav pressures in the 1850s. The Tsar's cautious foreign minister, Gorchakov, wrote in the autumn of 1876 that 'national and Christian sentiment in Russia . . . imposes on the Emperor duties which His Majesty cannot disregard.'[42]

Alexander II himself was not immune to the very same nationalist and pan-Slav feelings to which journalists like Mikhail Katkov and Fyodor Dostoevsky gave voice. After all, his grandfather had been given the same Christian name by his great-grandmother, Catherine the Great, in part at least to reassert the Muscovite claim to be the legitimate heir of Byzantium. His uncle, Constantine, had been even more obviously named for what turned out to be an elusive destiny – to be crowned in a recovered Hagia Sophia in a re-Christianised Constantinople. It was Alexander II's own references to the need to defend the Slav cause in November 1876, along with the rhetoric of Moscow as the Third Rome, which encouraged the Slavophiles. No longer inhibited by the pressures to grim conformity ever present in the reign of Nicholas I, Ivan Aksakov, for instance, took the Tsar at his word, albeit as a way of adding pressure on him to act in the Balkans, declaring

> The historical conscience of all Russia spoke from the lips of the Tsar. On that memorable day, he spoke as the descendant of Ivan III, who received from the Paleologi [or what was left of them] the Byzantine arms and combined them with the arms of Moscow, as the descendant of Catherine and of Peter [the Great] . . . From these words there can be no drawing back . . . The slumbering east is now awakened, and not only the Slavs

> of the Balkans but the whole Slavonic world awaits its regeneration.[43]

In addition to any desire by Alexander II to fulfil age-old dreams of recoupling rule over the Third Rome with the Second at Constantinople, Alexander II was clear that the whole purpose of his reign was to reform Russia so that his Empire could recover the position of predominance which she had enjoyed after her defeat of Napoleon until the calamity of the Crimean War. It was the need to wipe out the shame of that defeat which lay at the heart of Alexander II's decision to go to war in 1877. His reign had begun in the midst of a military catastrophe. The Tsar was determined to recover Russia's military reputation and freedom of action, that was the purpose of his reforms. The objections of his finance minister and the caution of his foreign minister – both of whom urged Alexander II to avoid the risk of another clash with the West – were brushed aside. The Tsar told his advisers, 'In the life of states just as in that of private individuals there are moments when one must forget all but the defence of honour.'[44]

Contact with Balkan reality quickly cooled the ardour of many Russian Slavophiles. In practice Russians and Serbs did not get on. There was a great deal of mutual recrimination, especially when their joint force was soundly beaten by the Turks. The Russian General Chernaiev did not repeat the easy victories in Central Asia in the 1860s which had won him his reputation. There, with only a few thousand men, Chernaiev had conquered legendary cities from *A Thousand and One Nights*, but in the battle against the Turks, his mixed Serb-Russian forces performed badly – though Chernaiev continued to send back optimistic newspaper reports long after the outcome was clear.[45]

The Russian consul in Belgrade, Andrei Nikolaievich Kartsov, wrote to his superior, Giers, in September 1876:

> I am sorry for our youth which is involuntarily disillusioned here after two or three days in the Serbian army. Drawn by the desire to take part in a military affair, they see that they are not among orderly troops but in some caravan or group of boastful cowards; and those who come because of sympathy for

> Slavonic brotherhood discover with bitter amazement to what extent his own skin is precious to this brother and how little he values the sacrifice and the very life of those of the same faith who arrive to spill blood for the Serbian cause.[46]

Certainly by Kartsov's account, Tolstoy did not exaggerate the drunkenness and shallowness of the motivation of many of the Russian volunteers.

The Serbs and later the Bulgarians were to discover that whatever the rhetoric about pan-Slavic solidarity, the Tsar was not fighting for altruistic purposes. At the time of the negotiation of the Treaty of San Stefano, his foreign minister, Giers, told the Serbian ambassador to St Petersburg, 'the interests of Russia come first, then those of Bulgaria, and only after them come Serbia's.' Needless to add, despite the willingness of Western statesmen like Douglas Hurd to accept at face value the pan-Slavist theory of ancient friendship between Russia and Serbia, this principle applied as much in post-communist Russia as in the pre-communist Tsarist state.[47]

After 1878, Russian support for individual Balkan states ebbed and flowed according to St Petersburg's estimate of their usefulness to the Tsar's ambitions. Bulgaria was now supported, then abandoned as its rulers tried to promote their own interests. Serbia was seen as part of the Austrian sphere of influence and the Russian legation in Belgrade was the focus of intrigue against both the Habsburgs and their local ally, King Milan. In the final analysis, the Russians regarded the Balkan Slavs as pawns, as did the Austrians, the British and the French. The region was a potential source of conflict between the Great Powers but they could not decide how to regulate it, which left the field increasingly open to the first Balkan ruler willing to play them off against each other for his own state's advantage.

The belief that the Ottoman system could be reformed on the Western European model was the great illusion of international mediation then and for decades to come. It was also part of the self-contradiction of the Great Powers' policy: all of them wanted the Balkans to calm down, but not one of them wanted to see Turkey revivified. In fact, it was the threat of effective reform in Turkey after 1908 that hastened the course of events which led to the First World War. Once the Young Turks came to power in 1908 with their programme of reform and modernisation, neither the Balkan states nor Russia or Britain was complacent about the status quo.

However, in the meantime, so long as Abdul Hamid reigned in Constantinople, Turkey's neighbours had nothing to fear. Little need be said about the effectiveness of the reforms imposed upon Ottoman Turkey under duress. The constitution of 1876 was annually reprinted for thirty years but the parliament it provided for met only once in 1878 and then only for two weeks without coming to any conclusions, let alone making proposals for effective reforms. Abdul Hamid showed a low cunning in ignoring Western demands for reform. He recognised that if his empire looked set on the path to recovery all the states most concerned for the well-being of his subjects would turn on him and destroy his inheritance. Instead he paid lip-service to their demands and, provided his debts to them were paid, they reproved his lack of progress with words and gestures only. After 1908, Turkey looked set to reform herself just as her neighbours, and especially the new regime established in Belgrade in 1903, were anxious to extend their territory and play the role of liberators of their still-enslaved fellow Slavs.

In the final analysis, the handling of the great Balkan crisis of the late nineteenth century can give little comfort to proponents of either the classic realist position or of morality in international relations. Disraeli's government survived the crisis but was nonetheless voted out of office in 1880 by the electorate, which in part at least was moved to return the Liberals by Gladstone's Midlothian campaigning on the morality of British policy as well as recession. However, Gladstone restored to power could do nothing to reverse the settlement in 1878, nor did he try to. Even in British colonial policy he was pushed along by events.

Russia too was left with little to crow about. Her victories turned out to be hollow and her erstwhile allies looked to Germany or Austria-Hungary for protection and investment. The Orthodox soul went back to sleep. Even the First World War did little to revive it. In fact, only with the death of 'scientific atheism' did politicised Orthodoxy spring back into life in Russia as in the Balkans.

5

From one World War to the Next, 1914–1941

World peace will not be any worse off.

Antonio di San Giuliano, the Italian Foreign Minister, on the assassination at Sarajevo.[1]

Even as the infant propaganda machines in London and Paris were cranking into action to promote the image of plucky little Serbia unjustly attacked by the beastly Austrians and Germans, Serbia was quick off the mark with making known her territorial demands in the event of an Allied victory. On 4 September 1914, Belgrade informed its Allies that in the event of a confidently expected rapid Allied victory, it would like to 'create out of Serbia a powerful southwestern Slavic State; all the Serbs, all the Croats and all the Slovenes would enter its composition.' Although Alexander and Pašić used the language of 'Yugoslavism' from time to time when it suited their efforts to bind Habsburg subjects to their cause voluntarily, they seem never to have doubted that Serbia's war effort would entitle her to act as conqueror and therefore to lay down the terms of South Slav unity to those peoples who had served the defeated Habsburgs.

In general, the Serb leaders were less concerned with Slovene or Croat public opinion than with the danger that their Allies might agree to a compromise peace which preserved Austria-Hungary or that France and Italy especially might sympathise with their fellow Catholics in the Habsburg Monarchy and promote a small South Slav state of Slovenes, Croats and Bosnians excluding Serbia.[2] Fortunately, Serbia existed as an international entity while the Habsburg subjects lacked any equivalent standing on the diplomatic stage. Furthermore, Montenegro's ruler, King Nikola, fatally blotted his copy-book by negotiating with the Central Powers and being found out, so Serbia's ambitions to absorb little Montenegro were hardly likely to be resisted by Nikola's deceived allies. However, the most favourable circumstance making for the establishment of a post-war South Slav state to Serbia's liking was the survival of the Serbian Army as a military force without rival in the territory of what would become Yugoslavia.

At first the chances of Serbia's resisting the Austro-Hungarian forces were regarded as slight at best. A combination of incompetence and poor planning rare even in Franz Josef's high command plus the courage of Serbia's battle-hardened veterans saw the initial Austrian invasion thrown back. But in 1915, with the aid of the Germans and the vengeful Bulgarians, Franz Josef's forces were finally able to conquer Serbia in the autumn of 1915. Rather than accept defeat and the end of his ambitions, Regent Alexander decided to retreat to Allied territory taking his father and as much fighting power as he could with him.

In late 1915, the retreat of the Serbian Army south-westwards through Albania to the Adriatic coast began. It was the stuff of legends. Old King Peter was carried in a litter drawn by oxen followed by his troops, officials, and a host of clergy and civilians. Despite terrible losses – perhaps as many as 20,000 died on the march – due to the bitter weather, disease and the harrying Albanians, the Serb Army reached the coast in reasonable order considering its ordeal and was taken off by British, Italian and French to the Greek island of Corfu. No one asked the Greeks whether they were willing to receive the Serb refugees there, but the Allies had not asked the Greeks for their permission when they seized Salonika as a base for operations against Germany's allies in the Balkans and settled Alexander and his remaining forces there.[3]

Life in occupied Serbia was grim. Disease as well as food shortages carried off hundreds of thousands of people. The occupying forces who partitioned the country treated it harshly, but none more so than the Bulgarians who were exacting their revenge for the Serb seizure of Macedonia and their defeat in 1913. The Bulgarians anticipated the most notorious horrors of the Second World War. In November 1917, the German Secretary of State, Richard von Kühlmann, described to a journalist how the Bulgarians gassed Serbian prisoners: 'They are brought to delousing stations for purposes of disinfection and are there eliminated by gas. That, he adds melancholically, is to be the course of wars in the future.'[4]

Many of the Serbs who survived the retreat into Albania were taken to French North Africa and settled in camps around Bizerta. For some these soon resembled prison camps. This reversal of fortune was the result of the worsening of the military situation for Serbia's allies over the next two years. By 1917, it was no longer clear that Alexander and his advisers had been right to put all their eggs in the Entente basket.

By the spring of 1917, the situation for the Allies was far from hopeful. Russia was in chaos. With the fall of the Tsar in March, the capacity of Russia to carry on the war became ever more doubtful. Even before the Bolsheviks seized power in November 1917, on the slogan of making peace at any price with Germany and her allies, the balance of power seemed to shift decisively towards the Central Powers and Alexander was not slow to recognise that if the Entente Powers lost the war he would not recover Serbia unless he could repair his relations with Germany and Austria-Hungary. Unless he was prepared to distance himself from the murderers of Franz Ferdinand, it was highly unlikely that he would be able to find a formula to satisfy the Central Powers.

Apis had never been a comfortable subordinate for Alexander. After all, after decades of exile in Montenegro, Alexander came as a virtual foreigner with his father back to Serbia in 1903. Apis had his own ideas about Serbia's future and what his own role should be. Naturally, his own ambitions could clash with Alexander's. Rumours abounded and still do that the colonel and the 'Black Hand' had plotted to remove the Karadjordjevićs. Whatever the truth of the matter, Alexander had reason enough to get rid of Apis.

Alexander knew that Apis was both untrustworthy and deeply sincere. Like many fanatics – like the Regent himself – Apis was so imbued with his sense of mission that he could behave ruthlessly and treacherously without feeling shabby. His eyes were always on the greater prize. When confronted with failure and the choice between damaging the Serbian cause which he had made his life's work or testifying against himself in order to preserve the legend, Apis chose the latter course. In 1917, Alexander accused Apis of plotting to kill him along with a group of confederates, as well as treasonable communications with the enemy – as good a case of guilt-projection as any psychologist could wish.

Even in the face of death, Apis refused to incriminate the Regent or Serbian government in the Sarajevo murders, taking the guilt on himself. Instead he went to his death without embarrassing his royal master. Greater fanaticism hath no man than to lay down his life for his murderer. The trial and stoic resignation to his fate of Apis prefigures that of so many Soviet communists in the 1930s at the hands of Stalin. Like the Soviet *vozhd*, Alexander Karadjordjević demanded unconditional loyalty to the idea which he embodied. Any sacrifice which Alexander demanded was deemed necessary and justified. Just as twenty years later Lenin's former comrades incriminated themselves in the great Moscow Show Trials as one last service and show of loyalty to the Party, so the victims of the Salonika judicial murders never uttered a word which might defend them at the expense of their *voivod*, Alexander. Encouraged to the end that he would be reprieved, Apis was shot on 26 June 1917.[5]

In midsummer 1917, the Central Powers looked close to victory. Russia was on the verge of collapse and even if America was about to enter the war, Alexander must have reckoned that a compromise peace between his Western Allies and Germany and Austria-Hungary was on the cards. If that happened, it would be easier for Britain and France to make concessions to the Central Powers in Eastern Europe and the Balkans in return for a German withdrawal from French territory and Belgium. Alexander knew that Nikola of Montenegro had been intriguing with the Austrians to recover his kingdom and must have feared that if he did not prepare his own escape route from blind loyalty to the Allied cause, Serbia and the House of Karadjordjević might be left high and dry, condemned to permanent exile without even the friendly Romanovs to rely on. By judicially murdering Apis et al., Alexander removed the guilty men and went some way to satisfying any potential Habsburg demands as well as silencing them in case they spilled the beans about his knowledge of the Sarajevo plot.

(Of course, it was typical of Alexander that he had less faith in the loyalty of Apis than the colonel merited.)

At the same time as Alexander was manoeuvring to dispose of the embarrassing Apis, Pašić was engaged in discussions on Corfu with the leaders of the émigrés from the Dual Monarchy. On 20 July 1917, Pašić and the Croat, Ante Trumbić, signed the Corfu Declaration which committed Serbs, Croats and Slovenes to the establishment of a postwar Yugoslav 'constitutional, democratic and parliamentary monarchy' under the House of Karadjordjević. Trumbić praised the key role of Serbia: 'As a state she has the absolute right to be called the Yugoslav Piedmont.' What was missing was Alexander's direct involvement. If the war continued to go badly he could disown the Corfu Declaration, but if the Allies won it would be difficult for its signatories to do anything other than follow his lead.[6]

In practice, as the tide of war turned both Pašić and Alexander became more assertive vis-à-vis the Slav subjects of the Habsburgs. The Croats seem to have expected that the proposed South Slav kingdom would be a federal affair, perhaps not entirely unlike the Dual Monarchy they were anticipating leaving – except with themselves having the position of the Hungarians to whom they had so long been subordinated. The Serb side made it increasingly obvious that they intended the new kingdom to be a unitary state.

The rapid collapse of the Central Powers in the autumn of 1918 gave the Habsburgs' Slavs little chance to organise themselves. Furthermore they, like the Czechs and Slovaks, had every incentive to act quickly to distance themselves from the defeated Dual Monarchy, otherwise they might be expected to help pick up the reparations bill which the Allies were clearly intending to deliver to the defeated states. Most Slovenes and Croats had little knowledge of the wrangles behind the scenes between the émigré Slavs from the Dual Monarchy and the Serbs. In any case, after Austria-Hungary's defeat, Italy's ambitions to control the 'Venetian heritage' along the Istrian and Dalmatian coasts meant that Serbia was an ally against a new foreign domination.[7]

The lack of direct contact between ordinary Croats and the Serb state meant that those who had advocated a Yugoslav solution to the political and cultural aspirations of the Habsburgs' Slav subjects soon found their naive expectations of a new era of brotherhood disappointed by the reality of Alexander's kingdom. Already at the Peace Conference, Prime Minister Pašić had argued that minority rights such as were being imposed on other new states were unnecessary in the new kingdom. Pašić dealt with the issue of minority rights at the Paris peace conference with typical Balkan sleight of hand. He insisted that such a problem could not exist in the new Yugoslavia:

> The Serb-Croat-Slovene state, composed of a single people with three names, three religions and two alphabets, by its very nature is called upon to practise the broadest tolerance . . . Consequently, the question concerning the protection of minorities in this state cannot have practical scope.[8]

Even if Pašić's rosy picture of intra-Slav relations could have been taken at face value in 1919, it was striking that he was blandly reassuring about the conditions of Yugoslav Muslims. According to Pašić, most were Serbs in any case and all, including the Albanians, were protected by treaty, but of course the Turkish signatory to the treaty with Serbia in 1914 had disappeared at the end of the First World War. As for the Macedonians: they did not exist, but were merely Serbs under another name. In any case, Pašić argued, Kosovo and Southern Serbia (Macedonia) had been integrated into the kingdom before 1914 and so should not be affected by the Paris Settlement.

In fact, Pašić denied the understanding of many of Serbia's wartime allies that victory had created a new state, 'Yugoslavia'. Belgrade preferred to see the 'Serb-Croat-Slovene Kingdom' as merely a natural extension of the Kingdom of Serbia, requiring no new foundation in international law. This theory of 'continuity' between Serbia and Yugoslavia was to bedevil the kingdom, since it raised and settled the acute issue of whether the non-Serbs were to be treated as equals with the Serbs or just as 'little brothers'. (In 1917, Pašić had told the non-Serb proponents of 'Yugoslavia' that its king would always have to be Orthodox by religion.)[9]

Under pressure from the Italian government, which was concerned about the fate of Italophone residents in Istria and Dalmatia as well as being itself under fire from D'Annunzio's proto-fascists for abandoning 'historic' Italian claims to territories in the New Yugoslavia, Pašić eventually accepted the minority protection demanded by the Allied Supreme Council. Implementing it proved to be altogether a different matter. The rhetoric of Pašić's Radical Party after 1918 made it clear that it was responsible for 'avenging Kosovo, resurrecting Serbia and uniting the Serbs'.[10]

The new kingdom was of course even more multinational than its title suggested. In addition to the ten million Serbs, Croats and Slovenes, it contained over half a million Germans (expelled after the Second World War) and just under half a million Hungarians and at least the same number of Albanians. What today would be called Macedonians or Muslims were counted among the Serbo-Croat speakers, though 150,000 Turks were recorded separately. There were also small communities like the 64,000 Jews and 20,000 Russian émigrés. In all fourteen languages were acknowledged, making the Karadjordjević kingdom no more homogeneous than the Habsburg Monarchy which it had done so much to destroy.[11] Royal Yugoslavia soon faced the same sort of political strife between its two largest peoples, the Serbs and the Croats, as Franz Josef's empire had endured between Germans and Hungarians. Although the Serbs were strong enough to dominate the new state, they were not numerous enough to swamp the Croats.

Hardly had the new state been proclaimed on 1 December 1918 than its constituent elements began to squabble. The elections to the first Yugoslav Parliament brought out not only the power of local loyalties among the Karadjordjevićs' subjects but also the depths of social divisions. The Croats felt deceived. Far from entering into a shared state, they found themselves subordinated to what was in effect a centralised Serb-run state. The chief agent of this policy was Svetozar Pribićević, a Serb from Habsburg Croatia, and minister of the interior in Belgrade after 1918. Pribićević's animus against Croats was no doubt based on resentments built up during his life as a subject of Franz Josef, but his harsh centralist policy did a great deal to sour Serb-Croat relations from the very beginning.[12]

Royal Yugoslavia never succeeded in developing political parties which operated on an all-Yugoslav level, at least not parties with any significant adherence. From the start, Serbs supported Serb-led parties and Croats followed their own leaders. It was much the same with other nationalities, in so far as they participated in politics at all.

Croat politics were dominated by the Croatian Peasants Party (CPP) which was in opposition to the new kingdom from the start. (Until 1925, it was called the Croatian Republican Peasants Party.) For a brief period from 1925 until 1927, the CPP provided ministers in the central government but only under virtual compulsion to do so. Its leaders, the Radić brothers and Vladdo Macek, had been imprisoned in 1925 to persuade them of the virtues of cooperation with the Vidovdan Constitution. But they soon left office and the rows between Serb centralisers and those they regarded as 'ungrateful' Croats went on more bitterly than before.

Even after the addition of Habsburg provinces with their industrial cities and ports, the Karadjordjevićs ruled over an overwhelmingly peasant and poor realm. In 1920, almost 80 per cent of their subjects were still earning their living directly from labour on the land. Five hectares of arable land was normally regarded as the minimum for a family, but almost a third of Yugoslav peasants lived off holdings of fewer than two hectares. About two-thirds of the rural population farmed below the desirable minimum of five hectares. Land reforms under Alexander I had little impact since they affected less than 10 per cent of holdings. The poverty of the average peasant is best illustrated by the fact that they possessed few animals. Whereas even in Bulgaria there was about one farm animal per capita, in Yugoslavia for every one hundred and forty people there were only one hundred animals. Fewer animals meant not only less meat to eat and fewer hides to work and sell, but also less manure. Agricultural economists at the beginning of the Great Depression estimated that 38 per cent of the rural population in Yugoslavia were redundant, but slow industrial and urban development had failed to absorb them and the crash after 1929 made matters worse.[13]

The Yugoslav government was well aware of the intractable economic problems which rural backwardness and the lack of foreign trade involved. At one of these interminable international economic conferences which made the early 1930s an eerie forerunner of our own time, the Yugoslav foreign minister, Marinković, regaled the assembled ministers and diplomats who urged poorer states to resolve their economic problems by liberalising trade with the following revealing anecdote:

> Last year, when I was in the Yugoslav mountains, I heard that the inhabitants of a small mountain village, having no maize or wheat on which to live, were simply cutting down a wood which belonged to them . . . and were living on what they earned by selling the wood . . . I went to the village, collected together some of the leading inhabitants and endeavoured to reason with them just like the great industrial powers reason with us. I said to them: 'You possess plenty of common sense. You see that your forest is becoming smaller and smaller. What will you do when you cut down the last tree?' They replied to me: 'Your Excellency, that is a point which worries us: but on the other hand, what should we do now if we stopped cutting down our trees?' . . . [14]

The fable was also political: inter-war Yugoslavia lived on the capital of its loyalties and built up no fresh loyalty to see it through the crises after 1941 when war broke out again.

The only apparent exception to the divisive nationalist basis of parties was the early success of the Communist Party. In the elections in November 1920, the newly formed Party gained 59 seats and was the fourth largest party in the Skrupština or Parliament. It gained almost 200,000 votes and had about 65,000 members. This vote reflected the deep-seated discontents among the still predominantly agricultural population, but the Party was at this stage still a supporter of the Yugoslav idea so it failed to support Croatian peasant rebellions around the same time, seeing them as 'reactionary' and 'nationalist'. The Party's high vote also showed how powerful Russophilia was among poor Serbs in particular, hoping for a miraculous transformation of their back-breaking lives such as was rumoured in the new Russia. However, police repression and the shifts and turns of Comintern policy towards Yugoslavia meant that the Communist Party's early success was never built on and it became an underground and factionalised party. Even before Stalin had achieved complete power in the Soviet Union in the late 1920s, already at the beginning of the decade the Comintern showed typical 'Stalinist' features: despite the theoretical equality of all communist parties as they sprang up in imitation of the successful Soviet model, in practice Moscow Centre dictated their policies and decided on their leaders even in ignorance of local conditions and personalities.[15]

This aspect of the Communist party favoured the rise to leadership within it of Josip Broz, better known as 'Tito'. Like many of his fellow Croats, Broz distinguished himself by his service in the Habsburg Army after 1914. He was decorated for gallantry fighting on the front against Serbia – a fact unmentionable in his official biographies after he came to power in 1944. However, like hundreds of thousands of his fellow Slav soldiers, Broz was captured on the Russian front and disappeared into captivity inside Nicholas II's empire which was tottering even more than Franz Josef's, despite its military successes against the Habsburg Army.

Like thousands of his fellow POWs (Imre Nagy, for instance), Broz was inspired by the Russian revolution which also released him from the prison camp. How and when he joined the Bolsheviks remains shrouded in myth as does so much of his life. Certainly he proved his usefulness and loyalty to the New Order before returning to Yugoslavia. So 'russified' did the future Tito become during his stay in Soviet Russia that ever afterwards he sprinkled his Serbo-Croat with Russian words and expressions. This led to the widespread rumour that the real Broz had died in Russian captivity and been replaced by a Soviet imposter!

Certainly, Broz's past was obscure. Like many illegitimate people, the future Marshal seems to have harboured fantasies about his parentage and later as Communist ruler liked to hint that his father had really been an Hungarian nobleman and not a common Croat. But it was his POW and post–1917 life which remained most shrouded in mystery. Even the date of his return to Yugoslavia after the war is much disputed. Later after his split with Stalin, Tito liked to play down his stay in the Soviet Union, but it may have lasted well into the 1920s.

What counted was his ability to act as an agent for the Comintern not only in Yugoslavia but also across Europe where the

Communist Party was uniformly unpopular with the authorities and banned in many places, not just Royal Yugoslavia, after 1921. As a courier and later senior official of the Comintern, Comrade Walter – as Broz's pseudonym then was – cut an unusual figure. Despite his absolute loyalty to the Stalinist line, he was far from conforming to the grey stereotype of the *apparatchik*. He wore smart suits and even dazzling rings on his fingers at the same time as he bustled in the backroom of revolution across the continent, one moment colluding with dubious Croat fascists in Vienna whose sole virtue was their hatred of Alexander's regime, the next paving the way for an underground railway to send volunteers to fight Franco in Spain on behalf of the Republic.[16]

It was 'Walter's' loyalty to the Comintern which was finally rewarded in December 1937, when he was appointed general-secretary of the illegal Communist Party of Yugoslavia with full powers to veto even its own Central Committee's decisions. The Comintern had handed Tito his first taste of absolute power, but it was only over the few thousand communists who belonged to the underground Party. With Hitler's power already casting a shadow across Europe, the tiny Yugoslav Communist Party was not even the chief concern of the Belgrade regime. Even though Belgrade was bitterly hostile to the communists, after 1921 they did not seem to present as dangerous a threat to the regime as that coming from the discontented nationalities inside the country.[17]

Despite the electoral blip of the communists in the first elections in 1920, it was the Croats and other recalcitrant nationalities who presented the major challenge to the new regime. It took two and a half years after 1918 for Alexander and Pašić to push through their model of a unitary state for the new kingdom. The fateful anniversary, 28 June 1921, was set for the proclamation of the constitution. It was too inviting a date to pass without incident. One Croat communist almost stifled the new constitution at its birth and threatened to plunge the country into crisis. He hurled a bomb into Alexander's carriage while he was en route to the Skrupština to attend promulgation of the Vidovdan constitution. It was seven years to the day since the murder of Franz Ferdinand, but the device failed to explode and Alexander survived with his sense of mission enhanced and his intolerance for non-Serb critics of the new order increased.

The brief parliamentary period proved how shallow were the roots of compromise and consensus in the country. Even if the Vidovdan constitution did not usher in an utterly pseudo-parliamentary period, the degree of real democracy was heavily circumscribed. Pašić's famous incredulity that Beneš's party could lose an election in new-born Czechoslovakia despite its control of the Interior Ministry revealed how far practising politicians were from playing by Westminster rules. Soon the growing gulf between the parties and their evident division along 'national' lines made parliamentary government impracticable. By 1928, it had become dangerous.

Meetings of the Skrupština came to resemble the sort of bear-garden which all contemporary extremists from communists to fascists so despised. Finally in mid-June 1928, proceedings were brought to halt by gunfire. A Serb deputy shot and killed among other CPP deputies Stjepan Radić, the most popular leader in Croatia. Radić's death was a disaster for Yugoslavia. However much he had been opposed in practice to the Yugoslav idea, his murder came to justify complete rejection of the state in the minds of many Croats. It helped to foster the atmosphere in which Croats who would not themselves carry out sabotage or terrorist acts against the Alexandrine state would do nothing to discourage them, certainly not inform the police.

Alexander I's use of political murder had not stopped with the killings at Sarajevo or even the judicial murder at Salonika but in all probability he was innocent of involvement in the assassination of Stjepan Radić, but it was certainly not unwelcome to the King. He was content for the politicians to discredit themselves. Their quarrels and violence paved the way for and justified the Royal Dictatorship established in January 1929. It was a regime against Serb parliamentarism as much as Croat separatism.

As ever, there were many voices who hurried to explain that Alexander had been forced against his will to establish a dictatorship because of the inadequacy of the parliamentary system. (Has any dictator ever seized power except to save the people from its unsuitable elected representatives?) Sir Nevile Henderson hurried to explain the new regime to R. W. Seton-Watson, whose acquaintanceship with the country and its peoples went back a great deal further than that of the future go-between of Chamberlain and Hitler: 'I find it difficult, in view of the ghastly mess into which the Parliamentary regime had brought the country, to see what other course the king had . . .'

The next few years saw a reign of terror against the King's enemies. However much Alexander might posture as sovereign of the newly named 'Yugoslavia', his rule remained essentially Serbian and his police took brutal measures against any threat to the integrity of his kingdom which might be posed by non-Serb political or intellectual forces. He placed all power beneath himself in his commander of the Life Guard who now took up the post of Premier and Interior Minister simultaneously. Alexander's favourite was the sinister Peter Zivković, who had played the key role in betraying Alexander Obrenović and his Queen in 1903 when he had been an officer of their guard. It was Zivković who had cut off one of Queen Draga's fingers in order to remove a ring from her slashed body. It was Zivković who had been central to Alexander's efforts to remove his brother Djordje – even trying to poison him. It was also Zivković who had persuaded his old comrade in conspiracy, Apis, to write the incriminating letter taking all the guilt for the Sarajevo murder plot on himself by promising him he would escape the firing squad and so ensured that Apis signed his own death-warrant at Salonika in 1917. So close were the two men and so unparalleled was the trust that Alexander placed in Zivković that it was rumoured they were lovers. Others believed that Zivković's knowledge of so many dark secrets gave him a hold over the King.

Whatever the reason for their close relations, Zivković pursued a policy of terror against any threats to his sovereign's power which badly damaged Yugoslavia's reputation with her former Western allies. The murder of scholars like Suflaj shocked men like R. W. Seton-Watson who came to detest Alexander's rule and even to muse aloud whether it might not be better if he were dead. The disillusioning reality of a Serbian stranglehold on political power under Alexander led Seton-Watson to complain that what had been created did not match his vision of a multinational liberal constitutional monarchy. Even before Sarajevo, Seton-Watson had warned of the dangers of a pan-Serb rather than a Yugoslav solution to the national aspirations of both Franz Josef's Slav subjects and of King Peter's peoples: 'The triumph of the pan-Serb idea would mean the triumph of Eastern over Western culture, and would be a fatal blow to progress and modern development throughout the Balkans.' Now his fears were confirmed and there was little the regime's loyal friends like Sir Nevile Henderson could do to disabuse Seton-Watson and others like him of their negative impressions – though he tried, just as later in his distinguished career he struggled from his post in Berlin to get across a positive picture of Nazi Germany to the British elite.[18]

Even before his dictatorship, Alexander had always faced the risk of assassination, but after 1929 the King was both hunter and hunted. His ambitions drove him on and made him ruthless towards his enemies, but they in their turn recognised that he towered above the regime and was its motor. Anyone wishing to destroy Yugoslavia had to kill Alexander. There were many who hoped to see him dead and to claim the credit. Communists, Croats, Macedonians and Albanians, not to mention some Serbs, had every reason to hate and fear Alexander. Ultimately, the first three groups seem to have coalesced in bringing about his destruction with the help of his foreign enemy, Mussolini.

His fate had all the inevitability of Greek tragedy. Alexander's assassination in Marseilles on 9 October 1934 should be as well-known as the murders at Sarajevo twenty years earlier. He died almost instantly from the bullet-wounds, but his host, the French Foreign Minister Louis Barthou, was abandoned in the panic and confusion and left to bleed slowly to death unrecognised in all the confusion. Barthou was the last robust French foreign minister before the Second World War. Fluent in German, he recognised the symptoms of Hitler's aggressive intentions early and might have prompted action, but after his death men like Laval took charge of French foreign policy. Barthou saw that France could not afford to treat both Germany and the Soviet Union as pariahs, and wanted to deal with Stalin. Alexander saw Italy and the Kremlin as his own *bêtes noires* and preferred to deal with Hitler. The assassin killed two contradictory approaches to the dilemmas posed by the decay of the Versailles peace settlement.

Alexander could never have come to terms with the Soviet Union. Its leaders had murdered his Romanov patrons and he himself had taken on the mantle of the inheritor of their post-

Byzantine ambitions. He planned to build a Patriarchal cathedral in Belgrade to match Hagia Sophia in Istanbul as a symbol of his claims. (It was completed under Milošević.) He established a military academy and other facilities for White Russian émigrés in Belgrade to prepare for the liberation of 'Holy Mother Russia'. Yugoslavia was a great Orthodox state, in many ways the greatest left since the fall of the Romanovs. Just as later in the twentieth century communist Yugoslavia seemed a smaller reflection of Soviet multinational reality, so Alexander's kingdom was intended to be a model of what Imperial Russia might have been.

As in the Soviet Union, the Yugoslav communists talked about the rights of individual nationalities to self-determination, but in effect they permitted that right only in pre-revolutionary states. Separatism was a good thing in Royal Yugoslavia because it weakened the power of the ruling classes and divided them against each other to the possible advantage of the left. After the revolution things would be different, but the communists did not say so yet. As the threat of Germany and Italy grew, the communists changed tack. Royal Yugoslavia had little interest in fostering the ambitions of the two openly fascist states to its own disadvantage, so suddenly it became preferable – at least in public. Tito's future chief ideologue after 1944, Eduard Kardelj, wrote in 1938:

> Although it is necessary to recognise the right of the Slovenes and the Croats to self-determination, nevertheless, every separatist action that at this moment attempts to break up Yugoslavia is in reality a preparation for new enslavement, and not for self-determination.[19]

Stalin was still publicly anxious to forge a Popular Front with Britain and France against Hitler so he promoted a positive attitude towards France's allies like Yugoslavia (even though it was not reciprocated by Belgrade).

This policy of promoting the idea of a Yugoslavia which for the present was the best option for all the constituent peoples was revived during the war and was the basis of the Communist Partisans' capacity to appeal to people in all groups in Yugoslavia. It underpinned the wartime declarations of the partisan front organisation, the Anti-Fascist Council for the National Liberation of Yugoslavia (AVNOJ), which sought to offer reassurances to all groups that their interests would be given free rein *after* victory. But the Comintern's policy was always 'dialectical' and its proclamations of resolute anti-Fascism or anything else should not have been taken at face value.[20]

Once it became clear to Stalin that the Western states would resist further German expansion in the summer of 1939, he lost interest in supporting the territorial integrity of France's East European allies. Now as Hitler would have a fight on his hands if he moved east, Stalin was happy to deal with the Nazi regime to promote a war which would help to speed up the disintegration of the capitalist states. The communists in Yugoslavia became proponents of national independence for the kingdom's constituent peoples once more and remained so until Hitler's surprise attack on Russia forced another rethink.

Like the Ustasha, the Yugoslav communists did not constitute a serious threat to the regime on the eve of the Second World War unless they could find foreign assistance. In October 1940, the Yugoslav Party had only 6600 members plus about 17,800 organised youth supporters.[21] But the Party was underground. What it could hope to appeal to was a vague pan-Slavism among ordinary Serbs, which was certainly stronger than it ever was sincerely felt by rulers of Russia or the Soviet Union who tended to conjure up pan-Slav feelings only when it suited their great power interests and drop them as soon as the situation changed.

Unlike contemporary fascist regimes, which were underpinned by mass movements, the Karadjordjević regime lacked a mobilised popular base. Alexander was too haughty to feel the need to base his rule on a party machine and Paul was too reluctant a ruler to throw himself into the machinations of a thoroughgoing dictatorship. Instead the regime relied on the police, army and bureaucracy to hold down opposition.

The Serb domination of all the institutions of Royal Yugoslavia was particularly marked in the military. Despite – or rather because of – the Croats' long and distinguished tradition of service in the armed forces of the Habsburgs, they were kept almost entirely out of high command under the Karadjordjevićs. More than 15 per cent of Franz Josef's generals and admirals had been Croats, but on the eve of Hitler's invasion of Yugoslavia its army boasted only two Croat generals, compared with 161 Serbs.[22] Since it is difficult to imagine an army performing more disastrously than the Yugoslav forces did in April 1941, an integration of Croats into the command structure could not have made matters worse and might have encouraged more resistance if Croat soldiers had been given more reason to identify with the state.

In other areas of state service, the favouritism shown towards Serbs was almost as marked. The position in the diplomatic service was much the same as in the Army. Out of 145 senior diplomats in 1934, Serbs provided 123 while Croats filled only 21 places. Only in the judiciary did the generally better-educated Croats do marginally better – over a quarter of judges were of Croat origin. Defenders of Royal Yugoslavia emphasise that despite their political and institutional dominance, Serbs as a whole did not profit economically from their hegemony. However, the gulf in economic development between Slovenes and Croats and their Serb fellow Yugoslavs only tended to emphasise the disproportionate political power of the Serbs. The relative backwardness of the Serb economy made the exclusion of their north-western neighbours all the more galling.[23]

Even after the Royal coup in 1929, there was no significant change to the Serb domination of the Yugoslav state. In so far as Alexander sidelined some Serb politicians for the rest of his reign it was because he resented their disobedience and ambition rather than because he wished to mollify the non-Serbs. What he hoped to do was to quieten all autonomous political life in his kingdom. In this aim, he was little different from his neighbour, King Carol of Romania, later in the 1930s. Alexander was simply more efficient at dictatorship than his flamboyant and irresponsible neighbour. What Alexander was very well aware of was Mussolini's greedy ambitions with regard to the Adriatic coastline and the fact that the Italian dictator was the patron of the authoritarian regimes in Austria and Hungary, neither of which were friendly towards Belgrade. In so far as Alexander took steps to pacify the discontent of his subjects along the western and northern fringes of Yugoslavia, it was so that they would be less willing to provide a fifth column to support his external enemies.[24]

Although it is commonplace to say Alexander (forgetting poor

Barthou) was murdered by Croats, in fact the trigger was pulled by a terrorist provided by the Macedonian organisation, IMRO. Alexander's rule was no more appreciated by Macedonian separatists than by the Croat Ustasha. Pavelić's men cooperated with and paid for the assassin's work. They hoped that Alexander's death would pave the way for their return in glory to Zagreb.

The nationalist enemies were not alone in wanting Alexander's downfall. In the conspiratorial world of opposition to the Belgrade regime which was strung out across Europe, peculiar alliances of convenience if not conviction were not unknown. Rumours constantly circulated that the communists too were involved in the background to the murder in Marseilles. This was not as unlikely as it later came to seem. It is easy to forget that in 1934 the communists still supported the disintegration of Yugoslavia. It was only in 1935 that Stalin decided to seek reactionary allies against Hitler and instructed the Comintern to back the post-Versailles regimes now threatened by Nazi expansion. But in 1934 the Party's line was still anti-Yugoslav. Even its organisation reflected this since it was divided into separate 'national' parties representing, for instance, the Croats.

Alexander distrusted Austria even in its reduced state after 1918. Vienna certainly was a hotbed of anti-Yugoslav feeling and by the early Thirties the Austrian capital seems to have housed from time to time both Tito and Pavelić as clandestine conspirators. The Austrian dictator, Dollfuss, was allied to Mussolini's Italy and so Alexander was not entirely out of sympathy with the Austrian Nazis who murdered him in July 1934. Although Dollfuss was killed, Mussolini's threat of intervention prevented Germany aiding the Austrian Nazis and their putsch was suppressed. Alexander permitted several hundred refugee Nazis to find asylum in Yugoslavia where they remained until the *Anschluss* in 1938.[25]

The murder of Dollfuss was followed only three months later by Alexander's own death. Perhaps he had gone to France to seek support against growing German power, but probably Italy remained his chief concern. Mussolini was indirectly involved in his death because of his subsidies to the Ustasha and the provision of training facilities. Anything which destabilised Yugoslavia served Mussolini's ambitions to extend Italian influence in the Balkans.

The assassination of Alexander failed to achieve its likely purpose. Apart from killing the King, the assassins and their various and disparate backers must have hoped that the deed would precipitate an internal crisis in Yugoslavia making it easier for them to achieve their goals. In fact, despite the minority of the new king Peter II, the Regency envisaged by his father took control of the situation in the aftermath of the murder. However, it was one thing to preserve public order but quite another to overcome the internal differences which divided young King Peter's subjects.

Alexander's cousin, Paul, has suffered a bad press. The new regent was alleged to have been pro-German. It is true that at the end of his rule in March 1941, Yugoslavia joined Hitler's Anti-Comintern Pact, but Paul had little choice short of facing the *Wehrmacht* alone, as happened disastrously ten days after his fall. Unlike Alexander, who had seen Italy as his main enemy, Paul recognised the dominance of Germany and had tried to find Western allies to counterbalance Nazi power in the region. He got short shrift from the British despite his well-known Anglophilia. Abandoned in the geopolitical jungle by the Western democracies, Paul tried to buy time. Even his adhesion to the Anti-Comintern Pact was on uniquely favourable terms including Yugoslavia's right to refuse the transit of German troops through its territory, which not even 'neutral' Sweden maintained in 1941.[26]

Meanwhile Paul had patched up a constitutional deal with the Croat leader, Macek. The '*Sporazum*' or Compromise was signed at the end of August 1939, just as Molotov and Ribbentrop were agreeing to the terms of the Nazi-Soviet Pact which would turn the Anti-Comintern Pact on its head for the next eighteen months as Hitler and Stalin acted as de facto allies against the Western democracies. By spring 1941, Hitler was anxious to have all the small European states locked into his system in advance of his attack on his erstwhile ally in the Kremlin.

Paul wanted to solidify Yugoslavia's internal political order by appeasing the resentful Croats and giving them in effect self-government across a broad swathe of territory including the historic Croatian kingdom plus significant parts of Hercegovina.

(The details of the boundaries were supposed to be settled by plebiscites which in fact were never held.) Unlike the other administrative units of Yugoslavia, only the Croatian *banovina* was based on the national principle and few people who would have identified themselves as Croats lived outside it (though Pavelić's supporters insisted the Bosnian Muslims were 'pure' Croats too). The *Sporazum* provided no constitutional guarantees for civil rights either in Croatia or the rest of Yugoslavia. It was implemented in a slipshod and dilatory manner and was hardly effective when war broke out in April 1941. What it did was to contribute to Paul's unpopularity with the Serb-dominated military, who saw him increasingly making concessions to both domestic and foreign opponents, whether Croat or German-speaking.[27]

By the spring of 1941, Hitler wanted to concentrate all his attention on the forthcoming achievement of his life's goal, the destruction of Soviet Russia. Already he was irritated by Mussolini's disastrous invasion of Greece which was drawing his forces into the Mediterranean theatre. The last thing Hitler wanted was another distraction. Naturally, Churchill and Stalin, who was not as naively passive in the face of the German build-up for Operation Barbarossa as is often made out, wanted the opposite.

The British intelligence and subversion agency, SOE, had built up an effective network in Belgrade. Its agents played upon the anti-German sympathies of many in the officer corps. At the same time, Soviet agents seem to have been making contact with similar circles in the hope of provoking a distraction on Hitler's southern flank. Ordinary communists in Yugoslavia were not fully informed of Stalin's strategy but as Djilas later made clear, they understood the Nazi-Soviet Pact as a temporary phenomenon and so were waiting for its abrogation – though they expected Stalin to make the first move. Of course when the Pact was first signed the Party activists had hurried to endorse it. Tito himself wrote in November 1940, '[The] Pact for Mutual Aid between the Soviet Union and Germany, and the entry of Soviet troops into western White Russia [i.e. eastern Poland], have aroused great enthusiasm amongst the broad masses of the Yugoslav population.'[28] Recognising its weak position, Prince Paul's government recognised the delicate balance of power by currying favour with both Moscow and Berlin.

On 5 April, Royal Yugoslavia and the USSR signed a 'Friendship and Non-Aggression Pact'. The Kremlin and Belgrade agreed that 'in the event of one of the contracting parties being the object of an attack by a third State, the other party undertakes to preserve a policy of friendly relations towards it.' The next day, Germany invaded Yugoslavia. When Stalin's Foreign Minister, Molotov, met Hitler's ambassador to receive news of the invasion he studiously failed to raise the Soviet Union's 'common interest to preserve peace' with Yugoslavia nor 'the friendship existing between the two countries', and shortly afterwards the Soviet Union de-recognised Yugoslavia, which had ceased to exist.

Shortly beforehand, local outrage, especially in Serbia against Yugoslavia's adhesion to the Tripartite Pact – as the Anti-Comintern Pact was called for politeness' sake after 1939 – had reached boiling point in Belgrade. Encouraged by British and possibly Soviet promises of assistance, a group of officers overthrew Paul's regime after the signature of the Anti-Comintern Pact. There was popular rejoicing in the streets of Belgrade.[29] For a few brief days, it looked as though the new Yugoslavia with the still adolescent King Peter proclaimed of age would escape Hitler's clutches. The Soviet Union had recognised the new government just as 'Operation Punishment' got under way on 6 April. (*Pravda* proclaimed the Soviet-Yugoslav Pact as evidence of the 'strengthening of peace' in an edition which reached the Moscow newsstands even as the Stukas were diving over Belgrade.) Churchill could take melancholy satisfaction in having engineered another front against Hitler. It lasted ten days.[30]

6

Wartime, 1941–44

> What would have happened if the glorious Red Army had not existed? What would have happened if this state of workers and peasants with Stalin, the man of genius, at its head, had not existed . . . and which with innumerable sacrifices and rivers of blood *liberated also our Slav nations* . . .? For this great sacrifice which our brothers in the great Soviet Union made, we other Slavs thank them. [Long-lasting ovations]
>
> Tito[1]

Hitler's 'Operation Punishment' was the most devastatingly swift of all his *Blitzkriege*. Within ten days of its launch on 6 April 1941, and for the loss of only 166 men, the *Wehrmacht* and its allies had overrun the whole country and all organised resistance ceased. The German Army rolled on through Greece and pounced on Crete at the end of May. With the Balkans apparently pacified, Hitler turned east to launch his showdown with Stalin a month later than planned. Whether the delay in launching 'Operation Barbarossa' was decisive has often been debated.[2] For Yugoslavia, the outbreak of war between Nazi Germany and the Soviet Union resolved any ambivalence among the local communists about how to react to the Axis Occupation. They would fight it.

Already other tentative resistance groups had sprung up around Yugoslavia as Hitler carved up the old kingdom with his allies, allowing annexation of coveted territories here and military occupation there, to Italy, Hungary and Bulgaria. Fatefully, it was also decided to establish the so-called 'Independent State of Croatia', whose dependence on the Axis was flaunted by the obsessive use of the word 'independent' by its representatives to describe it. The establishment of the Independent State of Croatia (NDH) had profound consequences both at the time and since. Although a would-be collaborationist regime under General Nedić was on hand in Belgrade and willing to provide a full quisling service to Hitler, the Nazis were unwilling to permit even the façade of satellite independence to the Serbs. The Croat regime, however, was initially permitted a wide leeway in implementing its own policies.

The savagery of the Ustasha's reign of terror shocked even the Germans. The German Army's approach to counter-insurgency had been one of calculated massive reprisals at least as far back as the Franco-Prussian War and soon enough the occupier began shooting hostages in response to any sign of defiance by the subject peoples of Yugoslavia, but the bestial and irrational nature of the Ustasha violence was too much even for Hitler's minions.

The cult of the knife among the Ustasha and in their folklore is well described by Vuk Drasković in his book, *Noz* (The Knife), though much of it could have been applied then or certainly now to elements among the Serb and non-Croat fighters. Describing the savageries of the internecine fighting in Bosnia-Hercegovina during the Second World War, one fighter propounds a philosophy of the knife:

> Our people possesses an instrument, which it can use better than anyone else in the world, and a word which we pronounce better than anyone else in the world. This not at all complicated instrument and this very simple word are our stamp, our trademark, our passport throughout history . . . We say: knife, and when we hear the word, we come alive, our eyes light up, our hearts beat wildly, something electric goes through the brain, we shudder . . . The word resonates in us, in these three letters [Noz] lies our whole history.[3]

A futile historical debate has gone on about whether the first violence was Ustasha against Serb or a Chetnik attack on a Croat or Muslim village. It overlooks the ideological and psychological intensity of Pavelić's regime on the one hand, and seeks to deny that some Serbs committed atrocities against Croats and Muslims just for their identity and regardless of their allegiance or lack of it to the Ustasha. The horrors of the Second World War have been reworked into a uniquely Serb experience and are used to justify revenge today on the descendants of the perpetrators of anti-Serb violence of fifty years ago – a little as if the Israeli air force was to bomb Vienna inflicting casualties on the post–1945 inhabitants on the off chance of scoring a direct hit on Dr Waldheim.

This tendency to talk as though the Second World War was yesterday was played up by the propagandists to reinforce national antagonisms. By refusing to let time pass, let alone wounds heal, the cult of Jasenovac was a direct stimulus to new atrocities. After all, if today's Croats were to be seen as the participants in genocide why should they deserve mercy now? Many Western Serbophiles seemed to accept the Serb propagandist line of argument and even to repeat it (even if they usually fell short of its logical conclusion). Derek Prag, the Conservative MEP for Hertfordshire, for instance, as late as the end of May 1993 (i.e. long after the horrors of ethnic cleansing against Muslims in his own time were well established) could still write that it was EC recognition of Bosnia that caused the problem:

> Anyone who knew the Serbs and knew the history of relations between Serbs and Yugoslav Muslims . . . knew what their reaction would be. The horrors of the Serbs' fight for freedom against the Nazis and their murderous puppet state of Croatia in the 1939–45 war, *in which most Bosnian Muslims sided with the Germans* [emphasis added], was too close to be forgotten.[4]

Mr Prag's presumption that because the savage response of the Serb paramilitaries to the breakdown of Yugoslavia was predictable seems to imply that it was therefore acceptable.

In August 1991, an exhibition of films was opened in Belgrade commemorating the massacres of Serbs in the so-called Independent State of Croatia between 1941 and 1944. The theme of the exhibition was 'Ustasha crimes do not fade with time', but the message was 'no people, except the Serbs, has experienced such a Golgotha'.[5] Dobrica Ćosić has given his immense authority to this notion of the Serbs as the uniquely martyred people even if he has not gone quite so far in identifying the nation's sufferings with those of Christ Himself. The elevation of the nation or country to divine status is a key to the fascistisation of a people. It is not the least irony of the Serbian portrayal of the Croats as genetically genocidal and inherently fascistic that this propaganda has itself taken on overtly fascist features.

Fifty years ago, there was no need to make propaganda about Ustasha atrocities, they were common knowledge. Determined to purify the population of Croatia and to impose his rule by exemplary terror, Pavelić sent out his supporters into the territories which he had been granted by Hitler (which included not only traditional Croatia but also Bosnia-Hercegovina) and they set about exterminating Jews, gypsies and Serbs as they came across them. The Ustashas combined a racialist hatred of Jews and gypsies with a religiously derived loathing of the Orthodox Serbs. Under slogans like 'Kill a third, convert a third, expel a third', Pavelić's supporters went on a killing spree. Although few in number in the aftermath of the collapse of the old system, the Ustasha forces were able to wreak mayhem on largely defenceless and disorientated populations. But their intended victims did not remain passive for long.[6]

It soon became apparent that Pavelić's policies were dangerously counter-productive. In the Serb-inhabited regions of the NDH, resistance groups sprang up. The district around Knin, the Krajina, was one hotbed of anti-Ustasha resistance as was the region of Bihać to its east. The Italians in particular were both disgusted by what they saw as the senseless savagery of their former protégé, Pavelić, and also alarmed by the impact on their forces of the growing resistance movements.

For all the unpopularity of Yugoslavia among Croats by 1941, the Ustasha regime led by Ante Pavelić would never have come to power without the German victory. The terrible savagery of the Ustasha and their leaders' hysterical insistence on the movement's right to rule indicated the underlying insecurity of Pavelić's power-base. Throughout his period in power, the regime was beset by resistance from Croats as well as Serbs and other minorities in the NDH. Among the Croats who joined Tito's partisans was the young Franjo Tudjman. Members of his family were killed by the Ustasha in reprisal for his opposition.

Even German soldiers and the SS were alarmed by the negative consequences of the Ustasha's brutality. In February 1942, one report noted,

> The atrocities perpetrated by the Ustasha units against the Orthodox in Croatian territory must be regarded as the most important reason for the blazing up of guerrilla activities. The Ustasha units have carried out their atrocities not only against Orthodox males of military age, but in particular in the most bestial fashion against unarmed old men, women and children . . . innumerable Orthodox have fled to rump Serbia, and their reports have roused the Serbian population to great indignation.[7]

The most notorious centre of Ustasha crime was the concentration camp at Jasenovac. The cult of the dead at Jasenovac has been so misused to justify more recent massacres by Serbs that it is easy to forget how much suffering was inflicted on Serbs between 1941 and 1944 in the NDH. Because Serbian propaganda so grotesquely inflated the number of victims in Jasenovac and instrumentalised the terrible name of the camp for crude propagandistic purposes, it is hardly surprising that some Croats questioned the 'official' Serb interpretation. The ghoulish repetition of frankly incredible allegations by Serbs whipping themselves up into a murderous fury should not however blind late twentieth-century observers to the crimes committed by the Ustasha.

It is only by contrast with the demographically impossible death-toll claimed by professional Serb genocidists that the probable scale of death as a direct result of the Ustasha seems smaller than the rhetoric might lead one to expect. This is the inevitable irony of the politicisation of a holocaust: it breeds the very revisionism it claims to combat, and it needs the revisionism to justify its own hysteria.

The facts are terrible enough and require no exaggeration, except by those who are not interested in the fate of real individuals. Probably about 325,000 Serbs were killed by the Ustasha in the NDH, including about 60,000 at Jasenovac alone. In other words about one in every six Serbs in Pavelić's realm was killed. This was the work of a force of about 30,000 Ustashas.[8]

Mihailović's Chetniks were self-consciously loyalists to the vision of Yugoslavia as a 'greater Serbia'. They regarded non-Serbs with suspicion at best and downright implacable hostility at worst. After all, the Chetnik organisation had its roots in the prewar Chetnik force which was in effect a kind of 'Black and Tans' on standby as much to suppress any defiance from suspect elements like Muslims or Albanians as to provide resistance to a foreign invader. The Chetniks waged an undiscriminating struggle against those whom they saw as agents of the dissolution of Yugoslavia and enemies of Serbia, which meant in effect the bulk of the population even though most areas were spared Chetnik activity.[9]

Throughout Yugoslavia, the death-toll has never been adequately estimated. But allowing for emigration and the much lowered birth-rate, probably about 900,000 people died as a result of the war and privations which went with it. The invaders may only have accounted for ten to fifteen per cent of these victims. The rest were killed in the internecine fighting between collaborators and resisters, Partisans and Chetniks.

Unlike both collaborators and Mihailović's Chetnik resistance, the communist-led Partisans were not nationally based.[10] Instead of appealing to the loyalty of one people in defunct Yugoslavia, Tito's men tried to appeal to all strata of the Yugoslav population to promote a common struggle against the invaders and their quislings and at the same time to give the communists a foothold in every area of the country as the basis for its eventual revolutionising on the Soviet model. Tito's chief comrades in arms were drawn from the different peoples of Yugoslavia: Djilas was a Montenegrin, Ranković a Serb, Hebrang a Croat, Kardelj a Slovene and Pijade was a Jew. The cosmopolitan mix of the communist leaders, combined with a judicial addition of prominent non-communists like Dr Ribar in the Anti-Fascist Council, made it much easier for Tito to appeal to people in every section of Yugoslav society than Mihailović, whose appeal was limited to Serbs.

Like Mihailović, the Partisans drew on the still lively tradition of resistance to the Turks and bandit warfare throughout much of the country. Djilas noted the cult of heroic self-sacrifice survived in his native Montenegro, and not just there, when he was a child: 'Survival was a way of life, and death in battle the loveliest dream and highest duty.'[11] He thought that the attraction of communism lay as much in its appeal to native rebelliousness in the local character as to any clearly understood ideological aims. However, as in many other parts of Occupied Europe the shattering defeat of the old order by the Nazis led to a widespread turn to the Left by people seeking a radical change from what had failed their country in its hour of need.

Not that the Partisans relied on positive attraction alone. Tito's forces quickly took advantage of the resort to a policy of reprisals by both Germans and Italians. The Partisans saw that if they attacked an Axis outpost the Germans and Italians were not inclined to inquire too closely among the local population who was responsible for it. They took savage reprisals regardless of guilt or innocence. This was exactly what the Partisans wanted because it forced the population to flee to the Partisans for safety. The Germans and Italians achieved in a systematic way what the frenzied brutality of the Ustasha had started: their firing squads were the best recruiting sergeants for the Partisans.

Djilas has described the savagery of the fighting many times. He is unapologetic. If he slit the throat of German prisoners then it was no more than their comrades or perhaps the victim himself had already inflicted on the invaded Yugoslavs. No mercy was expected from the occupiers and none offered. Even four decades on Djilas could take grim pleasure in the thought of the horrified bewilderment of the Italians in Mostar at the sight of the corpses of massacred Italian soldiers floating down the Neretva under the famous bridge.[12]

As far as the Allies were concerned the resistance forces on the ground in Occupied Europe were simply adjuncts to the overall strategy of defeating the Axis. Partisans or Chetniks were pawns in that struggle. London certainly was little concerned about the postwar consequences of the victory of one group or the other. In a moment of ruthlessness, necessary to win the war but unsettling to his reputation, Churchill put the point cruelly to his emissary to Tito, Fitzroy Maclean:

> Do you intend to make Yugoslavia your home after the war?
> No, sir.

> Neither do I. And that being so, the less you worry about the form of government they set up the better. What interests us is which of them is doing the most harm to the Germans.[13]

The criteria of the kill-rate undoubtedly favoured Tito's Partisans even if his sympathisers among communists and left-wing intelligence officers exaggerated the Partisans' effectiveness, as has been often claimed.

Certainly far fewer German forces were deployed in Yugoslavia in reality than the thirty or more crack divisions often cited in the 1990s. In practice, once conquered Yugoslavia was not a priority for Hitler, even though hatred of Serbs was one of the stronger hates which motivated the Führer. It was used for much of the time as a place to rest German units left understrength after hard fighting on the Eastern Front. Studying the formal number of divisions listed in the *Wehrmacht*'s order of battle in the Balkans is a very misleading way of trying to assess their actual manpower or their fighting effectiveness. The strength of most units in the region was far lower than their normal complement. Sometimes fewer than 15 per cent of a normal division's strength would be awarded the *Praedikat* of its own divisional number and if it was in the Waffen SS its own evocative name. The Waffen SS division 'Handschar', for instance, has become notorious – possibly because its distinctive fez head-dress distinguished it from more mundanely uniformed SS units. However, claims that it alone slaughtered more than 700,000 Serbs[14] grossly exaggerate the killing capacity of the unit.

Neither Chetniks nor communists regarded the defeat and the expulsion of the Axis invader as an end in itself. Victory over the occupier was only a step in the battle to control Yugoslavia afterwards. Both Mihailović and Tito recognised that in some circumstances Hitler's defeat would be to the advantage of his domestic enemy. Neither wanted to see his vision of a future Yugoslav state sacrificed because the other side – Partisan or Chetnik – was in a better position to profit from the Liberation.[15]

Both Mihailović and Tito recognised that their chances of determining the country's future depended upon the Allied attitude towards the Yugoslav resistance groups after the war. If the Western powers could be persuaded to come to the aid of the anti-communists then Mihailović would stand a good chance of dominating Yugoslavia, even if Stalin's forces dominated eastern Europe, but without Western military aid and support Mihailović would be destroyed by Tito's forces, as well as in action against the invader.

Mihailović's lack of direct operational control over many Chetnik groups meant that his reputation was at the mercy of local commanders who might choose to quieten down their locality and cut risks to their own men by making pacts, especially with the local Italian forces. (The Germans were unhappy about colluding with the Serb forces for a long time.)

Mihailović was defamed as another quisling. In fact, his contact with the Axis powers was far from unique. Tito's Partisans, too, occasionally came to terms with the invader and made local truces. In March 1943, Tito sent three of his most senior comrades to Zagreb to negotiate with the occupiers. For decades this meeting was denied and then grudgingly admitted though even then in terms so heavily qualified as to be completely misleading. It was only after Tito's death that the elderly survivors of this episode, Djilas and Velebit, confirmed its more serious purpose: it was to discuss what attitude the Partisans would take to a British landing on the Dalmatian coast as well as to arrange an exchange of prisoners.[16]

Tito's myth for a long time masked his own tactical deals with the Axis forces as well as his clear revolutionary purpose. In March 1943, for instance, he told his forces in Bosnia that en route to fight Chetniks in Montenegro 'do not fight Germans' and added, 'Your most important task at this moment is to annihilate the Chetniks of Draza Mihailović and to destroy their command apparatus which represents the greatest danger to the development of the National Liberation Struggle.'[17]

In fact, the Partisans were performing a task which the Germans had unsuccessfully urged their unenthusiastic Italian allies to perform.

At this time, Djilas and Velebit were actually in Zagreb negotiating with the Germans about the possibility of a cease-fire as well as the exchange of prisoners (including Tito's second wife, Herta, whom the Germans held, unbeknownst to themselves). When the German side asked what the Partisan response would be to an Allied landing on the Yugoslav coast, they were told that Tito's forces would resist such an Anglo-American invasion.

Tito must have been disappointed by the lack of Soviet assistance. His leading comrades were all deeply imbued with pro-Soviet, indeed Stalinist, assumptions and were loyal to the distant utopia. Yet still Moscow sent no help. Meanwhile the capitalist powers were trying to court the Partisans. Tito saw no reason not to take the Western aid if no strings were attached and it became clear that Stalin too thought that the National Liberation Struggle should be fought at the expense of the capitalists.

In fact, Stalin was worried that the Yugoslav Partisans were too fiercely communist to understand the tactical necessities of the situation. He complained loudly to Djilas that the Partisans wore the communist red star on their helmets and caps. To Stalin's eyes this was an unnecessary display of ideological loyalty which might put off the Western liaison officers and therefore lead to a cut-back in supplies to the Partisans. Of course, he need not have worried.[18]

By the spring of 1945, it was clear that Nazi Germany itself was about to be overrun by the Allied armies. Stalin's forces had crossed the Oder sixty miles from Berlin and were battering at the gates of Vienna. The Anglo-American forces in Italy were threatening to break out across the Po into Austria and Slovenia. The collapse of the Third Reich left no room for the survival of any of its satellites. The NDH had reached a dead end.

Unlike his role model, Hitler, who showed no inclination to survive *Götterdämmerung*, the *Poglavnik* was anxious to elude capture by the Partisans and unwilling to commit suicide. By late 1944, plans seem to have been laid with Croat representatives abroad including most importantly among the Red Cross and in the Catholic hierarchy to spirit Pavelić away in the increasingly likely event of defeat.

In April 1945, a large and heavily armed column of Ustasha left Zagreb moving north-west towards Austria where the rank and file might hope to find shelter among their erstwhile allies or at least better treatment at the hands of the Anglo-Americans than they could hope for from the Partisans. How far Pavelić and his chief henchmen knew that the Western intelligence agencies would turn a blind eye to their onward flight through Italy heading for Franco's Spain or Perón's Argentina still remains conjectural. Certainly, nothing seems to have been done to intercept Pavelić.

The fact that one of Hitler's most notorious allies was able to escape and then live out a fairly high-profile retirement (dying in 1957 after an assassination attempt) remains an unresolved mystery. Two main theories are repeatedly advanced to explain the ease with which men like Pavelić slipped through Allied territory. On the one hand, it has been argued that in the atmosphere of the start of the Cold War, suddenly at the end of the Second World War, Western intelligence agencies supported by the fiercely anti-communist Vatican saw the Soviet Union as the new enemy and regarded the East European collaborators with the Nazis as useful sources of information about countries now falling under Stalin's domination and possibly as future leaders of 'liberated' nations there.[19]

Certainly it is difficult to see how such loudly denounced and officially wanted men like Pavelić could escape without connivance from powerful figures in the Allied armies and intelligence. However, that does not explain why such radical anti-communists were willing to send back hundreds of thousands of ex-Soviet citizens and other East Europeans to a generally grim fate when they would presumably have been as willing to serve in a Western crusade against Stalin as they had been in Hitler's. The ex-quisling chiefs were not much use without their Indians.

The other argument put forward to explain the apparent complacency of the Western Allies towards escaping high-ranking Nazi collaborators is that it suited Stalin to let them escape. The fact that figures in the Vatican and the Catholic Church could be implicated in helping them would serve the Soviet leader's purpose of undermining a key Western institution. Already, Pius XII's failure to denounce the Nazis' genocide in unequivocal terms was becoming a controversial issue as the death camps were revealed. Evidence of collusion between Catholic clerics and the perpetrators of the Holocaust could only help to taint further the image of the Church.

Much has been made of the possibility that known Soviet agents like Philby, who held a key position in British intelligence and was on the spot in Austria for some of the time, might have influenced the passivity of the Western forces in letting slip the Pavelićs and his like. Since without their followers, who were in any case deported to their fate, these would-be Führers would be ineffective, it might well have suited Stalin to kill two birds with one stone: to discredit a key institution of the West and get his hands on many of his enemies. The fact that one of the key Croatian clergymen based in Rome who helped set up the 'rat-lines' by which Ustasha leaders escaped later defected to Tito's Yugoslavia does hint that Stalin might have penetrated agents into the Vatican in the inter-war period who then served his devious purposes.

Whatever may have been the truth about the postwar escape of Pavelić et al. and the return to their fate of thousands of his followers, plus many others whose only crime was to have fled Tito or to have been deported as forced labourers to Germany, it was an episode that leaves a bad taste in the mouth. Of course, the Yugoslav refugee problem was just part of the huge displaced persons (DPs) crisis at the end of the war, which the British tried to resolve by forcibly repatriating all and sundry to their presumed homes, by now usually under Stalin's control. No inquiries were made into individual reasons for wishing to remain in the West: no doubt, many were collaborators with Hitler who expected little mercy from Stalin, but countless thousands were victims of the war by any definition – forced labourers, prisoners of war or even people who had left their 'home country' decades before. All were scheduled for return regardless. Harold Macmillan wrote in his war diary about the situation in British-occupied Austria on 13 May 1945:

> Thousands of so-called Ustashi or Chetniks, mostly with wives and children, are fleeing in panic into this area in front of the advancing Yugoslavs. These expressions, U. and C., cover anything from guerrilla forces raised by the Germans from Slovenes and Croats and Serbs to fight Tito, and armed and maintained by the Germans – to people who, either because they are Roman Catholics or Conservative in politics, or for whatever cause are out of sympathy with revolutionary Communism . . .

But the key phrase in Macmillan's notes of this time was his comment, 'We have to look on, more or less helplessly, since our present plan of action is *not* to use force and *not* to promote an incident.'[20]

Any study of the British treatment of DPs cannot help being struck by how far it involved a roll-call of future *prominenti* in postwar Britain – from Brian Robertson at British Rail, through Charles Villiers at British Steel to Toby Aldington of the Dock-work Labour Scheme, and all presided over by Harold Macmillan. Other brilliant young men with future political greatness before them, like Denis Healey and Anthony Crosland were found on the north Italian front as war closed and witnessed the chaos. One British officer, who was later to have his fill of Yugoslav politics, who now came face to face with the DPs problem was the young Peter Carrington. Forty-five years later the future peace-mediator recalled,

> Everywhere people were displaced, frightened, herded into camps, *posing problems* to the exasperated and often bored Allies. In my own company area in the Rhineland we were responsible for a huge 'Displaced Person' camp. Largely containing Yugoslavs the place was divided between those who supported the Royalist Mihailović and reckoned a return to communist Yugoslavia meant sudden death; and those who felt differently.

In addition to the scores of thousands of Yugoslav DPs who were sent back to Tito's far from tender mercies, the British government sent back to Stalin's welcome hundreds of thousands of Soviet citizens and other Russians who had fled their homeland at the time of the revolution more than twenty years before the war.

It is commonplace today to deride claims by elderly Germans or Croats that they did not know of the atrocities committed in their names by Hitler or Pavelić, but it is worth remembering how few people in Britain or the United States knew about this forced deportation until it came to light in the late 1970s. Thousands of British soldiers played their part – at times resorting to force, at others witnessing Soviet machine-gunnings of those people who were handed over to them – but few of their friends and relatives heard about their shameful role.

Writing from the perspective of a statesman who had himself had to take hard decisions as well as from four decades' distance, Lord Carrington has argued that 'It is too easy, in the tranquillity of today, to condemn those in authority at that time who made harsh decisions in such matters with cruel effects . . .'

In addition to the residual wartime admiration for all things Soviet 'that people were understandably reluctant' to doubt, 'it is all too easy to forget that all over Europe were confused unsettled multitudes who created the need for some sort of decision and administration.'

Lord Carrington concluded in the late 1980s, 'It was an atmosphere hard for today's generations to conceive.'[21] Nowadays, his readers have seen the mass flight of two million people in and around Yugoslavia since 1991, and they may note with less sympathy and understanding the acute similarity between the British establishment's heartless response to its DP dilemma in 1945 when it preferred sending them back to a gruesome fate – 'We don't want them here, do we?' one civil servant minuted – and its successor generation after 1991, which decided to keep people 'close to their homes' in the Bosnian war zone.[22]

Lord Carrington made little bones that he knew about the horrors of war, some of them committed by himself.[23] On 6 February 1992, he recounted the following anecdote to Franjo Tudjman:

> Have I ever told you, Mr President, about the atrocities which I committed during the war. When I was in Germany, I saw, one night, the son of the house in which my company was quartered put some dynamite under my jeep. I immediately summoned his mother and gave her half an hour to evacuate the place. Afterwards we set fire to her home. I called my sergeant-major and gave him the order to douse the house with petrol. The non-commissioned officer carried it out, then he handed me a match. I lit it and threw it onto the petrol. Nothing happened. Then I took a second, then a third. Still nothing! The fire would not catch. That is the atrocity that I committed . . . and you, Mr President, how many atrocities have you committed?[24]

In all probability, no Western soldier could conceive the kind of savage struggle in which Tudjman and the other Yugoslavs of his generation were involved. The reality of an internecine civil war fought against the backdrop of Axis occupation was beyond the simplicity of the question, 'Who is killing more Germans?' At the same time, the survival of the Partisan army owed less to the mock heroics loved by Western wartime propaganda of wounded Partisans singing patriotic songs while their wounded legs were sawn off without anaesthetic.[25]

Opponents of intervention in Bosnia in 1992 constantly harped on the experience of the Germans in the region during the Second World War, but they showed little knowledge of events then and even less inclination to consider the implications of the differences between the situation facing Partisans and invaders in the 1940s and the position fifty years on. Even if the civil war parallel is accepted, the anti-Tito forces were numerically much weaker and also supported with a great deal less enthusiasm by the local population in their spheres of operation than either Croat or Bosnian forces would have been in 1991–92. In other words the basic condition of successful guerrilla warfare – support by the people so that the partisan can swim like a fish in water – did not exist fifty years later. Serb forces resorted to ethnic cleansing after 1991 precisely because they knew how little support they would enjoy outside a few well-defined areas in Croatia or Bosnia. Given the hostility of non-Serbs to their occupation by Serb forces in 1991–92, 'ethnic cleansing' was the only way for the numerically weak Serbian forces to protect their rear *against* partisan operations by their enemies. Far from being the likely source of guerrilla warfare in the 1990s, the Serb forces followed an anti-partisan strategy. It was that of Reinhard Heydrich, who on one occasion emptied a fish-tank of its water and left the fish writhing on the carpet to illustrate his notion of effective anti-partisan warfare: kill or drive out the civilian population and then the partisans will have no local sustenance and will not be able to operate.

The economy of Yugoslavia was much changed in the fifty years between one war and the next. By the 1980s, Bosnia was no longer self-sufficient in food. Television viewers of the war after April 1992 may have had the impression of a largely agricultural society, seeing sad pictures of refugees fleeing by horse-

and-cart, but in reality Bosnia was far from fertile. For instance, the republic produced only about 17 per cent of Yugoslavia's wheat crop and a mere three communes in Serbia's province of Vojvodina produced more maize than the whole of Bosnia-Hercegovina. In other words, even animal feed was far from abundant.[26] The scale of the humanitarian aid effort from the summer of 1992 onwards revealed that the most basic requirement of a successful guerrilla war did not exist for any side in Bosnia in the 1990s. Bosnia was dependent on food imports from other parts of Yugoslavia to feed its population. Even the Bosnian Serbs were soon dependent to a significant degree on UNHCR supplies. Of course, they tried to take more than they needed (and to hinder the UNHCR convoys in every way) as a tactic to undermine their enemies, but in fact without generous Western aid, the popular base among the Serb minority for the Karadžić/Mladić strategy in Bosnia might have crumbled.

Certainly the idea propounded by armchair anti-interventionists in Europe and North America that any force going to the aid of the Sarajevo government would face years of guerrilla resistance by a self-sufficient Serb partisan army was based on outdated thinking. On the contrary, the rations of Mladić's army as well as its weapons and ammunition would still have had to be supplied across considerable distances even within Bosnia and such supply convoys along with their necessary fuel dumps and supplies would have been very vulnerable to air attack, whether by planes or helicopters.[27]

Tito's Partisans never had to face a sustained aerial attack. In fact, the helicopter was not available to Hitler's forces. Apart from the famous parachutist raid on Tito's headquarters in 1944, neither the *Wehrmacht* nor the *Luftwaffe* made much use of air power in the anti-Partisan war, largely because Hitler could not spare it from much more important fronts where he was fighting Stalin or the Anglo-American Allies. Even the success of this offensive was overshadowed by Tito's escape, which in itself owed much to Allied air power.

Tito's forces survived because their destruction was never high enough on Hitler's list of priorities for the *Wehrmacht* to devote large-scale resources to attacking the Partisans persistently. Western arms drops helped to shift the balance of power within the

Yugoslav context decisively in Tito's direction. When the Red Army finally drove Hitler's forces back into the Reich, leading to the retreat of the German forces from the Balkans, it was left to Tito to liberate Belgrade and cover himself in glory.

Despite the small scale of Soviet help to the Partisan effort, Tito remained loyal to his Stalinist training. He recognised that it was better to milk the West until it saw the error of its ways than to draw off much-needed resources from the Red Army. But relations between the liberated Yugoslavs and the Red Army troops quickly soured. As elsewhere in Eastern Europe, Stalin's men had difficulty in distinguishing between conquered fascists and liberated allies: they raped women in Belgrade as readily as in Vienna or Berlin and looted as they passed westwards.

The puritanical Djilas complained to Stalin about the indiscipline of Red Army troops and received the generalissimo's unsympathetic reply:

> Imagine a man who has fought from Stalingrad to Belgrade – over thousands of kilometres of his own devastated country, across the dead bodies of his comrades and dearest ones! How can such a man react normally? And what is so awful in his amusing himself with a woman, after such horrors?[28]

What was to worry Tito more than Stalin's brutal indifference to the treatment of Yugoslav women was Stalin's apparent lack of faith in him. Although the Soviet media built up Tito as Stalin's most valued foreign comrade, the Yugoslav leaders began to detect signs that Stalin's classic divide-and-rule tactics were being deployed to split the Yugoslav Central Committee and perhaps to foster a rival to Tito. Tito had not survived the 1930s as a servant of the Comintern without learning how to read the signs of the times, and yet he had not lost his commitment to the Stalinist ideology which had served him so well. The postwar period was to test Tito's instinct for survival and his ideological fervour and that of his comrades.

7

Tito, 1944–80

> So it should be noted that when he seizes a state the new ruler ought to determine all the injuries that he will need to inflict. He should inflict them all at once, and not have to renew them each day, and so he will reassure his subjects and win them over when he grants benefits.
>
> Machiavelli[1]

Tito and the Yugoslav communists came to power by force. The inauguration of the new regime was marked by a massacre of its enemies. The savage destruction of the remnants of the collaborators with the occupiers went along with the start of a purge of those who had failed to side with the victors in time and increasingly even of those who had supported Tito only to discover their illusions about a democratic future for the Second Yugoslavia. Between 20,000 and 30,000 of the people handed over by the British in May 1945 died on a long death march without food or water which recalled the Turkish treatment of the Armenians in 1915 or the Nazi and Japanese destruction of their prisoners in the dying days of the war just a few weeks earlier.[2] Just as his contemporary Franco was able to live out a long life quietly because of the terror that his name still inspired even in senile decay so too Tito was able to live off the capital of fear which he stored up during the savage reprisals against his opponents after 1944. For as long as he lived, everyone in Yugoslavia feared, though few dared to say, that the old man might turn nasty again.

After years of an almost sensual longing for contact with the idealised men of the Red Army, the Yugoslav Partisans were bitterly disappointed by the behaviour of Soviet humanity in the flesh. As Djilas noted, the Partisans had imposed a rigorous and ruthless puritan morality on their own forces and the people under their control. They were shocked by the drunkenness and looting of the Soviet soldiers *in an Allied country*. Rape by Stalin's men was not at all uncommon in the 'liberated' areas of Yugoslavia, as elsewhere in Eastern and Central Europe as far as Berlin or Prague.

Djilas began to lose his faith not only in Stalin as the infallible guide of mankind to communism, but also in the effect of his system on his subjects. Their cynicism and corruption was in stark contrast to the idealised vision of Soviet people which he had adopted from Comintern propaganda. If Djilas was shocked by the everyday shabby and dishonest behaviour of the Soviet personnel with whom he met, including at the nocturnal drinking bouts presided over by Stalin himself, it was the sudden flashes of sincerity which alarmed even more because it brought to the surface the unconscious stirrings of doubt in his own mind. In 1944, 'late at night after supper . . . it was in the Red Army from the lips of General Korotayev that I first heard the stupefying thought, not entirely alien to me: when communism is victorious the world over, then wars will be fought with the ultimate bitterness.' Thinking back on the savage struggle against the Germans barely completed, Djilas realised that 'now a Russian who was also a communist, Korotayev, was entertaining the thought that wars would be especially bitter under communism – though under communism, theoretically, there would be no classes and no wars.'[3]

It was some time before any doubts which Tito might have entertained became public. For three years and more after the defeat of Nazi Germany, Tito remained in public Stalin's most devoted disciple. When he broke with Stalin, he needed the theoretical and moral revulsion for the Soviet way of communism which Djilas had thought through, but he needed it only as a weapon in his own struggle for power. However, the sudden denunciation of Tito and his regime by the Stalinists on 28 June 1948 helped to distance Tito from his Stalinist roots, particularly in the eyes of the West. His former liaison officers from Britain must have been in some embarrassment when Tito openly challenged British interests whether in Greece or at Trieste immediately after he had taken control of Yugoslavia.

Immediately after the defeat of Nazi Germany, Tito came close to an open clash with the Western Allies over Trieste. The city had a Slovene minority, but its incorporation into Yugoslavia would have created the kind of problem which Italian possession of Fiume (Rijeka) or the German demand for Danzig had created before the war. For several months an open clash looked likely between the Partisan Army and the British. Even the return of Tito's enemies who had taken refuge in the British occupation zone did not calm the issue. In fact, it ran on into the 1950s before it was regulated in 1954 (though it was only resolved, in so far as such matters ever are, in 1975).

Tito's involvement in the Greek Civil War was much more serious. It not only brought him into conflict with the Royal Greek government's British and American Allies, but also with Stalin himself. Having succeeded in revolutionising Yugoslavia through guerrilla warfare, Tito was determined to spread the revolution elsewhere in the Balkans. He saw himself as the head of a future Balkan Federation on the model of the USSR. Despite his assurances to the contrary, Tito began to intrigue to incorporate Albania into his Federation: it was one way of resolving the Albanian minority question in Kosovo, but also a step towards his aim of a pan-Balkan federation led from Belgrade.[4] Greece seemed to be the most important obstacle to this ambition as it lay outside the Soviet bloc. During the Second World War, a civil war between pro- and anti-communist resisters had taken place there, similar to the one which raged in Yugoslavia. It continued after 1944 when Churchill sent British troops to suppress resistance to the restored Royal government. Both Tito and the Albanian Party leader, Enver Hoxha, were more enthusiastic about helping the Greek communists than Stalin himself.

Whatever his global ambitions, Stalin was also very cautious in the immediate postwar period. He knew the Americans had the atomic bomb and he did not. He was also anxious not to antagonise West European centre-left opinion, which was still broadly sympathetic to the Soviet Union as a bastion against Fascism, by launching an openly expansionist drive. Stalin hoped to calm Western fears and to promote communism in the West European states without direct interference – after all the French and Italian communist parties were very strong.

Tito's enthusiastic support for the Greek insurgency was seen by Stalin as both a strategic mistake and a form of defiance of the Leader of Progressive Humanity. Stalin had a low view of the efficacy of guerrilla warfare against well-armed conventional forces. This was compounded by his respect for the awesome power of the USA.

In March 1947, the Greek partisans succeeded in putting such a strain on the resources which Britain was giving to Athens to back up its war effort that the Attlee government felt obliged to tell Washington that Britain could no longer continue to bear the cost, given its economic difficulties. This Partisan 'success' helped produce the Truman Doctrine in March 1947, and a flood of US aid and air power to reinforce the Greek government. It was precisely what Stalin had not wanted.

Although in 1947 Tito still seemed to be Stalin's favourite foreign son, tension was growing between them because of Tito's radical line and Stalin's morbid suspicion of any communist with his own power-base. In June 1947, Stalin's favour seemed confirmed when a replacement for the Comintern was set up with its headquarters in Belgrade. The Cominform united the Soviet bloc parties, plus others like the French and Italians, and was clearly intended to wield control over them as the Comintern had before 1943. If Tito seemed in favour, it was a typically Stalinist ploy. The Soviet leader was preparing to force Tito to back down over Greece and perhaps even to replace him with another leader in Belgrade.

In December 1947, he told Djilas and Kardelj,

> The uprising in Greece will have to fold up . . . They have no prospect of success at all. Do you think . . . the United States, the most powerful state in the world, will permit you to break their lines of communication in the Mediterranean? Nonsense. And we have no navy. The uprising in Greece must be stopped and as quickly as possible.

Stalin admitted that Mao was being successful in China despite Soviet advice to be cautious but added that the situation in Greece was different: 'The United States is directly engaged there.'[5]

Just as Allied support had helped swing victory for Tito in his own civil war, so US firepower had shattered the hopes of the Greek communists. Twice in the decade, the West had intervened in a Balkan civil war and each time the side it supported had won a decisive victory. Only a few advisers and liberal supplies of munitions plus air power had decided the issue in Greece. On the ground the fighting was done by supporters of the Greek government. It was a lesson which Tito learnt and the Anglo-Americans forgot.

Another legacy of the war was not so easily forgotten in the locality. The communists in Greece had been particularly effective in stirring up the border populations in Greek Macedonia and along the frontier with Albania. To Athens this was seen as a prelude to the annexation of those territories to the neighbouring communist states. Tito's establishment of a Yugoslav republic of Macedonia gave fuel to those worries, which survived for forty years, long after any dreams of a Balkan communist federation had died. By the 1990s, the Macedonian issue had become part of domestic Greek politics, where each of the two main parties vied with the other to stir up and win a Greek nationalist vote. Rather like the genuine historical roots of Serbian fears of Croat nationalism, the Macedonian issue loomed larger the further back in time its roots lay. Like Serbian nationalism, so Greek nationalism began to become aggressive against a spectre. But that lay four decades on.[6]

The winding down of the Greek Civil War coincided with Tito's dramatic expulsion from the international communist movement by Stalin on 28 June 1948. Tito was in an awkward position as Stalin knew: Tito's open support for radical communism in the Balkans had damaged his wartime reputation in the West as a patriotic guerrilla of the sort famous during the Peninsular War and celebrated in British schoolboy literature. However, when Tito turned westward again at the height of the Cold War, there were many willing pens waiting to rekindle his myth and perhaps bask once more in his reflected glory. 1948 marked the rebirth of the Tito myth which proved so dominant in establishment circles at Westminster and the universities for decades to come.

Few myths about Tito are more powerful still than the idea that Yugoslavia was liberated from Axis occupation by his Partisan army. Perhaps only the myth of Tito as the great 'Yugoslav nationalist' is more deeply entrenched in the West. If anything the collapse of the Titoite state has reinforced the nostalgia for the lost certainties of the past. But in practice, the Nazis and their collaborators were defeated by decisive battles taking place elsewhere in Europe. Even as the *Wehrmacht* retreated, the Partisans showed a marked reluctance to do more than harass Hitler's far-flung legions as they marched – they no longer had petrol – northwards from the distant Peloponnese and receding Aegean.[7]

Tito knew that the Anglo-Americans pouring into Austria and the Red Army storming across Hungary and the Danubian plain would remove the German threat to his power-base and leave him free to occupy the whole of Yugoslavia and to cleanse it of his enemies. Only Mihailović remained to defy Tito, but without supplies his Chetniks were a dwindling force. Few people, including Serbs, choose to be on the losing side of history if they can escape it. Maybe later they romanticise the loser. Certainly Serbs did, but from the autumn of 1944 Mihailović was increasingly on his own. Ultimately, he was betrayed into Tito's hands.

Mihailović's former admirers in the West who had switched their allegiance to Tito did little to save him. In fact, there was nothing they could do. The new communist regime could never have allowed the fallen Chetnik to live, even in prison, as a symbol of opposition to Tito – or even as a living embodiment of the past, which was going to be eradicated. With Mihailović dead and his supporters either gone with him, in camps, scattered out of Tito's reach, or having turned their coats, Tito had no internal rival other than another communist.[8] It meant that however much the West was disappointed in him, it had little choice but to back him in his struggle with Stalin. Better to have a Tito at odds with Stalin than a pro-Soviet Yugoslav leader. Supporting Tito again also made the West's wartime policy look less short-sighted. By chance it turned out Tito was on the West's side all along.

The West could now ignore Tito's grander visions, which had got him into trouble with Stalin, by antagonising them. If he had imagined a confederation of all the Balkan peoples under his own leadership, then it was not to be. In fact, Stalin's suspicion of other Balkan leaders who might have gone along with Tito helped to disrupt the Soviet bloc with savage purges and strange deaths after June 1948. The idea of Balkan federation was shared by Tito's Bulgarian counterpart, Georgi Dmitrov – with the slight modification that Dmitrov would be Comrade Number One.

Tito's ambitions to unite all the Balkan states into a federation which would be de facto under his leadership alarmed Stalin who did not like his subordinates to have ideas above their station. The Bulgarian leader, Georgi Dmitrov, was forced to back off from his tentative agreement with Tito and died not long afterwards. Stalin's thwarting of Tito's scheme was the cause of the Albanian leader Enver Hoxha's undying affection for the 'leader and teacher of progressive humanity'. Later on Hoxha turned against Soviet hegemony in the world communist movement but in 1948 Stalin anathematisation of Tito saved Albania from absorption into a Greater Yugoslavia.

Even after the open split with Stalin, Tito continued to push on with classic Stalinist policies like forcible collectivisation. Later on some Westerners challenged the idea that collectivisation had been a brutal procedure (just as their colleagues doubted that Stalin had 'blotted out' millions of Kulaks in the early 1930s), but the testimony of the enforcers of this early policy is convincing. When it was decided to relax the collectivisation policy in 1950, the Party leader in the Vojvodina, Jovan Veselinov told the chief planner, Boris Kidrić,

> The simple truth is that there is no wheat and we want the peasants to produce it out of nothing. Therefore, we are waging a regular war on them. Thousands of peasants have been arrested and sentenced to imprisonment. Some were killed. People are defending with axes the small amount of wheat they have harvested . . . In the liberation war, they were on our side, now they are our enemies.[9]

So long as the Soviet Union preserved its hostility, then the threat of imminent invasion remained. In those circumstances, Tito had anticipated relying on the methods of the Partisan war once conventional defence was overcome by the Red Army. Of course, if the peasantry were hostile, successful guerrilla warfare would be impossible. A relaxation of pressure on the peasants as well as an improvement in food production increasingly became priorities for Tito's regime if it was to outface Stalin's pressure.

Tito also used Stalinist methods to combat the local Cominformist supporters of the Moscow line. Not all the leadership supported Tito. The Croat, Hebrang, was the most prominent victim among the pro-Soviet group, but thousands were to die as a result of Tito's ruthless crackdown against would-be slaves of Stalin. A small revolt broke out in Montenegro and elsewhere discontent was evident, but nothing serious enough to shatter Tito's overall control and to justify Soviet 'fraternal assistance'. In any case, Stalin was cautious of an open clash with the USA.[10]

Despite his personal self-centredness and his obsession with having his person projected as the centre of attention, Tito's shrewd understanding of power relations never left him. He guessed that Stalin would not risk a direct assault on Yugoslavia, not because of the will to resist among the peoples there, but because of the Cold War situation. He told Djilas in the summer of 1948, 'The Americans are not fools, they won't let the Russians reach the Adriatic.'[11]

Stalin's fears that his charisma might wane in the face of the appeal of his younger ex-disciple was not entirely without a basis in fact. After all, when Wolfgang Leonhard, one of the most gifted of the East German communists, decided to defect from Ulbricht's DDR in March 1949, it was to Yugoslavia that he fled. Arriving in Belgrade as a refugee from Stalin's suffocating cult of personality, Leonhard was pleased to see that 'pictures of Marx, Engels, Lenin and Stalin were missing'. He was

> delighted to have found refuge in a country which had set itself the goal of establishing a socialist social system without the domination of a hierarchical *apparat* . . ., freed from terror and Stalinist purges . . . from the cult of the leader.[12]

Tito was not Stalin, but without similar methods to the Soviet *vozhd*'s he would not have survived. Even later, as he liberalised, Tito never relaxed the cult of his own personality even if it became a dead ritual for an old man a long time a-dying.

In place of Stalin's picture, Tito's now assumed unrivalled pride of place. The standard portrait of the Marshal-Liberator came to occupy a place in every public building (usually many more than one place) and he remained staring down on his subjects, the gaze slightly off centre, for four decades. Only in 1991 did Tito's image finally disappear from view and only then were the endless Titova streets renamed. In the meantime, Tito's struggle against the Cominformists went on.

The island concentration camp of Goli Otok embodied the savagery of the struggle between the Titoites and the Cominformists. More than ten thousand real or imaginary enemies of Tito's regime were sent to the island which was dry and baking hot in summer but bitterly cold and wind-swept in winter. Ranković's secret policemen not only treated their captives brutally but they also 're-educated' them to set them against each other. New arrivals in the camp were forced to run a gauntlet of the unleashed fury of the existing inmates. Terrible injuries were inflicted. The camp population was set to work quarrying inferior and unusable marble, allegedly in order to make the camp self-financing, but Goli Otok made no profit, though it did achieve its purpose of smashing pro-Soviet opposition.

Even after the camp was closed and the survivors freed, Goli Otok exercised an abiding terror. It was the unspoken but universally known crime of Tito's regime. Later in the 1970s, when underground Cominformists tried to organise them, Tito made a sinister allusion to Goli Otok: 'We have a place for them!' Ranković had the ex-inmates swear an oath of silence about their experiences and so long as he remained head of the security services there was little incentive to test his willingness to take reprisals.

Surprisingly it was not the outside world which protested about Tito's Gulag. Neither Stalin nor the Yugoslav émigrés made any play of the brutal conditions in which the Cominformists were held. It was Djilas and the writer, Dobrica Ćosić, who complained to the Party leadership about prison-camp conditions and the peculiar and perverse brutalities practised at Goli Otok. It was an early sign that the two men would fall foul of the regime, though in 1953 they were successful in persuading Ranković to close the camp.[13]

Despite his adoption of limited restoration of private enterprise and the development of what became known as 'socialist self-management', Tito never renounced his formal allegiance to communist goals. Economic reform did not reverse the uneconomic gigantomania which was so typical of all Marxist economic planning. Prestige projects were thought to go hand in hand with supposed economies of scale. Certainly the industrial labour force was concentrated in increasingly large enterprises. Even at the height of Yugoslavia's drive for industrialisation, the number of industrial enterprises declined as effort was focused on superplants: before 1941, Yugoslavia had had about 3400 industrial enterprises, but by 1959 they had been amalgamated into only 2500 even though new enterprises had been established. At the same time, compared with West Germany, for instance, which was already at the cutting edge of Western capitalist economic development, where the average enterprise employed only 128 people, Yugoslav plants had a workforce more than twice as large (around 360 men).[14]

As the Fifties went by, in the pursuit of hard currency Tito encouraged tourism to the beauties of his realm. To the astonishment of the Soviet leaders mass tourism had little impact on the regime's stability and brought in cash. Another departure from Soviet norms was Tito's decision to permit his subjects to travel abroad in search of work. It was a tacit admission that Yugoslavia had an unemployment problem as well as difficulty in matching people with suitable work, but the remittances from Yugoslav *Gastarbeiter* working for the old enemy, in Germany and Austria especially, shored up the economy as a whole.[15]

Tito's break with Stalin was of the utmost importance in the history of communism, but it did not mean Tito broke with the ideology and methods of Stalin, instead he turned them against his former patron. Mao was to follow Tito's example and then unleash the mass suffering of the Cultural Revolution. Ceauşescu, Pol Pot and even the arch-Stalinist Enver Hoxha, each in his own way owed a lot to Tito's example, and without it no other communist leader would have dared challenge the Kremlin's hegemony. However, unlike them, Tito preserved his regime through granting driblets of personal freedom, in the sphere of the economy and the right to travel. Even his liberalisation had its limits. Dissidents were imprisoned, or worse, and assassination of émigrés went on into the 1980s.

Tito's rhetoric was full of the humanist hypocrisy which distinguished all communists. Like Lenin and Stalin before him, and Brezhnev afterwards, Tito was always lauding his own integrity and the purity of his own motives while castigating the self-seeking purposes of others. On New Year's Day 1949, he attacked

> those who are appeasing their consciences with the reflection that 'the end hallows the means' . . . This dictum was particularly current among the Jesuits at the time of the Inquisition. Great things cannot be accomplished by dirty means or in a dishonest manner. Great things can only be created by honest means and in an honest manner – this is what we shall always believe.[16]

No hint that it was Stalin who precipitated the split and that Tito was forced to denounce the Soviet leadership in order to save his skin not his principles.

After Stalin's death Tito was able to restore his relations with the USSR in 1955. Stalin's heirs recognised the futility of the old man's antagonism of Yugoslavia and also saw that Tito was anxious to avoid becoming over-dependent on the West. In the same year, Tito laid the foundations of what became the Non-aligned Movement, allying Yugoslavia with newly independent ex-colonies like India or Burma. Cynics noted in retrospect that he had transformed Yugoslavia into a Third World country.

In 1956, Tito's revived friendship with the Soviet Union proved its worth to Khrushchev. Tito played a sinister part in the suppression of the Hungarian revolution. Even the Soviet leaders were taken aback by his cordial support for their policy of sending in the tanks. Khrushchev visited Tito in Brioni at the height of the crisis. Despite his normal distaste for the Russian practice, the Marshal demonstratively kissed Khrushchev. According to Khrushchev's adviser, Fedor Burlatsky, Khrushchev 'was pleasantly surprised: Tito was in favour of the immediate use of troops to rout the Hungarian counter-revolution'.[17]

When Tito's old comrade from the Comintern days, the Hungarian premier Imre Nagy, took refuge in the Yugoslav Legation, he was given assurances of his safety before being handed over to the Soviet forces and eventual death at their hands. Tito could not risk a bad example on his borders, particularly given the 400,000 Hungarians in Vojvodina, but the deceit towards Nagy rankled.

In 1968, too, Tito did not distinguish himself by supporting Dubček's liberalisation in Czechoslovakia. Although his visit to Prague shortly before Brezhnev's tanks arrived was seen as a gesture of support for the 'Prague Spring', in fact Tito advised Dubček to back away from political liberalisation. A few years later, Tito told a military delegation from the Czechoslovak Army: 'Formally we are not members of the Warsaw Pact, but if the cause of socialism, of communism, of the working class, should be endangered, we know where we stand . . . we hold our aims in common with the Soviet Union.'[18]

Tito's support for the Soviet Union during the two great threats to its Central European empire in 1956 and 1968 was not altruistic. His calculation was always that his own power-base would be safer if communism elsewhere was secure and yet less attractive than the model on offer from Belgrade. However, Tito's apparent public support for Dubček and the aftermath of the fall of Ranković weakened the discipline of the LYC in the republics. Hopes were high among non-Serbs for a better deal.

The grass-roots liberalisation culminated in the so-called Croatian Spring in 1971, when the reassertion of Croatian identity albeit under the tutelage of the local communists took on alarming proportions from the Titoite point of view. The reappearance of Croatian symbols and the emphasis on linguistic distinctiveness alarmed Serbs too. It was easy to portray these steps as a backdoor return to the Ustasha regime, however false those charges were. As twenty years later, the charge of Croatian neo-fascism was levelled at political leaders whose careers had been entirely within the Partisan-LYC bloc. The very fact that such charges came so easily to the lips and minds of Serb communists and others suggests that they too took for granted that the lip-service of the new Yugoslavia which had poured out of the mouths of communists of every background was in fact as shallow in Serbia as it was alleged to be in Croatia. In short, the idea of Yugoslavia was just a tool in the political struggle, not really an idea in which activists on either side of the Sava believed.

The Croatian Spring proved short-lived. But it was a severe

crisis for the regime. Nor was it merely an internal threat. Brezhnev offered Soviet 'assistance' to Tito to preserve the communist system in Yugoslavia. In practice Tito rejected the poisonous fraternal hand, but it forced him to recognise how vulnerable his state was to external intervention resulting from internal crisis. As ever, Tito moved carefully. Into the autumn of 1971 he was still speaking reassuringly, but once he was certain of his strength and had prepared his blow, he made clear his determination to suppress the reformers. In December 1971, Tito remarked, 'If we can't persuade them politically, we will adopt administrative measures.'[19]

Tito was as aware as ever that his regime rested in the final analysis on the army which had brought him to power in the first place. At the end of 1971, he made clear his willingness to resort to force if necessary to suppress dissent:

> There is also the question of the army's role in preserving the achievements of our revolution. Although its primary task is to defend our country against foreign enemies, our army is also called on to defend the achievements of the revolution within the country, should that be necessary. It cannot be otherwise . . . If it comes to shooting, the army is also here. This should be made clear to all.[20]

Few of his subjects needed reminding of that.

Having struck at the Croatian 'nationalists', Tito also purged Dubček-style Serb communists like Marko Nikezic and Latinka Petrovic in the 1970s. Ironically, this purge of the reform communists in Serbia probably paved the way in the long run for the eventual Serbian nationalist takeover of the Serbian communist party. Only in Slovenia and Macedonia was there much continuity in these years as Tito resorted to the classic manoeuvres of purging and shifting the cadres around.[21]

Tito's federal organisation of Yugoslavia and its division into six republics and two autonomous provinces of Serbia was intended as a sop to national feelings. Tito drew up the boundaries with attention to the linguistic, historical and ethnic realities on the ground, but he was never prepared to let them dominate his policy. In any case, Tito hoped to produce a Yugoslav identity when he adopted the federalisation of Yugoslavia. Like the Soviet communists, he hoped ethnic and religious, if not linguistic, differences would gradually dissolve into a new identity. In old age, he was less hopeful, but continued to see the republics not as national units. The communists were there to prevent separatism arising. Tito's deepest fear was always that a reform-nationalist tendency would usurp control of the LYC in a republic and shatter the country's unity. That was why he was severe towards both Serb and Croat reform communists after 1971. Reform was to be only according to the Titoite model.

Despite his abandonment of many features of the Stalinist cult of personality – such as the abolition of private property *in toto* – Tito's vanity precluded the abandonment of the outward signs of the cult of himself. The most obvious, lavish and absurd feature of this cult was the annual *Titova Stafeta*. Under Tito's regime every year the youth of Yugoslavia paid homage to its beloved Marshal by participating in their countless scores of thousands in a great baton race which passed through every part of Yugoslavia. It culminated on 25 May, the Marshal's official birthday (like any hereditary sovereign, Tito was not content with nature's timing – bad for parades). In the JNA stadium in Belgrade, the birthday celebrations would climax after the arrival of that year's decorated baton with a rousing chorus of 'Comrade Tito, we will never depart from your path'.

Whether Tito possessed any sense of irony or self-parody may be doubted, but otherwise it is difficult to explain the decision to rename the annual festival in his honour when he reached the normal retirement age in 1957; the *Titova Stafeta* was renamed – the 'youth race', naturally enough. At its peak in 1952, when Tito needed to conjure up a cult of his own personality to ward off Stalin's wiles, about one and half million of his subjects participated in the *stafeta* which covered a course of more than 130,000 km. (It was immortalised in one of the first sharp shafts of post-Tito irony permitted in Yugoslavia in Kusturica's 1985 film, *Papa is on a business trip* (*Otac na sluzbenom putu*) in which a seven-year-old Pioneer deputed to speak from a rural tribune cannot remember whether Tito was 'at the head of the Party' or 'the Party at the head of Tito'!) Gradually it declined and stabilised in the Marshal's old age at a manageable 100,000 participants covering up to 13,000 kilometres. By the death of Tito, a few days in advance of 1980's culminating ceremonies, no one knew how many of his subjects had carried the baton in his honour. This old man's cult of youth had an almost magical significance for Tito.[22] The baton was a symbol of life to ward off mortality. (More than 20,000 such batons were rumoured to have been manufactured for the individual relays of the annual pilgrimage runs and then stored in the Museum of 25 May – though only the presentation batons were on display.)

Tito's vanity and love of display had been evident even when he was an underground courier for the Comintern. Despite all the squalor and dangers of life as a Partisan, Tito had adopted the magnificent uniform of a Soviet Marshal. His outfit was specially tailored in Moscow and flown in at great risk to the Soviet aircrew who brought it to Bosnia.[23] Fortunately, alterations were not needed. What was ridiculed as evidence of mental imbalance or absurdity in a Wilhelm II or Goering was accepted without murmur in Tito. After all, he had invented the non-aligned movement. Tito's greatest achievement was to make into a virtue what other communists quietly did by stealth: he turned his country into a Third World state.

Like any other self-made dictator, Tito instinctively cultivated a sense of aloofness from his comrades in arms. He knew how to project his personality on his followers even in the difficult conditions of wartime. Distance was essential to his mystique. After 1944, he had many more possibilities to assert his unique role. Djilas describes how Tito arranged the decor and format of meetings to emphasise his separateness:

> Tito developed his own special style and protocol: his chair – which was always placed in the centre – was always different from all the others. He changed his clothes three or four times a day – according to the meaning or the impression which he wanted to leave behind.[24]

Just as Stalin's admirer, Enver Hoxha, confirmed Djilas' devastating portrait of the Soviet dictator in *Conversations with Stalin* in his own *With Stalin*, so Fitzroy Maclean's admiring picture of

Tito in *Disputed Barricade* matches Djilas' disillusioned impression of Tito's vanity and love of luxury:

> He takes pleasure in eating well, dressing well and living in agreeable surroundings. On his finger he still wears the handsome diamond ring which he bought in 1937 with the roubles he had earned by translating the official History of the [Soviet Communist] Party into Serbo-Croat; it reminds him, he says, of those difficult early days![25]

In many ways, Tito's glitzy style made him the object of the radical chic's admiration much as thirty years later the designer-stubble and Porsche sunglasses of Daniel Ortega led progressive souls in the West to imagine that his Sandinista movement was incorruptibly serving the Nicaraguan people.

Fidel Castro marked the transition for fellow-travelling style gurus from Tito's film-star glamour to Ortega's expensive grunge, and in the 1960s the cigar-toting Cuban overshadowed the paunchy Yugoslav as the most exciting new dictator. Tito was a man of his age preferring '40's film-star style and enjoying hobnobbing with Hollywood stars like Elizabeth Taylor.[26] In his old age, Tito remarked wistfully (and insincerely) in a television interview that, as a young man, he had thought of emigrating to the USA; 'Had I done it, I would have become a millionaire!'[27] Of course, as the owner of a whole country, Tito was far richer than any émigré could have hoped to become – but he also enjoyed the pleasures of power.

As head of the non-aligned Yugoslav state, Tito was the object of flattery from abroad as well as his subjects at home. He liked to keep count of the tribute paid to him by all and sundry. The Museum of 25 May in Belgrade contained all the gifts, domestic and foreign, which Tito had not retained for his personal use. Like Kim Il-Sung or Ceauşescu, Tito liked to display this tribute in the oriental fashion of emperors at the centre of the world. On average, the Marshal received eight presents each day. After Tito's death in 1980, it took the Yugoslav state four years to catalogue his possessions.[28]

In addition to the more or less valuable trinkets which his subjects gave him, Tito bestowed large parts of the country on its head of state for his own personal use. Palaces, hunting lodges (and the reserves which went with them) and whole Adriatic islands were cordoned off for the great man's relaxation, so that he could entertain his foreign admirers in the style which they clearly felt was appropriate to his status and theirs. The island of Brioni was only the largest of Tito's personal preserves. By the time he was re-elected to the Presidency of SFRY 'for an unlimited term of office' (like Hastings Banda of Malawi or other non-aligned local tyrants), Tito had 32 private residences. Some of them, like the White Palace in Belgrade, had belonged to the old royal family, but had been extended and embellished to meet the needs and express the importance of the great man. He also had two sea-going yachts and two Danube river-yachts plus his luxurious Blue Train.[29]

The complex interplay between Tito's ambition, his vanity and hint of decadence combined with extraordinary tenacity comes out in an anecdote told by Fedor Burlatsky about an incident on Brioni in October 1956: 'On a small terrace paved with marble stood a statue of a naked woman in an erotic pose . . . Approaching the figure, [Tito] affectionately patted her in a delicate place and the statue slowly and invitingly began to turn. "Pretty isn't she?" he asked us.' Then Tito revealed that even during the war as a Partisan he had decided to make Brioni his own. Seeing Burlatsky's surprise, Tito turned to Khrushchev's aide and informed him, 'Yes, young man. I did not doubt our victory for a minute, nor that I would become the country's leader.' Of course, possession of an island retreat worthy of Tiberius at Capri was one of the prerequisites of leadership in Tito's eyes.[30]

However much Tito was determined to hold onto power and to prevent the disintegration of the country which was his power-base, some of his reforms had long-term disintegrating effects. Tito's permission of local republican economic management created jobs for a loyal local *nomenklatura* in the short term, but promoted the fragmentation of the self-management system after 1976. The local communists began to operate enterprises for political and self-serving purposes on an even grander scale than before, at the same time the workforce saw little reason to support rational economic measures that required harder work.

But as Tito moved towards the end of his life, none of the

decay of his system was noticed by his Western admirers. Just as Mussolini was admired by some north Europeans for allegedly disciplining the Italians, getting the trains to run on time (at least over the tourist routes) and running a good show, so Tito attracted a similar unconsciously fascistic following. He kept those squabbling Balkan tribes down. Admiration of Tito for bringing order into Balkan chaos has often been expressed both before and after his death and the war. From the standpoint of the collapse of his beloved Yugoslavia, Sir Fitzroy Maclean concluded, 'I think firm government is certainly needed there.'[31]

Rather as the crude Khrushchev was loved in the West as a showman and even the bear-like Brezhnev was presented as essentially a cuddly fellow in the early 1970s, so Tito's vices appealed to Westerners. His corruption and buying of good publicity was seen as lavish hospitality. But the country had no long-term future without its host and master.

The roots of the eventual disaster may be traced back to 1966. The fall of the secret police chief, Ranković, in July 1966, was a turning-point in Yugoslav inter-ethnic relations. Tito announced that he was shocked to discover the extent of the UDBA's repression and surveillance of the population. Even he himself had been bugged by Ranković. In an apparently liberalising move, the secret police was radically restructured after Ranković's disgrace. Tito shifted internal security to the purview of the military intelligence (KOS). He could rely on the old Partisan hierarchy in the JNA. In the long term, this made little difference to Tito's subjects.[32]

Despite his apparently orthodox communist beliefs, Ranković had relied heavily upon his fellow Serbs to man the security apparatus, UDBA. After Ranković's expulsion from the Party, Croats and Albanians in particular felt liberated. The heavy hand of the UDBA was lifted. In Croatia and Kosovo, the local Serb *apparatchiks* felt insecure and often with good reason. Without their protector in Belgrade, the national majorities in the republics and provinces began to push Ranković's men around. Equally, the Serbs began to doubt the value of Tito's Yugoslavia as a guarantor of their interests. But until the later 1960s, they took for granted that Yugoslav and Serb interests coincided. For instance,

Dobrica Ćosić, who had enjoyed some influence with Ranković (as well as the benefits of his patronage) wrote in 1961,

> Today, the form of Serbian nationalism is often 'Yugoslavism' . . . They [the Serb Yugoslavs] are for unification. Unification is for them a creation of privileges for their language, and the assimilation of smaller nations, unification for them is never the overcoming of their 'Serbianness' . . . They are always for a strong unified state . . . [33]

In retrospect, the secret police chief became stylised as a victim of Titoism and 'Serbophobia'. His death in 1983 was marked by outpourings of Serb nationalism. Ranković had been the 'lost leader' of Serbia's sidelined communists. The posthumous cult of him as a victim of Tito – the Croat – was an early symptom of the symbiosis of Serb communism and Serb nationalism, which Milošević came to personify. Oddly, the promoters of the myth of Ranković as Serb victim overlooked the fact that so many of his victims – and an absolute majority of the inmates of Goli Otok – were Serbs and Montenegrins. For a people with long memories, Serb propagandists' recall can be remarkably selective.

After the fall of Ranković economic liberalisation went ahead, but with limited success. It was usual among admirers of Tito to argue that his system was fundamentally different from the Comecon approach. However, looking back after the breakdown of communism across Europe in 1989, the similarities leap to mind more than the differences. Not least was the fact that as the revolutionary dynamic declined so did labour discipline and output throughout the region. No efforts to revive the revolution could reverse this decline. In fact, fanatical Stalinists like Ceauşescu set in train an even sharper rate of decline than the more relaxed world-weary Tito. The mentality of 'they pretend to pay us and we pretend to work' was almost as universal in Yugoslavia as it was in the Soviet bloc.

Ljubo Sirc remarked that 'the downfall of the Yugoslav "socialist market" is not due to any Yugoslav peculiarities, but to problems with economic first principles.'[34] In any case, as even Tito admitted the much-vaunted system of self-management often did not function at all in reality: the system was largely illusory and at the mercy of bureaucratic decisions made on high by communist officials. 'Despite the wide self-management and delegational basis, many decisions are in essence not taken in a self-management manner, although they formally pass through a self-management procedure.'[35]

Towards the end of his life even Tito began to hint that the system which he had created was incapable of resolving the problems facing Yugoslavia. Occasionally, in the midst of self-congratulatory rhetoric, the Marshal would let slip comments like his remarks to the Yugoslav TUC in November 1978: 'We are confronted with the question of why almost exactly the same problems and weaknesses arise in our economy year after year.' It was all rather like the plaintive criticisms of Brezhnev and his comrades in the Soviet Union on the eve of perestroika. As his life was already evidently draining away in March 1981, less than a year after Tito's death, Leonid Brezhnev contributed the insight that 'the economy must become economic'.[36]

Just as Brezhnev's aides kept him in a quasi-mummified state, propped up for state occasions, fearing for their careers if he was ever to be formally certified as dead, so Tito's epigoni struggled to preserve his authority as the grave beckoned. Like Franco in Spain a few years earlier, Tito's last days were spun out by every device of advancing medical science. (Unlike Franco, Tito did not complement his doctors' skills and their tubes and electronic flummeries with relics and rosaries.) What agonies Tito went through during his prolonged passage from this life in the spring of 1980 can only be guessed at. For his hand-chosen inadequate successors, it seemed every second's delay in announcing that the Marshal had lost his final battle was a worthwhile sacrifice to avoid assuming responsibility for his legacy.

Tito would have enjoyed his funeral. Apart from *Schadenfreude* at his successors' growing difficulties and their inept response, there can have been few pleasures for Tito beyond the grave. The showman in him would have liked the send-off which his subjects gave him. The vain old man would also have enjoyed the guest list: Brezhnev, plus three kings and thirty other heads of state, Margaret Thatcher and fifteen other prime ministers, along with hundreds of lesser lights from Yasser Arafat to Willy Brandt. Tito would have appreciated the irony of Kurt Waldheim's presence. The only snub was Jimmy Carter's decision to send his mother Lilian along with Vice-President Mondale.[37] Many tears were shed – all broadcast live to fifty-two countries. Many more tears were to come – and more than 170 countries would witness them.

8

After Tito: The Breakdown of Yugoslavia

> Six Wonders of Socialism;
> 1. There is no unemployment, but no one works.
> 2. Nobody works but everyone is paid.
> 3. Everyone is paid but there is nothing to buy.
> 4. There is nothing to buy but everyone owns everything.
> 5. Everyone owns everything but all are discontented.
> 6. Everyone is discontented but all vote for the system.
>
> Osmica (December 1989)

Until May 1980, people used to joke that Yugoslavia had seven frontiers, six republics, five nationalities, four languages, three religions, two alphabets and one boss. The death of Tito left Yugoslavia without its guiding figure. Only the Army, which the Marshal had shaped and which his very customary title showed was his own preferred institution in the country, remained as a real all-Yugoslav body. The League of Communists and the Federal Government were soon revealed to be hollow with only the republics possessing any real identity.[1]

On Tito's death, the 'unlimited mandate' came to an end and the provisions of the 1974 constitution came into effect. Tito's pupils loyally carried out their master's will but his design was faulty – perhaps he guessed that none of them would be able to juggle with carrot and stick as he had done. The problem with the success of the wartime partisan generation, the so-called 'Club 1941', was that they had both dominated the system – even in their quarrels after 1945 – and had grown old and sickly together. In the meantime, frustrated ambition and cynicism had driven younger and abler people out of politics, leaving only the time-servers. Whatever Tito's intentions and expectations, he left a most peculiar system of government to his successors. Only the engineers of a united Europe seem to have taken it as a model since.

To understand the flaws of the Titoite legacy, it is necessary to imagine a federation composed of several different nationalities, many of whom had taken different sides in the Second World War, now forming one state with a single currency, but widely differing levels of economic, social and cultural development. Determine that the presidency of its federal government should rotate at regular intervals between the nominated representatives of mutually competitive republics. Throw in an economic crisis whose effects are felt more by some nations than others among the population, and which is therefore supposedly alleviated by arbitrarily set 'cohesion' funds taken from richer areas and disbursed – with corrupt pickings en route – to their poorer counterparts, frequently ancient antagonists, and the recipe for the breakdown of civil order is almost complete.[2]

Symbolic of the failure of the Titoite project of uniting and integrating the peoples and regions of Yugoslavia was the fiasco of the so-called 'Brotherhood and Unity Motorway', intended to criss-cross the republics bringing them ever closer together. In fact, much of it was never built and most of it did not connect with other parts of the system. A haphazard series of motorway sections dotted the landscape without integrating the transport system. The Slovenes, for instance, would have preferred to improve their communications across the Alps into the markets of Central Europe rather than build an asphalt symbol of subsidies draining southwards.

Many of the 'modernising' projects were wasteful and absurdly grandiose. For instance, the Feni nickel-smelting plant in Macedonia cost $300 million to complete but processed such low grade ores that it could never hope to make a return on the investment. However, the works' managers and visiting dignitaries could enjoy Feni's splendid pink marble foyer and staircases and forget about the balance sheet. It was the sort of project which impressed the *apparatchiks* of the IMF, World Bank and eventually the EBRD.[3]

Most importantly, the gap between rich and poor grew steadily. Instead of diminishing the gulf between the relatively developed (former Habsburg) territories and the largely backward parts of

Yugoslavia, the federal schemes for development had the opposite effect. Whereas the average Slovene was half as productive again as the average Yugoslav in 1947, by the eve of Tito's death Slovenes were more than twice as productive as the Federal average. By contrast, Kosovans sank from being roughly half as productive as the national average in 1947 to less than a third as productive by 1978. In the 1980s the gap widened still further. Unemployment was already a severe problem in the underdeveloped regions at Tito's death and it was closely associated with national identity: Albanians were four times more likely to be unemployed than the Yugoslav average. The fact that investment and hiring and firing decisions, despite the rhetoric of self-management, often lay disproportionately in the hands of one 'nation' rather than another made for bitter disputes about favouritism and prejudice.[4]

Not unreasonably, the communists in Belgrade wanted to overcome the disparities in the levels of economic development and standard of living which distinguished the different parts of Yugoslavia. Their assumption was that as economic convergence progressed it would erode the national differences. Like their Soviet counterparts, they lived in the increasingly disappointed expectation that at some point in the future, the ethnic and linguistic constituents of their socialist federated republics would blend into one. By Tito's death, even the great capitalist model of the melting-pot theory, the USA, was showing signs of overheating, but both in the USSR and Yugoslavia by the 1980s it was clear to all – except many of those paid in the West to study such matters – that the socialist experiment had not only failed to diminish national differences, but actually worked to exacerbate them.

In the richer republics of Yugoslavia resentment at the transfer payments grew. Far from promoting 'cohesion', these funds provoked indignation among the Slovenes and Croats who lost out and saw valuable investment flowing into the southern 'black holes'; but they did nothing to benefit the southerners. Despite everything, the gulf between the developed parts of Yugoslavia and the so-called developing parts widened after 1945. (Of course, the EC's cohesion policy has led to Greece getting relatively poorer vis-à-vis north-western Europe despite huge inflows of ECUs.)

While Western tourists in Istria or Dalmatia could enjoy outstanding value on their package tours to the one communist country which offered edible food as a matter of course along with sunshine and sand, the economists employed at both federal and republican level were more and more aware of the growing disparities between state expenditure and popular expectations and the declining competitiveness of the Yugoslav economy as a whole. The hyper-inflation of the late 1980s was only the most obvious symptom of the underlying economic problems, but it brought out tensions between the republics too. Slovenes wondered why they should have to carry around six-figure banknotes to do their daily shopping when much of the inflationary expenditure went on other republics or the People's Army, which aroused less pride in Slovenia than in Serbia for instance.[5]

So long as the West had seen Tito's state as a valuable buffer between the Warsaw Pact and what NATO liked to regard as its own sea, the Mediterranean, then international institutions and governments had been willing to lend generously. With Gorbachev the strategic climate changed. Yugoslavia was less necessary, though nobody could foresee its demise. Just as with the Soviet Union itself, the common error of thinking that there existed a Yugoslav 'nation' blinded Western leaders to the fragile nature of those states.

Although the West had no desire to precipitate a crisis inside Yugoslavia, and its leaders and 'experts' thought that economic reform would restore stability to Yugoslavia's politics, the strict diet of spending cuts and financial prudence demanded by Western creditors were a key ingredient in undermining Federal Yugoslavia. Once the gravy train stopped, there was little incentive for the individual republics to pay for repairs if they could hope to continue their journey without the others. Austerity encouraged the tendency, long apparent, for each republic to focus on its own interests. It also made the communists redundant. Not only had they got the republics into a mess but the retrenchment at republican level made a pan-Yugoslav institution suspect. It was hardly surprising that the first nationalists in Yugoslavia were so often communists, quick off the mark at sensing a new era; they were after all politicians who had made their careers sensing which way the wind would blow next, under Tito and afterwards.[6]

What was most remarkable about Tito's creation was not that it collapsed in floods of blood and tears but that it took eleven years to unravel so disastrously. In retrospect, everyone can see what was clear to so many people inside Yugoslavia and some outsiders too, that the years after Tito were wasted. Fearful that any innovation would shatter the stability of the house of cards, the same policies were pursued after Tito's death as had marked his last years, but without the authority implied by even his moribund presence.

Like any dictator Tito had left no room for greatness in his shadow. His successors avoided the worst mistake of diadochi and did not fall out among themselves and start a civil war, but the succession of anonymous *apparatchiks* who rotated through high office in the years after 1980 failed to grapple with any of the problems bequeathed by the Marshal. The economy continued to consume more resources in investment than it could use properly. Inflation and unemployment fluctuated but the trend was ever upwards.

In retrospect, some of these difficulties were good practice for the problems of survival during the exigencies of war after 1991. To Westerners, life with hyper-inflation is barely conceivable. Yugoslavs had learned to live with the Deutschmark as the parallel currency and increasingly as the currency of choice throughout the 1980s. Throughout Tito's rule the black market and under-the-counter deals had been everyday ways of meeting one's needs. Western governments and 'experts' remained in thrall to the naive idea that Yugoslavia's problems were primarily economic and therefore believed that if only prices could be stabilised or output boosted without inflation, then the political tensions inside the Federation would melt away. However much endemic economic crisis and the disputes which it generated between the republics made matters worse, the essential crisis was one of power. The question was who should rule after Tito and on what the new ruler's authority would be based. The waning of any legitimacy which even the lip-service to communist ideals had once possessed raised the spectre of an alternative basis for authority. Ironically, what that new source of legitimacy would be became clearer with the death of Tito's comrade who had seemed the most communist in his Politburo.[7]

Three years after Tito's death, Alexander Ranković died. Whereas the mourning for the Marshal in 1980 had been backward-looking and state-sponsored, the scenes at Ranković's funeral were unprecedentedly spontaneous. Certainly, huge numbers of Yugoslavs had been swept up by emotion at the death of Tito, but many of the tears were as much about the passing of a sense of personal certainty and security which had survived so long as the Old Man ruled as for Broz himself. The emotions aroused by Ranković's death were forward-looking, ominously so.

Although he had lived quietly in retirement since his fall in 1966, enjoying the privileges of a high *nomenklaturist* even in disgrace, Ranković had become without any effort on his part the symbol of the mounting resentment of the Serbian *apparatchiks* at what they saw as their diminished standing in the Yugoslav state. The disorders in Kosovo since 1981 only added to the lustre of Ranković's name in the eyes of those Serb officials and policemen who recalled with nostalgia the order which had reigned under the UDBA's boss.

Tens of thousands of people gathered at Belgrade's new cemetery on 22 August 1983, in an atmosphere more like a revivalist meeting than a funeral. They chanted Ranković's old revolutionary *nom de guerre*, 'Marko, Marko'. No acclaim for Tito. In fact, the funeral crowd for Ranković was the first open demonstration in Serbia against Tito's legacy. It was clear to all that it was Ranković as Serb strongman who was being hailed. He had represented the sort of Yugoslavia which Serb communists had wanted. With Tito gone, Ranković's passing away reopened the debate about what sort of Yugoslavia Serbs wanted and what sort of leadership.

So far as is known, Slobodan Milošević was not at Ranković's funeral, but he cannot have been unaffected by the atmosphere aroused by it, nor can he have missed the renewed charge coursing through his fellow Serbian communists. It was only a year later that Milošević entered full-time politics and joined the Belgrade party committee. At the time, Milošević was still building his career on the back of the patronage of the Serbian Party leader, Ivan Stambolić.

In the debate about what is the precondition for a successful demagogue – the existence of a crowd to hand or the innate charisma of the leader – the Milošević example can be read both ways. Certainly nothing in his career until the mid–1980s suggested that Slobodan Milošević could sway a crowd with his words, but then none of his contemporaries had tried to do so either. A child of the Second World War, Milošević like scores of thousands of other Yugoslavs had grown up with the Titoite state and had benefited from its sponsorship.

At first sight Milošević seemed set on the classic *apparatchik*'s curriculum vitae. Despite his peculiarly morbid family background – both parents and an uncle committed suicide – nothing seemed to diminish his drive for success. If anything these family tragedies spurred on the ambition within him. Born in 1941 at Požarevac in Serbia, he studied law at Belgrade University and was an activist in the university party committee, becoming chairman of its ideological committee. After completing his studies in 1964, he moved into the Party apparatus, joining the LYC as a full member in 1969.[8]

By then he had shifted sideways into the management of the State-owned energy company, Tehnogas. He was quickly on the fast track in the new 'business-orientated' Yugoslavia of late Tito. Whereas most future leaders of a communist party entered the *apparat* early on in their careers, moving up from secretary of the Youth League by a succession of party posts to the very top, Milošević was the sort of 'new communist' beloved by the academic prophets of convergence between capitalism and communism. He was a technocrat, a practical man, not an ideologue.

Of course in practice his move to Tehnogas and his rapid promotion there owed much to his political patron, Ivan Stambolić. Convergence theorists would no doubt prefer to describe this relationship as part of an 'old boys' network' rather than as a typically communist patron-client relationship. Whatever description one chooses, it helped Milošević rise rapidly. Five years after joining Tehnogas, he was its general-manager. Then in the late 1970s, he moved into banking. As director of Beobanka, Milošević became a minor figure on the international banking scene. His house was a typical product of the fringe of reformed Yugo-communism, a state-owned operation run for profit, where the *apparatchiks* in business learned how to act like entrepreneurs, even though they were not.

During his time at Beobanka, Milošević spent a lot of time in the West, especially New York, where he perfected the peculiarly sinister heavily accented English which became so well known after 1991. It was also during this time that his relations with the security services strengthened. As in other communist countries, Yugoslav overseas business and especially banking operations were intimately linked with espionage and in the case of KOS activities with surveillance of émigrés. Milošević's contacts with the peculiar world of expatriate Yugoslav business was to stand him in good stead after 1991 too, when propaganda activities on behalf of the Serb government were frequently conducted and paid for by Western-based companies and businessmen.

Despite his fluent English and his travels, Milošević did not become Westernised. This is not to say that he remained some sort of archetypical devious Balkan politician as is often urged in explanation of his behaviour. Rather Milošević became what the communists used to call in their days of hope 'a man of a new type'. He was the first really effective post-communist *apparatchik*. As it began to dawn upon them that the communist system might be waning once Gorbachev liberalised criticism both at home in the Soviet bloc and by extension among Western academics who had feared to cross the Party line for their own reasons, then Westerners tried to anticipate what the future political order and its professional politicians would look like. All too often, they took the reform communists as the harbingers of the new politics rather than as the liquidators of the old. It was difficult for West Europeans and Americans who implicitly accepted the obsolescence of nationalism to comprehend that it could be instrumentalised by someone other than a backward-looking and therefore doomed demagogue. Milošević has almost single-handedly shattered the complacent assumptions of Westerners about the path which history was supposed to be following into the future. Instead of an inevitable progression to greater brotherhood, harmony and cooperation, he began to chart a viable course into a darker future.

At first Milošević himself may not have been clear about exactly which course to follow. When he entered Serbian politics at the beginning of the 1980s, he and his wife were still fiercely orthodox Marxists. They shared the desire to reinvigorate the teaching of Marxism-Leninism in the universities, making it obligatory again for all students whatever their courses. His wife, Mirjana, remained a true Marxist-Leninist even after Slobodan Milošević found new truths to parrot in support of his ambition.

The decay in the regime's legitimacy was brought into sharp focus in 1985, when the Serb historian, Veselin Djuretić, produced a book, *The Allies and the Yugoslav War Drama*, which argued that the Partisan movement and the role of the Western Allies in Yugoslavia during the Second World War had been essentially anti-Serb. Only a year later, the Serb Academy of Sciences put together its Memorandum, which echoed the view that the Serbs had been the peculiar victims of the Second World War.

Behind the rediscovery of Serbia's victimhood during the war lay the contemporary reality of the running sore of the Kosovo crisis. Ever since Tito's death, the political situation in Kosovo had gone from bad to worse. Belgrade had imposed heavy-handed and often brutal measures to control the discontents of the Albanian majority, but all to no avail.[9]

While the Albanians provided the classic alien threat, being both non-Slav and non-Orthodox, the Muslims of Bosnia and their co-religionists scattered through southern Serbia particularly in the Sandjak presented a different threat to Serbian minds. Unlike the Albanians, the Muslims were Serbo-Croat speakers and generally ethnically Slavonic. (Relatively few Muslims traced all or most of their ancestry as opposed to their religion to the Ottoman conquerors.) Many Serbs and some Croats liked to deny the national status of Muslims as a constituent people of Yugoslavia, insisting that they were 'really' Serbs or Croats who just failed to recognise their true identity.[10]

To many West Europeans the idea of political status based on religious affiliation (even when it was nominal) was an odd if not unacceptable idea in a secularised age. However, in the Balkans the idea had a tradition rooted in the Ottoman millet system whereby the religious leaders of the given faiths of the Sultan's subjects were held responsible for their co-religionists and their good behaviour. People had been classified as Orthodox, Catholic or Jews as well as true followers of Islam. When Tito decided to acknowledge the Muslims as a 'nationality' in the 1960s, the term might have seemed incongruous to those who associated 'nation' with race (even subconsciously), but in a post-Ottoman context it was hardly unrealistic. The tragedy of it lay in the fact that West European exclusive notions of the synonymous nature of nationality and state allegiance dating from the nineteenth century were being fostered again in Belgrade and then in Zagreb. These left little place for a religious or cultural identity, even one sincerely and wholeheartedly felt.

Serb nationalists like Dobrica Ćosić denounced the idea of a Muslim 'nation' from the start. In 1968, he denounced the decision of the Central Committee of the LYC to recognise 'the Muslims as a separate nation'. On the contrary, according to Ćosić it was a 'senseless' decision. This defiance of Tito's line led to the expulsion of Ćosić from the Party. In 1971, the census offered the chance to declare oneself a Muslim 'in the national sense'.[11]

In Bosnia the Muslims constituted the largest single population group, though until the Serb nationalist backlash in the 1980s, many 'Muslims' had preferred to identify themselves as 'Yugoslavs'. In 1981, 1.2 million (about 5.5 per cent) of the population designated themselves as Yugoslavs. It was a fourfold increase, but it was most striking in Bosnia where the number of 'Yugoslavs' rose from 44,000 to 326,000. Rapid rise in numbers of 'Yugoslavs' in Bosnia may be read as evidence of the waning of Islam. Despite all the clamour in the Serb press about fundamentalists, they were not gaining ground, nor would they have done unless the secularisation of Bosnia had been shattered from outside. It was the Serbian offensive in the late 1980s which began the process of return to the religious fold, rather as Jews like Schoenberg ostentatiously visited the synagogue to spite the Nazis.[12]

Just as growing religious freedom elsewhere led to the revival of church attendance and religious activities, so Islam enjoyed a renaissance too in the 1980s. This was regarded as a very sinister development by Serbia in particular. Hostility to the Muslims united both Serb communists and dissident opposition. They were seen as the descendants of traitors to the Serbian cause and a fifth column of Islamic fundamentalism. Since by definition the Muslims could not deny their Ottoman heritage without renouncing Islam, in the eyes of Serb nationalists they remained obdurate traitors whenever they celebrated their religion or their past.

It was not the least of the ironies of Tito's Third Worldism that all the contacts which he fostered with Middle Eastern regimes had the effect of strengthening anti-Arab and anti-Islamic feeling among many of his subjects. Although the strict orthodoxies of Saudi Arabia had little appeal for most Yugoslav Muslims, the willingness of the Saudis and other oil-rich Arab regimes to pay for the building of new mosques was appreciated. In retrospect the willingness of Riyadh to fork out cash for religious projects may be seen as foreshadowing its indecisive role during the war: the Saudis were always happier paying for someone rather than taking action themselves.[13]

Although the politicisation of Bosnia after 1989 was marked by the establishment of the Muslim Democratic Action Party (SDA), led by Alija Izetbegović who had been a frequent victim of Tito's heavy-handed justice for his religious views, it was far from a purely revivalist movement. The prominence of Fikret Abdić in its counsels was striking. He remained very popular in his home region. His frauds after all were classic white collar crimes which seemed to hit institutions not people, or at worst other people living somewhere else in Yugoslavia. It was not the people of his native region of Cazinska Krajina who had been defrauded. However, they had lost their jobs and blamed Abdić's persecutors for their difficulties rather than their boss. Against this local background, Abdić was able to continue his transformation from member of the Central Committee into local godfather, known as 'Babo' (Daddy). Many Bosnians seem to have thought – rather naively – that Abdić possessed the business skills needed to revive the republic's economy. In the Bosnian elections in 1990 Abdić obtained more votes than Izetbegović but Izetbegović was elected to chair the presidency, which was on the standard Titoite rotating model.[14]

Even the involvement of very unfundamentalist figures like Abdić in Muslim politics could not dissuade those Serbs who saw an Iranian-style mullah-led nightmare coming. For the true conspiracist, the very fact that men like Izetbegović could profess

Islam yet endorse a pluralist society and dismiss the idea of their daughters wearing the chador on the grounds that they were Muslims not folklorists was simply a deception. Rather as anti-Semites had argued before 1945 that Jews could not be assimilated and secularised and were always deeply alien (symbolised by incomprehensible rabbinic chants and outlandish ringlets), so the anti-Muslim theoreticians in Yugoslavia could not get away from their fear that every Muslim in a business suit was just waiting for his chance to turn into a whirling dervish.

Serb suspicions of Islam were matched by fears of a Catholic revival. The decision of the Virgin Mary to appear to six Croatian children in 1981 was exactly the sort of phenomenon that alarmed defensive Orthodox Serbs. Although the Virgin refrained from repeating her anti-communist message at Fatima in 1917, her affiliations were as *Pravda* might have remarked 'well known'. By 1987, scores of thousands of pilgrims were making their way to the site of the apparitions near the Hercegovinan town of Medjugorje and the Bosnian authorities decided to permit it as a tourist attraction bringing in valuable cash. The extensive accommodation constructed for the pilgrims was to turn out to be useful refugee shelter after 1992 too.

As an institution the Catholic Church had always been suspect to the communists, not just because they promoted scientific atheism, but also because the Church's internationalism cut across their own. Despite the charges that Catholic clergy *en bloc* had actively supported the Ustasha regime, Tito was careful to emphasise at the start of his own regime that the Catholic clergy could expect better treatment if they became 'more national' and less Vatican-orientated.[15] Of course, that did not stop him arranging the show trial of Cardinal Stepinac and persecuting the clergy as well as trying to discredit Rome as a way of undermining the institution.

However, once his clash with Stalin exposed him to a clear and present danger, Tito began to relax his pressure on the churches. In the 1950s they even began to receive subsidies to maintain their buildings and a *modus vivendi* was worked out, but in ideological terms at least the organised churches remained condemned as yesterday's ideology. It was only as the collapse of the system became apparent that, for instance, in Slovenia in 1989 Christmas Day could be made into a public holiday again.

By then Yugoslavia was already in effect a confederation with each republic deciding many of its policies and making laws with little concern for the others. Even while communists ruled in every republic, the clash of interests between them had become so acute that self-interested and mutually conflicting policies were pursued. When Mikhail Gorbachev visited Slovenia in 1988, he is said to have remarked that if life in the Soviet Union could reach the same standard he would be satisfied. Unfortunately, Slovenia was not Yugoslavia and the Soviet Union resembled the Yugoslav totality more than any individual part.

Although Yugoslavia had her dissidents, ranging from the doyen of ex-communists, Milovan Djilas, through to the wild bearded anti-communist figure of Vuk Drasković in Serbia, and taking in the self-proclaimed human rights activist, Dobroslav Paraga in Croatia as well as Izetbegović in Bosnia, as elsewhere in the communist world it was only when splits appeared among the communists themselves that real change became possible – but then it came quickly.

The debate about the future of Yugoslavia revealed the fissures within the League of Yugoslav Communists. As early as April 1989, the Central Committee of the Slovene Communist Party had abandoned its claim to a monopoly of power. Throughout the communist world, the insistence that the Communist Party as the 'vanguard of the working class' had the right to the 'leading role in society' undercut all the paraphernalia of civic rights and elections enshrined in written constitutions from Ljubljana to Pyongyang. Little Slovenia led the way in the abandonment of the dictatorship of the proletariat. A little over a year later, even the Soviet Communist Party was ready to accept competition from other parties. (In March 1989, multi-candidate elections had been held in parts of the Soviet Union, but many republics obstructed a choice and the CPSU remained the sole legal political party.) The Slovene communist leader, Milan Kučan, resembled Mikhail Gorbachev in his turn from Leninist rhetoric to endorsing some form of pluralistic social democracy. Unlike Gorbachev, Kučan seemed willing to go the whole way in accepting the logic of pluralism and the need for the communists to compete for office against other parties.

The repluralisation of politics also got under way in Croatia. The local Croat communists tried to curry popular favour by symbolic nationalist acts like restoring the statue of the Ban Jellačić to his podium in the main square in Zagreb in March 1990. This sort of action released the pent-up nationalism among Croats by both admitting Croat national feeling as respectable for the first time and simultaneously encouraging more of it. If the Croat communists thought that a few nationalist gestures would rescue them at the polls when they followed the Slovene example and agreed to multi-party elections for May 1990, they were mistaken. But then so were the Slovene communists. However, Kučan's supporters proved more adept at riding the tide against them and dealing with the newly elected kaleidoscopic DEMOS alliance than their Croat comrades.[16]

By their own preference, but pushed from below too, the Slovene and Croat parties had come to promote ever more devolution within an increasingly watered-down Yugoslavia. Milošević's solution to the Yugoslav crisis was to recentralise the state. This offered the best possibility to combine control of the LYC with the instrumentalisation of Serb nationalism for his purposes. After all, as Ćosić and others had pointed out, Serb nationalism regarded an integrated Yugoslavia as part of its heritage, cruelly stolen by the Croat Tito and the Slovene Kardelj.

Milošević used the *langue de bois* of communism in his rhetoric justifying de facto Serb hegemony. He affected surprise that anyone could doubt the benefits of what he called 'homogenisation' but revealed his totalitarian mind-set:

> I . . . ask the critics of homogenisation, why are they disturbed by the homogenisation of peoples and human beings in general if it is carried out on the basis of just, humane and progressive ideas . . .? Is this not the meaning, the aim to which humanity has always aspired? Surely the sense of human community is not to be unhomogeneous, divided, even when its aspirations are progressive and humane?[17]

However, if the other republics were unwilling to accept the

Serbian model of tightened centralisation, there was always another option according to Milošević. By midsummer 1990, his legal experts had drawn up a new constitution for Serbia with a strong concentration of power in the hands of a directly elected president. It clearly established the sovereignty of Serbia and left the republic's secession from the rest of Yugoslavia a possibility if the other republics would not toe Belgrade's line. Milošević told *Politika* at the end of June, 'Taking into account the strong confederal disintegrative tendencies it would be irresponsible towards Serbia and her citizens, if we had only one recipe for the Yugoslav crisis. Therefore this constitutional draft has also taken into account the other option: Serbia as an independent state.' The new order in Serbia was endorsed by the customary 98 per cent of the electorate and Milošević took this as endorsement for the final abolition of any vestiges of Kosovan autonomy in July 1990.[18]

Because the Western states only turned their attention to the breakdown of Yugoslavia once the guns had started to fire and were then overwhelmed by the pace of events, it is hardly surprising that their leaders never caught up with the background to the disintegration. But anyone paying heed to what Milošević was saying a year or more before the fighting began could see that he was preparing for two possible scenarios: either the preservation of a restored totalitarianism throughout Yugoslavia, or more probably the declaration of Serbian independence with the demand for territorial concessions from Croatia and Bosnia-Hercegovina. Since the West overlooked Serbian policy until the fat was already in the fire it was natural for EC and American statesmen to accuse the Slovenes and Croats of initiating the breakdown of Yugoslavia as though they had suddenly come to that decision in a fit of midsummer madness in June 1991.

The reformed communist, Milan Kučan, did not make a good bogeyman for the Western Yugo-preservationists. It was difficult to portray him as a sinister throw-back to nineteenth-century nationalism. An experienced bureaucrat, Kučan was too like an EC commissioner to be diabolised. With his Croatian counterpart after the May elections, Franjo Tudjman, Yugoslav propagandists and their Western audience had more to work with. Tudjman's rhetoric was undeniably nationalistic and any kind of Croatian nationalism faced a century and a half of deep-seated progressive distrust compounded by the memory of the Ustasha regime during the Second World War. Furthermore, personally Tudjman was stiff and awkward to deal with. Despite his two decades as a communist *apparatchik* in the service of Tito, Tudjman had not learnt how to 'relate' with his Western counterparts. His English was not as fluent as Milošević's and he tended to stand on his dignity as Croatia's first democratically elected leader.[19]

Despite his reputation as an uncompromising nationalist, even after his party's victory in the Croatian elections, Tudjman talked of developing further 'Tito's concept of federalism which also included some elements of confederalism'. After all, Tudjman was not certain of his popular support. His Croatian Democratic Union (HDZ) had won a clear majority of seats with only 42 per cent of the vote only because of the communists' miscalculation that their adoption of the British-style first-past-the-post system would guarantee *them* a majority on a minority vote. Tudjman's party had to bring into line the supporters of other parties, including the communists who still held key posts throughout the republic.[20]

The alterations to the Croatian constitution which the HDZ introduced were probably much less significant in alienating the Krajina Serbs than subsequently made out. Certainly the issue of symbols was irritating. The restoration of the chequerboard flag and Latin script were instantly denounced as a reversion to Pavelić's methods. But despite the constant Serb talk of a return of genocide, what violence there was in 1990 in Croatia seemed to come from Serb militias who were ominously well prepared for a clash. In their response to Serb roadblocks and attacks on public buildings and the new national flag, the Croatian authorities showed a revealing combination of heavy-handedness and under-equipment which boded ill for their capacity to maintain order. Increasingly, the Croatian authorities had to rely on the good offices of the JNA to preserve peace, but the JNA was at best neutral in the clash between the elected authorities and local militias in the Krajina and at worst some of its officers and men sided with their fellow Serbs.

Tudjman's cautious approach in practice to the assertion of Croatian sovereignty along with his government's cooperation with the JNA was undoubtedly judged as weakness in Belgrade. Serb contempt for Croats persuaded Belgrade that when push came to shove the Croats would back down rather than face a civil war which they lacked the equipment, training and will to win. However, despite his fumbling diplomacy, Tudjman's vision of an integral Croatia left no room for conceding any of its territory to Serbia or any other republic. Apart from anything else, his own electorate would not have accepted that the first act of a sovereign Croatia, even as part of a continuing Yugoslavia, should be to cede land.

Even if Tudjman could have agreed to renounce significant areas of territory to Serbia because they were inhabited by Serbs in the main, this would not have resolved the problem that most Serbs in Croatia lived in areas with a Croatian majority. Nor would territorial concessions by Zagreb have done anything for Bosnia-Hercegovina except render it unviable as either an independent or federal republic, since it would have meant that Serb-controlled territory surrounded large parts of Bosnia and would have encouraged secession among the neighbouring Serb communities inside Bosnia. To put it another way, Croatian territorial concessions would have signed Bosnia-Hercegovina's death warrant even before its birth certificate had been made out. The consequence would have been the creation of a Greater Serbia which might in any case have then turned on Croatia and demanded more territory along the Adriatic since Serb ideologists' definition of Serbian land extended well beyond the areas where Serbs actually lived in large numbers.

All of Tudjman's negotiations about some form of a vague confederal Yugoslavia which would satisfy Croat desires for sovereignty while permitting a common economy and infrastructure were rejected by Milošević, who was willing to accept only a recentralised Yugoslavia or a Greater Serbia carved out of the other republics. Both those options involved subordinating non-Serbs to Serb interests. There was to be no compromise.[21]

Meanwhile in the Krajina, the local Serb forces felt strong enough to move against the Croatian authorities. At the end of February 1991, they declared themselves autonomous. Clashes occurred between the Croatian police and Serb militias when the Serbs seized police stations and disarmed the local police. The

JNA moved, ostensibly to maintain order but in practice to provide a protective shield for the developing Serb mini-state. The JNA even fired on the Croatian police. It was a sign of the growing extra-constitutional role of the Army. Just as on 9 March it intervened on the streets of Belgrade to back up Milošević without any authorisation from the Federal Presidency, so increasingly the JNA acted on its own authority in Croatia, albeit hand-in-glove with local Serb militias.

It was the violent and intimidating events on the ground in Krajina which overshadowed the discussions of the politicians. Talk about reform from Milošević palled in the face of a heavily armed allegedly persecuted minority taking control of its localities and facing down the powers in Zagreb.

The critical Slovene sociologist, soon to be foreign minister of that republic, Dmitrij Rupel, saw through the rhetoric of reform of the federation emanating from Belgrade. It was merely echoing the demands of the Memorandum of the Serbian Academy. Behind the demand for a coherent approach to planning the economy and infrastructure lay clear political goals:

> The worst is the request for a unified legal system which in fact suits those who claim that liberal-nationalist and other hostile elements have been tolerated too much in some parts of the country and that, for instance, this system should be simplified so that Draconian sentences such as those pronounced in Kosovo are pronounced in Slovenia too.[22]

For all that the fighting in the first two years of the Yugoslav war went on outside Kosovo, Kosovo remained the core of the problem. The fact that Milošević's Serbia had made the destruction of the province's autonomy a keystone of its policy had clear implications and consequences for the rest of Yugoslavia. It was not only the costs of military occupation and the distaste for sending their sons there to hold down the Albanian majority which antagonised other republican elites and peoples. It was the lesson taught by Milošević's repression that alarmed a cross-section of non-Serbian communists, from the neo-social-democrat Slovenes to the previously complacently Titoite leaders of other republics. It was not only dissidents like Rupel who saw the symbiosis of Milošević and the Serbian Academy's approach to Kosovo as ominous for all Yugoslavs.[23]

9

Kosovo: Myth in the Service of Aggression

> Serbia is not a state, it is Kosovo; and Kosovo is a tomb, the tomb in which everything is buried, and the resurrection can only spring from the tomb, because there is no resurrection without death.
>
> Isidora Sekulić[1]

Kosovo is more than a blood-soaked battlefield. It is Serbia's national shrine. The defeat of Tsar Lazar by the Ottoman army on the Blackbird Field on 28 June 1389 still rankles. That disaster has become the stuff of legends. The martyrs of Kosovo are more real to the Serbian Orthodox Church than most of the other saints in its calendar. The fact that Lazar's defeated army was composed of soldiers of many different nationalities including Albanians is ignored in Serbian history books. Long before the policy of forcible depopulation was introduced into Yugoslavia, the history of the Battle of Kosovo was 'ethnically cleansed'.

Self-pity and self-glorification run through the Serbian understanding of Kosovo. Historical reality has largely been abandoned to make way for a mythic interpretation of the battle's significance. Many Western historians regard it as much less significant in the development of Ottoman hegemony over the Balkans than other later events. After all, Tamerlaine's irruption into the Ottoman heartland in Anatolia set back the Turkish conquest of both Constantinople and the Balkans by decades. It was only after the fall of the last Roman emperor in 1453 that the Turks could really force through and consolidate their conquest of the whole Balkan peninsula. But later wars lacked the clear-cut, epic quality of Kosovo. After 1389, there was too much compromise and intrigue and even downright collaboration with the Turks to provide an undiluted moral.[2]

Not that the moral of the Kosovo epic aroused universal respect. After all, central to the story was the role of the assassin, Milos Obilić, one of Tsar Lazar's paladins, whose loyalty was doubted by his lord. Obilić's disappearance from the Serbian host on the eve of battle seemed to confirm the suspicions against him, but in fact although he had crossed over to the Turkish camp it was in order to slay the Sultan Amurad. Pretending to make his obeisance to the all-conquering Ottoman, according to legend Milos Obilić suddenly produced a knife and stabbed Amurad to death.

This suicidal act did not deflect the Turks from their military objective. Lazar's army was routed and the Tsar himself taken prisoner and then executed for having defied the dead Sultan's offer before the battle of his life in return for his acceptance of Islam and Ottoman sovereignty. However, it was not the noble Lazar's preference for a heavenly crown instead of earthly subjection to the infidel which lived on most vividly in the folk-memory, but Milos Obilić's cunning murder of the Sultan. The glorification of this act by nineteenth-century writers had obvious consequences and helped to stimulate the cult of political murder at the beginning of the twentieth. The grand futility of Obilić's act became its fascination.[3]

Defeat at Kosovo and the successive waves of Ottoman conquest in the fifteenth century led to the heartland of Serbian medieval culture falling under Turkish control. Kosovo housed the seat of the Patriarch of the Serbian Orthodox Church at Peć. Although Catholicism, or Islam for that matter, played a major role in establishing the cultural identity of those peoples who adhered to its tenets, its universal aspirations conflicted with nationalism. On the other hand, the Orthodox Church developed along national lines from an early stage, and fostered a fusion between tribe and religion. Orthodox Christianity in Byzantium as well as later in Russia was very much a state-dominated church. In the West, however precariously at times, the Papacy established itself as a separate and often rival centre of authority to the state. Although at the local level – bog priests in Ireland or Franciscan friars in Hercegovina – the Catholic clergy might identify their religious faith with their tribal identity, Rome was always uncomfortable with nationalism.

The Orthodox Church tended to be much more inward-looking. It sought to preserve its faithful and their liturgy rather than to proselytise. In fact, fear of Catholic evangelisation has been a recurrent theme in Orthodox attacks on the Vatican. For centuries there was no contradiction between being a Serb and being Orthodox. Indeed, so obvious was the conjunction, that until well into the twentieth century many Serb peasants would regard their religion as the only necessary statement of belonging. To be Serb was to be Orthodox and vice versa. Speakers of the same language who were not Orthodox were by definition renegades to be regarded with all the loathing reserved for apostates.

Centuries of subjection by the Muslim Turk and then decades of domination in Bosnia-Hercegovina by the Catholic Habsburgs were not simply a humiliation, but perversions of a divinely ordained state of affairs. The reuniting of all Orthodox believers under a devout Tsar was the implicit programme of the Orthodox Church, and above all the recovery of Kosovo, the original Garden of Eden of Orthodoxy with its monasteries and other places associated with the spiritual development of the Church. (In everyday practice, however, Orthodox hierarchs generally found it easier to operate under Ottoman than Habsburg rule: the Sultan preserved the Patriarchate at Constantinople and other elements of the hierarchy to facilitate his rule, whereas the Catholic Habsburgs tended to promote conversion which was easier from Orthodoxy to Catholicism than to Islam and therefore a constant trauma for the Orthodox.)

Given the biblical quality of the historical myths about Kosovo which grew up in the Orthodox Church and were then taken over in secularised form by nineteenth-century nationalists, it is hardly surprising that the reconquest of the area in 1912 should have been marked by scenes of religious fervour and crusading brutality towards the non-Serbs and Muslims who actually inhabited the territory at the start of the twentieth century.[4]

The ethnic cleansing of the last decade of the twentieth century has a long and brutal history, above all in the precedents set in Kosovo in 1912 and after. Just as the Serbs came into their own promised land again with the final collapse of Ottoman power in Europe, so the Albanians were aroused to seek their own state out of the ruins of the Turkish Empire. A classic problem of incompatible claims appeared. To Serbs, not only Kosovo but much of what was to become the new state of Albania had anciently and therefore today by right belonged to Serbia, including access to the Adriatic Sea. But this claim could not go unchallenged by the Albanian majority which actually lived in the territories demanded or actually occupied by the Serbian Army.

A guerrilla war broke out between the Serbian liberators of a medieval Kosovo that no longer existed and the Albanians. It was fought as ruthlessly as any colonial war against a recalcitrant native population unwilling to accept the logic of the Gatling gun. Even by the standards of contemporary colonial wars it shocked West European and American observers, not least because of the disjunction between the Serbian government's claim to be the decolonising liberator and its actual policy of expelling native inhabitants and destroying their homes and economy to persuade them to go. Investigators for the Carnegie Endowment reported:

> Houses and whole villages reduced to ashes, unarmed and innocent populations massacred en masse, incredible acts of violence, pillage and brutality of every kind – such were the means which were employed by the Serbo-Montenegrin soldiery, with a view to the entire transformation of the ethnic character of regions inhabited exclusively by Albanians.[5]

The violence had the effect of alienating former supporters of the Serbs, including Enid Durham, who had travelled widely in the region and organised humanitarian relief for the victims of the war against the Turks.

After the First World War, resistance to Serbian domination flared up again. The response of Belgrade was to expel hundreds of thousands of Albanians from the province across the border into Albania proper. The Albanian-speaking population fell from upwards of 800,000 to 439,657 in time for the first pan-Yugoslav census. At first the Serbian authorities tried to Serbianise the Albanians by enforcing education in the Serbian language and forbidding it in Albanian, but it was quickly decided that any education only stimulated Albanian resistance so state-promoted illiteracy became the preferred weapon against Albanian identity. One Serbian official proudly noted in 1921 that the Kosovar Albanians 'will all remain backward, unenlightened and stupid; nor will they know the state idiom [Serbian], which would help them to fight against us.' He concluded, rather optimistically as events have turned out, 'It is in our interest that they remain at the present level of their culture for another twenty years, the time we need to carry out the necessary national assimilation of these areas.' By 'assimilation' the Serbian authorities clearly did not mean absorbing the Albanians into the Serbian community, but rather artificially building up the Serb element in the population as a prelude to an irrevocable 'final solution' of the Albanian problem in Kosovo – probably another mass expulsion.[6]

The assassins of Franz Ferdinand at Sarajevo in 1914 did not just want to liberate Bosnia-Hercegovina from Habsburg rule, but were deeply imbued with the ethos of Kosovo and the Obilić myth. It was natural therefore for a surviving member of the plot to kill the Archducal couple, Vaso Čubrilović, to devote his energies after 1918 to the Albanian question. Čubrilović revived the idea of 'the expulsion of the Albanians' in a lecture to the Serbian Cultural Club in March 1937 which served as the basis for a memorandum to the Regent's government in Belgrade. Paying particular attention to the international situation and the indifference of the Western powers to Hitler's anti-Semitism or Stalin's de-Kulakisation, Čubrilović argued, 'At a time when Germany can expel tens of thousands of Jews and Russia can shift millions of people from one part of the continent to another, the shifting of a few hundred thousand Albanians will not lead to the outbreak of a world war.'[7]

For all his devotion to the Serbian cause, Čubrilović was an extraordinary political chameleon. He survived the Second World War and entered Tito's government, still advocating the expulsion of the Kosovar Albanians. When Tito fell out with Stalin and Stalin's loyal disciple, Enver Hoxha, in Tirana, Tito gave up his ambitions to incorporate Albania into his Yugoslavia. Men like Čubrilović and Tito's Security Chief, the Serb Alexander Ranković, enjoyed free rein as any Albanian nationalist was clearly an enemy of the Marshal as well as the Serbian right to Kosovo. Čubrilović lived to a ripe old age (dying in 1990) and was one of the spiritual fathers of the revival of Serbian nationalism after Tito's death. A member of the Serbian Academy, Čubrilović's influence was an essential prerequisite for the Academy's famous Memorandum in 1986.

Fifty years after his appeal for the expulsion of the Albanians of Kosovo, Čubrilović could take senile satisfaction in the tone and content of the Memorandum. However, the most interesting aspect of Čubrilović's thinking about how to deal with the Albanians was the justification of the brutal measures required. He complained that the Serb authorities had been too weak and 'Western'. Serbia ought to learn from her old enemy: 'Turkey brought to the Balkans the customs of the Sheriat . . . Even the Balkan Christians learned from the Turks that not only state power and domination, but also home and property are won and lost by the sword.' He argued that since the Albanians still outbred the effects of Serbian recolonisation, 'the only way and the only means to cope with them is the brute force of an organised state, in which we [Serbs] have always been superior to them.' The necessary precondition for a mass expulsion of Albanians from their ancestral homes was 'the creation of a suitable psychosis'.

In order to create an atmosphere of fear and a willingness to leave, the Serbian state ought to use very un-Balkan tactics: 'The law must be enforced to the letter . . . fines and imprisonments, the ruthless application of all police dispositions, such as the prohibition of smuggling, cutting forests, damaging farmland, leaving dogs unchained, compulsory labour and any other measures that an experienced police force can contrive.' In addition, property titles should be questioned and business permits withdrawn. Islam should be harassed and the daughters of Muslims forced into schools with boys. But all of these measures were only the background to state-sponsored terror: 'We should distribute weapons to our colonists. The old forms of Chetnik action should be organised and secretly assisted.' The Montenegrins should be unleashed on the Albanians – 'This conflict should be prepared by . . . our trusted people' – and then once the Albanians replied to force with force, 'the whole affair should be presented as a conflict between clans.' Čubrilović recognised the need to pacify Western opinion with the argument that any violence was just an old-fashioned tribal war. He therefore preferred to keep the Serbian Army out of action except when it was 'secretly burning down Albanian villages and city quarters'. Chetniks should be used to suppress the Albanians whenever the action was under scrutiny so that the tribal nature could be emphasised.[8]

The social and individual psychology of the 'Turkified' Serb nationalist will one day receive a thorough study. What is clear is the deep underlying self-hatred which runs through it. In order to rid oneself of the domination and even the legacy of the hated 'Turk', his worst features must be assimilated into the Serbian character. Ottoman brutality had to be matched or even surpassed in order to save Serbdom from the Turkish legacy of an Albanianised Kosovo.

Dušan Simić, the president of the city council in Priština, the capital of Kosovo, told *Newsweek*, 'Serbs fought here to save Europe from Islam. And we are still fighting to keep Islam from spreading into the heart of Europe.'[9] In practice in the 1990s, Serb policies were likely to revive the very kind of Islamic fundamentalism which they were supposed to combat. The psychological need to create one's ideal enemy to justify one's own savagery is again apparent. Albanians and other Muslims are hated as much for not living up to their stereotype as for conforming to it.

Čubrilović complained that the government in Belgrade spent money on roads and other developments but not on his scheme. The underlying mentality of his 'ethnic cleansing' was this sense of betrayal by even Serb authorities. After the Second World War, Tito's mixed non-Serb origins made him the butt of Serb complaints that they were the victims of government indifference to their plight, in reality to their ambitions. However, it was not just the inadequacy of these measures to counter the demographic trends in Kosovo which made the appeal of violent measures so strong to the likes of Čubrilović both then and now: it was their very violence that became an end in itself. Humane 'ethnic cleansing' is a contradiction in terms because those who wish to carry it out want it to be a brutal and degrading process in order to cleanse their own sense of centuries-old humiliation and betrayal by their own kind.[10]

Just as the 'ethnic cleansing' in Croatia and then Bosnia after 1991 was masterminded to a great extent by Mihaly Kertes,

Milošević's 'Hungarian' security chief, so even in Kosovo itself Belgrade's rule depended upon Albanian collaborators at every level in the administration until very recently. It was only late in the day that Milošević decided nothing more could be squeezed out of them and tossed them aside, even turning on them and persecuting his former servants as 'traitors'.

The theme of the betrayal of the Serbian people by the Croat Tito, but also by his Serbian hirelings, ran through the Academicians' complaint in 1986. Ironically, it was an idea taken up by Milošević when he distanced himself from the Serb communists who had originally promoted his political career. On the field of Kosovo, at Vitvodan in 1989, Milošević recalled the

> concessions which many Serb leaders made at the expense of their people [which] could be accepted by no people on earth, neither historically nor ethically. Especially since the Serbs throughout their history never conquered or exploited anybody else. Their whole national and historical being throughout their history, through the two world wars as well as today is liberating.

It was a classic statement of the victim-aggressor mentality which the Kosovo myth encouraged among Serbs. In essence, it was the self-justifying notion, 'How can we who have been wronged so often in the past, be wrong in our actions today?'

Victimhood became the tool of Milošević's mobilisation of the Serbian people. Already in November 1988 Milošević told a rally in Belgrade:

> There is no time for sorrow. It is a time for struggle . . . We shall win the battle for Kosovo regardless of the obstacles facing us inside and outside the country . . . We shall win despite the fact that Serbia's enemies outside the country are plotting against it along with those in the country. We tell them that we go into every battle with the aim of winning it . . . And there is no battle in the world that the people have lost.[12]

In 1986, the Serbian authorities had already forced the local Kosovan government to prevent any Albanian settlement in the few still purely Serb settlements in Kosovo. The German Yugoslav expert, Viktor Meier, an early critic of Greater Serbian chauvinism in Kosovo, called this policy 'Klein-apartheid'.[13] Although every effort was made to reverse the population decline among the Serbs, neither economic incentives nor even the waves of Serbian refugees from the war zones in Croatia and Bosnia produced any serious demographic impact. Despite all the propaganda about Kosovo as the heart and soul of the Serbian nation, by the early 1990s it had lost its appeal as a place of residence.

Once the fighting had started elsewhere in Yugoslavia, the official Serbian approach to the Kosovo problem took on all the features of a Balkan parody of the fascist obsession with the birth-rate. On 28 June 1993, the Orthodox Church announced a new medal, the 'Majka Jugovica' which any Serbian mother bearing four or more children in Kosovo would be entitled to receive. It was named after the legendary Serbian mother, Jugovica, who was supposed to have lost her nine sons on the Blackbird Field fighting against the Turk six hundred and four years before.[14] Hitler and Mussolini doled out similar 'Mutterkreuze' to the fecund among their subjects, but failed to boost the German or Italian birth-rate markedly. What such awards illustrate, however, is the fascistic obsession with fertility, or rather the lack of it.

The deification of the nation is a key feature of authoritarian nationalism. However, in the case of Serbia, the exultation of the nation-state to a quasi-divine position in nationalist propaganda had certain peculiarities. When nineteenth-century German or Italian nationalists worshipped their states it was usually as a revitalised pagan god in revolt against Christianity and the Church which was held to have debilitated and divided the naturally united Germans or Italians. In Serb nationalist theology, Serbia is identified with Christ. The Serb nation's sufferings through history are seen as a parallel Golgotha. Recurrent defeat and conquest make Serbia into an eternally recrucified Christ. The result of this theological politics has been to reinforce a spirit of militant self-righteousness and self-pity among Serbs.

Kosovo is the central text in this Serbian New Testament. To take one example of many such invocations, it is worth pondering on Matija Bećković's *Serbian Gospel*, for instance:

> The battle of Kosovo was never finished. It is as if the Serbian

> people had waged only one battle – by widening the Kosovo charnel-house, by adding wailing upon wailing, by counting new martyrs to the martyrs of Kosovo . . . Kosovo is the costliest Serbian word. It was paid by the blood of the whole people . . . Kosovo is the equator of the Serbian planet. The ceiling of the lower and the foundation of the upper world. Here the conscience of the Serb people was split into the period before and after Kosovo. Kosovo is the Serbianised story of the Flood – the Serbian New Testament.[15]

If Kosovo was the divine womb of the Serbian nation, then alien defilement of it was all the more blasphemous. Great emphasis has been laid in Serb propaganda on sexual imagery, particularly on identifying Albanians as the archetypal perpetrators of sex crimes. Serbian portraits of Albanian life have long denigrated it as the product of sexual violence and chaos. On the eve of the First World War, the Serb politician and public health reformer, Vladan Djordjević, informed German readers that Albanians were little better than troglodytes, conceived and living 'in incest'. More than half their brides were no longer virgins, but their husbands were hardly likely to live long enough to care since 70 per cent of men, Djordjević insisted, died violent deaths in blood feuds. He dismissed the idea that these sex-crazed primitives could lay claim to a political or national identity with further colourful claims: 'And some would wish to claim that people who do not know what salt is and who mistake sugar for snow . . . know what a Fatherland is and that they would be ready to die for this exalted concept.' It was hardly surprising that Djordjević concluded that such people were both multiple religious apostates without any sincere beliefs and at the same time marked out by their religious fanaticism![16]

Another pre–1914 Serbian writer, Jovan Hadzi-Vasiljević, argued that Muslim Albanians had swelled their numbers when they 'seized and Mohammedanized Serb girls' as a prelude to grabbing Serb land.[17] This charge echoed down the decades to the 1990s and was applied elsewhere to argue that no Slav-speaking or descended Muslim could really exist since their ancestors had been forcibly converted. Vojislav Šešelj proclaimed at the beginning of August 1991 that 'the Muslims in Bosnia are Islamicized Serbs and part of the so-called Croats are Catholic Serbs.'[18] Ratko Mladić himself repeated this charge which both turned Muslims into Serbs and yet still justified killing them: 'Serb mothers watched children taken away by the *Musilmani* to become sultan's kids to be sold as slaves . . .'[19]

Why the Serbs of Kosovo should have let themselves be Albanianised as well as converted to Islam has never been adequately explained by the Serb promoters of the idea that there is not a real Albanian majority in Kosovo because many 'Albanians' are in fact the descendants of forcibly converted Serbs. After all, the Muslims of Bosnia and other parts of Yugoslavia did not necessarily adopt the Turkish language when they adopted the conqueror's religion. Without a substantial Albanian population already in situ in Kosovo it is difficult to explain the alleged Islamicisation and Albanianisation of Serbs there.[20]

Although many ethnographic historians have accepted that the Albanians' Illyrian ancestors were the early inhabitants of much of the western part of modern Yugoslavia, where they appeared two or three centuries before Christ, to official Serb historians and propagandists the priority of the Albanians over the Slavs anywhere is vile heresy. Violent abuse and even physical attack have been the fate of those who pointed out that the Slavs, from whom Serbs, Croats et al. are descended, appeared on the Balkan scene only seven centuries later. Milan Šufflay, the Croatian Albanologist, had his skull smashed open in 1931 after years of abuse and threats for promoting an uncontroversial opinion of the ethnic past of the south-west of Yugoslavia – uncontroversial, that was, outside Alexander's Kingdom. Šufflay's end was a chronicle of a death foretold. He had received a threatening letter from a 'patriotic' group known to have close contacts with the Ministry of the Interior and on 24 January 1931, three weeks before his body was found, the newspaper *Nasa Sloga* announced, 'We are going to cleave skulls.'[21] Šufflay's was not the last to be 'cloven' for his views on ethnicity in Yugoslavia.

Undoubtedly, inter-ethnic tensions and the violence associated with them played their part in the escalation of the Kosovo problem. But the Serb media often wilfully distorted the facts or suppressed inconvenient aspects of a story so that its message would be one of undiluted anti-Albanian force. Take for instance the case of the murder of a Serbian teenager, Danilo Milinćić, shortly before the Twelfth Congress of the LYC in 1982. Adding spice to the story, it was reported that the unfortunate boy's father, Slavoljub, had himself been murdered fifteen years before. Any reader could be forgiven for concluding that the Milinćićs had been the victims of a cruel Albanian vendetta against them. In fact, it transpired that the father, Slavoljub, had been murdered by another one of his sons, Miroslav, acting together with an in-law! Far from being evidence of a race war in Kosovo with the Serbs the perennial victims, this case was in fact yet more grim evidence of Kosovo's violent and unsatisfactory society, which made life so unpleasant for Serbs and Albanians alike.[22]

Until the collapse of the last openly Stalinist regime in the world in neighbouring Albania in 1991, the Albanians of Kosovo always faced the undesirability of secession. The poverty and oppression of Enver Hoxha's Albania were even less attractive than Serbian domination. Belgrade, therefore, had little interest in seeing successful reform in Albania.

As Sabrina Ramet has pointed out, the Kosovo question is more like the Palestinian issue than any European model (Spanish-Basque relations, for instance): 'Two ethnic communities with distinct languages and religious traditions lay claim to the same territory with competing historical arguments as evidence.'[23] However, there is a striking contrast with Palestine. Whereas the inflow of Zionist settlers in the twentieth century displaced some of the resident Palestinian Arabs, Christian and Muslim alike, creating an embittered Palestinian diaspora unable to return because of the might of the Israeli state, the crisis in Kosovo has been embittered by the continued emigration of Serbs despite the political and military hegemony of their own state over the province. The hysteria of Serb propaganda about Kosovo is a by-product of the reality that enthusiasm for the cause and a willingness to sacrifice oneself for it are much less widespread among Serbs than their (self-proclaimed) leaders will admit. However aggressive and dominant, Serb nationalism is a tribal religion with more chiefs than Indians – a fact which Western statesmen have been unwilling to recognise.

Belgrade or Zagreb might have enjoyed the blessings of a Western-style feminist movement, but outside the big cities, especially in the southern republics and provinces, violence against women and their humiliation were commonplace. The police and the local authorities showed little interest in rape or other crimes against women. One observer noted 'the repeated refusal of the Yugoslav police in the less developed republics . . . to move in cases of rape, unless the rape in question "was motivated by nationalist motives". . . . Most rapes within the same national group remain unreported or at least underreported . . .'[24]

The Serbian police tended to a chauvinistic indifference to women's claims of rape unless they kindled the desire to put the blame on Albanians. Not unreasonably, Bogdan Denitch thinks 'It is a scandal that the official women's organization of Serbia has only raised the issue of rape when it affects the rape of Serbian and Montenegrin women by Albanians.' In October 1988, the Serbian women criticised the other women's organisations for not protesting against the peculiar outrage of Albanian men raping Serbian women.

These allegations of rape against Albanian males were taken up and used by Milošević himself, who understood the deep resonance they would find among otherwise patriarchal and chauvinist Serb men. In their minds it was for them to maltreat their own women, not others. Milošević spoke to a Serbian crowd in the Kosovan town of Uroševac, during a factory visit in April 1987, but his words were addressed to the recalcitrant Albanian majority in the province. The speech was to provide a classic text in the school of political blindness to the beam in one's eye:

> It is just and moral that every nation, and *its own most progressive people before all others, should struggle against their own nationalism* [emphasis added]: against all those terrible and inhuman actions which offend and degrade others. For these terrible and inhuman things, in the end, offend and degrade the nation itself, and those of its members who perpetrate them.
>
> The Albanian nation must defend not only Serbs and Montenegrins from the shame of those things which its nationalists do, but themselves.
>
> With every assaulted Serbian child a stain falls on *every Albanian* [emphasis added] who has not prevented such a shameful thing.

Milošević rammed home the idea of collective guilt and the imputation that revenge might be taken on the Albanians as a whole for sexual or other crimes against Serbs by adding: 'The safety of Serbian and Montenegrin children, here in Kosovo, ought rather to be the concern of every Albanian mother and father, rather than that of the [Serbian] police.'[25]

As to the reality of the problem, according to the Yugoslav Forum for Human Rights in 1987, only 9.6 per cent of the rapes recorded in Kosovo between 1982–1986 were committed by Albanians against Serbian women. As in any society most rapes in Kosovo were acts of domestic violence by men who knew the women or girls concerned.[26] But the potent mixture of racial stereotypes and sexual fears and fantasies were stronger than any statistics.

Whatever else General Ratko Mladić may have been accused of, his masculinity has not been impugned. However, even the redoubtable 'cleanser' himself revealed that he shared Serbian fears of the Albanian birth-rate. Like any Boer or Southern Klansman, Mladić got excited by the Muslim's secret weapon, their fecundity: 'The Islamic world does not have the atomic bomb, but it does have a demographic bomb. Atomic bombs are under some kind of control. Their enormous reproduction is not under any kind of control.'[27]

The allegations of rape against Albanian men fitted into this nightmare vision of subversion of Serbia by breeding. Nonetheless, whatever the truth of particular charges of rape the police showed remarkably little interest in pursuing their investigations. What mattered was to publicise the charges and to exacerbate the public mood.

One particular case became notorious and illustrates the Serbian authorities' lack of interest in uncovering the truth. In May 1985 a Serb farmer, Djordje Martinović, was found with a broken bottle thrust up his anus. He claimed that he had been attacked by a group of Albanian-speaking men who had tortured him in this way. The case was immediately widely publicised, as perhaps was inevitable given the sensational nature of the charges. However, it was not only the press who took up the case and retailed its lurid and distressing details to a fascinated and alarmed Serbian public. If that had been all, then no doubt it would have been a three-day wonder – even if, as was the case, the police signally failed to find the alleged perpetrators of the crime. However, the Martinović case was taken up by politicians anxious to exploit the Kosovo issue. Even members of the Serbian Academy took up the case. In their famous Memorandum in 1986, the Academicians specifically mentioned this case as an example of the Albanian genocide against Serbs.

The key charge made by the Academy was not only that Martinović had been the victim of a crime 'which recalls the darkest periods of Turkish impalements', but that the case was significant because of the 'tenacious failure to discover and acknowledge the truth in regular court proceedings'. This was indeed true, but the Academy used the failure of the police and judicial authorities to clarify the case as another plank in its claim that Serbs were the victims of a treasonable indifference by their own government to what was happening to them.

To confound anyone trying to discover the truth about this incident, Albanian sources made their own lurid charges: far from being the victim of a racially motivated and humiliating attack, Martinović was accused of engaging in a perverse sexual practice which had left him with his injuries. Since Martinović was taken to Belgrade immediately after he reported the incident and kept out of public view but also away from any judicial inquiry, the truth of the case never emerged, and Martinović's reputation remains under a cloud. His case, however, served a purpose. Apparently, Martinović's undoubted sufferings (whatever their cause) have been immortalised in a painting of the crucifixion now hanging in the Serbian Academy in Belgrade.[28]

The failure of the economy was most striking in a province like Kosovo. As much as inter-ethnic tensions it accounted for the drift and then the flight of Serbs from the region. The exodus has been exaggerated because Serbian propagandists do not like to admit their precarious demographic rights in Kosovo to begin with, but nevertheless, between 1971 and 1981, about 18,000 Serbs and 4500 Montenegrins left the province. However, it was not only Serbs who left in search of a better, safer life. Bogdan Denitch admitted the unpalatable truth, blotted out by Serbs anxious to see their kinsfolk as the victims of 'ethnic cleansing' *avant la lettre*: 'Of course, the breakdown affects the Albanians in Kosovo as well; massive numbers of Albanians have migrated from that underdeveloped province.'[29]

In the same period as the much-publicised departure of at most 30,000 Serbs and Montenegrins from Kosovo, 250,000 Albanians left the province, looking for work elsewhere. After all, even ethnically blind statistics showed that Kosovans were over three times more likely to be unemployed than the average Yugoslav. Unemployment statistics also illustrate the severe relative disadvantage of Albanians in Kosovo. Although they made up four-fifths of the working-age population, Albanians held only 60 per cent of the jobs. By contrast, Serbs and Montenegrins held a third of all jobs – more than twice their proportion in the population. Only 109 Albanians per thousand Kosovans held a job, but 228 Serbs per thousand and 258 Montenegrins per thousand had work before the wars in the north began.[30]

As in many other Third World countries, mass education in Yugoslavia exacerbated social and inter-ethnic problems rather than alleviating them. Even allowing for the province's continued higher than average levels of low academic attainment, Kosovo's university grossly over-produced graduates with an education almost unusable in the area. Priština University had around 37,000 students before Milošević moved against it – far too many to be absorbed by the local economy.

Many Albanians took up jobs or refuge in Slovenia and Croatia. Ironically, although the Slovenes were anxious to preserve a demarcation between themselves and the other southern Slavs, let alone poor southerners like the Albanians and Macedonians, and despite the fact that many quasi-refugees from Kosovo in Ljubljana did not feel welcomed, nonetheless their presence and their stories of Serbian heavy-handedness after 1981 kindled Slovene apprehensions about the mood in Belgrade and its long-term purposes. The fact that the federal defence budget was hiked by $350 million not long after the Kosovo riots in 1981, which in turn required Ljubljana to increase its contribution to the federal budget by 30 per cent, was taken by most Slovenes as evidence that other Yugoslavs were having to pay the price of Serbia's unwillingness to acknowledge Albanian rights to autonomy and self-administration.

Even a student of Yugoslav affairs more inclined to accept

some of the Serb charges about Albanian pressure on the Serbs in Kosovo found their charges of 'genocide . . . a monstrous and chauvinist exaggeration'. As Bogdan Denitch remarked, 'When the responsible political leadership of the Serbian LCY and government and leading intellectuals and academics took over that grotesquely abused term from a hysterical yellow press, [then] . . . the danger point was reached . . . After all, genocide cannot be discussed; it has to be fought with arms if necessary.'[31]

The inflation of the rhetoric of human rights abuse was a key element in the heating-up of the political atmosphere in Yugoslavia. Given the increasing repression of them in the 1980s, especially after 1989, it is hardly surprising that the Albanians saw themselves as the victims of an incipient genocide, or at least of an impending brutal mass expulsion like those already experienced earlier in the twentieth century. But it was the increasingly dominant Serbs who despite their hold on political and police power continued to cast themselves in the role of victims.

It was the opponents of Tito's heirs who first took up the theme of an Albanian 'genocide' against the Serbs of Kosovo. Even Milošević's future victim, Vuk Drasković, the only prominent opponent of the Serbian president after 1992 who was prepared to risk life and limb to denounce his policies, had originally made use of the Kosovo issue to undermine the communist regime. Even during the war against Bosnia, Drasković could still not envisage self-determination for the Albanians in Kosovo even if he otherwise wished to grant them full civic rights in a 'democratic' Serbia.

However, the chief corrupter of political language in Serbia was the arch-ideologue of eternally suffering Greater Serbia, Dobrica Ćosić, who went so far as to compare the Serbs as a 'people of martyrs' with the Jews during the Second World War: 'The Serb is the new Jew, the Jew at the end of the twentieth century.'[32] Alain Finkielkraut was moved to remark that this sort of rhetoric suggested that the Nazis of the late twentieth century were confusing themselves with their victims.

Whatever hysterical and self-pitying rhetoric came from the ideologues about the Kosovo issue, Kosovo taught the JNA and the Serbian political class a fateful and misleading lesson.

Because the deployment of a massive paramilitary force and the evident willingness to use it had cowed open rebellion by the Albanians in the province after 1981, the JNA's generals and Milošević's political allies concluded that the threat of force and the occasional salutary use of it in localised form would suffice to intimidate any separatists in the other republics. After all, in 1981 alone, perhaps as many as 300 people were killed before order was restored, but the disturbances were quelled and nothing comparable occurred for more than a decade afterwards.[33]

For Ćosić, the fault for the failure to restore anything resembling the rule of law or democracy lay with the Albanian majority. Their 'struggle' had led to the 'persecution of Serbs' which 'entailed the intervention of the army and the police and repressions'. Unfortunately, according to Ćosić it was impossible to bring the Albanians to their senses because of foreign support for them: 'In the name of protecting human rights, the Albanians are strongly supported . . . by certain circles in the US Congress and Senate, the European Parliament, centres of Islamic power, Albanian lobbies financed by the drugs trade and weapons trade . . .' among others. Human rights were simply 'an alibi for an anti-Serb ideology and policy which is destabilising Yugoslavia'. For Ćosić as for Milošević, Yugoslavia was a flexible idea: sometimes it embodied the sacrifice of Serb interests on the altar of anti-Serb ideology, but at others it was the bastion and legal basis of Serb claims over other peoples within the Federation. At any given moment, Yugoslavia could mean good or bad, it was up to the Serbs and them alone to decide.[34]

Serbia's relations with her two other neighbours – the northern province of Vojvodina and Macedonia to her south – present far fewer deep-seated psychological and historical problems. The Macedonian question, unlike the Kosovo question, does not arouse deep-seated emotions among Serbs. Even if the average Serb might occasionally give way to the blasphemous private thought that Kosovo is not worth all the cost of keeping, it is difficult for any discussion of Serb-Albanian relations in the province to be put other than in emotionalising propagandistic terms. Macedonia is different.

Although Serb historians have denied the existence of a separate Macedonian nation, preferring to insist that the Macedonians are South Serbs whether they like it or not, in practice Serb political attitudes towards their southern neighbour are based on strategic and economic criteria rather than nationalist myth. In any case, there are too few self-identifying Serbs in Macedonia to make a Krajina or Bosnia out of the republic without too much trouble for Belgrade.

However, Serbia today faces the same strategic problem which she faced before 1912. Her northern and western neighbours are hostile and so her most secure route to the outside world lies southwards through Macedonia. Even if Serbia ideally would like a port of her own on the Aegean, a friendly Greece controlling Thessaloniki makes a tolerable second best. This is especially true since for their own mythico-nationalist reasons the Greeks cannot form an alliance with the Macedonians, but on the contrary look to Serbia to help hold the new republic in check.

Sandwiched between Serbia and Greece, Macedonia has little option but to cooperate with Belgrade. However much her own independent status may depend upon UN approval, Macedonia has learnt that UN guarantees count for little in the Balkans and therefore she has accommodated herself to Serbia's needs. Macedonia provides the chief conduit for sanctions-breaking so that Greek firms can continue to export to Serbia despite the UN blockade. So long as Skopje conforms to Serbia's requirements, it is unlikely that Belgrade will throw her to the nationalist wolves in either Serbia or Greece.[35]

The most potent threat to Macedonia comes not from her tiny Serb and Greek populations, but from the intertangling of her substantial Albanian minority in the continuing crisis in Kosovo. Serb policy towards Kosovo and Albania proper, as well as towards the Albanians of Macedonia, seems torn between maintaining the status quo in Kosovo with a heavy hand and provoking the Albanians into an uprising which in turn would justify a 'final solution' of the problem. Serbia can count on Greek support for almost any conceivable action which might be taken against the Albanians. The problem for Macedonia would be that her own Albanians would probably be drawn into any race war in Kosovo and this would draw in the Greeks who might try to dismember Macedonia at the same time, if only by offering Bulgaria inducements in the form of titbits of Macedonian territory.

Just as the Kosovo problem lay at the start of the unravelling of the Yugoslav Federation, so the long-awaited explosion there could shatter the only republic (apart from Slovenia) to have preserved, despite the war, its original pre–1991 borders, now as a sovereign if fragile state. The tragedy for Macedonia is probably that it will not be granted the breathing space necessary for the new state to develop before separatist and aggressive tendencies tear it apart too. Whether the Macedonian majority will continue to feel 'Macedonian' if that happens or seek shelter in somebody else's identity remains to be seen. However, recent history suggests that new national identities may be modern formations but they quickly develop a life of their own even if the new state fails to survive.

Serbia has never faced much of a problem with the members of one of Europe's oldest continuous states now living within its boundaries. The Hungarian minority in the Vojvodina used to belong to the elite race of the Crownlands of St Stephen until the collapse of the Dual Monarchy in 1918. Disgruntled before the Second World War and glad to be reincorporated into Horthy's Hungary in 1941, after Tito's victory the Hungarian minority in the Vojvodina never seem to have seriously entertained the idea of seeking reunification with Hungary herself.[36]

If the Hungarians in the Vojvodina have not posed a problem to Serbia, the Serb regime has increasingly been a source of trouble to them. For one thing, Hungarian lack of ambition to reunite with Hungary may be genuine – after all, there are too few Hungarians, 20 per cent of the province's population, to make revolt viable and Hungary herself is much weaker than Serbia and surrounded by suspicious neighbours. But of course to the men who stirred up the Krajina and set Bosnians at each others' throats, the Hungarian minority looks like exactly the sort of issue which they could set ablaze if they were the rulers in Budapest. The Hungarian minority in the Vojvodina can be as law-abiding as it may choose, it cannot alter the fact that its very existence is a defiance to the logic of the ethnic cleansers who rule them.

Possession of Vojvodina, like Kosovo, is not just an ideological imperative for Belgrade. Whatever national myths justify control of these territories, they also have great economic value for the

Serbian regime. The poverty of Kosovo should not disguise the fact that it possesses considerable mineral wealth. Non-ferrous metals do not excite much public interest and their extraction and refinement disfigures the Blackbird Field, but by ruling Kosovo Serbia keeps control of a significant and rare asset.

The agricultural fertility of the Vojvodina makes continuing control of the province essential to a regime facing international sanctions, however ineffective. It is food from the Vojvodina which helps to feed the war effort elsewhere. The efficiency of Hungarian farmers is more valuable than ever in wartime, but it is precisely in the tense atmosphere of war that the more hysterical nationalists seek to displace the non-Serbs in the province and bring in 'ethnically pure' if more primitive farmers from the south and west.

Milošević's regime faces the tensions between its own rational if ruthless interests and the ghosts of ethnic cleansing which it has summoned up and loosed on the country. The myth of Kosovo enshrines the cult of self-destruction and even cynical exploiters of it may be drawn into its logic and not be able to avoid the tendency to go step by step towards its own doom. Its very resonance with opponents of Milošević like Vuk Drasković might tempt the Serbian president down that path hoping once again to fracture his opponents by stealing their nationalist thunder. Given the West's very public assurances that it could not accept a Serb onslaught against the mass of the Albanian population, even if the Serb forces were able to use their massive military superiority against the Kosovars, such an operation might precipitate long-threatened American-led intervention or at least open assistance to the Albanians from outside the country. Tsar Lazar might not be the last Serbian ruler to fall over Kosovo. Victory in a second Battle of Kosovo could prove as elusive as in 1389.

PART THREE:

War

The outbreak of war on the territory of Yugoslavia produced an unprecedented flurry of international peace-mediators. The wars in ex-Yugoslavia at the military level were marked by a reversion to crude battlefield tactics as well as primitive savagery towards captured combatants and civilians alike. Only in the field of international interference could anything new be detected: a host of EC, UN and other international organisations sent out an unparalleled array of cease-fire monitors, peace-mediators, humanitarian helpers and the like, but with no effect on the killing. The contrast between the actual conduct of the war, which was cruelly purposeful and effective, and the meandering self-importance, shabby hypocrisy and moral cowardice of the representatives of the international community was the most striking feature of this first post-Cold War war in Europe.

10

The War in Croatia, 1991–92

Serbia has no pretensions to territory of other republics.

Slobodan Milošević[1]

The fighting in Slovenia turned out to be a ten-day wonder. It taught the JNA that the old Yugoslavia could no longer be held together. However, another lesson was taught by the Slovene 'war'. A Serb-led army could rely on the divisions among the republics to prevent the different ethnic groups ganging up against it. Even if it had failed to defeat Slovenia, it was not at all clear that any of the other republics had learned how to defeat the JNA. Their passive response to the JNA's bungled operation to seize Slovenia's border crossings was an ill omen. Few of Serbia's neighbours understood the ironic imperative of any successful secession from the Federative Socialist Republic of Yugoslavia: they had to act in unison. The failure of the Croatian government to intervene on the side of the Slovenes was a testament to its caution, its unwillingness to risk human life and even its preparedness at the twenty-fourth hour to negotiate some sort of future for Yugoslavia. It was not a testament to President Tudjman's foresight.

Despite the fact that Tudjman's Croatia had indeed declared independence at the same time as Slovenia, and the incessant insistence of the Serb-based media that under German and Vatican influence he was bent on the immediate and total destruction of Yugoslavia, the government in Zagreb had shown willingness to compromise and avoid bloodshed. Despite the evidence of bitter hostility among ordinary Croats to attempts to move JNA forces through Croatia to attack Slovenia after 26 June, Tudjman's government resisted the pressures to side with the Slovenes.

Already the JNA had shown itself far from neutral in the violent incidents which had taken place in Croatia between Serbs and Croats since the victory of Tudjman's HDZ in May 1990. It would have been wiser for Croatia not to have waited until it was the victim of a Serb attack. Certainly, Tudjman's restraint won him no brownie points from the EC or its mediators.

For all Tudjman's bombast on the electioneering trail, he proved remarkably acquiescent when Kadijević's ministry had demanded that Croatia turn over weapons belonging to the local territorial defence and even the police force in the spring of 1991. Large quantities of automatic rifles, but more importantly mortars and artillery pieces were handed over to the JNA along with anti-tank missiles and other sophisticated equipment, which could have played a decisive role in defeating an armoured attack on the republic. Unlike Croatia, Slovenia had frustrated the JNA's efforts to disarm that republic at the same time.[2]

Whether the Croats handed over all the arms available to them must be doubted, but the loss of two hundred thousand infantry weapons was not an insignificant reduction in the republic's capacity to defend itself. Over the next few months, it became increasingly clear that JNA and other Serb-dominated security services were stirring up trouble among the Serb minority in Croatia, especially in the two areas with Serb-speaking majorities, the Krajina south of Zagreb and in eastern Slavonia bordering Serb territory in the north-east.

Although Tudjman himself spoke optimistically about 'Europe' not allowing the JNA or Belgrade to use force against Croatia even after the fighting in Slovenia, some members of his government made contingency plans. In the run-up to the crisis, Belgrade television made relentless use of grainy film of the Croat defence minister, Martin Spegelj, in a beery smoke-filled backroom apparently conspiring some form of violent attack on communist and JNA officials to show that the Croatian government was plotting a massive and sinister attack on Serbs and the army. This film was first shown in January 1991, and in practice much of the armament available to the Croatian police and National Guard was handed over after this film was shot, so it suggests that any wild schemes for a Croat rising were abandoned before the JNA's intelligence service released it to the public.

Whether the bugging of Spegelj produced an authentic account of this infamous meeting remains fiercely debated – even among Croats. Even if it were true that Spegelj and his boozy friends were cooking up some kind of scheme, it soon became apparent that the local Serb militias and the JNA were also prepared to take the military initiative. In fact, whatever the truth of the allegations against Spegelj they served a classic propaganda purpose: the Croats were accused of planning to launch the very kind of military offensive and ethnic cleansing which the Serb forces were about to embark on.[3]

Even before the fighting began in Slovenia, local Serb forces backed by the JNA and other Yugoslav security agencies had begun to dislodge the police and other authorities loyal to the Tudjman government. Soon after the victory of Tudjman's HDZ in the May 1990 elections, violent incidents took place, especially in the Krajina and even in coastal towns below that mountainous region. Violent incidents in places like Split were striking, because although there were Serbs resident there, much of the evidence pointed to outside trouble-makers coming into coastal towns both to assert their Serbianness, to intimidate Croats, and to frighten off lucrative tourists.

In Dalmatia, the Serb minority was small and largely the product of recent migration to take advantage of the economic opportunities there. Similarly, big ports like Rijeka and Pula with their dockyards and naval presence had Serb minorities, but of recent origin. The Krajina was different. Eleven of its communes had large Serb majorities. (In eastern Slavonia, too, there were places with clear Serb majorities, but also many areas or individual villages with Croat, or even Hungarian and Czech absolute majorities.)

The Krajina or border region had developed out of the struggle between Christian and Turk. From the mid-sixteenth century, the border between the Ottoman Empire and Croatia, which had fallen to the Habsburgs, like the remnants of Hungary after 1526, had remained broadly static, even if the scene of raids and constant insecurity for at least two centuries more. The devastated area was repopulated largely with Orthodox believers who had trecked out of the Ottoman Empire. They provided a military-peasant community to defend the border region. So useful were they to the Habsburgs, that their normally fierce counter-reformation zeal to convert everyone in their power to Catholicism was tempered by prudence.

The exact ethnic origin of the Krajina Serbs is much disputed. Nowadays, it would be foolhardy in the extreme to suggest in Knin that they were descended from Serbianised Vlachs; only a pure Serbian origin (whatever that may be) will do. In any case, what matters is the insistence of the locals on their Serb identity. At first, in the aftermath of Tudjman's election victory, it seems that the bulk of the Krajina Serbs accepted the propaganda picture of his government as the wartime Pavelić regime restored. The bulk of Serbs living in Croatia (more than 75 per cent were resident outside the Krajina) seem to have been less alarmed, but many of them were postwar arrivals from other parts of Yugoslavia and so had less easily aroused local wartime nightmares. The Krajina had been the scene of some of the Ustasha state's worst atrocities.

The restoration of the traditional red-and-white chequerboard flag of Croatia, the sahovnica, was a natural step for newly democratic Croatia. Everywhere in eastern Europe, the red stars and other symbols of the communist order were being scrapped in preference for older, more historically legitimate symbols of statehood. What seemed natural to Croats was easily taken as a threat by the Krajina Serbs because of Pavelić's use of Croatian national symbols to cloak his own regime with some legitimacy.

At first, the Krajina Serbs chose to stick to Titoite symbols as their identity. Into 1991, red stars were proudly worn on the caps and helmets of the local militias which sprang up, fostered of course by the JNA and the local communists defeated in the May 1990 elections. In Serbia itself, the nationalist anti-Croat or anti-Albanian style was all self-consciously Chetnik. In the Krajina, the Partisan myth was still strong. Before the twentieth century, there had of course been Chetnik bands in the region, but when it came to the choice between Mihailović and the communists, the local Serbs had proved much less Chetnik than subsequent myth-makers would have liked. Eventually, Chetnik chic won out in Krajina too, though its roots there were pre-Mihailović.

The flaunting of communist/Titoite flags and symbols also

made local sense, since an immediate effect of Tudjman's victory was a widespread purge of Serb communists from public office, particularly in the local security forces which they had dominated. Naturally, the new jobless rallied to the flag which had cost them their employment and hoped that still powerful Serb-Yugoslav forces would restore them to power and privilege. The existence of a mountainous and recalcitrant region like the Krajina suited them well.[4]

Attempts by the new boys in the Croatian police and nascent National Guard to assert their authority misfired badly. They were easily provoked and poorly organised when push came to shove. Some Serbs enjoyed rattling them with the odd volley of shots from a safe distance. Violent incidents around Krajina were fostered by the largely self-proclaimed leadership of the Krajina Serbs as it moved openly towards secession. Milan Babić, the local boss, was a dentist and black-marketeer turned patriot. At the time it was normal to ridicule his pretensions, but soon enough he was to seem typical of a certain post-communist breed of local politician. With folk-memories of Ustasha violence easily aroused, in 1990–91 Babić's demand that the Serbs of Krajina should decide their own future and should not be separated from a Yugoslavia containing Serbia proper probably had general support in the region, but as the fighting went on and corruption and arbitrariness became the norm in Krajina, there was a drift of Serbs away from the region. These people were refugees not from the Croats but from the reality of a policy defining as Serbia wherever Serbs lived.

Although Krajina was as near to a compact ethnic territory as was likely to be found in the overlapping intermingling of peoples where religions and dialects of Serbo-Croat met, it was also an island of Serbs surrounded by Croats and Muslims (in neighbouring Bosnia). So long as Federal Yugoslavia existed, it was possible for the JNA and KOS to give direct aid to the Krajina Serbs to promote the disruption of Croatia, but in the event of war it would be more difficult to send aid direct from Serbia. Slavonia, on the other hand, bordered Serbia directly.

The population mix in eastern Slavonia was much less clear-cut than in Krajina. Its major cities, Vukovar and Osijek, contained significant Serb minorities. These were less easy to stir up than solidly Serb areas in Krajina or Serb villages along the Danube. In May 1991, the village of Borovo Selo was shaken by savage violence. Although the Serbs, including those in Belgrade, claimed the overwhelmingly Serb village was attacked by the Croatian police, the balance of casualties suggests otherwise.

Borovo Selo was one of the places in which a local Serb defence force had been established. On May Day, two Croatian police cars visited the village after dark. As a finale to their celebrations of the workers' holiday, someone opened fire on them. They fled. The next day, a police bus came back to Borovo Selo accompanied by the undamaged car from the night before. When the police reached the centre of Borovo Selo, they came under fire. Twelve Croats and three Serbs were killed in the ensuing gunfight. Three of the dead Croatian policemen were savagely mutilated. If it was a victory over the Ustasha, it was not without a certain similarity with Pavelić's methods.

The slaughter of Croatian policemen naturally both alarmed ordinary Croats and created a wave of protests demanding the punishment of their murderers. The radicalisation of Serbs was only one purpose of the violence promoted from Belgrade. It was also necessary to promote extremism among the Croats. A classic purpose of propaganda as well as political action is to turn one's designated enemy into what it has been claimed he was all along. Random and brutal attacks on Croatian officials were intended to force Serbs to take sides with the Serbs committing the violence but also to promote a fascist response among Croats which had been lacking thus far. If Belgrade's propaganda machine depicted the Serbs of Croatia as being the victims of a renewed fascism, it would help if there were real Croat fascists on hand to back up the story.[5]

If the Serbs made capital out of fears of revived Croatian fascism, the would-be Croat fascists themselves proved sparse on the ground. The chances of a seizure of power by Dobroslav Paraga's Party of Rights (HOS) were constantly written up in the Western press but Croats showed less enthusiasm for him than the hacks looking to recycle the old story of Croat fascism.

Having abandoned his previous stance as an advocate of human rights (in which he mirrored his more successful Serb counterpart, Šešelj), Paraga liked to posture surrounded by paramilitary guards and once the serious fighting began the HOS proudly announced its dispatch of volunteers to the front. It may even be that its claims that HOS members distinguished themselves by their peculiar courage were not without foundation, though they were usually put in an unconvincingly grandiose way: braggadocio and bravery rarely go hand in hand. In any case, the only thing that Paraga and his opponents were agreed upon was the inflation of the numbers of his supporters and their activity at the front.

So long as the fighting against the JNA and its allies was the main task, the Croat government and the official defence forces, the HVO, cooperated with the HOS troops and even put up with their grabbing of the headlines and insubordination. Ultimately, however, Tudjman moved to suppress the independence of the HOS volunteers and to integrate them into the HVO while also acting to stifle Paraga's activities as a politician. As with so many of Tudjman's actions, in the eyes of the West he could never get things right. So long as Paraga was allowed free rein, the Croatian government was accused of turning a blind eye to an openly fascistic demagogue, but once he had been charged with various transgressions and his movement effectively silenced, Tudjman was accused by his professional critics of suppressing free speech.[6] However, all that lay in the future. As we have seen, the West Europeans had difficulty grasping that the violent incidents in remote parts of what was still Yugoslavia could have any great significance.

It was only the direct intervention of the JNA in Slovenia which began to break down the EC's complacency. Even after that, the Brioni Agreement on 7 July was taken as a sign that the Slovene war had been a perverse exception to the general rule that diplomacy particularly under the influence of the affluent West would calm any irrational tendencies towards violence. In fact, Slovenia was just a prelude (as the war in Croatia was to be to the struggle in Bosnia). By cutting its losses in Slovenia, the JNA was able to concentrate on what many of its officers saw as the old enemy, Croatia. At the same time, it was easier to coordinate the activities of the JNA and the Serb militias now that they had a common goal to thwart Croatian independence.

Throughout July and into August, a form of low casualty shadow-boxing went on in the border regions of Croatia as the

Serbs asserted themselves and pushed out Croatian policemen from both the fringes of Krajina and eastern Slavonia. One eye was still fixed on the West. Neither Belgrade nor the JNA, let alone the local Serb leaders, could be certain how the European Community countries would react to an open, all-out war against Croatia. Meetings in Belgrade and on Brioni must have helped give the Serbs the measure of the guardians of the new Europe. They were paper tigers. Looking further west, Bush and Baker gave no sign that even after the Brioni Agreement (7 July) would the USA be prepared to recognise the break-up of Yugoslavia. It took another nine months and more than ten thousand dead to persuade Washington to recognise the independence of the breakaway republics.

During this period, and for a long time afterwards, the JNA insisted that its forces were simply trying to maintain the peace whenever they opened fire on the Croats. However, the fact that the JNA moved to occupy strategic points, such as the bridges across the Danube linking Serbia with Slavonia, suggested that it was preparing to pour aid into the hands of the Serb militias and to deploy its forces there too. Milošević too denied that his government had anything to do with the 'civil war' in Croatia.

Just as later in Bosnia the Serbian government vehemently denied all connection with the fighting while all along supplying and giving strategic guidance to the local Serb forces, the tactic was refined during the fighting in Croatia. It meant that Mr Milošević could play the injured innocent when asked to Lord Carrington's peace conferences while ensuring that the local warlords did not get out of his hands. Once he had achieved his basic goal of establishing Serb-controlled puppet states in Krajina and eastern Slavonia in Croatia, Milošević dropped his claims to have had nothing to do with the war. At the end of February 1992, he told journalists that Serbia had helped in the war, 'first economically and politically . . . but finally, when all this proved insufficient, with arms'. Of course, the actual chronology of aid was reversed: the Serb authorities and JNA supplied arms to begin with, only later giving open political support and then providing economic aid to the embattled regions.

During the war, Milošević also took an increasingly important role in directing military actions. At first, the strategy and tactics of the war were left to the JNA and local commanders, but they proved slow-moving and slow-witted in their approach. Caution cost the JNA any chance of a *Blitzkrieg* against the ill-armed Croats. Learning the wrong lesson of the failure of its tanks to intimidate the Slovenes, Kadijević and Adzić moved ponderously to prepare a combined armour, artillery and infantry assault on Croatia. The failure of their strategy and its counterproductive effects on international opinion led Milošević to intervene in military decision-making.

After his fall from even the shadow of power, the last Federal Premier, Ante Marković, released tape-recordings of Milošević ordering the Yugoslav Air Force not to engage in bombing on a particular day because it would clash with a meeting of the EC. Even Milošević took a while to get the full measure of the impotence of the EC and felt the need to restrain his less politically sensitive generals from committing an atrocity which might influence the West Europeans to take action. Ironically, the EC had far more potential influence than it knew and Milošević's caution about its response encouraged him to purge the JNA leadership. Of course, this also strengthened his control over the armed forces, making any political threat to his power less likely.[7]

The Western elite's summer holidays resumed with the Balkan bushfire apparently extinguished. Meanwhile events in Moscow were moving towards their farcical climax with the coup of 19 August. Certainly, Kadijević and the JNA hardliners had looked to the Red Army to guarantee Yugoslavia against any NATO attempt to impose a peace settlement or to support Slovenia or Croatia. But Bush's slap in the face to separatists in the Soviet Union delivered in Kiev a few weeks earlier must have encouraged them to think – even after the de facto collapse of the Soviet Union with the failure of the Moscow coup – that the United States would still not back the separatists. Milošević was shrewder in his dealings with Moscow and avoided publicly nailing his colours to the hardline mast. Belgrade put a lot of effort into massaging its relationship with the new men in the Kremlin even before Yeltsin formally usurped Gorbachev's functions at the end of December 1991. But July and August was a time of prodding and testing Western resolve by the JNA. It was soon found wanting.

It was most inconvenient for Western political leaders that the Yugoslav crisis should have grown in seriousness during the summer vacation season. In 1990, Saddam's invasion of Kuwait had cut short many a well-earned rest. Now, the Balkans threatened to interrupt their leisure. (By 1992 interrupted summer holidays had become almost routine – though Mr Major made his irritation clear when he had to interrupt a visit to the Barcelona Olympics in order to dampen down demands for action over the Bosnian crisis.) The best opportunity for Western intervention passed hardly noticed in the capitals of the holidaying democracies in August 1991. President Bush and his EC allies had resolutely set their faces against acknowledging Slovene and Croat demands for independence for fear of setting a bad example to the Soviet peoples. Suddenly on 19 August, they were aroused from their slumbers to be told that Gorbachev was no more and the hardliners in power. Even in this crisis, clearly of world importance, they wobbled. It was only *after* it became clear that Boris Yeltsin was not under arrest too and was mobilising opposition to the putsch that the Bushes, Majors and the rest began to issue clarion calls to defend democracy – though not before President Mitterrand had managed to pen a message to 'Cher M. Yanaev'.

In the days and weeks after the collapse of the coup it became clear that the Soviet Union itself was falling apart. Instead of taking firm steps to resolve the Yugoslav crisis while the Belgrade leadership was uncertain of Moscow's stance and aware that its natural supporters there were under arrest, the NATO leaders prided themselves on their resolution and congratulated themselves on their bloodless victory in the Cold War. All the time the war in NATO's backyard was gathering pace.

Unarmed EC monitors, quickly dubbed the 'icecream-men' because of their absurd white uniforms, had been deployed after the Brioni Agreement, but at first only in Slovenia where the fighting had stopped. As it spread in Croatia, even the Zagreb-based monitors could not avoid its implications. As early as 16 August, an EC helicopter was hit by gunfire. It was a sign that the combatants, particularly the Serbs, were no respecters of self-important international institutions. (They were also no respecters of the international media: as the war went on across ex-Yugoslavia, journalists and particularly press photographers became favourite victims of snipers. Serb forces regarded the Western media as enemy propagandists because they reported what went on, and therefore fair game.)[8]

Belatedly in September 1991, first the EC then the UN imposed an arms embargo on former Yugoslavia. It was the first sign that the 'international community' was in effect backing the Serb side, since the JNA controlled the arms stockpiles and most of the weapons-making capacity of ex-Yugoslavia. There were loopholes, but the Serb cries that only the Croats were smuggling arms proved wrong. Swedish weapons and spare parts continued to reach Serbia.

The Croats, aided by their émigrés and taking advantage of the ex-Warsaw Pact weapons washing around Central Europe, were able to import large quantities of firearms and ammunition. Unlike the Bosnians the following year, the Croats had the advantage of extensive international frontiers and a long coastline. However, probably the most significant source of weapons for the fledgling Croatian Army came from the JNA itself. Some Croats still in the JNA deserted, bringing their equipment with them, as it became clear that their commanders intended to use them to fight their fellow Croats. But the main source of weapons came from blockaded JNA barracks and stores in Croatia.

In some places, local people had already blocked the exits of JNA garrisons at the time of the Slovenian fighting. This became a regularised tactic as the summer progressed. The JNA command claimed that the (largely non-violent) sieges of their bases justified their intervention in Croatia in order to protect servicemen, but without the JNA's earlier actions and clear intentions, the blockades would not have started. Although ultimately in October 1991, Lord Carrington was able to achieve one of his few successes by persuading both sides to accept an end to the 'war of the barracks', in practice by then the JNA had destroyed any military equipment remaining in the barracks still held by its troops and the Croats were satisfied with the contents of the fifteen bases which had surrendered.

Elsewhere the war was hotting up. Whereas most of the blockaded JNA bases lay deep inside Croatia, the main fighting was taking place along its borders as JNA forces crossed into the republic in battle formation from Serbia and still-Yugoslav Bosnia. The JNA was still confident that its existing resources would flatten Croat opposition and end the war.

On 20 September, an enormous convoy of JNA tanks began to move against Sid in Slavonia. Despite its massive superiority, it soon became clear that the motivation of the JNA rank and file was low. From its height under Tito, the JNA had declined in size by 1991 to a standing army of about 150,000. Already in March 1991, Slovenia refused to permit its young men to be conscripted. Croats and other non-Serbs were increasingly avoiding military service. Even young Serbs, especially from Belgrade, were unwilling to do their time in Tito's '9th federal unit'.

Lenin had a dictum: 'Better fewer, but better.' In its own way, the Serbified JNA had learnt Lenin's lesson. What mattered was the quality as much as the quantity. Reliability was more important than skill. One mortar-operator willing to shoot from a safe distance at civilians and ill-armed militiamen was worth more than half a dozen unreliable and unwilling conscripts who might in the crunch either run away and create a gap in the line or, worse, side with the army's enemies.

In the 1980s, the JNA had suffered from the general economic decay of Yugoslavia. Its share of the Federal budget sank from about 70 to 50 per cent. Its strength fell from 220,000 to the roughly 150,000 men in arms it could boast in 1991. However, Tito's vast array of weapons factories and arsenals had survived him. Yugoslavia was a major arms exporter before 1991 and the JNA directly supervised production and sale of weapons abroad. As with other communist armies – in China, for instance – the interweaving of the People's Army with the arms trade was a key feature of Yugoslavia's export drive.

Although Tito and his successors had built up an enormous stockpile of weapons and ammunition in order to provide for resistance to any foreign invasion, in practice during the war after June 1991, the JNA and its surrogate militias did not call upon the full arsenal by any means. On the contrary, arms exports were used to pay for hard currency imports like oil and luxuries for Milošević loyalists.[9]

Despite Yugoslavia's much-vaunted 'non-aligned status', Soviet arms imports provided the vast bulk of the high-tech weaponry which Belgrade could not manufacture for herself. In the event, the Mig–29 fighters which Yugoslavia had received before any of the Kremlin's Warsaw Pact allies and the T–72 tanks built under licence from the USSR played little part in the fighting. Against lightly armed Croatian militiamen the Mig–29 was little use and even tank crews proved reluctant to risk falling foul of mines or daring attacks and in practice the JNA's armour restricted itself to the role of mobile artillery rather than as a battering ram making the way clear for rapid advances.

Oddly enough, Western governments and their observers on the spot do not seem to have shared the local estimate of the low morale and fighting quality of the JNA in 1991. Despite clear evidence of its inability to turn its superior firepower into a decisive war-winning weapon, and the unwillingness of the Serb infantry to go in for the kill even in battered Vukovar after weeks of bombardment, Western governments silenced the already growing demands for intervention in the late summer and autumn of 1991 by conjuring up the historical myth of the invincible Serbian peasant soldier in fighting doggedly for his own home.[10]

Despite the timidity of NATO top brass and their 'expert' advisers, the whole experience of warfare since the end of the Cold War has cast serious doubt on the fighting capacity of Soviet-type armies and their weapons. Certainly, from Krajina to Tadjikistan, Soviet weaponry has proved deadly against civilians but in Iraq and in Yugoslavia, the weaponry and proficiency of forces largely trained and equipped on the Soviet model have proved very ineffective against even less well-equipped but determined opponents, let alone professional NATO forces.

The fiasco of the JNA's armoured thrust in September 1991 was made worse by the defiant resistance of the garrison of the Danube port-city of Vukovar. Given its strategic location, Vukovar had been an object of Serb-JNA assault from August onwards. Although the besieging forces were able to capture much of the town by late September, a key sector in the west held out until 18 November. Vukovar was stylised as the Croatian Stalingrad. That may have been too grandiose a title, but certainly the cost in blood and ammunition of taking the city ended any optimism about conquering Croatia in the JNA.

Vukovar was defended largely by a local militia of about 5000 men. It was besieged by a JNA and Serb irregular force of up to 40,000 men. Artillery was used to level Vukovar. Stories about the fanatic determination of the Serbian Chetniks were not matched by the reality. The Serbian forces avoided hand-to-hand fighting relying instead on a slow but steady battering by cannon and mortar to shatter the Croat defences.

Many Croats, and not just locals from Vukovar, felt that the government in Zagreb did not do enough to relieve the city. It is possible that in autumn 1991 Tudjman's government still had its eye on an expected Western intervention and thought that the savage bombardment of Vukovar from land and air would arouse Western opinion. (The concurrent attacks on Dubrovnik were beginning to concern the Western press at any rate.) The obvious disparity in firepower between Croat and Serb ought to have rallied international support to the underdog.

On the other hand, the Croatian government probably recognised that its own forces lacked the tanks and artillery to break the siege. The Serb guns would have turned on any relief force, which would have to approach across the flat, open land of Slavonia rather than using the ruins of the city as cover, as the defenders were able to. Whatever the reason for the failure to rescue Vukovar, its fall was not a complete disaster for the Croat cause. The long resistance had blunted the Serbian war effort.

However, the conquest of Vukovar was accompanied by the clearest evidence of a practice which was typical of the Serbian war effort. 'Ethnic cleansing' was an old Balkan concept, but new to the comfortably multicultural West Europeans. Only when television pictures were shown, not only of columns of the surviving defenders of Vukovar being marched off to an obscure fate, but also of Croatian civilians, women and old men predominantly, equally disappearing under Serb guard, did many Westerners realise that the war was not just about conquering territory but also about removing its unwelcome peoples.[11]

Elsewhere direct terror frequently inflicted by bands of 'volunteers' up for the weekend from Serbia or Montenegro, caused people to flee their homes, once a few exemplary acts of brutality had made the point. In other places, which the sinister Chetniks and other militias could not reach without too much risk to themselves, artillery and aerial bombardment encouraged Croats to 'cleanse' the area themselves before Serb forces arrived.

There were a hundred thousand refugees in Croatia by the end of August 1991. The figure would never stop rising. Serbs in Croatia well away from the contested area began to leave the republic in turn and go to Serbia. In the atmosphere of crisis, Serbs could easily be accused of acting as a fifth column for Belgrade, though in fact it was remarkable how little anti-Croatian terrorism or subversion of any kind, took place among the Serb communities in cities like Zagreb where most Croatian Serbs lived. At no time was Zagreb like Belfast.

If the sinister pictures of the aftermath of the fall of Vukovar shocked Western public opinion, they had less effect on their governments. Massacres were alleged and gunshots heard by the journalists. Months later mass graves were discovered. The EC could not decide who was in them. Despite the atrocities committed during the fighting, little Western attention was aroused because it took place away from the cameras, usually after Serbian capture of a town when the victims could be both killed and then disappeared. Western governments and their intelligence agencies were of course better informed than the international press or public but they were also anxious to avoid inflaming the atmosphere by revealing their inconvenient knowledge. This approach had a long tradition.[12]

In Bosnia, either self-confidence or stupidity, perhaps both, led the local Serbs to permit television cameras into detention camps. The JNA officers supervising the treatment of prisoners did not make that mistake. Although the bulk of those massacred by Serbs after their victory were killed by irregulars, without the connivance of the JNA's leadership their fate would have been less anonymous and perhaps the example of their murder would have stirred an international reaction like the one which followed nine months later when the Bosnian Serbs flaunted their mistreatment of prisoners before the international media (albeit with minimal response).

Two years later, it suited Milošević to discredit some of the hardmen leading the militias or even standing on the sidelines in JNA uniforms. In January 1994, to the embarrassment of Western governments who had shown no enthusiasm for pursuing war criminals despite high-sounding UN resolutions, Belgrade suddenly began to point the finger of blame and to admit that atrocities had taken place after the fall of Vukovar.

It was a harsh reflection on the West's sensitivities that the savage destruction of Vukovar aroused much less concern among opinion-makers than the threat to Dubrovnik, the 'pearl of the Adriatic'. By October 1991, the Western media were reporting daily on the Serb bombardment of ancient Ragusa. Aficionados in the press back in London worried more about the fate of the Titian *Assumption* than casualties among the local people and the flood of refugees from the Dalmatian hinterland.[13]

Although the old city of Dubrovnik itself was relatively unscathed by Serb-Montenegrin bombardment, its suburbs where most of its people had lived and where its tourist hotels were largely located had been destroyed and frequently looted by the enemy. Everyday life in the city was also made extremely difficult not only by the hazards of enemy fire but also by the shortages and irregular supply of daily essentials. If the siege of Dubrovnik lacked the full horrors of Vukovar or Sarajevo after it, it should nonetheless not be downgraded just because the old buildings largely survived after all.

The Serb attack upon the Dalmatian coast was clearly aimed at Croatia's economy and her heritage, since her chief source of hard currency, the Dalmatian beaches, was next to the glories of her heritage, the towns along the Adriatic coast, which occasionally the tourists came up from the beach to see. Destroying or damaging a Šibenik cathedral discouraged tourism certainly, but the Serbs' campaign went further. It was an attempt to destroy what they did not have.

The Renaissance towns along the coast were the epitome of the historical differences between Serb and Croat. Catholic cathedrals and church spires were natural targets for bored gunners, but there was the added spice that they symbolised the cultural difference between the two sides. It may well be that the ex-communists in charge of the Serb war effort saw Catholic buildings as symbols of their old enemy, religion, but it was an appeal to the half-remembered ancient religious antagonisms which probably appealed to the ordinary foot-soldiers in their war. Also simple primitive vandalistic urges were unleashed by the war. The legacy of more than four hundred bombed-out or burnt-down churches will stand as poisonous symbols. The same forces went on to destroy mosques in Bosnia with similar glee and the same result.

Only one attack on historical buildings had a military or political purpose. On 7 October, the Yugoslav Air Force bombed the historic upper city in Zagreb, badly damaging the Presidential Palace. At the time President Tudjman was negotiating with Ante Marković. Somebody clearly wanted to kill two birds with one stone. They missed but blew away much of the infuriating chequerboard roof on St Mark's church.[14]

For all its destructiveness, the Croat-Serb war was not as bloody as the physical damage inflicted might have suggested. Of course, it was deadly enough. About 14,000 people were killed, but thousands of others, mainly Croats, disappeared unaccounted for. Their graves are slowly coming to light. It is not difficult to predict that the mass graves of 1991 will most likely be as insidious a legacy among Croats as the unquiet dead of 1941 were among Serbs.

But by the end of 1991, both sides had fought themselves to a standstill. Neither wanted to inflict the kind of casualties which prolonged trench warfare and infantry assaults would surely lead to. The Serbs were certainly aware that nationalist fervour was sustained only by low casualties. Draft-dodging in Serbia and the emigration from Krajina and Slavonia of disillusioned Serbs encouraged Milošević to accept the UN mediator Cyrus Vance's terms, which favoured the status quo brought about since June. The Croats could expect little foreign help if they refused 'peace', and needed a breathing space to organise their state and its armed forces.

During the serious fighting which presented a clear threat to Croatia's existence, there was a general political truce inside Croatia, which may have been exploited by more far-sighted members of the HDZ to entrench themselves in positions of influence. But the end of the formal war after January 1992 – even if by no means of daily gunfire and mortar bombardments across the cease-fire lines – put Tudjman's government in the position of having to face uncomfortable criticisms about its conduct of the war. Tudjman proved unhappy with the idea of criticism, let alone its practice, but despite his personal popularity, questions about why Croatia had been so apparently ill-prepared for war and how places like Vukovar came to fall remained unanswered, though persistent.

Later on, in 1993, it became clear that Tudjman's government was uneasy about press criticism of its growing involvement in the fighting between Croats and Muslims in Bosnia and that through a variety of measures it was moving to gag vociferous critics or even to conscript them into the front line. Using the excuse of privatisation of state property, the HDZ managed to transfer many formerly state-owned media outlets into private concerns run by their supporters. In the dying days of communism, Croat journalists had become accustomed to almost complete press freedom, but now they found their new proprietors anxious to exercise influence and usually downright control over their editorial judgements.[15]

In retrospect, for all the natural scepticism about any political leader with a highly developed sense of his own destiny as national saviour, what was remarkable about the development of Croatia under Tudjman was that despite wartime conditions and the all too easily manipulated legacy of communism – including the opportunities for influence and corruption offered by the privatisation of state property – elections in which the opposition's votes were not miscounted or spirited away took place. In fact, although Tudjman himself retained the presidency easily when re-elected in 1993, the emergence of strong regional variations in voting suggested that in the long term a normal peacetime democracy could develop in Croatia; but as quasi-wartime conditions existed, the danger of internal dissension remained real. At first, the external threat from the JNA and Serbia might have pushed Croats together, but the fact that, after January 1992, their pressure was very differently felt around the republic undermined its unity. Despite the Vance Plan's high principles, in practice it left the Serb forces in control of the territory which they had occupied during the fighting, which posed a serious threat to the viability of Croatia and hence to long-term peace.

However, from the point of view of the international media, the war in Croatia came to an end with the acceptance of the Vance Plan. The details of the plan were hardly public before the growing disorder in Bosnia distracted attention from the Krajina and Slavonia. But the Vance Plan's weaknesses were to be repeated in Bosnia with more deadly results.

The deployment of the UN 'Blue Helmets' in between the opposing forces came as a welcome relief to the Serb generals as they contemplated the need to shift the focus of their war efforts into Bosnia. The UN forces acted as a buffer between Croats and Serbs. The international community could be relied upon to restrain any Croat move to recover territory, if only because the Blue Helmets would be caught in the middle.

A key part of the Vance Plan which had made it acceptable to the Croats was its emphasis on the need to reopen the communications inside Croatia. The Serb artillery in Knin had effectively split the republic in two from its mountainside positions only a few miles from the sea. The destruction of the road bridge at Maslenica linking the two halves of Croatia was a sore point. Despite assurances to the contrary, it was not brought back into service with the cease-fire.

Although Serb heavy weapons in the 'pink zones' monitored by UNPROFOR were put into store, the guns were neither spiked nor destroyed. As events turned out, in January 1993 they could easily be recovered by the Serbs and put back into service when the Croat Army occupied the Maslenica bridge area. This thin strip was strategically vital to Croatia since it was the only road-link between Zagreb and the bulk of Dalmatia. The latter area in turn was vital to any rapid recovery of the Croatian economy since its tourist potential offered the quickest way of gaining hard currency. Few tourists were likely to visit the area, however, despite the official cease-fire.[16]

Every day in 1993 somewhere along the thin strip of Croatian territory, bullets, artillery shells or mortar bombs whizzed across from the Serbian-held high land. The Serbs were being excessive in their efforts to remind the Croats of their vulnerability. Even a shell at monthly intervals on Zadar or Šibenik would have been enough to discourage foreign tourists and to satisfy the beggar-my-neighbour imperative behind the firing.

Against the background of the savagery and misery of Bosnia after April 1992, the daily exchange of fire across the pink zones between Serb and Croat naturally did not grab the headlines, but the state of 'no war, no peace' was inherently destabilising. However much Tudjman might countenance an adventure in Hercegovina as a way of compensating Croatia for her losses, in practice Dalmatians and many other Croats wanted strong action to relieve the daily pressure on the region.[17]

11

The Peacemakers

I labour for peace, but when I speak unto them thereof they make them ready to battle.

Psalm 120

The confident departure of Jacques Poos and his two colleagues, Gianni di Michelis and Hans van den Broek from Luxembourg at the end of June 1991 was the first of countless international interventions in the Yugoslav war. Rarely has there been so much peacemaking and so few survivors. In addition to the cost in terms of dead and wounded, Europe's backyard war inflicted terrible damage on the reputation of the West's statesmen. However, if the peacemakers failed to produce even the semblance of peace, they remained invincible in one respect: no matter how disastrous the consequences of their ill-thought-out and frequently high-handed interventions, nothing could shake their own self-esteem. The modern peace-mediator is invincibly proud of his achievements. After all, any failures are always the fault of the locals.

Even as the publics of their own countries came to despair of the endless relay of EC or UN or CSCE negotiators, mediators, cease-fire observers and spill-over monitors, no disaster seemed able to shake their pride in being the world's 'best and the brightest'. As late as March 1992, US ambassador Warren Zimmermann assured an audience in Belgrade (of all places), 'It is hard to find a more dedicated and more able group of international public servants than those who are devoting their talents to the problems of Yugoslavia.[1]

The assumption that the 'great and good' of the international community had only to bark and the squabbling Balkan tribes would stop their disruption of the peace marked the opening phase of the conflict. It was not just M. Poos who assumed that 'If there is one problem which the Europeans can solve, it is the Yugoslav problem.' The briefers at the EC Summit in Luxembourg worked overtime to get the message across that the crisis in Yugoslavia was auspicious and would permit the Community to put behind it any lingering shadows of its inept and divided response to the Gulf War six months earlier. The press repeated the up-beat briefings about the capacity of the Community to knock heads together in the Balkans. For instance, the BBC's John Simpson reported, 'The Community has a great deal of influence over Yugoslavia and over the governments of the two republics [Slovenia and Croatia].' Viewers were assured that the swift dispatch of the *troika* contrasted sharply with the dithering before Operation Desert Storm. 'It wasn't bad. Only six hours after the start of the summit, the Community had dispatched a diplomatic task-force to try and sort out the problems in the backyard.'[2]

The statesmen gathered at the Luxembourg Summit were 'cheerful', according to the BBC's John Cole, particularly because of the Community's successful rapid response to the Yugoslav crisis.[3] Only one European statesman did not share the euphoria at Luxembourg. Douglas Hurd was cautious about the likely success of European mediation. 'A solution cannot be imposed from outside.' The visible disintegration of Yugoslavia alarmed Hurd because he took for granted that what the Balkans needed was a heavy hand to maintain order: 'Yugoslavia was invented in 1919 to solve a problem of different peoples living in the same part of the Balkans with a long history of peoples fighting each other.' After the Second World War – incidentally, *pace* Hurd, the only time when the Yugoslav peoples had fought each other on their own account in recent times – communism had kept them from each others' throats until now. The future looked grim to the Foreign Secretary. It did not require too much perspicacity to see that Hurd did not see national independence for Slovenia or Croatia as a viable solution.[4]

Hurd even anticipated the brutal ethnic cleansing. For him, independence for Slovenia and Croatia meant 'you would have to move thousands and thousands of people and that doesn't happen peacefully and easily. The prospect is a frightening one.' Hurd insisted 'I don't deceive myself' and showed foresight about what was coming. Even as the fighting in Slovenia was still a straight confrontation between the JNA and the Slovene defence forces, the British foreign secretary saw the tidal wave of inter-communal violence already on the move. He expected primitive instincts to 'assert themselves', including the urge 'to drive people of a different tribe out of your village'. To add to this grim foreboding, Hurd warned that in 'Eastern Europe where these disputes have been frozen under communism' the inter-ethnic 'disputes' were bound to re-emerge, adding, 'Yugoslavia is not the only one.'

Hurd's rare foresight was matched unfortunately by defeatism. There was nothing the West could do to stop primitive brutality except talk, regardless of the sincerity of its interlocutors and the sufferings some of them were planning to inflict on other Yugoslavs. Repeatedly, Hurd predicted the Lebanonisation of Yugoslavia and then backed away from accepting any responsibility for halting the slide into chaos. 'The worst fear which we must struggle to avoid is Yugoslavia settling down into a chaos, fighting, a number of small statelets all bankrupt, all relying on the West in one way or another, trying to involve other countries in their fighting . . . We really ought to be able to do better than that and the European Community . . . acting together ought to try if we can to avert that . . .' But it would not be possible to use force. Instead the EC would use the 'economic screw'. But 'politics prevail over economics in these matters'. Hurd's conclusion was that negotiation must lead to some form of renewed Yugoslavia, acceptable to the very parties whose primitive passions he had just described.[5]

Even as the British Foreign Secretary was airing his doubts about the prospects of restoring peace, his EC colleagues in the *troika* were criss-crossing the battle zone from Ljubljana to Belgrade and Zagreb. Their key proposal was consistent with the Community's position before the outbreak of hostilities: the secessionist republics should accept a moratorium on independence while the JNA halted its operations so that Federal and Republican authorities could negotiate a reconstituted mutually acceptable Yugoslavia. The prime pressure was put on Slovenia and Croatia to compromise despite their previous experience of negotiations with Belgrade in the run-up to the outbreak of fighting, an experience which the EC ministers ignored. The two republics knew that international recognition was vital to their prospects of establishing viable states in the international economy, so they had little choice but to accept the EC's terms, particularly as the United States and Soviet Union were even less friendly.

The Brioni Agreement on 7 July was regarded as a triumph of European diplomacy, but in practice it was the result of Milošević's recognition that trying to keep Slovenia in Yugoslavia was more trouble than it was worth. The JNA had proved incompetent in its operations in Slovenia and therefore the non-Serb Yugo-federalists in its high command had lost their power to influence policy in Belgrade. Both Milošević and the JNA leadership could agree on the impossibility of permitting Croatian secession. It was important to buy time for the redeployment of forces against the Croats. While the EC was celebrating the *troika*'s successful mediation without the involvement of the Americans, the preparations for a real war were under way.

Many observers were surprised by the reluctance of the United States to get involved either directly through its excellent contacts in Belgrade or indirectly through the United Nations. Instead Washington seemed content to let the EC take centre stage. Some thought this was because the Americans believed that Europe had come of age and would be able to deal with the crisis. Others thought James Baker wanted to give the Twelve enough rope to hang their ambitions to act as a superpower equivalent of the USA, even in their own backyard. Certainly, two years on Baker drew the conclusion that Europe had failed and that without US leadership nothing could be achieved. By July 1993, the former Secretary of State could note with all the distance of an impartial observer, 'The sad story of European inaction on Bosnia reveals that *only American leadership* can bring Europe together on this issue.' It was a pity that Baker had not recognised as much two years earlier, though it should be remembered that he added a Hurd-like caveat to justify the long US inaction under his stewardship: 'That does not mean America should be the world's policeman.'[6]

The outside world resisted recognising the new reality inside Yugoslavia. Most member states of the UN face either active or potential separatists. Few enjoy full democracy and certainly even some of the democracies would not tolerate local majorities challenging the state's borders or sovereignty. It was hardly surprising therefore that many states at the UN opposed any kind of international intervention in Yugoslavia. There but for the grace of God went India, Zimbabwe or China. European countries faced challenges to their frontiers too. Italy had barely resolved the South Tyrol question with its German-speaking minority and was increasingly beset by the revolt of the Northern Leagues against the corruption of the centralised states, embodied in the portly figure of Foreign Minister Gianni di Michelis. In Corsica, for instance, the French government faced endemic terrorism by Corsican nationalists, so it was hardly surprising that Roland Dumas, Mitterrand's Foreign Minister, should declare 'It is not the role of the EC to promote the independence of peoples.'[7]

The dream of putting the South Slav Humpty-Dumpty back together again still lived on if only in Paris and Brussels, but as fighting spread in Croatia it became clear that the Community's united front would come under pressure from below. Public opinion began to doubt the wisdom of the EC's manoeuvrings, especially in Germany. Contrary to Serb propaganda assiduously repeated by French and British politicians and other Serbophiles, Kohl and Genscher had originally supported the EC's commitment to a united Yugoslavia. Genscher's telephone-diplomacy with Zagreb was intended to restrain the Croats from declaring independence. However, under the impact of television pictures from Croatia when Germans saw places with which they were familiar as holiday-makers under bombardment, public opinion in the newly united Germany began to make itself felt. After all, many Germans asked, if they themselves were entitled to self-determination, why should Slovenes and Croats be denied it?

For the first time in his career, Hans-Dietrich Genscher found his popularity waning as his public questioned the morality of the saintly figure in his trade-mark yellow pullover. Already in June, one of Genscher's sidelined rivals in the FDP, Martin Bangemann, the vice-president of the EC Commission, had publicly questioned the Twelve's dogmatic commitment to Yugoslav unity regardless of popular opinion:

> [We] should not conclude from the correct principle of non-intervention in the internal affairs of a state, that the united Yugoslav state should be preserved at any price . . . We ought to support the Yugoslav population, regardless of how they want to be ruled in the future . . . The EC should not exercise external influence on the evolutionary process only by offering help to a united Yugoslavia.[8]

Sensitive as ever to press criticism and public opinion, Chancellor Kohl began to edge away from the EC's consensus. But it was not Germany that decided what happened on the ground in Croatia. It was the growing Serb revolt in the Krajina and Slavonia openly backed by the JNA and its air force which made reconciliation impossible – as it was intended to.

Meanwhile the EC's *troika* continued on its task of mediation, oblivious to the harsh realities on the ground. Cease-fire monitors were dispatched in bright white uniforms and blue baseball caps with the Community's twelve stars on them to observe the cease-fire in Slovenia where the fighting had stopped before they arrived, but in Croatia they waited until the beginning of September before setting about monitoring the breakdown of successive cease-fires, though never pointing the finger of blame. Indeed they insisted it was not their function to do so, which made it difficult to see what the point of the expensive 'monitoring' was. At £39,400 per annum plus expenses each monitor of transient cease-fires did not come cheap, but a Community which could squander billions purchasing and storing unwanted food, thereby keeping the Euro-peasantry in a style to which it had become accustomed, saw nothing incongruous in establishing an 'intervention fund' to provide scores of retired EC diplomats and soldiers with something to do at someone else's expense.

As part of the Brioni Agreement, the Community had organised a conference at The Hague (the Dutch had rotated into the Community's presidency) to discuss peace and reconciliation while Croatia burned. The conference opened on 7 September, two long and deadly months since Brioni, but nothing, not even war, could be allowed to disturb the traditional vacation season of the Twelve, whose elite had no intention of sunning themselves with the Euro-proles on Adriatic beaches in any case. Over the vacation period, great events had occurred which ought to have altered the Community's approach.

The farcical coup in Moscow on 19 August had swiftly collapsed, plunging the Soviet Union into its death throes and rendering it incapable of intervention in support of Belgrade. The hardline counterpart of Kadijević, Marshal Yazov, had fallen with the other plotters. Any realistic threat of Soviet military aid to the JNA had disappeared with the failure of the putsch, but neither the European Community nor NATO were able to grasp the moment to assert their authority in the Balkans by making it clear that they would enter the power-vacuum, issue an ultimatum and impose peace terms if the parties to the conflict would not genuinely cease fire according to a peremptory timetable. The Soviet military was winded by the August events, but the West's statesmen and planners were caught even more off guard and unable to respond decisively to the revolution in the strategic environment. The chance of swift and probably bloodless intervention against the slow-moving and vulnerable columns of JNA armour and vehicles as they advanced ponderously across Crotia was lost. Allied air power which had shattered similar forces in the Gulf seven months earlier sat idly in its hangars while Bush, Major and Mitterrand covered up their flustered response to the coup by celebrating 'their' victory in the Cold War.

The stately pace of the Community's peace process had an air of treading towards inevitable disaster as it missed a unique opportunity to act decisively. Instead of assembling EC heads of government, with the power of decision, the *troika* opted for a classic EC measure, a talking shop. So used were the Twelve to finessing any internal disagreements by putting off the evil hour of decision and holding another conference instead, that the members of the *troika* backed by the consensus of the Twelve seem to have thought that a civil war could be put on the back-burner in the same way.

It is no easy task to keep a multi-lateral discussion going for as long as possible. It requires rare talents, tact and a quiet but firm determination, a devotion to duty which few men or women possess. The Hague Peace Conference needed a suitable chairman who could take on the almost full-time burden of persuading the recalcitrant South Slavs to see reason but also cover the

Community's rear in case its venture into foreign policy turned sour. Britain may not have been uniformly successful with her exports to the Community, but the next two years were to show that when it came to producing the very model of a modern peacemaker, Britain still led the world.

Whatever their differences in style and temperament, Lord Carrington and Lord Owen met the requirements for the perpetual pursuer of a frustrated peace. The chairman of Christie's, Peter Carrington had had a lifetime's experience at the centre of Britain's own graceful decline. He possessed the sort of unruffled aristocratic charm which hid a steely determination always to see the other chap's point of view and never to take sides with the angels when compromise with Beelzebub was still possible. A lesser being would have refused such a thankless task, but *noblesse oblige*. A cruder man would have given it up sooner in disgust or shame, but breeding will out and no humiliation seemed to perturb Lord Carrington as he went about the task of negotiating with what he later described, in a rare moment of uncharacteristic forthrightness, as 'liars'.

For the best part of a year it seemed nothing could shake the noble lord's faith in negotiation as the magic key to peace. Neither deception nor falsehood, insult to his person nor even atrocity against civilians could shake his pursuit of negotiation. The 'peace process' became an end in itself, what happened on the ground a mere backdrop to the perpetual round of discussions and communiqués. 1991 passed into history and 1992 staggered forward as the fighting spread from Croatia into Bosnia, but still the credo of the mediators was chanted with as much fervour as ever. Carrington told an interviewer:

> Cease-fires are negotiated and then broken. Agreements are signed and then broken. And you just have to persevere. It's no good starting on this if you abandon the attempt at the first setback, or setbacks. Eventually, people will realise . . . that they are not actually going to gain their objectives, not going to gain anything settled or final by simply attacking their neighbours, killing their neighbours, and at that stage they will say, well now we need a plan, we need an agreement, we need a forum, we need negotiation, and it is at that point that the EC

> – Europe – can in fact be useful and that stage will come, I believe, in Bosnia as it came in Croatia.[9]

People in Bosnia might be forgiven for thinking that 'killing their neighbours' was a pretty 'final' way of going about things. The dead cannot negotiate even at an EC-sponsored peace conference, but to the EC foreign ministers this was a regrettably short-term way of thinking. The willingness to put up with shameless breaches of the cease-fires did not seem to undermine the self-esteem of either Carrington or Hurd. If Waterloo was won on the playing fields of Eton, then the EC's diplomatic ambitions were lost there. The patrician indifference to humiliation and debacle which they showed even when spat upon by not deigning to wipe away the spittle but continuing polite conversation with their assailant as though nothing had happened, compounded the growing contempt for the West and its chosen representatives. Unfortunately, in the real world if anyone lets himself be treated with contempt, it is not only the uncouth who learn to despise him.

However much the EC leaders liked to think in the long term – charting the future of a continent like master mariners setting forth on the great ocean – the leaders of the Twelve proved remarkably lacking in foresight when it came to anticipating events in the Balkans. Not only were they taken by surprise by the flare-up of fighting in Slovenia, but they refused to be distracted from each fresh outbreak of violence to consider the big picture. For instance, already in July 1991 the government of Bosnia-Hercegovina was so alarmed by the scale of the fighting along its north-western borders inside Croatia and the involvement of JNA and militias based in Bosnia that it asked the EC to engage in preventive diplomacy by sending a corps of monitors to observe developments in the republic. The Twelve displayed sovereign contempt for Sarajevo's attempt to distract them from their central preoccupation. The foreign ministers of the Community informed the Bosnians 'at this stage the European Community must concentrate on the situation in Croatia and on the Serb-Croat problem, which is at the heart of the Yugoslav crisis.' Those Bosnians would have to wait their turn for Brussels' attention.[10] Buffeted by the high tide of history, the Twelve continued according to routines better suited to calmer waters.

The Conference on Security and Cooperation in Europe (CSCE) was supposed to have established ground rules for the peaceful development of its 35 member states. Based on the principles of unanimity and rotating chairmanship which all international bodies favour as a substitute rather than a mechanism for decision-making, the CSCE's flaws were revealed within days of the setting in place of the keystone of what was grandly entitled Europe's new 'security architecture'. On 19 June 1991 the CSCE agreed in Berlin to establish a fully-fledged 'conflict prevention mechanism'. Needless to say, the midwives of this procedure were taken by surprise when Yugoslavia immediately gave birth to a conflict. The Yugoslav delegate at the Conference, backed up by the Soviet Union and Romania, blocked the necessary unanimity for any CSCE action. However, the CSCE was now able to agree to pass the burden for peace mediation to the EC, as conflict prevention was already obsolete.

Even the imposition of an arms embargo took weeks to secure. Sweden for instance was anxious to complete contracts for missiles and other equipment which Belgrade had with Swedish firms before adopting its usual sanctimonious stance on the trade in death. Ironically, it was only when the representative of the Federal Government signalled that Yugoslavia would support a UN role, in late September 1991, that some of the members of the Security Council were prepared to support an arms embargo. Of course, Belgrade wanted an arms embargo not to damp down the conflict but to keep the balance tilted in favour of the JNA and Serb militias. After all, it was Croatia which lacked control of arsenals and needed to import weapons or scavenge them at home. In fact countries like Sweden continued to supply sophisticated weapons and spare parts to Belgrade months after the fighting began. (Under Olof Palme, Sweden had been an honorary member of the non-aligned movement which meant that at conferences promoting world peace and development, the Swedish premier encouraged – even bribed, it is alleged – Third World statesmen to buy Bofors rather than US weapons.)[11]

The role of Lord Carrington quickly became farcical. His shuttle diplomacy for peace was supposed to remind observers of a latter-day Henry Kissinger at the height of his powers. Instead it soon acquired the attributes of an Ealing comedy, 'Carry on Carrington'. With hindsight – a quality which has distinguished his career from Crichel Down to Croatia – Lord Carrington recognised quickly that some of his interlocutors were not sincere. Two years on, Carrington told Channel 4 News,

> Well, I think I found very quickly that you really couldn't rely on a word they said. They were quite prepared to sign any bit of paper you put in front of them without the smallest intention of doing anything about it and, er, *after a couple of times of cease-fire, after a couple of times you got a cease-fire* and so on you realised that they were completely unreliable people and they were out for their own agenda.

What a surprise! People killing each other 'for their own agenda'! Whatever next![12]

However indignant Carrington may have been, at least the noble lord was always even-handed and never vulgar enough to point the finger of blame at any one side. For instance, at The Hague on 25 October 1991, Carrington managed to conflate his rebuke to the *absent* General Kadijević for his coordination of the onslaught on Dubrovnik – 'I wanted to say these things to Kadijević himself'! – with sharp words to the dutifully present Croats for minor infringements by local forces of the 'cease-fire'.[13]

What Carrington's even-handed approach meant in practice was not distinguishing between victim and aggressor. Even at a practical level in the autumn of 1991 it was obvious that the Croat forces lacked both the firepower and the command-and-control available to the JNA, so to condemn as equal violations the odd Croat sniper and a Serb artillery barrage was objectively to side with the more powerful force. Despite his military experience, Lord Carrington does not seem to have recognised that joint action by the JNA and the Yugoslav Navy plus air attacks by Yugoslav jets by their very nature had to involve high level coordination and central ground control.

The tragi-comic implications of the EC's even-handed approach to violent breaches of the cease-fire which its representatives had negotiated reached its nadir on 7 January 1992. As if to prove beyond all doubt its ice-cold impartiality, the Community's representatives refused to point the finger of blame even when one of its own helicopters was shot down by a Federal jet killing all five EC monitors on board. One spokesman referred to 'the accident'.[14] Mr Hurd hurried to say that the incident should not be allowed to hinder the peace process which was probably precisely what it was designed to test: the Community showed its lack of seriousness by its handling of the shootdown. It even did so in the face of denials of Yugoslav Air Force involvement and the absurd suggestion that it might have been the work of specially fitted-out 'sports planes' flown from Austria. If Croats had become cynical about the Community's apparent willingness to carry on negotiating regardless of their suffering at least it showed how even-handed it was now by not permitting the deaths of its own personnel at the hands of Federal forces to halt the peace process for more than a moment's silence.[15]

The Serbs had recognised early on that the mentality of the EC's statesmen left them vulnerable to the charge of partiality. Desperate to maintain their status as umpires, any allegations of taking sides led the EC's representatives to shift towards taking a more positive view of their detractor. Of course, the accusations of partiality were redoubled with every success in bringing the EC into a more pro-Serb position.

The Community also came under fire from other international bodies. If the CSCE had descended into inaction on the Yugoslav crisis from the start, the UN had ruffled feathers. For decades it had been the UN's task to provide the venue for fruitless and dishonest peace talks and its new activist Secretary-General, Boutros-Boutros Ghali, was not about to cede responsibility for such activities to a regional body which took no account of his prerogatives. Soon journalists were reporting that 'There is a feeling at the United Nations that the European Community has allowed itself to become too closely identified with Croatia.'[16]

Yugoslavia's long courtship of the Third World, combined with its diligent involvement in the UN bureaucracy, gave Belgrade great advantages in New York over Zagreb and Ljubljana.

The German decision to recognise Slovenia and Croatia as independent states by Christmas 1991 gave the Serbs a weapon with which to beat the allegedly partial EC. In fact, of course, even though the Brioni compromise had expired on 7 October, the Community had still refused to recognise the two republics, but also had insisted on not considering what the consequences of either recognition or non-recognition would be both for them and the other republics, particularly Bosnia and Macedonia. The French proposal to set up a commission under one of President Mitterrand's former ministers, Robert Badinter, to work out a constitutional and human rights test for would-be independent republics seeking EC recognition was intended as a time-wasting exercise. It was also an expression of wounded Gallic pride: Paris was increasingly distressed by Britain's provision of the EC peacemaker and wanted to share what passed for the glory of managing the peace process.

In practice, Badinter produced a set of conditions with admirable speed by Community standards – though to determine that the EC would only recognise states with a pluralistic democratic constitution which guaranteed minority rights could have been established in a morning. Croatia was held not to have met every requirement down to the last jot, but its parliament enacted amendments which then did so. However, Slovenia, Bosnia and Macedonia did meet the requirements. Unfortunately, the majority in the Community did not want to recognise any republics except the Yugoslav Federal state.

Furthermore, to compound the problem, Greece began to make noises which threatened to derail the Community's approach altogether. From the start of the war, West European newspapers had begun to receive a flurry of Greek communications, sometimes from ambassadors, sometimes from ordinary Greeks, denouncing in ever more florid terms the idea that there could be a Macedonian state which was not part of Greece. It soon became clear that Greece was openly colluding with Serbia to break the various embargoes put upon her. The EC's obsession with its own consensus meant that it was at the mercy of a maverick. Rather than admit that Greece had broken ranks, the other eleven closed ranks around the Greek position. If Greece would not recognise Macedonia, nor would they.

Whatever basis the Greek mistrust of Yugoslav Macedonian intentions might have had in the late 1940s, the hysteria whipped up inside Greece in 1991 revealed how shallow were its commitments to many EC principles. Given the Greek refusal to acknowledge the existence of its own Slavic or Vlach minorities plus its policy of employing only registered members of the Orthodox Church in the civil service, police and judiciary, it is highly unlikely that Greece could have met the Badinter criteria for EC recognition, but then Greece was also a member of the Council of Europe despite its flouting of its key principles. The West Europeans seem not to have noticed the motes in their own Community's eye when pontificating about acceptable behaviour in the Balkans (north of Greece). To people there it suggested the EC's seriousness was not all that it might have been.[17]

Chancellor Kohl's announcement at his Party Congress in Dresden in December that the recognition of Slovenia and Croatia was a great 'victory' for German foreign policy set off alarm bells in London and Paris. For decades, Whitehall and the Quai d'Orsay had been used to the German poodle doing as it was instructed in foreign policy matters at the risk of being reminded of its Nazi past if it stepped out of line. Despite his subsequent admission that 'after two cease-fires' he had recognised the futility of his mediation, Lord Carrington showed remarkable irritation with any alternatives, complaining bitterly that German recognition of Slovenia and Croatia in December 1991 (more than 100 cease-fires into the war) had 'torpedoed my conference'. Even after Genscher's broadside, Lord Carrington remained on the diplomatic trail until the end of August 1992. Probably his devotion to public service outweighed any vanity in the elder statesman's persistence in a lost cause.

One influence on Lord Carrington was undoubtedly Fitzroy Maclean. An admiring profile of Maclean in the *Independent*[18] told its readers, 'Lord Carrington consults him occasionally, and Sir Fitzroy is in fairly regular contact with the Foreign Office.' Other influential Tory old-timers like Julian Amery went on pilgrimages to honour the hero of the Chetniks. The unavoidable whiff of a policy made in White's, as policy was sixty years ago, runs through much of the background to the British government's decision-making about the Balkan crisis. Pity the Serb leaders turned out to be so unclubbable, though for much of the time the clubsmen in St James's gave the impression that it was the victims – whether Croats or Bosnian Muslims – who were being such a bore for not giving in. Maclean was also a vocal proponent of the Fourth Reich theory, appearing on television to warn against German ambitions.

The fact that Britain's influential clubland heroes and foreign policy establishment reverted to a gut anti-Hun stance was very revealing. A strange disassociation seemed to flourish in certain minds: on the one hand they wanted Britain to be at the heart of Europe but on the other they feared that big bad Helmut was about to throw his weight around again. A similar problem beset the French elite. Mitterrand's *faux pas* in drawing attention to the German-Croat wartime alliance was typical. Even as Maastricht approached and the British and French governments insisted on signing up to a common foreign and defence policy with the newly assertive Germany, they jibbed at the consequences.

In practice Germany proved a paper tiger. Its recognition of Slovenia and Croatia was followed by a few quiet days at the front. Perhaps the Serbs believed their own propaganda and thought that recognition meant that the *Luftwaffe* was on its way to bomb Belgrade again. If so, their paranoia was soon relieved. Chancellor Kohl was capable only of gestures. As events were to show, Germany was still intimidated by its past and reluctant to undertake military missions abroad, possibly even at home in defence of herself. Certainly Kohl's government happily accepted a self-denying ordinance that said that if German troops were ever to be deployed as peacekeepers on behalf of the UN, they could never operate wherever Hitler's *Wehrmacht* had been in action. Reunited Germany might have dwarfed the other European states in terms of population and economic power, but it soon transpired that it was a timid giant. German passivity after recognition suggested that indeed it was a new Germany and a worthy member of the New Europe.

By December 1991 the UN had been able to interpose itself into the peace process in the shape of former US Secretary of State, Cyrus Vance. Vance was able to claim the credit for brokering a more viable cease-fire between Serbs and Croats which came into effect despite the shooting down of the EC monitors on 7 January 1992. In practice, it was the solidification of the front line rather than any diplomatic magic wrought by Vance which led to the establishment of a UN-monitored armistice.

With the spring approaching and the Bosnian government clearly anxious to avoid being abandoned within a Serb-dominated rump Yugoslavia, Belgrade wanted to redeploy its forces and attention towards Sarajevo. The deployment of UN forces provided a valuable buffer between the JNA and any Croat counter-attack.

Far from setting the foundations for peace, the Vance arrangements along the Serb-Croat front line simply made war more viable in Bosnia, particularly as neither the UN nor the EC had any intention of taking any more action to pre-empt fighting there than they had in Croatia. Although the UNPROFOR operation in Croatia was run from Sarajevo, that was a state of affairs which lasted only as long as the fighting was in Croatia rather than Bosnia. Once the situation was reversed, the gaggle of international observers, monitors and UN troops with few exceptions redeployed themselves to Zagreb away from the line of fire. For a while the UN commander, General Satish Nambiar, still insisted that the outbreak of fighting in and around Sarajevo would not affect his plans for peacekeeping, using the Bosnian capital as his headquarters to control deployments in Croatia. 'The bad developments and the spreading clashes are not going to influence the planned arrival and deployment of UN peace forces.' But this determination proved short-lived.

As the war in Bosnia unfolded step by step, the EC clung to its tried and failed formula of the Hague Conference. No one need have doubted the sincerity of Serb warnings that they would not accept any referendum result in favour of Bosnian independence, but the renewed war still seemed to take European leaders by surprise. So much anachronism in one country seemed incredible. As late as April 1992 Lord Carrington was still optimistic that the horrors of war would make all sides see sense. Coming away from Belgrade, he assured journalists, 'I think they were all really rather scared by the level of violence.' Of course, those organising the violence intended to frighten others and not just the gentleman from Christie's . . . [19]

The advance of the Serbs and the accompanying atrocities, most of which went unreported by the world's press but enough of which hit the headlines in the West, shook even Washington out of its complacency. The Bush administration shifted suddenly from its refusal to recognise Slovenia and Croatia into a blanket recognition of the four non-Serb republics, leaving only Serbia and Montenegro in a diplomatic limbo. However, the change in US policy on recognition was not accompanied by any action, so the fighting continued. The arms embargo was maintained in place, giving the Serb forces an even greater advantage versus the infant Bosnian Army than they had possessed against Croatia.[20]

International sanctions had little effect on the capacity of Serbia to continue the war, but the decision to exclude the Yugoslav national football team from the European Soccer Championships due to be held in Sweden caused great excitement among EC leaders. Denmark, which held the presidency until the end of June 1992, was selected to replace the pariahs. At the EC summit in Lisbon to discuss among other things the Danish 'No' to Maastricht and the war in Bosnia, the Danish Foreign Minister, Uffe Ellemann-Jensen, seemed to regard the fact that Denmark had replaced defunct Yugoslavia in the European soccer championships as the most important development. He came wearing a football scarf and took a portable television into the summit meetings so that he could follow the score. His Prime Minister, Paul Schluter, and the German Chancellor also followed the final on mini-TVs during the crisis session devoted to Bosnia! Ellemann-Jensen even showed his toy proudly before the cameras after his colleagues had ruled out intervention to stop the slaughter in Sarajevo. The dying in Sarajevo might be forgiven for thinking that he did not care.[21]

As ever anxious to avoid tackling the main problem head on, but careful to give the impression that he was on top of events, Douglas Hurd called for the 'immediate dispatch of international monitors' to Kosovo to 'prevent an explosion of unrest'. In other words as a bandage for the problem rather than a cure for the basic reasons why Albanians there were discontented. 'If there were some explosion in Kosovo, all would be lost and we would be back at the beginning,' said Hurd. He had talked 'persuasively' to Milošević about the need to uphold human rights there.[22]

However, the start of the new British presidency of the EC was overshadowed by a *coup de théâtre* from President Mitterrand. Without informing his partners, who admittedly were preoccupied with the football, the French President flew to Sarajevo from Lisbon. His dramatic visit was intended to obscure his inglorious role as one of the chief proponents of doing nothing. Of course, he had no intention of taking action to halt the slaughter, but Mitterrand knew the media well enough to know that by bravely coming to do nothing in person, and avoiding saying anything of substance, his tarnished image would be smartened up.

Unlike Mitterrand, British politicians on their visits to Sarajevo could not maintain a sphinx-like silence. Instead of a silence interpreted as inscrutable profundity, they gabbled in front of the cameras, giving aid and comfort to the Serbs besieging the city. Douglas Hogg was a master of the British way of crisis management: he approached every problem with an open mouth. For instance on 13 August Hogg assured the world's press in front of an armoured personnel carrier in Sarajevo, 'I explained very clearly . . . that there was no cavalry over the hill. There is no international force coming to stop this.' Even if President Izetbegović did not get the message, the Serb gunners around the city certainly did.[23]

At first, Douglas Hurd seemed about to change British policy when he set off in Mitterrand's footsteps in his capacity as President of the EC Council of Ministers for a trip around the Balkans. He declared, 'We have to do our utmost to stop this suffering continuing. It is not just a matter of relieving those who are already suffering, it is trying to prevent this going on in the future.'[24] In Sarajevo two days later, Mr Hurd said that the EC would not accept the partition of Bosnia nor any alteration of its borders by force.[25] Hurd told a press conference in Sarajevo, 'I don't believe that Serbia will be able or will wish indefinitely to continue in a position without trade, without friends, without any position in the world.' Serbia still had considerable sanctions-busting trade and that showed she had friends – some of whom, like Greece, were friends of Mr Hurd too. It was the 1930s illusion again: even if an aggressor is identified (in this case very reluctantly and late in the day), it does not mean that he will be ostracised because self-interest or sympathy may well motivate others to aid him. Greece and the Ukraine for instance did not share Mr Hurd's inhibitions.[26]

Unlike some of his colleagues who still preferred to find responsibility for the conflict difficult to allocate, Douglas Hurd told journalists that 'we believe that it is possible . . . for the authorities in Belgrade effectively to influence what happens, what the Serbs do in Bosnia.'[27] But it was left to Belgrade to carry through any influencing. After his visit, Hurd admitted, 'I now have quite a different and much more vivid impression of what it's all about. I'm bubbling over with impressions at the moment which will take a bit of time to sort out.'[28] But of one thing he was certain. He regretted that the EC monitors seemed largely forgotten and proposed sending more.

By midsummer 1992, the level of violence had become even more frightening. On 15 July, Carrington received Karadžić and the others at Christie's, a venue no more surreal than the peace process itself. Dr Karadžić offered a cease-fire and corridors for humanitarian aid. Carrington told a press conference held in a room littered with empty gilt picture frames, each waiting for a portrait of a peacemaker,

> Everybody has agreed to a cease-fire a great many times, but the cease-fire doesn't happen and I think that we have certainly come to the conclusion that perhaps the best way of getting a cease-fire is to find some constitutional agreements which would render the hostilities unnecessary.[29]

Even Lord Carrington felt that an international military presence on the ground might assist in stopping the fighting, but his approach brought him into conflict with the UN Secretary-General, always jealous of his prerogative and apparently angry about being treated as a 'wog' by British officials. On 22 July, Boutros-Boutros Ghali publicised a letter refusing to cooperate with Lord Carrington's latest cease-fire and requiring another 1100 UN monitors to supervise the heavy weapons of all sides. The UN Secretary-General was piqued that Lord Carrington had had the gall to announce the agreement before sending the details to him in New York. It was a minor classic of the tendency of the angels of peace to stand on their dignity and squabble over correct form while whole cities burn.

On 20 July, the thirty-ninth Bosnian cease-fire broke down. It was difficult for even the unflappable to deny that European mediation had led nowhere and the situation was getting worse. The French were sniping openly at Carrington's ineffective role and calling for a new and grander peace conference, even hinting that the UN should replace Lord Carrington. John Major had to act if Britain's EC presidency was not to be marred by the loss of its chairmanship of the EC Yugoslav Peace Conference. Lord Carrington's characteristic injunction that 'we should not be too optimistic but not too pessimistic either' was hardly calculated to reassure those hoping for anything concrete to come out of his negotiations.

Anxious to avoid the humiliation of seeing Britain's hold on the peacemaker's position snatched away by France, John Major, fresh from his election triumph, decided to trump any criticism of the Hague Conference and Lord Carrington's approach by summoning a bigger and better conference to London at the end of August. A weary Lord Carrington was left with the task of preparing for it, but found himself snubbed by Milošević.

As a preliminary, Lord Carrington held his last EC conference also in London at the end of the second week in August. Milošević did not come. A US diplomat speculated on his reasons:

> I am not sure that Milošević did not attend yesterday's session because he was embarrassed about all the international criticism of Serbia's ethnic cleansing policy in Bosnia and the detention camps. I think it is because he has contempt for the EC because he knows it has no clout.[30]

In addition to the need to protect Britain's *amour propre* as President of the EC until the end of December, John Major had another reason for summoning the London Conference. By July, public disquiet about the level of brutality in Bosnia was fed by television pictures on a daily basis. Then the media discovered the Serb detention camps. Although the UN, Red Cross and Western governments had known about them, their public exposure through television put pressure on the West, which had just defeated Saddam, to do something to stop the violence. Unfortunately, leaving aside any military scruples, neither Britain nor the United States was willing to spend the cash in a time of recession (compounded for President Bush by imminent elections). Whereas the Arab states had paid for Britain's contingent in the Gulf, domestic recession seemed to rule out sending a force to Bosnia, particularly as the government deficit looked set to hit fifty billion pounds in 1993.

An unwonted passivity came over the victors of the Gulf War. The language of inaction of the West's political leaders was striking and consistent throughout the crisis. The representatives of powerful states spoke only in the passive mode as though waiting for someone to tell them to act rather than being the decision-makers themselves. The United States was the world's remaining superpower, but Dick Cheney, its defense secretary, could only announce on 28 May 1992, 'We are not contemplating at present – because we have not been asked to [!] – any deployment of US troops.' It was an extraordinary state of affairs that the 'only superpower' had to wait to be asked before it could 'contemplate' deploying troops.[31] The European Community countries mustered well over two million of the most heavily armed forces in human history but could do nothing until the international community made a decision.

Military options were written off before they were seriously considered. The UNPROFOR commander in Bosnia, Lewis Mackenzie, who was later openly to demand the appeasement of the Serbs, showed an uncharacteristic preference for citing history as the justification for doing nothing – apart from deliver groceries and appear on television:

> If we read our history, it is one extremely difficult place to fight and you want to make pretty sure what you want to achieve before you go in there and better be prepared to stay for a long time.

It seems to have escaped Mackenzie and Bush that the Bosnian Serb commander, General Mladić, was finding it rather easy to wage war in Bosnia, but then he wasn't fighting NATO forces.[32]

To counter public opinion, which seemed to be increasingly turning to the idea of Western intervention to prevent at least the worst excesses of attacks on civilians, Mackenzie and others began to cite the enormous numbers of troops which they claimed would be necessary to carry out any effective intervention. However, on closer inspection Mackenzie's estimates seemed to have been plucked from the air for journalists' sake rather than based on precise planning. He scattered six-figure numbers about with little regard for precision and when challenged explained that he had not 'thought through' the strategy yet! The impression grew that Mackenzie may not have been Canada's first military genius but he was certainly a media genius as he sounded off ferociously and wittily in his command bunker at Sarajevo airport.[33]

Certainly no attempt was made to draw on real historical experience of previous operations in the Balkans. Neither the Austrian occupation of Bosnia in 1878 nor the Central Powers' regime from 1915–18 was studied. Above all the Axis occupation from 1941–44 was tabu. Studying the lessons of the *Wehrmacht*'s lightning conquest of Yugoslavia and then the brutal period afterwards was a particular blindspot for the Germans themselves. Their otherwise bullish defence minister, Volker Rühe, refused to countenance any *Bundeswehr* study of the past or the transfer of such material to NATO.[34]

From the very start of the conflict in Yugoslavia, Douglas Hurd had cited the precedent of the British deployment of troops to Ulster after 1969 as a reason for avoiding intervention in ex-Yugoslavia. He repeated this argument regularly as did his colleagues at the Ministry of Defence. Whether the noticeable upsurge in IRA activity reflected the terrorists taking heart from the suggestion that the British government was wearying of its commitment to Northern Ireland remains to be seen, but constant references to the Ulster precedent must have encouraged the Serbs. However, they were more concerned about US intentions since Britain or any other West European country was hardly likely to intervene alone.[35]

Serb propaganda made great play with 'history' and the Vietnam parallel. Milošević and his henchmen saw very clearly that victory in the Gulf War had not lifted the shadow of South-East Asian defeat from the shoulders of the American Gulliver. Far from it. If anything the miraculously bloodless victory over Saddam reinforced the trauma. Bush and his generals could not believe their luck. Their laurels were won cheaply and they feared tarnishing them by risking their good fortune again so soon after liberating Kuwait.

Even when pictures emerged of emaciated and ill-kept prisoners from Serb concentration camps at the beginning of August

1992, Bush made it clear that he continued to be haunted by the fear of a quagmire even if he talked about the Holocaust, which was a 'burning memory for all of us'. In the same breath, the President could utter the following: 'The pictures of the prisoners rounded up by the Serbian forces and being held in these detention camps are stark evidence of the need to deal with this problem *effectively* [emphasis added].' Undoubtedly the fact that television showed scenes of shaven-headed prisoners so evocative of fifty years earlier put pressure on the US administration, but the President demanded that someone give him an aim, as if it were not the President's task to set goals for US policy:

> Before I'd commit American troops to battle, I want to know what's the beginning, what's the objective and how the objective is going to be achieved and what's the end and I learned and I'm old enough to remember Vietnam, I'm old enough to remember World War Two having participated in it. (Syntax as broadcast.)

The President bemoaned the burden of office as, in election year, he drew his audience's attention to the fact that he had to take decisions which might risk 'someone's son, or someone's daughter' in battle, concluding 'I do not want to see the United States bogged down in any way into some guerrilla war. We lived through that once.'[36]

The President's capacity to utter sentences containing mutual contradictions as well as unfinished sub-clauses was well-known by this stage in his career, but his mangling of the English language after putting the Sixth Fleet on alert while enunciating a classic diplomatic passive exactly mirrored the intellectual and moral confusions in the mind of the West's leader. From the White House briefing room the following Bushism went forth:

> I am appalled at the human suffering and the killing in Sarajevo and we will do *what we are called upon to do*. But right now *we are not prepared* to use those forces and, yes, I hope *that sends a signal to people over there that we're serious*. [Emphasis added.][37]

Bush's circumlocutions contrasted with the clear statements of

Bill Clinton, his Democratic rival for the presidency. But every Serb knew that even if elected Clinton would not act for another six months at the earliest. This time factor left John Major's London Conference as the only show in town. Already on the fringes of the preliminary conference leading up to Mr Major's London Peace Conference, Western voices expressed their hopelessness about action. A NATO diplomat told the *Financial Times*: [38] 'Either we go in and saturate the place or we stay out. There is no room for half-baked measures. In any case, it is probably too late because the Serbs have gotten what they want.' He added, 'They are likely to allow aid convoys in now.'

In the meantime, the existing UNPROFOR deployments came under pressure and revealed their weaknesses and lack of cohesion. Wearing the Blue Helmet did not automatically instil a common approach. Nor did it inspire much respect among the snipers and mortar-operators in and around Sarajevo. Two Dutch UN officers were suspended for refusing to remain at their posts in the Marshal Tito Barracks in Sarajevo after they were shelled on 20 August.[39]

Ukrainian and Russian Blue Helmets were prone to taking sides as well as bribes (as we have seen). If Western states did not want to recognise the analogy between the collapse of Yugoslavia and the Soviet Union, then it did not escape the Russian peacekeepers. One Belgian peacekeeper told *Le Figaro* that his Russian counterparts 'only talked about that'. When fighting broke out in the newly independent republic of Moldova in the south-west of the former Soviet Union in June 1992, the West showed remarkable understanding for the active role of the Russian 14th Army, despite the situation's alarming similarity to events in Krajina and since. Margaret Tutwiler, James Baker III's spokeswoman, assured the press, 'We recognise President Yeltsin's concern for the safety of ethnic Russians.' In fact, at that stage Yeltsin was still strong enough to seek to rein in the aggressive Russian communist-nationalists in charge of the 14th Army. Unfortunately, Foggy Bottom did not seem to recognise the same manipulative strategy at work in the Trans-Dniestr district of Moldova as in former Yugoslavia. Or, perhaps, James Baker's strange policy reflected understanding all round.[40]

JNA officers tried to appeal to their history of a common

struggle against fascism, now represented by 'West Germany', as the Serb general, Biorcević, called the enemy to the north. In public, the Russians insisted that any past alliance was history and that 'henceforth we are neutral'.[41] That neutrality did not forbid the old allies from holding a joint parade to mark the anniversary of the defeat of Nazi Germany in May 1945.

While the objectivity and value of the Blue Helmets was called into question, the obdurate maintenance of the arms embargo on Bosnia at the insistence of John Major and François Mitterrand continued despite article 51 of the UN Charter which explicitly states: 'nothing . . . shall impair the inherent right of individual or collective self-defence if an armed attack occurs against a member of the United Nations.' Although the Anglo-French axis claimed to be upholding the spirit of the UN Charter when they resisted all efforts to persuade the Security Council to lift the arms embargo on Bosnia, in fact a reading of the UN Charter casts doubt on their obstructionist position. After all, a key principle of the Charter was that aggression should not be allowed to succeed. Underlying the drafting of the Charter was the experience of the 1930s and the failure of the League of Nations to protect its weaker members – China and Ethiopia – against stronger powers – Japan and Italy.

Like the high-minded appeasers in the 1930s, the EC's leaders could not conceive of the utility of force in politics. Brought up under the shadow of the Second World War, the European Community's statesmen were in thrall not to its causes but its consequences. Far from learning the Churchillian lesson, they adopted the Chamberlainite view of the futility of war. Churchill of course once cynically if grandly remarked in his ancestral home, Blenheim Palace: 'Chamberlain says war produces nothing, but look at all this.' In the real world outside the cloistered conference chambers of Brussels and Luxembourg, there are still ambitious men who are also ruthless.

Douglas Hurd could not stop repeating the phrase 'sooner or later negotiations'. Unwillingness to apportion blame led Euro-statesmen like Jean-Pierre Cot, leader of the Socialist Group in the European Parliament and representative of President Mitterrand there, to insist,

> If the Yugoslavs don't want peace, and if *both* parties don't want peace, I'm afraid that . . . our main problem now is trying to contain this within limits. We refuse to internationalise the conflict after all history has shown us. Yugoslavia is a pretty dangerous place to internationalise a conflict.

Cot went so far as to justify action with the remarkable phrase 'this is a precedent for all Europe, as we all know'. Why the veto on international policy should lie with the most belligerent party to the conflict was never fully explained. Perhaps the appeasers of Belgrade could not admit their reasons to themselves, but the trump card was left in Milošević's hand.[42]

The *Financial Times*, a reliable monitor of Foreign Office thinking, subtitled its montage of map and dramatis personae to illustrate its coverage of the London Peace Conference: 'Yugoslavia: everyone's a loser'. It was another invocation of Churchill's dictum that 'jaw-jaw is better than war-war' which was endlessly repeated and misunderstood. Certainly, the combination of fighting and negotiations that actually developed did little good except to buy time for Serb advances. Forty years of peace in Europe combined with the Vietnam syndrome had rendered the West incapable of understanding the belligerent mentality. Cyrus Vance insisted that 'War is not the answer. It will be ruinous for all sides.' Perhaps, but certainly much more ruinous for the loser. The bitter reality of war is that it usually ends when one side defeats the other. It is pious fallacy to insist that in war there are no winners. What ought to matter is which side wins and to whose advantage that victory works. As time went by the suspicion grew that some people in the Foreign Office had decided that on balance they wanted Serbia to win.[43]

What Mr Major wanted was less clear. His evident pride in the forthcoming London Conference – 'the largest of its kind' – suggested that the conference was becoming an end in itself. As Mr Major's rigid adherence to the financial orthodoxy of the ERM dragged Britain deeper into recession and closer to the rocks of a forced devaluation, the Prime Minister's resemblance to Ramsay MacDonald became more pronounced. MacDonald had had an even less advantaged childhood than John Major and like the embattled Conservative his lack of well-travelled worldly-wise manners had led to snobbish and hurtful comments, but also had encouraged a fatal love of the international stage. Malcolm Muggeridge's comments on MacDonald's delusions about his effectiveness as a statesman and peacemaker could as well be applied to his successor sixty years on.

In 1932, MacDonald had given vent to the opinion, 'Europe is not settled. Europe is very unsettled. Europe is in a nervous condition.' Muggeridge commented,

> With this feeling in his heart, it is not surprising that he eagerly approved a proposal to summon one more conference, bigger, more comprehensive in its range, with a more distinguished and more numerous attendance than even the Diasarmament Conference . . . over which he would preside, and which would surely not fail – 'The direct representatives of this Government, that Government and the other Government, brought face to face . . . will much more quickly and much better, as a piece of workmanship, find the accommodation which will lead to a great world agreement.'[44]

As if in conscious parody of his predecessor, Major ran through all the delegations who would be attending the London Conference for the benefit of an interviewer, including the 'EC, UN, CSCE, IOC . . .'[45]

Unlike Margaret Thatcher, who had proved a thorn in his flesh already by pre-empting him and demanding safe havens for Kurds in 1991 and now was pressuring him to take military action to halt Serb advances in Bosnia, John Major seemed determined to prove what reason and diplomacy at the highest level could achieve. Unfortunately, the previous year of diplomacy suggested that even the word of honour of heads of republics was of little value when a life-and-death struggle was under way.

Whatever their misgivings about the proposed conference, the former Yugoslav republics all sent delegations headed by their presidents. Federal Yugoslavia was not overlooked either. Its delegation provided a chance for the new Federal Premier, Milan Panić, to show himself off before the world. Panić was a Serbian émigré who had built up a pharmaceutical company in California which had a subsidiary in Serbia. His appointment as Federal

Prime Minister took most people at home and abroad by surprise. His personality proved even more astonishing. A voluble figure, sometimes as incoherent in Serbian as he could be in English, Panić was taken very seriously by Western leaders. Even his tantrums inside the Queen Elizabeth II Conference Centre were regarded as statesmanlike expressions of authority. Only Milošević seemed to treat him with silent contempt. Milošević had accepted Panić as Federal Premier because he might prove a useful distraction for the West without exercising any real power. All serious institutions like the Army and police had already been taken into the control of Serbia rather than the Federal institutions.

With Panić's clowning providing light relief, the London Conference moved effectively through Mr Major's agenda guided by his firm hand but willing to sign anything in any case. All participants accepted the British-drafted Declaration of the Principles of Civilised Conduct. If the Geneva Convention had been almost unanimously ignored, it was unlikely that the London Principles would lead to a change of heart among the combatants. In addition to outlawing the clear breaches of international law involved in 'ethnic cleansing', the participants in London agreed that they would not accept the partition of Bosnia-Hercegovina or any territorial conquest.

Despite all the rhetoric, the only immediate change at London was the retirement of Lord Carrington and his replacement by another former British foreign secretary. At first sight, the new EC mediator was as different from Carrington as the British establishment could imagine. Time would tell whether the installation of the sharp-tongued former Labour MP into Lord Carrington's chair would change the great outsider of British politics into an oligarch after all. First signs were promising. Lord Owen told the *Sunday Telegraph* that he believed that the 'London Conference was the turning point. Serbia learnt what it meant to be an international pariah – that the world was not prepared to sit back and shrug off its territorial acquisitions.' At the same time, the new peace-mediator thought that the 'Serbs are turning to Panić . . . as a preferable leader to President Slobodan Milošević'. Turning to the fate of the Muslims in Bosnia, Owen insisted that 'we have to convince them that they are not going to be the victims of *Realpolitik* . . . if we allow it to happen to the Muslims of Bosnia the whole of Islam will react – and rightly so.'[46]

Lord Owen had made his presence felt in the Bosnian matter by demanding that NATO use its air power to halt the Serbs, just as Lady Thatcher had done. Perhaps he was still of the opinion that force might be necessary, but over the next few months the fragility of his decisiveness became apparent. In any case, even before the London Principles had been enunciated, they were undercut by Douglas Hurd who made giving the Serbs no incentive to pay heed to the preaching of the international community into a fine art. At the end of July, as the Conference was being mooted, Hurd told the BBC, 'I suppose all options will be discussed, but one option that I don't think is feasible, and having been to Yugoslavia I am even more clear about it, and that option is using military force against hostile opposition to impose a particular solution.' Hurd was confident that the London Conference would not lead 'to a solution which is imposed against force by force'.[47]

Ruling out the use of force against any recalcitrant party to the war, of course, simply left it open to that side, particularly if it was winning, to attend the London Conference (courtesy of the British taxpayer) and still carry on the war. Douglas Hurd's public pronouncements in the run-up to the London Conference must count among the most inept series of diplomatic signals ever dispatched by a holder of his high office. Hurd had nothing to offer but talk: 'Talk has to continue . . .' There were objectives – a cease-fire, political arrangements, etc – 'but you only reach them by talking'. Victory is not a word to be found in Mr Hurd's vocabulary. He has been one of life's natural second-bests. Unfortunately in war, coming second means losing.[48]

If the London Conference really did shock the Serbs by confronting them with worldwide condemnation (as some journalists claimed), John Major moved swiftly to relax the pressure on Milošević, which in any case was left vague by the failure to set a timetable to the London agreement.[49] Instead of emphasising the obligation to abide by the agreements signed by Milošević and agreed to by Dr Karadžić, the British Prime Minister began to make excuses in advance for any failure to abide by the text: 'We can't necessarily rely on the fact that everything that has been undertaken will be delivered speedily or in the form in which it has been undertaken. Some people may not be able to deliver immediately or in full.' The problem was that 'some people' ('who' was left unclear) might choose not to act on their word rather than being prevented from doing so by *force majeure*. Mr Major's Conference had been intended to mark a break with the past, instead it offered more of the same which unfortunately for people in Bosnia and throughout Yugoslavia meant worse.[50]

12

The War in Bosnia, 1992–93

> Alexander the Great, anxious to conquer Leucadia, first made himself master of the neighbouring towns and turned all the inhabitants into Leucadia; at last the town was so full of people that he immediately reduced it by famine.
>
> Machiavelli[1]

In Bosnia, it all began at a wedding. It would have been more appropriate if the first killings had been at a funeral instead of staining someone's nuptials, but the fighting in Bosnia never obeyed the rules of propriety, let alone the unfortunate thirteen 'principles of civilized conflict' drawn up at the London Conference at the end of August 1992. Who started the killing in Bosnia was instantly debated. Did the Muslims or the Serbs fire first? The shooting at a Serbian wedding in Sarajevo on 1 March 1992 – when the revellers, some of them waving Serbian flags, were fired on by gunmen who killed the groom's father – seemed to answer the question. Muslims fired first.

However, like so many questions about origins the fierce dispute about who fired the first shot in Sarajevo missed the point. Even though the first fatalities were on the Serb side it soon became apparent in Bosnia as it had already in Croatia that the self-styled victim minority was armed to the teeth and well-prepared for war while its 'oppressors' were foolishly poorly armed and badly deployed if they were intending to carry through what the Serbs proclaimed were their genocidal plans. Of course, in any society a few foolish and self-destructive people can easily be provoked into taking actions which no rational person would adopt. In all probability, the wedding shootings in Sarajevo were the result of Muslim folly playing into waiting Serb hands. An excuse would have been found for an uprising soon enough in any case as the weather improved and the fighting season started again.

Ever since the hollow Vance Plan had come into force in Slavonia and Krajina, the JNA had been redirecting its deployments to help the Bosnian Serbs. As far back as the late 1980s, local arms dumps and underground militias had been set in train, but in the winter of 1991–2, preparations went on feverishly to prepare a Bosnian Serb force for action. Without a clear swathe of Bosnia under their control the Serb commanders in the occupied parts of Croatia would not have a secure rear or even reliable communications with Serbia proper. As much as any local ambitions for a 'Bosnian Serb Republic' the strategic imperative was for the Serbs to break up any independent Bosnia-Hercegovina in order to guarantee their gains in the war against Croatia. Without a corridor linking the Krajina's rear across northern Bosnia via Banja Luka to Serbia and Serb-occupied Slavonia, the Krajina would be economically and militarily unviable.[2]

In March 1992 at the latest the militias who had proved their worth at Vukovar (by comparison with the conscripts of the JNA) were moving into Bosnia. The implementation of the Vance Plan covered their rear. It was important for the strategy of creating a 'Greater Serbia' that a corridor across northern Bosnia should be created to link the rear of the Krajina with Serbia proper, but the JNA also wanted to occupy the bloc of territory running along the border of Serbia herself. This area contained a mixed Serb and Muslim population but it also would provide Serbia with a strategic buffer to protect both Serbia and Montenegro from the direct effects of war. Arkan's men were sent to occupy the area running south from the Brcko gap, especially the towns of Bijeljna and Zvornik. As Mark Mazower has argued, Arkan's men were necessary because despite the propaganda about ancient animosities between local Serbs and Muslims it was difficult to get local people to start the fighting. Outsiders were needed who would kill anonymous victims without compulsion and thereby polarise society and force people to take sides.[3]

The process of terrorising non-Serbs into leaving their homes got under way *before* the international recognition of Bosnia, which Serbs and their supporters insisted was the spark which ignited war. Militias like Arkan's needed no outside signal to set about killing and plundering. In fact, their activities were the detonators of a wave of terror and counter-violence. This drew local Serbs into the fighting, as was anticipated by the strategists who had been preparing for the conflict for some time.

Already in the summer of 1991, the JNA treated the territory of Bosnia-Hercegovina as a rear area in its war against Croatia, but it also began to detach whole districts from Sarajevo's control. In July, the local command ordered the mobilisation of Bosnian Serb army reservists in ten municipalities in the Bosnian Krajina against the wishes of the government in Sarajevo. Some of these men were used in fighting inside Croatia, but others began to establish a system of power parallel to the constitutional one. All the time the propaganda machine rumbled on about Serb fears of persecution just as the Serb militias were taking hold of a far more formidable armoury than anything that Sarajevo could hope to possess. With the international arms embargo on the whole of ex-Yugoslavia after 25 September 1991, the government in Sarajevo had little chance to build up its own forces as a deterrent to the violent secession of the Karadžić forces. Dr Karadžić had little reason to accept any compromise with the other parties in Bosnia because his forces had all the big guns.[4]

Far from single-mindedly pursuing independence from Yugoslavia, Izetbegović and his colleagues in the SDA were only too well aware of the explosive potential of the mixture of populations and allegiances in Bosnia. Their dilemma was how to establish a viable democratic Bosnia inside a Serb-dominated Yugoslavia. Once the fighting broke out in Croatia in the summer of 1991, the grim likelihood of an extension of the war into their republic became cruelly obvious. Sarajevo's efforts to involve the UN or the West in deploying effective forces to pre-empt an extension of the war into Bosnia were snubbed.[5]

Throughout the run-up to independence, the Bosnian interior ministry cooperated closely with the JNA in maintaining order. At one level this was a form of appeasement by those soon to be denounced as bloodthirsty Islamic fundamentalists. Rather as Tudjman's government in the spring of 1991 had done a great deal to put itself at a disadvantage in the event of war, so Izetbegović's presidency let the Interior Minister, Alija Delimustafić, hand over large quantities of the weaponry and munitions belonging to the Bosnian Territorial Defence to the JNA. Delimustafić seems to have played a double role. According to *Vreme* he was a KOS agent and therefore in league with Belgrade all the time. Certainly, treason makes a more rational explanation for his disarmament of the Republic than any confidence in the good intentions of the JNA's officer corps.[6]

Repeatedly, Karadžić offered to negotiate with the Muslims in Bosnia though not with the Hercegovinan Croats. It was a crude ploy to split the non-Serbs. Meanwhile one of the Bosnian Muslim leaders, Muhammed Filipović, noted on 6 August 1991, that 'the Serbs are armed to the teeth, they have created a state within [the] state in Bosnia-Hercegovina . . . It is possible that a conflict between Serbs and Muslims will break out any day.'[7]

The Muslim population in Bosnia was a provocation in the eyes of Serb nationalists. To them, there were no 'real' Muslims, only 'forcibly converted' Serbs. (I was forcefully reminded of this during a studio discussion programme, 'Whale On . . .', when a Serb resident of Britain screamed at a Bosnian Muslim who had dared to identify himself as such, 'You were forcibly converted', meaning of course that five hundred years or more earlier one of the man's ancestors had been obliged to turn Muslim, which may or may not have been the case.)

In the mind-set of the Serbian fighters, every injustice ever done by the Muslims or alleged against them had taken place only yesterday. Of course, Turkish rule had not been a bed of roses. Certainly, it seems reasonable to assume that many people converted to Islam at least partly to restrict the tax burden on themselves and to avoid other Ottoman levies. The most important of these was the *dervshirme*, the conscription of Christian boys into the Sultan's service. Most of these boys went into the janissaries, the celebrated elite troops of the Ottoman Empire, but the most intelligent were recruited to serve the empire as administrators. Despite their recruitment at an early age, these boys were bitterly resented as renegades by the Serbs.

The Serb forces had already destroyed well over four hundred Catholic churches and religious monuments within range of their artillery in Croatia. But in Bosnia the onslaught on the Muslim heritage was even more merciless. More than 800 mosques were destroyed by the summer of 1993 and they included some accorded the accolade of UNESCO registration, including the great late sixteenth-century mosque in Banja Luka.[8] In November 1993, the Hercegovinan Croats completed the destruction of Bosnian cultural identity when their artillery destroyed the Old Bridge in Mostar whose graceful arch had symbolised the city and republic for four hundred years.

It was not only the physical monuments to the centuries of Muslim culture in Bosnia which were the targets for destruction. The Serbs also set about exterminating those people who embodied the separate identity of the Muslims. Muslim clergy in particular in the towns and villages overrun by the Serb forces were frequently killed on the spot or later separated out from other prisoners to be murdered. Along with the religious elite, the educational and social elite of the Muslim community was particularly savagely attacked. The deliberate murder of lawyers, doctors and teachers gave the lie to the propaganda claims that the Serbs were not bent on anything more than protection of their own people and were happy to let the Muslims enjoy autonomy in their own areas. By eliminating so many members of the Muslim elite, the Serb forces were engaged in an attempt to render any kind of Muslim society unviable. Combined with the destruction of mosques and other holy places, the onslaught against the Muslim elite seemed to fit the definition of genocide given in the UN convention forbidding it and empowering the international community to act to stop it. But to stop 'a specific intent to destroy, in whole or in substantial part, a national, ethnic, racial or religious group' requires more than words of condemnation, but they were all the West had to offer.[9]

The horrors of the war in Bosnia were generally explained as being deeply rooted in a history of conflict, running back hundreds or even, as one distinguished British diplomat, Sir Crispin Tickell, put it, 'thousands of years'. Certainly it is true that the greatest twentieth-century Yugoslav novelist, Ivo Andrić's, literary oeuvre is dominated by the theme of Bosnian fanaticism and savagery. Even before his *Bridge on the River Drina*, he had pondered what he saw as the innate tendency of his fellow countrymen towards irrational animosity. He anticipated the argument of the 1990s about the 'disease' of nationalism: 'This uniquely Bosnian hatred should be studied and eradicated like some pernicious deeply-rooted disease. Foreign scholars should come to Bosnia to study hatred . . . just as scientists study leprosy.'[10]

British proponents of the myth of inherent savagery unique to the Yugoslavs like Edward Pearce were fond of quoting Andrić, but, in awe of the literary power of Andrić's fiction, ignored the facts of history. In fact, Andrić's writing was drenched in an almost sadistic pleasure in the cruelties which he described. This transmitted itself vicariously to his readers. Even if some of the defenders of Bosnia painted an over-rosy picture of inter-communal harmony, the idea of an eternal local struggle (only halted temporarily by the late Marshal's iron grip) was an even more unrealistic picture of the modern history of Bosnia.

Although Serb propaganda liked to hint that the Muslims lacked a historical right to any say in Bosnian matters because of their apostasy to Islam, men like Izetbegović had a longer Bosnian ancestry than many of the Serbs who loudly proclaimed their devotion to their native soil. It is striking how far outsiders from other parts of Yugoslavia were prominent in the promotion of a Bosnian Serb republic. The leader of the Bosnian Serbs, Radovan Karadžić, was the most striking case in point. He was a classic rootless minor intellectual with a yearning to belong and therefore an exaggerated sense of nationhood. He came from Montenegro to Sarajevo to work as a psychiatrist. He was an outsider even more devoted to the local Serb myths than many local Serbs who could trace their ancestry in Bosnia a long way back. Many of the radicals were people without strong local roots. The same was true of other parts of Yugoslavia including still peaceful Vojvodina. Often long-term Serb residents resented the loud and bullying tone of the newcomers, but backing from Belgrade and the KOS meant that the locals' preference for restraint was sidelined.

Without the inflow of Chetniks from outside Bosnia and the help of JNA professionals who stayed on in the republic after Belgrade's nominal withdrawal of 'outside' forces, the local Serbs might not have prosecuted the war into largely non-Serb territories – allowing that there might have been some form of violence to begin with. However without the JNA's legacy of tanks and artillery, any intra-village rivalries would have remained local unpleasantnesses. It required professional officers like Ratko Mladić, who had played the role of radicalising outsider in the Croatian war, to return to his native republic along with other non-Bosnian Serb radicals really to set one community at the throats of another across the republic.[11]

Within a few short weeks of the outbreak of fighting the strategy of terror had produced a wave of refugees. The scale of the exodus was enormous. Within a month the UNHCR talked of more than a third of a million people on the move. Before midsummer's day the figure had reached three-quarters of a million and was rising. Although there were Serb refugees, as the strategists anticipated, who provided pathetic pictures of human misery to counter growing outrage in the West about the Serb Army's atrocious methods and who also would prove a recruiting ground for vengeful troops, the great bulk of the displaced population was Muslim. This was also a classic strategic manoeuvre. The refugees fled to areas still under government control. Their presence in huge numbers led to the collapse of the local economies as thousands of extra mouths demanded food and housing.

The widespread raping of Muslim women and girls was a peculiar feature of the strategy of ethnic cleansing and ritual exorcism of past Muslim domination. Although rape has always been commonplace in war, and Stalin's troops, for instance, were encouraged to violate German women as the prize of victory and in revenge for the sufferings inflicted on the Soviet Motherland, it has very rarely been used as an instrument of war-fighting. After all, as we have seen, Stalin's troops raped liberated and conquered alike in Yugoslavia at the end of the war. Setting their men onto Muslim women was part of the Serbs' overcoming their inferiority complex towards the Muslims.

An important element in the Bosnian war was the revival of old antagonisms between town and country, literate and uneducated, which had been largely overlaid by twentieth-century developments. Even if there was little to choose between Serb and Muslim in terms of education or standard of living by the 1990s, Serb nationalist propaganda did a great deal to instil a sense of grievance: the Muslims still had not been paid back for the centuries when they had lorded it over the Christians. The cruellest way in which Serb men could strike the pose as lords of today was to rape Muslim women. Defiling Muslim women struck at the whole idea of a separate Muslim community. In the eyes of Serbs they were renegades and their wombs ought to bear Serbs not 'Muslims'. Although official Serb sources denied the charges of rape camps and the organised violation of Muslim women – as did apologists in the West – captured Serb soldiers admitted it, but more importantly Serbs at liberty boasted of their prowess.

Undoubtedly, Serb women were raped on occasion by Muslim soldiers whether out of pure lust or for revenge, but the balance of outrage lay heavily against the Serb forces. They captured many more women and they had a psychological-ideological motive to commit the crime. It was punishment for the Muslims' ancestors reneging.[12]

The other factor putting heavy responsibility on the Serb high command for crimes against the civilian population was the simple fact that whereas the supporters of the government in Sarajevo had to organise themselves on an ad hoc basis to form the BiH Army and local defence forces, the JNA command structures were taken over *en bloc* by the so-called Bosnian Serb forces. General Mladić took charge after his successes in the war versus the HVO and inherited a regular army of about 80,000 men.

When Serbia and Montenegro formed the new Federal Republic of Yugoslavia in April 1992, Belgrade ordered JNA members from both republics to leave Bosnia and the territory of other republics. However, this much-publicised command was primarily for Western consumption. Firstly, the large contingent of Bosnian Serb forces, regular and conscript, was not affected. They carried on and took over the JNA and territorial defence weapons and ammunition. Furthermore, although about 14,000 troops left Bosnia in the period before the fighting, their withdrawal was largely cosmetic because of the build-up of local Serb forces to replace them and the arrival of 'volunteers' from Serbia, many of them from outside the ranks of the JNA, though the BiH forces captured or killed JNA men from Serbia and Vojvodina, including Hungarian conscripts, over the next few months. The removal of the last non-Serb professional JNA officers in the spring of 1992 also made the Serb Army in Bosnia a more reliable force for the sort of savage campaign Mladić intended to pursue.

Although the fledgling BiH Army inherited some former professionals, mainly Muslim, from the JNA, it was so disadvantaged by its lack of armour and heavy artillery that even skilful regulars would have had difficulty thwarting Mladić's conventional thrusts towards his strategic goals. In any case, there was always an element of distrust surrounding the ex-JNA senior officers. Certainly, in relations with Croatia and the local Croats, memories of Muslim officers in the JNA loyally obeying Serb orders over the previous year when Croatia had been the target discouraged trust and cooperation between Croat defence forces and BiH ones under such command.

The speed with which Mladić's forces were able to surround Sarajevo and create effective corridors linking most of the territories which had been earmarked as the basis of a Bosnian Serb Republic not only illustrated the imbalance of forces, it also showed how decisive conventional firepower was in a war in Bosnia. Even as armchair experts in the West and nostalgics for Tito's heroics were holding forth to governments and in the media on the impossibility of a conventional army conquering, let alone holding territory in Bosnia against the wishes of its inhabitants, Mladić's men were showing how it could be done. The war in Bosnia revolved around Mladić's determination to hold key roads and clear the non-Serb population from their vicinity. The roads were vital as troops, armour and their supplies, particularly the huge number of artillery shells which the Serb Army used, were transported by motor vehicle. Such had been the profound change in the agrarian economy of Bosnia that even if Mladić had wished to imitate Tito's methods, he could not have found pack animals to transport his men and supplies. Without his tanks and artillery, his men would have only been able to advance by launching risky and costly attacks themselves, but despite their heroic rhetoric, the Serbs showed great caution about risking their own lives in hand to hand combat, preferring the prolonged artillery barrage and blockade to do their work.[13]

In response to the savage attacks on the non-Serb areas of Bosnia, the West set in train the machinery for sanctions and withdrew the vestiges of recognition from Yugoslavia. On 12 May, the EC monitors in Sarajevo left the city as early as possible before news of the withdrawal of EC ambassadors from Belgrade the day before reached local Serbs. In practice their hell-for-leather flight turned out to be unnecessary as they were waved through successive checkpoints without difficulty.[14] Two days later the UN announced it was pulling out its personnel too. The retreat of the international community was covered by a barrage of statements and condemnations from the chancelleries of the richest and most powerful countries in the world.

So long as the fighting had been in Croatia, Sarajevo with its modern communications infrastructure from the 1984 Winter Olympics had made an ideal headquarters for UNPROFOR, but as fighting intensified nearby the staff were withdrawn to peaceful Zagreb. A token force remained to guard Sarajevo airport. It was the Canadian garrison of this easiest and safest route into the besieged city who became the object of much media coverage. Their commanding officer, Lewis Mackenzie, made his name by firing from the lip with as little hesitation as he showed reluctance to be drawn into shooting from the hip. In fact, whatever his personal intentions, Mackenzie's stream of interviews equating all sides as sharing a similar burden of guilt for the war made him into a strategic ally of the Serbs, cordially loathed by the besieged population. The fact that Mackenzie's UN mandate and the firepower at his disposal condemned him to inaction does not excuse the fact that he seemed to approach every fresh crisis with an open mouth. However, his successors as local UNPROFOR commanders shared Mackenzie's penchant for inaction if not his gift for the soundbite, so perhaps Canada's hero should not be too harshly judged. He was just a typical representative of the kind of soldier bred up by NATO during four decades preparing for Armageddon.[15]

Fighting around the airport – which was surrounded by different suburbs of Sarajevo, each dominated by forces loyal to the BiH government or to the Serb regime established in Pale overlooking the city – meant that communications and aid supplies to the city were frequently cut as both sides struggled to control the key area and its routes into the city. By midsummer, the Western states seemed about to give up the stuttering aid effort when the French President, aware that his domestic position was ebbing fast as anti-EC feelings and disillusionment with his Socialist regime spread, decided to perform one of his best stunts.

He flew secretly from the EC summit in Lisbon, which had discussed football and Bosnia with roughly equal seriousness (see above), to the besieged Bosnian capital.[16]

François Mitterrand's publicity-grabbing lightning visit to Sarajevo on 28 June achieved nothing to halt the fighting, but it shamed some of his fellow EC leaders caught on the hop by the French President's unexpected jaunt into agreeing to try to fly in humanitarian aid. This began two days later. The media began to talk about the 'lifting of the siege of Sarajevo',[17] but in practice the fighting began again even on the first day of the aid flights. Once it was clear to the Serbs that the West was primarily concerned with calming its own public and media concerns about human suffering rather than stopping the fighting, their forces resumed the offensive.

Soon enough, the Serb forces and then their rivals learned that the UN humanitarian aid was an easy source of supplies and funds for their war efforts. Even when troops were deployed in their sky blue helmets to protect the aid convoys, they had orders not to use force against local groups trying to stop them delivering food or other supplies. From the start, those responsible for aid made (tacit) agreements with the forces besieging Sarajevo about how much and what sort of aid would be delivered. For instance, food was let through but not the fuel to cook it. A cat-and-mouse game was played between besiegers and besieged over when and how much electricity would be permitted in the Bosnian capital. Instead of using 'all necessary means' to deliver the humanitarian aid, the UN forces preferred to bribe their way through the lines. A regular set of tariffs was drawn up and periodically changed to take account of shifts in the value of the dollar or the importance of the cargo. Cash from the UN's aid effort became a vital ingredient fuelling the war effort of the competing armies in Bosnia, but especially the Serb Army's coffers. In addition to cash, petrol and other fuel stuffs were acceptable in exchange for letting aid through.[18]

The British government laid great emphasis on the importance of humanitarian aid and regularly claimed that it was saving scores or even hundreds of thousands of lives. If ever an audit can be done of the net effect of the UN aid effort, its outcome might be less than flattering to those who saw it as a substitute for action to stop the fighting or to reverse ethnic cleansing. Without the bribes and syphoning-off of UN and other aid made possible by the softly-softly approach, the war machines might not have been able to function and carry on killing people and destroying their heritage.

Throughout the following period, the understandable desire to protect those forces engaged in delivering humanitarian aid from unreasonable risk was debased into a desperate effort to avoid any risk. Since they were professionals who had often joined the armed forces precisely in order to take risks, albeit in a highly disciplined way, the obsession with the safety of their forces on the part of the British government in particular did not ring entirely true. There was a growing feeling that their deployment served the political purpose of blocking any more decisive action just as much as genuinely humanitarian purposes.

Under the blanket of avoiding unreasonable danger to HM forces and other Blue Helmets, a host of measures to make more effective humanitarian aid were not taken. The key negative decision was the persistent refusal to use the large ex-JNA airfield at Tuzla which was in the BiH Army's hands. Instead of flying in aid to Tuzla's swollen population, convoys of heavy goods vehicles made irregular and lengthy, not to mention dangerous, journeys to the unoccupied north-east of Bosnia. Of course, following this route obliged them to pay the 'customs tolls' levied by the armies in between the Croatian ports where aid was disembarked to Tuzla itself.

During the Srebrinica crisis in the spring of 1993, when French then Canadian Blue Helmets set up a perimeter around the last Muslim-held town in eastern Bosnia, suddenly Tuzla was used so that the UN personnel could receive aid and be flown out for treatment when sick or wounded. A few Muslims were also helicoptered to the base for treatment. This showed the viability of using Tuzla airfield as an aid route, but the precedent was not followed up. It led to dark mutterings that the West, and the British in particular were using aid, and the withholding of aid, as a weapon to pressure the Sarajevo government to accept peace on the Serbs' terms.

Despite the experience of the Croats, the BiH presidency, led by Alija Izetbegović, seems to have put its faith in external intervention. Once its makeshift forces had established defensive lines around the few areas left under BiH control – those which Mladić did not wish to risk large casualties in storming – each side sat it out to see whether the West would come to the aid of the Bosnians before they were starved into surrender. Permitting the passage of UN aid, however grudgingly, was one way in which Mladić avoided direct confrontation with the West without in practice giving too much assistance to his enemies.

The BiH presidency hoped that the evident human suffering and the gratuitous bombardment of civilians in Sarajevo would pressure NATO to use its military power to reverse the situation. But even the massacring of bread queues and then of mourning relatives failed to stir any official response. Certainly, it horrified public opinion, but all the classic forces which would have mobilised it for action went strangely silent over Bosnia. The official peace movements in the West were inactive on the Serb side, with many of their once stentorian voices raised in explanation of how much the Serbs had suffered in the Second World War.

By contrast, many of the fellow travellers of anti-war movements from Vietnam to the Gulf among the intellectuals and the artists of the West took up the cause of Bosnia. Sarajevo became a symbol of an embattled multicultural ideal under assault from ranting nationalist troglodytes. From Susan Sontag to Bernard-Henri Levy, a pilgrimage to Sarajevo became a must as once Hanoi had been. Whatever their motives, the inhabitants of Sarajevo probably found their morale uplifted by the motley crew of jet-set blockade runners. At least the intellectuals did not come like Douglas Hogg to advise surrender since the 'cavalry' were not en route to the rescue.

1992 was the fiftieth anniversary of the swinging of Hitler's Final Solution into full gear. But Western politicians who could be relied on for a routine condemnation of fascism were strangely reticent about drawing comparisons with the current tragedy. 'Never again' had been repeated for fifty years and had turned out to be an empty promise. Of course, by comparison with the Nazis' industrialisation of mass slaughter, the Serbs' use of cruder, more ancient methods rendered them less capable of murder on a Hitlerian scale, but only those obsessed with not drawing comparisons with the Nazis could avoid recognising the symptoms of genocide abroad in Europe again.[19]

Of course 1992 was not only the year of Bosnia, but also of the Olympics, which took up a lot of Mr Major's time, as well as the US presidential elections. Although he campaigned mainly on domestic issues, Bill Clinton recognised that the growing disaster in the Balkans was a sign that George Bush's assumed mastery of foreign affairs might also prove a weak point in the President's record. A master of easy promises and slick rhetoric, Clinton soon had the President under fire for inaction while Sarajevo was bombarded.

It was not only Clinton who encouraged Bosnian resistance. Belatedly recognising that it had been lied to and deceived, his predecessor's administration began to speak out against aggression. George Bush announced on 21 May 1992:

> We now recognise the full sovereignty of Slovenia, Croatia and now of Bosnia and we stand in solidarity with their people. And let me make this clear: we will not recognise the annexation of territory by force, that aggression cannot be rewarded. We must stay involved trying to find a peaceful answer.[20]

The last sentence was still the key one: aggression would be reversed by all available *peaceful* means. Even rescinding the one-sided arms embargo was going too far along the road to war for George Bush and his allies.

The real pressure for foreign intervention and a lifting of the arms embargo came with the public's discovery of the Serb-run concentration camps later in the summer. Of course Western governments and 'humanitarian' agencies had known about them for some time, but had not publicised them for fear of offending the Serbs and damaging the 'peace process' as well as because of the embarrassment it would cause to them as the proponents of the policies which helped to create the environment in which mass ethnic cleansing could take place.[21]

It was striking that it was a Serb public relations blunder which led to the media publicity about conditions in their camps. The Serb propaganda machine had recognised the importance of getting Western opinion on their side or at least confusing it by promoting the equivalence argument, whereby victim and aggressor were much of a muchness because the *méchant* Muslim dog was fighting back after being attacked; but even propagandists have to believe something and it is often their own propaganda. Having denied the existence of concentration camps for Muslim men and insisted that ethnic cleansing was not taking place, Karadžić seems to have convinced himself that his forces held only prisoners of war and those in good conditions.

An accomplished liar, Karadžić showed remarkable lack of insight into the mentality of his own fighting men and particularly of the sort of person who would become a concentration camp guard. Believing in the complete justice of their cause and with utter contempt for their opponents and their rights, the bull-headed guards at Trnopolje or Omarska could not conceive that anyone authorised to visit them would come to a different point of view. Pictorial evidence of maltreatment and malnourishment threw Karadžić onto the defensive. After his denials of the evident facts could no longer be sustained, he denied responsibility and threatened those who were.

Radovan Karadžić liked to posture as the supreme commander of the Serb forces in Bosnia and for a long time he was treated as the man in charge of the war. His grandiloquent threats of condign punishment for those who disobeyed him were taken seriously. (Just as Milan Panić's equally categorical and meaningless declarations were fed to the Western media by cynical governments and mediators as authoritative statements proving that he was 'our' partner in peace.) John Kennedy, Conservative candidate for Barking in the April general election, as well as a diligent lobbyist for the Bosnian Serbs, told Channel 4 viewers on behalf of Karadžić,

> He's been quite rigorous when announcing this cease-fire in making it perfectly plain that he expects military leaders in the field to obey political direction and if they don't *they will suffer sanctions of a severe nature* and I think he's absolutely determined to rein them in and bring them under control and doesn't want to see forces running around and acting on their own initiatives.[22]

The military commanders ignored these blood-curdling threats of punishment for those who defied Dr Karadžić, but then they knew where real power lay in the Bosnian Serb Republic, which was something which the Western leaders preferred to ignore.

No one was punished, needless to add, and in any case the international community stepped in to resolve the problem by agreeing to provide transport to deport the camp inmates from their places of detention out of Bosnia into Croatia where they could be interned for the duration of the war in what were politely called refugee camps. Naturally, many of the survivors of Serb detention welcomed the chance to escape to Croatia where many of their remaining relatives had sought sanctuary, but the UN-sponsored and Western-approved and organised resettlement of the inmates was a severe blow to the West's own claims to be determined to reverse 'ethnic cleansing'. In fact, it was one of the first major episodes in which the international community actively promoted the process.

Behind the scenes, Western diplomats had long favoured some sort of population exchange and mass resettlement programme as the 'final solution' to the Yugoslav problem. However much the impetus for mass flight and ethnic cleansing came from within Yugoslavia, the international community's readiness to tolerate the principle of forced relocation of peoples, with all that implied with regard to the murder and rape of the weak, the halt, the lame and the old as well as the destruction of property and cultural heritage, certainly encouraged the cleansers to carry on.

The farcical non-implementation of the London 'Principles of Civilised Conduct' and the failure of each successive peace conference which foundered on the Serb unwillingness to accept any Bosnian state or to renounce the gains of ethnic cleansing showed how little respect the Serb leaders felt for the values of those mediating peace. The only real pressure on Milošević was his calculation of whether it was worth bearing the burden of sanctions despite their loopholes or whether he should agree to a peace deal in bad faith in order to get them lifted and then return to his project of conquest afterwards.

By the time of the Athens Conference at the beginning of May 1993, Milošević seemed to have come down on the side of calling a (temporary) halt to the war if only to avoid putting the new

President of the United States to the test over his threats of intervention. But Mladić and the Bosnian Serbs had got too used to victory to care much about the outside world. The economy of the Bosnian Serb Army and politicians was based on loot and conquest. An end to the war would require an abrupt change in their lifestyle. Karadžić could be persuaded or bullied into going along with Milošević's acceptance of the Vance-Owen Plan, but many of his parliamentarians and Mladić himself could not.[23]

After the rejection of the Athens Agreement by the Pale Parliament in May 1993, it became obvious that Karadžić had no real power base in Bosnia capable of challenging Mladić and that his external support came from Milošević. Western journalists laid great emphasis on Milošević's apparent humiliation by the Bosnian Serbs. However, since he strengthened his control over Serbia immediately afterwards it seems it did not weaken his position. He also let loose his tame journalists on the recalcitrant Bosnian Serbs – except for General Mladić, significantly enough.

In May 1993 also, the Belgrade press began to publish serious allegations of corruption and misappropriation of funds by the Bosnian Serb leaders. This was of course part of Milošević's campaign to make the Bosnian Serbs accept the Vance-Owen deal – or at least to be seen pressuring Karadžić, et al. to do so. The government newspaper, *Politika*, reported on the authority of the 'circles in power' that Radovan Karadžić had lost 300,000 Deutschmarks in a single night in a Belgrade casino. If that story was true, few could doubt where the money came from. The tolls charged to let humanitarian aid pass had found their natural home in the croupier's purse. Other leaders of the Serb Republic along with Karadžić had acquired well-appointed flats in the *nomenklatura* suburbs of Belgrade, including the Shakespeare scholar, 'Vice-president' Nikola Koljević, 'Foreign Minister' Aleksa Buha and other members of the Pale establishment. Other reports attacked Karadžić's children for their self-indulgence and arrogance. His son, Sasha, was alleged to have demanded that he and his dog, Ajka, be found places on a helicopter supposed to transport the wounded.

Another of Karadžić's close allies, Biljana Plavsić, the 'Passionara' of Pale, was also criticised for spending too much time in Belgrade. She was almost in tears at her harsh treatment: anonymous telephone calls and threatening letters made life worse than in Sarajevo! Milošević's wife, Mirjana Marković, actually went so far as to compare Dr Plavsić with Dr Mengele, adding that the 'latter was a psychopath though at least not a Serb'.[24]

Of course, it was not only the Serb leaders who were corrupted by war and the easy pickings of the black market for those with the right connections. The decay of civil society was also acute in the government-controlled areas. The age-old traditions of Balkan corruption reinforced by four decades of communism made a good ground-base for the full-scale mafiaisation of the supply side of the economy under war conditions. In besieged Sarajevo, the black market flourished under its natural conditions.

As in any situation of crisis and shortage the black market performed a dysfunctional service. For those individuals who still had hard currency or valuables to buy scarce items of food, fuel and medicine, the spivs were a good thing. The racketeers knew where vital supplies were and how to get them. Not only did they bribe officials within the city, but also made their arrangements with the besieging forces and the privileged international personnel who came and went from the city. In a war which resounded as much to the rhetoric of fanaticism as to gunfire, the willingness of men who had slit their opponents' throats for their circumcision to turn a blind eye to supplies entering Sarajevo in return for a cut was an even more depressing revelation about human nature. It is one thing to murder a man in the white heat of ideological conviction, but to do so and then take a kickback from his brother is a thoroughly depraved way to behave.

For all that individuals, still able to afford the sky-rocketing prices of the black market, must have welcomed its provision of the otherwise unobtainable, as a social phenomenon the black market was a contributor to the general decay of the quality of life. It eroded the solidarity of people under siege and gave power to a mafia class. It flattered the esteem of the black-marketeers inside Sarajevo, who, like many urban crime barons, began to pose as patriots and the representatives of their people. This had the effect of undermining the relations between the different groups making up the population of the besieged city. In the scramble for survival, these was a tendency for Muslim, Croat and Serb within the loyalist area to be set against one another in any case, but the activities of the local barons of the black market only exacerbated the process.

As tensions rose inside the besieged city as it went deep into a second year under blockade, reports began of murders of non-Muslims. These were routinely attributed to an allegedly growing degree of fundamentalism within the Muslim population of the city. The born-again fundamentalists were supposed to have been picking upon people they regarded as inherently suspect, i.e. Croats and Serbs. This may have been the case, but it was also the case that black-marketeers in and outside the official BiH forces were engaged in battles over turf. Protection rackets and control of supplies naturally encouraged violence in an enclosed urban world beset by the threat of external bombardment at any moment. In retrospect, what may seem most striking about Sarajevo under siege is not the flaking of civil society under pressure, but its remarkable robustness despite all the forces pushing it towards total breakdown.

Another vital ingredient in the corrosion of society was the stationing of the UN troops and other personnel in the region. Already in Croatia, the Russians, Ukrainians and the African contingents had made their names through their willingness to barter for anything with local people, but especially with gunmen and preferably warlords who usually had the ability to pay in hard currency. What made the Bosnian deployment of UNPROFOR distinctive was the evident corrosion of the discipline of the Western professional forces too.

No doubt, even in peacetime all armies are composed partly of a network of soldiers nicking and trading items belonging to the stores, but the humiliating idleness imposed on most UN troops by the nature of their mandate seems to have pushed UNPROFOR as a body over the edge into the outright exploitation of the beleaguered populations whose territory it occupied. All military bases attract prostitutes but what made the situation around the French barracks so distasteful was the evident fact that many of the girls were reduced to selling their bodies to French soldiers in order to feed themselves, often to the same soldiers who were selling UN rations on the black market at exorbitant rates. UNPROFOR's involvement in the black market was a highly visible symptom of the flawed morality underpinning its ineffective presence. Why shouldn't troops who were not in Sarajevo to protect the population but only themselves, and various visiting dignitaries passing through to tell the Bosnians to renounce all hope, feel liberated from any responsibility to behave decently towards the civilian population?

General Morillon's table in the French officers' mess was famous for its fine wines and ripe cheeses. It was further evidence of the strange priorities of the airlift. No room could be found for fuel for Sarajevo's operating theatres – ostensibly for safety reasons, but in practice because the Serb Army forbade it – but the General's cellar could not be allowed to suffer. Until late in the day, Morillon carried on the tradition established by Mackenzie, and it was only after he was surrounded by the desperate people of Srebrinica that he relaxed his opposition to UNPROFOR or any other action which might risk a clash with Serbs. However, even in Srebrinica, despite his ringing quotation of Macmahon after his capture of the Malakoff bastion in the Crimean War, 'J'y suis, j'y reste', he promptly left the town and it sank into anarchy after its brief 'salvation' in April 1993.

The corruption of the Ukrainian Blue Helmets produced absurd situations. On one occasion, a company was unable to leave its exposed position when it came under fire because all its fuel had been sold to spivs, possibly the same people firing on it. The short-sighted troops had to sit out the firefight in their static fighting vehicles. The partiality of the Ukrainian contingent was hardly surprising.[25] Their government in Kiev had long since learned that the West was only interested in the politics of gesture. Provided the ex-communists controlling the Ukrainian government made the right noises about support for sanctions and the peace process, Kiev could get on with trading with Serbia.

From the imposition of UN sanctions onwards, the media reported that Ukrainian vessels were regularly sanctions-busting up the Danube. Since Ukraine had had no serious economic reform despite the collapse of the Soviet Union and the alleged change of heart of its *nomenklatura* rulers, it is difficult to believe that oil barges and other supplies could have been sent from Ukraine up the Danube to Belgrade without official approval. Even the barges themselves were still state-owned after all.

Anatoly Zlenko, who had made a smooth transition from the

communist *apparatchik* holding the post of bogus foreign minister of the Soviet Ukraine to the foreign minister of an internationally recognised sovereign state, indignantly denied the allegations and evidence of sanctions-breaking in the autumn of 1992: 'We don't have any people who break sanctions – absolutely not . . . There are no violations.'[26] However, before long Mr Zlenko was making a rather different case to justify Kiev's continuation of diplomatic relations with Belgrade and Ukraine's ostentatious refusal to recognise Bosnia-Hercegovina. This had been a 'far-sighted step' since the Bosnian government 'was unable to control its own territory', which of course meant that 'it would have made no sense to recognize it'.[27]

Throughout the fighting in the rest of Bosnia, the enclave around Bihać remained firmly under Muslim control even though surrounded by Serb territory. The Serbs made no effort to capture it and indeed permitted the people to trade with their territory and even more surprisingly with Croatia beyond their lines. The failure of the Serbs to snuff out the Bihać enclave was not surprising: it was ruled in effect by Fikret Abdić, the sort of Muslim with whom Milošević could do business, and indeed the sort of late communist spiv to whom Western statesmen gravitated when looking for a partner. As 1993 progressed, Abdić, encouraged by the respect paid to him by Western statesmen and media alike, began to act more and more like an independent potentate. But not all the Muslim forces in the Bihać pocket were prepared to accept de facto secession from Bosnia-Hercegovina, however profitable such a course of action might be for 'Daddy' and his supporters. By the autumn, Abdić seemed to have avoided war with the Serbs only at the risk of promoting an intra-Muslim conflict inside the enclave.[28]

Abdić was not the only person who seemed able to carry on making money during the war, but the revival of his Agrokomerc empire as the focus of a cross-border trading system which made profits by selling through no-man's land was a grim reminder of the survival of communist corruption and business ethics into the post-communist mayhem. When it came to adapting to the new realities, the old *apparatchiks* were second to none.

What Abdić overrated was the degree to which the loyalty of his fellow Muslims in the enclave could be bought. The more he became the public proponent of acceptance of the Vance-Owen carve-up, the more splits appeared even among the defenders of the Bihać pocket. The ugly little civil war between loyal supporters of the government in Sarajevo and Abdić's men (supported with supplies from the neighbouring Serbs) which started with Abdić's acceptance of the role as the favoured Muslim partner of the international mediators and spluttered on through the winter was just another symptom of the breakdown of Bosnia which was fostered by the 'peace process'.

By midsummer of 1993 the options available to the Bosnian Army were clearly limited, but the Washington Deal clarified matters. For all their loud talk about not accepting this and rolling back that, it was clear that the Western states had abandoned any idea of the 'international community' asserting itself and enforcing the London 'Principles'. Difficult as it was for men brought up in provincial Bosnia to comprehend that men masquerading under the title of President of the United States of America or Her Majesty's Principal Secretary of State for Foreign and Commonwealth Affairs were shameless creatures boastfully proclaiming one thing while shabbily conniving at precisely the opposite, the realisation that Balkan duplicity was not unknown among the pressed suits of Western Europe and North America naturally did little to discourage cynicism. If the West had no intention of reversing ethnic cleansing, as clearly it had not, then the Bosnian Army would have to shift itself in the struggle for the survival of its people. The Hurd doctrine had triumphed in the UN Security Council and now its corollary would triumph on the ground: in a three-way contest for survival, the weaker parties would seek to destroy each other since neither could take on the strongest and hope to win, but at the same time, the Serbs though strongest did not wish to make the necessary further sacrifices in blood for total victory, when they could wait and see Croat and Muslim undermine each other in the struggle for survival.

By discrediting Western policy and Western ideals, the parties to the Washington Deal set in train the next series of horrific events on the ground in Bosnia. Already the Vance-Owen Plan had encouraged the war of each against all in the scramble for land, but now it intensified. The Croat-Muslim fighting took on the character of a full-scale war too. Mate Boban and the Hercegovinan HVO overestimated their firepower vis-à-vis the Muslim forces, seeming to have expected an easy victory in their attempt to establish full control over Hercegovina and Croatian enclaves inside Bosnia. At the same time, those in the BiH Army who thought that the Muslim strategy of survival depended on conquering a viable block of land cutting south-westwards from Tuzla rather than in direct confrontation with the firepower of the Serb forces around Sarajevo, turned their attention to seizing and securing that territory. The recent history of an unhappy and unsuccessful working relationship between Croat and Muslim forces in their joint struggle against the Serbs had embittered relations between the two groups. Each side blamed the other for its defeats at the hands of the Serbs. Muslims accused the Croats of failing to try to lift the siege of Sarajevo, while Croats regarded the flood of Muslim refugees from elsewhere in Bosnia into areas they regarded as their own as a prelude to effective Muslim control. The Serb strategy of ethnic cleansing played a vital role in splitting Croats and Muslims by upsetting the balance between them in the areas into which the refugees flowed. (It was another reason why the neat plans for population transfers did not work in practice.)

Just as the JNA was central to the Bosnian Serbs' war effort, providing everything from the directing brains to the ammunition, so the HVO was to the Hercegovinan Croat campaigns in the west. Hercegovinan Croats were central to the inner decision-making elite on military matters in Zagreb, too, and along with their wealthy émigré counterparts exercised a baleful influence on Tudjman, appealing to his childish Machiavellian side. Belatedly recognising that power politics was the only thing that seemed to work in the Balkans and certainly that power politics was all that the West respected (as the Vance-Owen Plan showed), Tudjman shifted back from his anti-Serb alliance with Izetbegović towards the fantasy of compensating Croatia for what had been lost to the Serbs in 1991 by taking land from Bosnia-Hercegovina. Milošević had played up to Tudjman's geopolitical daydreams already in the spring of 1991 as a way of trapping the Croatian President into discrediting himself in the eyes of the West and as 1993 progressed was to find it all too easy to lure Tudjman back into the same trap.

Croatia's Defence Minister, Gojko Šušak, was himself an émigré from Hercegovina who had returned to Croatia (after a successful career at running pizzerias in Canada) and like so many émigrés from a thousand exiles in the past showed little sign of having learnt anything and every sign of having forgotten nothing. His influence in redirecting the Croatian war effort compounded the undoubted local tensions between Croats and Muslims, which the influx of refugees from elsewhere constantly worsened.

Perhaps because it was a struggle between two losing sides (each humiliated by its failure to defeat the Serbs), the fighting between Croat and Muslim became as bitter as any yet seen. It was a crude struggle for survival between two groups fighting to avoid the fatal relegation to third place. Most Serbs had never faced such a direct threat of annihilation, whatever Dr Karadžić had claimed on their behalf, but the crisis meant that Croats in Central Bosnia and Muslims in Hercegovina lived on an ever sharper knife-edge.

From spring 1993, the struggle for control of Mostar became increasingly brutal. The HVO forces drove the Muslims across the Neretva from the west side of the city into a pocket in the east. It was the classic preliminary of ethnic cleansing. Muslims of military age, including those who joined the Croat forces to fight the Serbs, were rounded up and disappeared into grim makeshift concentration camps. The survivors were eventually driven from Hercegovina with the aid of the UN who shipped them abroad. 'Humane' ethnic cleansing as ever required a brutal prelude.

By August 1993, the Muslim enclave in Mostar was in a desperate condition. A little military aid was smuggled into the besieged garrison through the mountains from BiH controlled territory, but large-scale food supplies had been blocked by the Croat forces. When eventually a UN convoy escorted by Spanish troops entered the city, local people blocked its departure, causing much bad blood with the Spaniards who clearly resented the ingratitude of the desperate inhabitants and refugees.

Although the Muslim enclave survived the onslaught, because the HVO proved as unwilling to fight street for street as the JNA had in Vukovar two years earlier, the city of Mostar suffered irreparable damage. Most of all, its symbol, the very bridge which gave the city its name as the crossing of the Neretva was destroyed on 9 November. As ever, the vandals were too ashamed of their act to admit it, and like the Serb mosque-killers elsewhere in Bosnia, the Croats indulged in shabby lies to avoid confessing that their artillery had bombarded the elegant span of the Stare Most until it collapsed into the river below. It had been built in 1566, on the site of an older pre-Turkish bridge, and had survived even the savage fighting in the Second World War. The destruction of the old bridge was a self-defeating act, typical of the brutal nihilism unleashed by the war. Far from promoting the Croats' cause, the broken arch of Bosnia's tourist trademark provided a useful symbol for those demanding sanctions against Croatia.[29]

Against the background of Croat-Muslim fighting in Hercegovina and especially around the media enclave provided by the grocers of Vitez, which produced news reports and film so convenient for the Foreign Secretary's anti-intervention message, the Serb forces resumed their operations well aware that UNPROFOR and its political masters were desperate for the war to stop and therefore wanted a Serb victory as the quickest route to removing the embarrassing coverage from the television screens of Western electorates.

By the beginning of August 1993, General Mladić was displaying utter contempt for the international community. In the presence of UN observers, he flew in his personal Gazelle helicopter from command post to command post around Sarajevo to visit fresh conquests and direct the artillery fire onto the UN's largest 'safe haven'. Although NATO jet-fighters flew regularly above Sarajevo to patrol the UN Security Council's decreed 'no-fly zone', Mladić flew with impunity. The committees required to decide on UN action and then pass on authorisation to NATO in Brussels which could in turn unleash a thunderbolt from the international community's aces-in-the-sky over Bosnia never came, at least not before the General had touched down and gone on, accompanied by press (and UN monitors), to continue the battle.

Contempt for the UN 'no-fly zone' was hardly surprising.

Britain and France had only agreed to it in the first place provided that no force was used to impose it! By mid-March 1993, it had been breached 465 times. By the time Mladić was flying around Sarajevo in his helicopter in order to direct his attacks more effectively, the count of breaches of the 'no-fly zone' had been given up.[30]

As Bosnia disintegrated into zones controlled by the Bosnian government, Serbs and Croats – with those areas in turn often in effect under the authority of local militias and warlords – the position of Bosnia as an internationally recognised member of the UN became even more surreal. Stranger still was the fact that by autumn 1993 two ghostly flags fluttered outside the UN building in New York: on the one hand the fleur-de-lys of Bosnia, but not far away on another flagpole the blue, white and red banner with a red star at its centre of Yugoslavia. The refusal to derecognise Yugoslavia was one of the key indicators of the insincerity of the international community. How it could recognise newly independent states like Bosnia or what it condescendingly entitled 'The Former Yugoslav Republic of Macedonia' and yet continue to treat 'the Socialist Federative Republic of Yugoslavia' as a full member passed understanding, especially as the Serbs and Montenegrins had themselves de-recognised it![31]

13

Last Chances for Peace

> Diplomats are just as essential to starting a war as soldiers are to finishing it. You take diplomacy out of war and the thing would fall flat in a week.
>
> Will Rodgers

If those responsible for the killing in Bosnia never seemed to weary, then the diplomats 'jaw-jawing' away in Geneva or wherever they could put a conference together showed equal pertinacity. No setback or humiliation could deflect the mediators and their staffs from talking to the parties to the conflict, briefing international organisations (UN, EC, WEU, IOC, etc.), consulting governments and leaking the latest position to the press. For the peacemakers it was never too late to talk some more and always too soon to despair. Shuttling from one negotiation to another became a way of life. It was self-contained and self-justifying: mediation became an end in itself. No matter how much killing went on or how many promises were broken, there was always another last chance for peace.

Lord Owen's appointment as the EC's peace-mediator was supposed to mark a dramatic shift in the intensity of the Community's determination to achieve an end to fighting in Bosnia. Instead of the languid old aristocrat, Lord Carrington, the Twelve had accepted the short-tempered doctor turned statesman, who had already sounded off vigorously on the subject of what to do *to the Serbs* if they refused to play ball. However, from his first statements in the job it became clear that Lord Owen was only a new instrument playing the old tune. His comments to journalists on the steps of the Élysée after meeting President Mitterrand must have rung with hollow familiarity in Balkan ears. All the favourite themes were there:

> The new countries that are emerging in what was formerly Yugoslavia have to live within Europe and they have to live with the reality of the European Community and the European Community was founded on democratic principles. It will not accept ethnic cleansing. It will not accept racist pressures. It will not accept that you can achieve territory by force of arms. These are principles which we will stick to not just for weeks or months but for years.[1]

Needless to say these principles were dead within nine months, but Lord Owen's mission survived the abandonment of these grand phrases. It turned out that what the appointment of the dynamic and thrusting Lord Owen instead of the sixth baron Carrington meant was that the EC had abandoned laid-back old-style appeasement for a new 1990s style of aggressive appeasement. Lord Owen turned out to be capable of being tough – as the Muslims increasingly discovered.

Lord Owen's old friend Cy Vance continued in office as UN mediator. Vance had been Secretary of State under Carter when Owen had enjoyed his brief spell as Foreign Secretary under Callaghan in the last days of Labour rule in Britain. Vance was almost a father-figure for Owen who has praised him as second only to George Marshall among postwar US secretaries of state. However, whereas Owen had become more robust (in speech at any rate) as a result of his tenure in King Charles Street – making him unique among postwar British foreign secretaries – Vance was a dyed-in-the-wool opponent of the use of force as his resignation from Carter's administration rather than support the rescue of the hostages held in the US embassy in Teheran had showed. But Owen's respect for Vance's judgement (combined with the obvious fact that John Major had raised him up to a high profile job again with a very clear mandate not to oppose Whitehall policy) meant that Owen's status as a male Thatcher manqué was about to be put to the test and found wanting.

Vance was dead set against both military intervention and lifting the arms embargo, so Owen had to explain away his previously robust statements on the need to be prepared to use force to impose peace if necessary:

> It was a fairly sophisticated way of trying to increase the pressure in a variety of different ways, during that time that pressure has increased in many ways, all of which I think offers a real possibility that with detailed work we may be able to bring this situation to a tolerable level fairly soon.[2]

The speed with which Lord Owen moved from his former robust stance to adopt the full mediating mentality astonished his one-time admirers and gratified his previous critics.

Owen was not prepared to set a deadline for agreement. He argued, 'there [have] been too many deadlines set in the past.' At first he set a piecemeal agenda, but soon the peacemaker's need to hype his own efforts led to the same fatuous optimism which had marred the EC effort from the start. By November 1992, Owen was confident that the Geneva peace conference set up after the London jamboree was getting results because of his new tough-minded approach: 'We in the Geneva conference tend to make very limited agreements and nail them down and by and large they stick.'[3] Over the months, Lord Owen found an agreement was about to stick on more than one occasion as the glue revealed itself to be just hot air. If he had turned his talents to the racing world, his career as tipster would not have lasted as long as his role as mediator.

As humiliation and failed agreements followed each other like 'confetti', as Owen was later to admit, it became cruelly clear that even with his personal reputation on the line, Lord Owen was a natural EC mediator for whom neither time nor failure set a term to the 'peace process'.[4] Unsalaried, but reinvigorated by assuming his apparently natural role at the centre of great events, Lord Owen set about the task of peacemaking with a rare will. Britain could take a certain melancholy pride in the fact that after producing a Lord Carrington, it was able to turn to an Owen. Few of her European partners could boast as much.

There were differences between the approach of Owen and Carrington. At heart, Lord Carrington seems to have found all his Balkan interlocutors unconvincing and certainly uncongenial. In his world-weary way, Carrington did not expect to win over any of them to his point of view. Lord Owen, who had always shown a certain weakness for rubbing shoulders with men of power, like the Chinese leaders whom he has defended, sought out Milošević as the key player. This was true of course, but to believe any peace worthy of the name could be based on Milošević's promises was an illusion. At best it would offer a way out for the EC and UN from their embarrassing imbroglio.

To accuse Lord Owen of cynicism from the start seems unfair. He set about his task with all the enthusiasm of a boy scout given a copy of Machiavelli instead of Baden-Powell by mistake. Owen set about making his play for Milošević. In March 1993, he told the press about a recent conversation with Milošević: 'We said, you have substantial influence and the world holds you in part responsible for what is happening in Bosnia and Hercegovina. You may think it unfair, we told him, but that's the way the world sees it.'[5] Already in an interview with *Foreign Affairs* in February 1993, Owen had revealed, 'I have been fortunate . . . in my working relationship with him . . . Vance and I always sought him out, *even when he was electorally unpopular* [emphasis added], because we could see he was potentially a very powerful figure.' In fact, 'Milošević is the most important person in the whole region.' So central was Milošević to Owen's peacemaking strategy that he was prepared to admit that in effect his first few months in office and the repeated negotiations then had been merely shadow-boxing while Bosnia burned: 'It seemed to me unrealistic to expect him to have helped the peace process in December [at the time of the Serbian elections], which would only have benefited . . . Milan Panić.'[6] At the time, of course, Lord Owen and the rest of the 'international community's' gaggle of mediators and statesmen had all proclaimed Panić as the best bet for peace and sneered at those who suggested that he was an absurd figure without any serious chance of toppling Milošević.

In the run-up to the December elections in Serbia, the West had held out the prospect of lifting sanctions if the Serb people voted for Panić. Afterwards it became clear that the angels of peace had cynically calculated that the real effect of UN sanctions would be to rally Serbs around Milošević rather than give in to pressure. The former US secretary of state, Lawrence Eagleburger, admitted that his support for sanctions had been despite the fact that he knew that they would reinforce Milošević's position unless firm actions were taken to reverse Serb aggression on the battlefield: 'Yeah, of course I did and I don't give a hoot . . . I'm sure it helped . . . I think he would have won anyway, but yes, I think I gave him some more votes.'[7] With enemies like Lawrence Eagleburger, who needs friends?

After Milošević's re-election as president, the fighting intensified in Bosnia. Meanwhile the peacemaking duo unveiled their plan to cantonise Bosnia-Hercegovina. It sparked off fresh fighting between Croats and Muslims as well as Serbs and Muslims as each side struggled for control of 'their' cantons, as was predictable. But Milošević's stock as a potential ally in peacemaking rose all the time. By Easter, Lord Owen felt it possible to remark about Milošević, 'In his own way, he is interested in peace.'[8] At Athens a few weeks later a nod of Milošević's head was enough to indicate peace was at hand.

Even the failure of Milošević to deliver peace did not damage his hold over Lord Owen's imagination. For the mediator, Milošević was the Moses of the peace process waiting to lead his people back to the promised land of 'Europe': 'Milošević is now prepared to take on the *hard right*, he is prepared to deal . . . and he is heading towards leading Serbia back into the European family. I have no doubt of that.'[9] Lord Owen does not seem to have asked himself what sort of family would want an unrepentant Milošević back in triumph. In fact, the idea that Milošević's quarrel with the 'hard right' represented anything more than a power struggle was unlikely. Just as when Hitler purged his Nazi rivals in 1934, *The Times* and other appeasers latched onto their judicial murder as a sign of the Führer's moderation, so Owen and his fellow mediators saw Milošević's falling out with Šešelj as proof that their man, Slobo, had been a moderate all along. The same sort of thinking had led the Bush administration to save Saddam's face and his power-base in the spring of 1991 when Assistant Secretary of State Richard Murphy argued that it was 'better for us if he is in power than if he is martyred'. Milošević was never likely to be martyred by the West, but by 1993 he had become its preferred partner for peace. This inversion of values required Izetbegović and his people to be martyred for their obstinate refusal to kow-tow to Belgrade and its Western partners in the peace process.[10]

However much Lord Owen's brash style might not have seemed

to suit the role of Balkan gravedigger, he rose to the challenge marvellously. But not even his talents were enough to persuade or intimidate the losing side into capitulation. The British government began to lose faith in its appointed appeaser. The more desperate the position became and the more obvious the failure of the Carringtons, Vances, Owens and their ilk to negotiate anybody's way out of the hole which diplomatic efforts had dug so deep for eighteen months, the more obsessed Mr Hurd became with finding a peacemaker who could finesse an end to the bloodshed. By mid-April 1993, the British Foreign Secretary was even prepared to trample on the feelings of past and present distinguished persons, declaring, 'We need an *international heavyweight*, someone *who can knock heads together* [emphasis added], to bulldoze through the obstacles . . .'[11] The world, however, was running out of patience as well as superannuated grandees.

Cy Vance was the first to throw in the towel. Even all the comforts of sanctions-breaking hotels in Belgrade could not disguise the strain on the aged Vance.[12] There was even a hint that he was not prepared to go the whole hog in the matter of conceding Serb demands. If Vance began to liberate himself from the internationally recognised necessity to appease Belgrade, his successor showed from the start all the hallmarks of an effective mediator. Fatal equidistance was immediately evident in the initial remarks of Cy Vance's replacement as UN peace envoy, the former Norwegian Defence Minister, Thorvald Stoltenberg. A former Norwegian diplomat in Belgrade during the early 1960s, he showed an acute sympathy for the hurt feelings of Serbs: 'The occasionally unilateral condemnations of Serbia by the international community wound the Serbian soul.' In practice, guilt was shared for the 'bloodbath, the violence, the thefts and rapes'. In so far as the new UN umpire was prepared to attribute responsibility, Stoltenberg admitted that since 'Serbia was the biggest country' involved it must have 'the greatest responsibility'.[13]

At the same time as Stoltenberg was criticising international partiality against the Serbs, Radovan Karadžić was insisting that the Bosnian Serbs 'might cancel further cooperation with those who behave partially and openly demonstrate anti-Serb policies'.[14] Every well-meaning Scandinavian expression of rebuke for lack of evenhandedness simply served to reinvigorate Serbian rhetoric of victimhood and therefore helped to justify further acts of violence and Serb demands for special consideration by the international mediators. It is a reflection on the inversion of the moral universe that the powerful aggressor's sensitivities were treated with kid gloves while the victims were routinely accused of shooting their own people and put under pressure to make concessions.

Backing up the bullying tactics of the international mediators, whose eyes seemed more often on the Nobel Prize than the prize of peace itself, was the pack of international bodies who had got themselves involved in the Balkan crisis and resented anyone who made ripples which could disturb their own operation. A pattern of whines appeared. Each successive toe in the water aroused pipes of rage from the groups already operating more or less ineffectively in the area. The aid workers protested that they would be put at risk if troops were sent in by the UN to act as escorts for aid. The politicians who were risking their electorate's disapproval by sending troops to ride (unloaded) shotgun complained whenever anyone suggested that their mission would be more efficacious if more troops and a more aggressive mandate were applied and so on. Some of the Blue Helmets complained that civilians tried to take cover in their barracks and thus exposed the sacred insignia of the UN to the risk of shell and shot.

Certainly, the belated dispatch of Western troops – Canadian, French, British and Spanish – was played down by their political masters as far as possible. British ministers in particular distinguished themselves by the amount of media time they took up with insisting on their well-laid contingency plans for retreat. This was hardly an approach likely to intimidate marauding bands of brigands. But the Western governments took pride in the inefficacy of their half-measures. According to one diplomat, 'By doing it under UN command, we avoid any appearance of military aggression that the name NATO might conjure up and we do not compromise the safety of thousands of UN peacekeepers who are in Yugoslavia'[15] – as if it was not precisely the utter ineffectiveness of those thousands of UN personnel which was the origin of proposals for more effective intervention rather than more of the same.

Finally, in February 1993, the UN Security Council took steps to coordinate the various agencies and forces which it had dribbled into dying Yugoslavia. Different rules of engagement threatened chaos with so many different units of Blue Helmets rubbing shoulders in the middle of a war. 'The result of this successive deployment was a legalistic maze,' according to one Western diplomat, 'since the rules of engagement were different in Croatia, in Sarajevo and the rest of Bosnia-Hercegovina, and in Macedonia. Now we will have the same rules for everybody.'[16] However, the same rules meant that thousands of Blue Helmets became ineffective in a standardised way rather than each nation failing to bring peace in its own way.

Some of the Western states who deployed Blue Helmets, like Sweden, were essentially post-military societies. It was hardly surprising that soldiers drawn from a comfortable welfare state found it alarming to be put at risk in a confusing and alien Balkan conflict, but other troops came from more robust societies. The real reasons for the British government's reluctance to let its professionals do their job properly remain obscure. Of course, John Major's purchase of his narrow general election victory in 1992 left his government with a daunting hangover of a vastly inflated public sector debt of around £50 billion and growing, so that even modest expenditure in the Balkans risked exploding the government's financial position. Certainly, the Conservative Party's own rocky finances made it beholden to generous Greek benefactors who might have been no less pro-Serb than their fellow countrymen. But the humiliating strategy of grin-and-bear-it which John Major, along with Douglas Hurd and Malcolm Rifkind, imposed on the British Blue Helmets led to professional British soldiers being spread-eagled and disarmed by gunmen whom the too-well-disciplined squaddies regarded as less than rabble. The humiliation of the British Army in Bosnia (against the will of the ordinary soldiers) may yet turn out to be a significant factor in threatening the security of Britain in the future.

A lexicon of timidity could easily be composed from the statements of Her Majesty's ministers expressing deepest caution about the risks of military involvement. As early as June 1992, John Major had assured the House of Commons, 'It would take only one ground-launched missile to cause serious loss of life.' A year later, his defence secretary insisted that 'Every single UN soldier in Bosnia is within range of Serb artillery. If there were attacks on Serb positions, it is entirely within the power of the Serbs to retaliate by shelling British forces . . . They are, I repeat, all within range of Serb artillery.'[17] No doubt the squaddies were touched by the politicians' concern for their well-being, but what lesson potential aggressors would take from such statements by a government willing to pay for a nuclear deterrent that might risk rather more severe consequences for Britain as a whole seems to have been left uncontemplated in Whitehall.

Of course, ministers hid behind the courage of the ordinary soldiers whenever their policy was criticised. Naturally, it takes great courage as well as discipline for soldiers to obey such fatuous orders as Whitehall issued for Bosnia; and just as in Ulster, British troops behaved remarkably well in a stressful position. But the fact that their political leaders imposed such humiliatingly passive conditions on them so as to frustrate even their role as the delivery boys of humanitarian aid means that they are more likely to be challenged on the battlefield in the future and perhaps by a more formidable foe than the Chetniks.

Once Bill Clinton was elected, he sought to impose on his European allies his campaign promise to take effective action to stop the slaughter in Bosnia, but he was also hamstrung by his own election promises to put America first and his use of Bush's allegedly too active foreign policy as a stick with which to beat his defeated Republican rival in November 1992. As events showed subsequently in Somalia, Clinton preferred to endure a humiliating fiasco at the hands of half-armed natives rather than see through a tough policy. Naturally, alerted to the risks of 'another Vietnam' in Bosnia, he was always determined to avoid putting American boys on the ground. Clinton's assessment of the school of American youth of 1993 as being no more willing to risk their lives than he himself had been a quarter of a century earlier will turn out to be a major factor in the challenges to US security in the coming years.

However, at least Clinton was prepared to offer US air support to a West European ground force. Even if the West Europeans were not prepared to intervene in the war, Clinton was also willing to provide air power to enforce the UN resolutions providing for the delivery of humanitarian aid through the use of 'all necessary means'. But Major and Mitterrand were against even doing that job properly because of the risks it posed to their troops and to their reputations if they bungled matters. Warren Christopher, the US Secretary of State, admitted that the British, French and Canadians had pressured the USA not to agree to arm the Bosnians because that would put their troops in a 'gravely endangered' position. Clinton's stance changed to conform to that of his allies: the newly elected US president intoned the ritual mantra that only a negotiated settlement could resolve the matter and that a settlement would not be 'imposed'.[18]

Colin Powell, the desk-bound hero of the Gulf War, succeeded in imposing his narrow view of the criteria for using US military power. As a staff officer in Vietnam, Powell seems to have been as scarred by that experience as the draft-dodging president. By the time he retired in summer 1993, Powell had stymied any US military involvement. His successor as chairman of the Joint Chiefs of Staff, John Shalikashvili, could not reverse a year and a half of energetic inaction by his predecessor, but he did give vent to the suspicion that the anti-interventionists had overestimated the fighting capacity of the Serb forces. After all, the US Army and its NATO allies had been preparing for Armageddon for four decades. The Serb Army was not a 'first-rate, fully combat-capable outfit like we have been preparing [to fight] for I don't know how many years'. Shalikashvili admitted that any campaign involved risks: 'Never underestimate the mess and the nastiness you can get into, but I think we have had too much overestimating [of the Serbs].'[19]

Like Germany's political class with its heart-rending appeals for someone else to bear the burden of rolling back aggression, so Bill Clinton and his colleagues undermined US prestige by posturing about the need to act but insisting that US forces would only do so from a safe distance several miles high in the sky. Whatever George Bush's failings as a decisive statesman, Bill Clinton seemed determined to show that he could surpass his predecessor's capacity for meaningless public declarations. By mid-May 1993, after months of flip-flops over Bosnia (and most other issues), Clinton assured the press, 'I realise it's frustrating . . . but we're not vacillating. We have a clear strong policy.' Whatever its clarity and strength, that policy was a firmly kept state secret.[20]

Clinton's vice-president, Al Gore, admitted that the one-sided effect of UN sanctions had been to aid Belgrade. 'The world community has in essence sided with Serbia . . . They have unlimited ammunition . . . The world community is preventing the other side from arming itself.'[21] It is the traditional job of the vice-president to keep his mouth shut and go to state funerals. Gore's statement of the truth made no difference to US policy and suggests that he would have done better to say nothing if he was not willing to attend the funerals in Bosnia of those encouraged to fight on by his empty words.

If no conceivable government of the United States was capable of risking professional US ground forces to uphold its loudly proclaimed principles, then other less powerful states and alliances might be forgiven for failing to match words and deeds. Certainly, Serb propaganda claims about German or Turkish plans to resume their domination of the Balkans were without foundation (except in the minds of a coterie of Tory and Labour MPs who travelled to Belgrade together to sip in the fountain of truth there and learn about the evil machinations of their own allies and partners in the EC or NATO).

Ordinary members of the British public were inclined to ask, not unreasonably, why their 'boys' were expected to go to Bosnia or their taxes provide aid when the Muslim countries did little that was evident to help. This attitude exaggerated the degree to which Bosnia was a Muslim state, but the question in itself gave the lie to the bogey of international Islamic fundamentalism. It was revealed to be a paper tiger used by the Serbs to frighten Westerners (who had a mixed-up fear of Khomeiniism and their local Asian shopkeepers), but like most unfounded fears no amount of evidence could relieve it. After all, if evidence were required for such anxieties they would not exist in the first place. The Serbs and their Greek allies – playing on the ignorance of the West and its self-righteous prejudices – conjured up a powerful picture of the mujahedeen of pan-Turkic Ottoman revanchism in league with the demons of Islamic fundamentalism swarming northwards determined to stable their horses in Westminster

Abbey and turn St Paul's into a mosque. But neither Suleiman the Magnificent nor the Invisible Imam marched to the aid of Bosnia.

If the EC's pressures on Serbia proved remarkably ineffective, its bullying of the Turks, in which the British distinguished themselves, was highly effective. The Turkish elite was so desperate for approval from its Western role models that it seemed prepared to accept any humiliation at their hands. Although any credible chance of entering the Community itself had long since disappeared for Turkey, Ankara remained besotted with the idea of European acceptance of Turkey as a partner. Even the shabby treatment of Turkey during the Gulf War, when not only Germany made clear how reluctant she was to uphold NATO obligations towards its south-eastern bastion, or the failure of leading Western statesmen to attend the funeral of President Ozal after his sudden death, could not liberate the Turkish elite from its deference to Europe.

The West's failure to act effectively over Bosnia did not pass unremarked among Turks, however. By currying favour with a Europe which appeased Serbia, despite her small size, the Turkish government undermined its own standing and the prestige of the whole Westernising project begun under Ataturk. By weakening the authority of the Westernised elite in Turkey, the West's Balkan policy may yet produce the nationalist or fundamentalist backlash which the West claims to fear and to wish to forestall. (Open EC, especially French, support for the military coup in Algeria in January 1992, intended to prevent the election of an Islamic party, the FIS, has, needless to say, simply radicalised and brutalised the population there and made an eventual anti-Western government more likely.)

If Bosnia turned out to have as few willing friends as Croatia, then Serbia proved to be far from the lonely victim of a worldwide conspiracy which Belgrade projected herself as. The world community contained many states who sympathised with Serbia. In September 1992, three members of the Security Council – China, India and Zimbabwe – objected to the proposal to send more troops to Bosnia to distribute humanitarian aid. They saw it as a precedent for the interference in the internal affairs of states.

Each had skeletons in its own cupboard – though none more so than China.[22]

As the war went on, Russia took a more and more openly pro-Serbian position. Gorbachev's former spokesman turned deputy foreign minister, Vitaly Churkin, one of the new-look young blow-dried hardliners in Moscow, argued repeatedly for a lifting or at least a moderation of sanctions against Rump Yugoslavia, even as he insisted on imposing them on Croatia as the breakdown in relations between Bosnian Muslims and Croats led to more internecine fighting in 1993. (Oddly enough, a leaked Foreign Office document suggests that the British government was willing to support Russian proposals to lift sanctions against Serbia as early as October 1992, but seems to have thought twice – either for fear of offending the Americans or perhaps so as not to undercut Milošević's populist anti-Western election ticket before he had been put back where the FCO wanted him, in power.)[23]

The insistence that all measures to promote peace or humanitarian aid in former Yugoslavia had to be approved by the United Nations meant that even when the Security Council was able to pass resolutions it was only after horse-trading which meant that Serbia's friends were assured that the new measures would be as ineffective as those that had gone before. The deals behind the scenes at UN headquarters in New York also meant that countries with flagrantly dreadful human rights records like China were not only allowed to play a sanctimonious role in proceedings but to turn them into a farce for anyone with eyes to see – which of course excluded the Western diplomatic elite. Naturally, Peking demanded a higher price than the mere pleasure of participating in charades which made the UN's moralising more absurd than ever. When a full account of the cost of the UN's role in Bosnia is made, it may be found that the human suffering which China was encouraged to continue inflicting within its imperial boundaries outweighed even the costs of the war in Yugoslavia itself.

Of course, the European Community's general line that the war in Yugoslavia was everybody's fault encouraged the inaction of the UN's members. No government cast a plague on all Balkan houses as vigorously as the British. Like Douglas Hurd, Defence Secretary Malcolm Rifkind laboured long and hard to put across the message that everyone was to blame for the war in Bosnia.

Even when Croats and Muslims had at last signed the umpteenth version of the Vance-Owen map, Rifkind still could not see, or (since he is a clever lawyer) gave an excellent impression of not comprehending that by insisting that all three sides agree as the precondition of peace, he was giving to the Serbs a veto over when to end the fighting. Rifkind told British television viewers in March 1993 that a precondition for peace was 'a clear desire on the part of the people of Bosnia [for it]'. If Vance-Owen failed, 'that implies the people of Bosnia are not prepared to make peace'. It escaped the learned parliamentary silk that no one had asked the people of Bosnia or even Serbs, Croats and Muslims who lived there whether they wanted peace. Of course, the Rt. Hon. Malcolm Rifkind QC MP, did not want to ask such a leading question because it might lead to an embarrassing conclusion: that only a minority even of Serbs wanted the war. The Defence Secretary had already made clear (not least for the benefit of Dr Karadžić's public relations consultants in London watching for any weakening – i.e. strengthening – of the British position) that 'We are not interested in a combat role' and 'You do no good by implying that there is a military solution', so it was obvious that he could not conceive of doing or saying anything which might hinder a continuation of the war.[24]

As the war went on so did the peace plans. The longest shelf-life belonged to the Vance-Owen Plan. From the late summer of 1992, it seemed no humiliation nor any dishonest signature could do away with the duo's scheme for peace. (Lord Owen, who as David Owen had suffered ridicule as one of the 'Two Davids' with the Liberal leader David Steel during the general election campaign in 1987, seemed complacent about his double-billing with Cy Vance.) Their plan to divide Bosnia-Hercegovina into cantons was complicated by earlier assurances that the UN, EC, CSCE et al. would not accept a partition of the republic. Vance & Owen originally had the services of a senior Finnish diplomat, Maati Ahtisaari, who insisted that there would be no 'green line' dividing Sarajevo or any other part of Bosnia. But Fred Eckhard, the duo's spokesman, seemed to undercut that principle by the uncomprehending competence that he gave to the cantons: 'The local governments will be able to safeguard ethnic rights, such as education and culture, with protection of minorities.'[25]

It seemed to escape the UN spokesman that the 'local governments' all too often would be composed of the very people who had done so much to make life hell for the 'ethnic minorities'. What sort of Muslim was expected willingly to grant Dr Karadžić control over life and limb? No clear plan for external, international monitoring of human rights was included in the UN plans concocted in the autumn of 1992.

Tadeusz Mazowiecki saw the basic flaw in the Vance-Owen Plan: whatever its originators intended it was seen as an 'ethnic cleansers' charter'. He told *The Times*,[26] 'The peace plan according to which Bosnia-Hercegovina would be divided along ethnic lines has been used in order to create ethnically homogeneous areas.' Although it was repeatedly denied that this was the intention of the Vance-Owen Plan, everyone in former Yugoslavia and even the mediators and their staff themselves fell into talking about cantons controlled by Serbs, Croats or Muslims. Lord Owen told Channel 4 News in November 1992, 'The idea of having provinces . . . is a way of ensuring that some of those provinces may be *Muslim-controlled . . . Obviously* [sic], *some will be Croatian, some Serbian*, but the idea of going to seven or ten provinces was *to prevent a three-way carve-up*'![27] (Emphasis added.) Unfortunately, no better way could have been devised to encourage a naked and brutal scramble for land.

The same savage measures to 'cleanse' cantons were increasingly inflicted by troops from all three sides. In April 1993, Lt.-Col. 'Bob' Stewart of the Cheshire Regiment remarked from the scene of one massacre near his base at Vitez in central Bosnia, 'The Vance-Owen Plan requires this country to be polarised and as you can see here . . . it causes these people to deal with this in the only way they know how.'[28]

Even as Bosnia was descending further into the abyss of mutual slaughter and the United States' European allies devoted most of their energy to thwarting any American-led intervention to knock heads together, Lord Owen was operating in a parallel universe in which the 'European Community . . . [has] remained very steady for the last eight months and I have no complaints at all, but we have now found a much greater unity between the United States and the European Community. I find the international community . . . is tending to speak more and more with one voice and *it is a very determined and resolute voice*'! Despite talking about bringing 'diplomatic, economic and military' pressures to bear, Owen immediately added that there were 'a lot of difficulties' with any military action.[29]

Lord Owen's rock-solid international community had already lived through the disappointment of seeing peace apparently at hand in Geneva at the beginning of 1993 only for it to dissipate once it became clear that the incoming Clinton administration had no intention of taking immediate action on its anti-Serb campaign rhetoric. Over the next four months after Karadžić's rejection of the Geneva version of the Vance-Owen Plan on 12 January 1993, America blew hot and cold about taking action and Douglas Hurd must have doubted at times whether he could hold the line he set out in February that 'Everybody can see there is going to be no military intervention.'[30] After Easter, the mediators felt the chances of another peace conference were looking up.

The Greek Prime Minister, Constantine Mitsotakis, like his great rival and nemesis Andreas Papandreou, knew the weaknesses of West European statesmen and had based his policy on exploring the EC's obsession with consensus and its loathing for the outsider. His advice to Milošević, his strategic ally against both Albania and Macedonia, was clearly that the Community wanted to get out of its embarrassing involvement in the Balkans. If Milošević would accept its face-saving formulations, he would get a second chance to pursue his goals afterwards. Mitsotakis also needed to show his own people that his government, which was upsetting vested interests inside Greece by its policy of economic liberalism, could achieve nationalist aims and so head off the revival of Papandreou's national-socialist PASOK party. Bringing together the warring parties plus the international busybodies in Athens at the start of May was intended to kill several birds with one stone.

Athens brought out all the shallow optimism which had marked each failure of the peace process. Lord Owen's words expressed it perfectly, if not clearly: 'This is a happy day. A day in the Balkans. A day in Athens. Sunshine. Let's hope that this does mark the moment of an irreversible peace process.'[31] A lot of comment at the time emphasised how helpful Milošević had been to the mediators and how much pressure the Serbian president had put on the Bosnian Serb delegation, led by Karadžić, to agree to less than their maximum demands. However, since the dishevelled and weary appearance of Dr Karadžić seems to have owed more to a long night of wining and dining in Belgrade with a group of sympathetic British MPs that did not end until 3am on the morning he set out for Athens, than to any bullying by Milošević, the plaudits won by the Serb president as the man of peace seem to have been exaggerated.

In any case, the sunshine in Athens was soon followed by the pall cast in misty Pale by the decision of the Bosnian Serb parliament to reject the plan. Some people interpreted the whole episode as play-acting. From start to finish, Milošević had no intention of accepting the Vance-Owen Plan, according to this interpretation. All that he had achieved was to get the measure of the West once more. By apparently distancing himself from the Bosnian Serbs, Milošević could achieve his goal of getting sanctions lifted while his Bosnian puppets took the blame for the failure of the peace plan. Perhaps this was the case, but more likely it was a genuine disagreement on tactics. Whereas Milošević recognised that the European Community states were desperate to resolve the Bosnian crisis and would happily lift sanctions and withdraw their troops once a deal was signed, leaving the way open for a resumption of Serbian expansion afterwards, General Mladić saw no reason to halt his drive for conquest and reckoned – rightly as it happens – that the West's bluff could be called again. Mladić also was developing into a political personality in his own right and possible rival with Napoleonic ambitions in the long term, so it suited him to face down the public appeals of the most powerful Serbian politician.

Whatever the machinations behind the scenes at Pale, Mladić's estimate of Western pusillanimity proved correct. Far from increasing pressure on the Bosnian Serbs, their rejection of the Athens Settlement marked a decisive shift in Western policy towards open appeasement. A month later, Douglas Hurd repeated his hollow ritual of endorsing the Vance-Owen Plan, this time to the Foreign Affairs Committee of the House of Commons, but even as he praised the Plan he buried it with his insistence that 'We are not talking about an operation enforcing the Vance-Owen Plan by pushing the Serbs out of areas which they now occupy. An essential part of the Plan is that they withdraw *by agreement*.' (Emphasis added.)[32]

Briefly it appeared that President Clinton was going to act on his loud words about lifting the arms embargo and launching air strikes against the forces besieging Sarajevo, but it was not to be – though the White House briefing room echoed to his grandiloquent concern for the Bosnians many more times. Clinton's tortured syntax suggested that he had inherited more than George Bush's job when he entered the White House.

Many Western apologists object to the term 'appeasement' when applied to the EC/NATO capitulation to Serbia, even though the most powerful alliance in history (according to its order of battle) had previously demanded compliance with UN resolutions which it now reneged on. Defenders of the Major-Mitterrand line supporting the dismemberment of Bosnia and the dispossession and deportation of the bulk of its population which the Vance-Owen Plan implied, denied that it was a shameful re-enactment of Hoare and Laval's plan for Abyssinia or Chamberlain and Daladier's abandonment of Czechoslovakia at Munich. Of course, it was not: in the 1930s, Britain and France refused to risk war against powerful states on behalf of weaker ones. By the 1990s, an old Vichy civil servant like Mitterrand (who continued to send an annual wreath to Pétain's tomb till the press kicked up a fuss in 1993) and Britain's premier from the postwar generation, who admitted to his nostalgia for Baldwin's Britain, had reached a deeper pit of moral and political decay: they appeased the *weak* but vicious.

Lord Owen had always laid great emphasis on his family's proud tradition of opposing appeasement. In his memoirs, *Time to Declare* (a title which he failed to take to heart), he recalls that he was born into a radical West Country family in the year when appeasement reached its high tide with Chamberlain's sell-out of Czechoslovakia at Munich: 'To this day, Mother refers contemptuously to Chamberlain waving "that silly bit of paper".' (Fifty-four years on, Chamberlain's lineal successor, John Major, proudly claimed that he had obtained Dr Karadžić's signature at the London Conference without which Owen would not have entered on his degrading comeback to big time politics.)

As a young man at Cambridge in his first term in 1956, Owen felt the humiliation of the impotent response of the West to the Soviet suppression of the Hungarian Revolution deeply. He wanted to imitate the volunteers who had gone to Spain as volunteers around the time of his conception. Twelve years later, he was already Navy Minister as the Soviet tanks rolled into Czechoslovakia to suppress the Prague Spring: 'Again, I felt the frustration that we in the West were not prepared to respond more vigorously . . . I believe there should have been serious sanctions.'[33] Lord Owen's indignation about the comparison between himself and past appeasers was therefore understandable, but it is difficult not to feel that a younger Owen would have been in the front rank of those scorning the prematurely aged world statesman.

Hurd's minister of state, Douglas Hogg, told the House of Commons, accurately for once, that 'it is very wrong to regard Serbia as posing anything like the strategic risk that Germany posed to Europe in the 1930s.'[34] Condemning silly direct comparisons between Hitler's mighty Nazi Germany and Milošević's impoverished Serbia (if anyone had actually made them) was a typical politician's cheap jibe at an Aunt Sally. The son of Quintin Hogg ought to have been better informed about the 1930s parallels: Paddy Ashdown and others, who compared the failure of Western resolve over Bosnia to the earlier 1930s, pointed out the step by step retreat of the British and French in the face of *weaker* powers, or the farce of 'non-intervention' in the Spanish Civil War. Here the Western states hindered military aid to one side while the fascists poured it into the other, all of which happened before Munich but were essential ingredients of the mind-set which disastrously misjudged relations with Hitler. Appeasement of weak states by Britain and France along with US isolationism encouraged the more powerful in their aggressive ambitions.

If Hogg stuck to a rather unimaginative and apologetic version of the 1930s, it was left to Lord Owen to put up the most original line of defence. He had not been foreign secretary for nothing, so he cleverly pointed out that there could be no analogy between 1930s appeasement and the 'peace process' because 'Munich was signed *before* World War II had begun . . . We are trying now in

1993 to bring about an end to a bitter war well under way.'[35] What Lord Owen seemed to be struggling to distinguish was the difference between appeasement and abject surrender.

In any case, even if Vance and Owen were hurt and outraged by the accusation of appeasement, some of the staunch supporters of their approach were open about accepting it. General Lewis Mackenzie, who enjoyed the distinction, unusual even in the Canadian Army, of being promoted to full general without achieving a success on the battlefield – only in the UN's media briefing room in Sarajevo – publicly urged appeasement of Serbia and the acceptance of the rule of force in international affairs: 'Force has been rewarded for the last twenty centuries. That's the reality . . . *Stop the killing by appeasing*. It's distasteful in the extreme but stop the killing.'

Cynics might suggest that the former Blue Helmet was so favourable to giving the Serb forces what they wanted because of the lavish funding of Mackenzie's lecture tour in the USA by a Serb-American lobby group, but as the General insisted, he had always held these views, even before he was getting US$10,000 for each speech on the theme. Balkan conspiracy theorists attribute too much morality to Western appeasers when they try to find financial inducements at the root of their selling-out of Western values. Appeasers have principles too: they do not need to be bribed to advocate giving in to force. It is what they believe in.[36]

Even after the debacle of his plan at the hands of the Bosnian Serb Parliament in Pale, Lord Owen tried to talk his way past the fiasco with tough words: 'If the world community is prepared to be rolled over by the Bosnian Serbs, well of course that would be the end of [the peace process]. But I don't think they are.'[37] But Owen was simply whistling in the dark. It was not only his bluff that had been called.

So flaccid had the West European 'great powers' become by the 1990s that in their horror at the thought of taking action they looked to anyone to assist them in hindering the apparently impetuous Americans. The Pale Parliament's decision was a direct challenge to the West. It could not go unanswered. Apart from a suddenly robust Jacques Delors, who perhaps really believed that 'Europe' could be a superpower, the leaders of the EC were united for inaction and terrified that Washington might do something in their stead – with Europe then dragged in the United States' wake. The EC statesmen seem to have taken Clinton's open-air therapy for his acute concern about Bosnia at face value, unlike the Serbs. Fearful that the Americans might take action and show up the impotence of the EC states for what it was, as well as putting their penny-packets of troops serving with the UN at risk, the Europeans fled east for protection. Suddenly, despite all their domestic difficulties and upheaval, the Russians were able to return to the centre of the world stage with the EC states clutching at Mother Russia's skirts for protection from the belligerent Americans.

Britain in particular had been currying favour with the Russian restorationist group in the Yeltsin camp. The Western media focused so much attention on the lunatic hardliners in the Russian parliament gathered around Vice-President Alexander Rutskoy and Speaker Ruslan Khasbulatov, that the really powerful group of military and diplomatic figures in Yeltsin's government who supported the restoration of a Russian empire in the territory of the former Soviet Union were overlooked. Even at the height of the crisis between Yeltsin and his rivals at the start of October 1993, this hardline group within his government was able to veto the attempt by Russia's former Warsaw Pact allies in Eastern Europe to apply for membership of NATO. Immediately after the rout of Rutskoy's supporters, the Russian military announced that it was giving up its former doctrine of no first use of nuclear weapons. Russian troops then entered Georgia and that ex-Soviet Republic signed up to join the Russian-dominated Commonwealth of Independent States. While the media devoted a lot of attention to the antics of the Soviet nostalgics who were rioting in the streets of Moscow, it paid less heed to the careful and skilful manoeuvring of the level-headed and clear-sighted hardmen in the Kremlin, who had no nostalgia for an ideology which had failed and were bent on replacing it with something which would succeed.

Both the Russian foreign minister, Andrei Kozyrev, and his deputy, Vitaly Churkin, were typical representatives of the new elite in Russia. Youngish, English-speaking and fashionably coiffeured (at least in Churkin's case), they had all the trivial features of a Westerner which led their US and EC counterparts to see them as just like themselves. (Of course, the Eagleburgers of the West had had to admit belatedly that they had seen the English-speaking 'banker', Milošević, in the same light.) But behind their façade of Westernisation, both of Russia's chief spokesmen on foreign affairs showed repeatedly that they understood that their task was to promote Russia's power and influence whatever its domestic travails. In December 1992, Kozyrev sent flutters through the Western dovecotes with his infamous 'spoof' speech at the CSCE review conference in Stockholm in which he demanded a sphere of influence in the former Soviet Union and asserting Russia's ties of friendship with Orthodox Serbia. Soon enough, and despite Yeltsin's clash with the Parliamentary hard-liners, Kozyrev's little joke became indistinguishable from Russian policy.

Since Britain supported the restoration of Russian power in the former Soviet Union as a factor for stability and her diplomats derided the chances of the republics achieving viable independence, it was hardly surprising that Whitehall and the Kremlin agreed on policy towards Yugoslavia. Mitterrand too regretted the disappearance of Yugoslavia and lost no chance of urging its restoration even on the Slovene ambassador when he received his credentials in the autumn of 1993! Churkin was the chief spokesman of Russian policy in the Balkans. Although he was described as a mediator by the West and its press, his statements larded the normal guff about the peace process with clear threats to the Bosnians and the Croats to accept Serb conquests or face the consequences.[38]

Marshal Shaposhnikov, then commander-in-chief of CIS joint armed forces (now one of Yeltsin's advisers), was even clearer when he ruled out peacemaking by Russian or other armed forces in ex-Yugoslavia: 'I am categorically against resolving any problems by force, including the Yugoslav problem, and I do not think that all the political methods of resolving this problem have yet been exhausted.'[39]

This sounded like Hurd, but of course the Russians were less self-deceiving about the consequences of ruling out military intervention.

No Russian statesman engaged in the kind of hollow rhetoric

beloved of their British counterparts. Did Douglas Hurd really believe his assurance to the House of Commons on 29 April? 'Military conquest in Bosnia cannot achieve gains which are accepted.'[40] Negotiations apparently were the only way to achieve an internationally recognised peace. At least that was Douglas Hurd's line then. It was still holding a month later when he told the listening public, 'The Bosnian Serbs need to realise what Mr Milošević appears to have realised already that they are not going to be accepted, that they are not going to be able to retain acceptably to the outside world what they have simply grabbed by force. How long it will take for the penny to drop, for those withdrawals to take place, I cannot tell you.' Soon enough the penny was going to drop for the Foreign Office mandarins, but Hurd and his ilk would carry on speaking categorically about their rejection of the legitimacy of the conquests which in practice they were conniving with. In his swansong as a Foreign Office minister, Tristan Garel-Jones managed an excellent example of the genre of the international community in full Churchillian pose. On 6 May 1993, he told the House of Commons, 'The international community is *absolutely determined* that *no territory gained by conquest* . . . shall be accepted . . . As my Rt. Hon. friend the Foreign Secretary said in his speech, these *so-called* conquests by the Bosnian Serbs will prove to be empty conquests – *I have no doubt about that.*' (Emphasis added.) Even in a thin House in May, Garel-Jones' lack of doubt was too rich to inspire much faith.[41]

Even as they were denying that they would ever accept a forced revision of the Vance-Owen Plan, the European statesmen were cobbling together better terms for Belgrade in cahoots with Kozyrev. By the end of May 1993, Andrei Kozyrev was taking the initiative. He was even thinking aloud about the possibilities of making 'certain changes' in the borders between the former Yugoslav republics.[42] His deputy, Vitaly Churkin, also began to make bold statements. Churkin made it clear that Croatia would have to adjust itself to the de facto loss of Krajina.

West European blundering in the Balkans made possible the most startling result of the crisis: the return of Russia to the centre of the diplomatic stage and its elegant interposing of itself into the gulf which developed between the United States and her

European allies. The Washington Deal on 23 May 1993 may well come to be seen as the 'diplomatic revolution' of the late twentieth century. For more than four decades, Soviet leaders from Stalin to Gorbachev strove fruitlessly in their different ways to decouple the West Europeans from the United States. The cruel humiliation inflicted by the ganging-up of Kozyrev, Hurd, Juppé and their Spanish colleague on new boy in the White House, Bill Clinton, will probably be seen as the turning-point in the souring of trans-Atlantic relations.

Such was the confusion and incapacity of the Clinton administration to come to a firm conclusion that the USA's European allies and Russia were able to come to Washington itself and dictate the new terms. The Washington Agreement (23 May) was presented as yet another peace settlement for Bosnia. Of course, it was nothing of the sort. The Bosnian Serb Army ignored it, as it had previous toothless deals. What the Washington Agreement marked was the passing of US hegemony in the Western alliance. America no longer led and Clinton's increasingly desperate and foolish statements showed this. Threats of US air strikes followed for several months but they were the death rattle of Clinton's foreign policy. At the beginning of August 1993, the US State Department was reduced to the humiliating position of announcing that the administration's latest hint that air strikes were on the way was 'not a bluff'! It was power politics as the theatre of the absurd.[43]

As the hopes for the peace process faded so the rhetoric of the international community's leading representatives became more and more fevered. Alleged war criminals were warned of their impending prosecution. At the end of May 1993, the UN Security Council passed a resolution establishing a war crimes tribunal. The US ambassador, Madeleine Albright, admitted that 'sceptics, including the war criminals who deride this tribunal because the suspects may avoid arrest, should not be so confident.' However, Her Excellency did not have any nasty surprise for them. She could not, for instance, threaten them with high-tech snatch-squads descending on Belgrade and the backwoods of Bosnia bent on getting their man. On the contrary, the worst fate which the representatives of the world's only remaining superpower could threaten was that men like Milošević would remain trapped 'for the rest of their lives within their own land'. She overlooked that Slobo showed little inclination to foreign travel and being imprisoned in a country one owns is rather less onerous than being a refugee stuck in an alien out of the way corner.[44] The more loudly Western representatives talked about bringing mass murderers to trial, the more that dim prospect receded.[45]

Along with the fuss about war criminals, the Washington Deal set off another round of actions designed to disguise the fact that the West was determined to do nothing. After the French general, Morillon, had captured the headlines by visiting the besieged town of Srebrinica and refusing to leave it until a tiny token force of French Blue Helmets had taken up residence there, the buzz alternative to stopping the war was for the UN's forces to set up 'safe havens' inside Bosnia around which the war could continue.

At first the Washington decision to set up safe havens was seen as a further step of Western involvement in the fighting rather than as part of its disengagement. Douglas Hurd moved quickly to calm any fears that the Washington Deal meant anything other than a step towards capitulation to the Serbs by the 'international community'. Explaining that the Deal required more troops to be sent to protect 'safe havens', the Foreign Secretary insisted that no more British troops would be deployed to back up the plan. As for the proposed safe havens, it soon became clear that they were to be safe only for UNPROFOR, *not* the local inhabitants or refugees seeking asylum in them. Even the USA was prepared to act if UNPROFOR forces in the 'safe havens' were attacked but not if the refugees were under fire. When the point that the West would not respond to attacks on a safe haven which did not involve UNPROFOR was put to the Foreign Secretary, he replied, 'Indeed . . . the protection is for UNPROFOR troops if they were attacked.'[46] As the people of Srebrinica were already discovering, their haven was safe only for the UN troops who were not protecting them.

Indeed, Douglas Hurd's justification of the Washington Agreement was that it did not involve Britain sending more troops to Bosnia – 'it is in the paper'. His policy had been summed up more than a century and a quarter earlier by one of his predecessors in the Foreign Office, Lord Clarendon: 'We are willing to do anything for the maintenance of peace except committing ourselves to a policy of action . . .'[47] Hurd's junior at the FCO, Douglas Hogg, said Britain would do its 'utmost' to reverse Serb conquests. Mr Hogg clearly employs a different dictionary to other English-speaking people since his 'utmost' certainly did not include lifting the arms embargo on Bosnia let alone sending troops in to aid the Muslims.

It was not only British ministers who became involved in terminological inexactitude when they swore their devotion to the cause of right in Bosnia even as they abandoned the peoples there to their fate. At the beginning of July 1993, the occupant of the most powerful office in the world conjured up his own helplessness. Bill Clinton wailed, 'I care just as much about those Muslims in the heart of Bosnia as anybody else in the world and I would do *anything* to bring an end to ethnic cleansing.' But the 'anything' which President Clinton was prepared to undertake was soon qualified to mean nothing concrete. He explained, 'I do not believe that the United States and Europe should send huge numbers of soldiers to the civil war there to bring an end [to it].' As ever, the question with President Clinton was not what did he not believe, but what *did* he believe in?[48]

Clinton concluded his comments by remarking that the crisis in the Balkans 'has not been resolved in the way I would have hoped'. It was a classic diplomatic passive: the resolution of crises presumably requires action, but the post-Cold War statesman never acts alone. Instead he leaves it to vague groups, not people like himself to decide. The 'international community' or the UN are supposed to make decisions which only the president or foreign secretary passing the buck is in fact in a position to make. However, instead of biting the bullet – admittedly not something Mr Clinton ever showed much inclination for – the diplomatic passive is invoked: something should have *been* done, but never 'I should have done something.'

Ruud Lubbers, the Dutch prime minister, continued to insist at the EC's summit in Denmark that the Community would do its 'utmost' for the Bosnians.[49] This suggested that he had done little more than learn his fluent English from Douglas Hogg. The Dutch no more than the British were going to change course three years into the crisis. Lubbers made that clear too. In various interviews at the Copenhagen summit, he gave the impression that the Netherlands would have done *more* to stop the fighting in Yugoslavia if only the other EC members had permitted it. However, it soon turned out that what Lubbers meant by doing more was in fact doing less than the Community had done. Left to itself, the Netherlands would *not* have recognised Slovenia, Croatia or Bosnia![50]

In fact, all that Lubbers made clear was that by the end of June 1993 – two years after the European Community's disastrous impulsive decision to interfere in the Balkans – the unanimity of the Twelve was collapsing as members struggled to distance themselves from the debacle. It was not by chance that at the Copenhagen EC summit, the Dutch foreign minister at the start of the carnage, Hans van den Broek, seized the photo-opportunity presented by Alija Izetbegović's presence on the fringe. The Bosnian President must have been getting used to European statesmen distancing themselves from their own irresponsibility over the previous two years. After all, a few days earlier, now as he was effectively out of power, François Mitterrand told Alija Izetbegović that he had favoured military action all along.[51] By the end of the banquet on the first night of the Copenhagen summit for the visiting Euro-statesmen, eight of the Twelve had let it be known that they would no longer support the UN arms embargo against Bosnia – though, of course, they were not proposing to end it. (At least, Douglas Hurd remained consistent for inaction, but then he is a man of honour.)[52]

The new French government had already announced a bold scheme to avoid 'future Yugoslavias'. But the bold proposal put forward by M. Balladur's recently elected government amounted to little more than saying that the European Community should agree to guarantee the security of those countries least likely to be affected by the sort of conflict which was most likely in the new Eastern Europe. In other words, it was simply a re-hash of the EC's do-nothing approach presented with more Gallic panache than before. Furthermore, it was a typically French manoeuvre to distance the West Europeans from their American protectors. Given the tensions between the Clinton White House and the Twelve it could hardly have been less timely, or at least inappropriately named. As active Russian influence throughout Europe grew, it was hardly wise to contribute to the diminution of US influence which was already waning and showing every inclination to decline further.

A month after the Washington Deal, Owen and his partner, Stoltenberg, cobbled together another deal at Geneva in the Palais des Nations, the shrine of moral cowardice in the twentieth century. By the end of June, both Lord Owen and Secretary-General Boutros-Boutros Ghali were publicly pressuring the Bosnian Presidency to accept whatever terms the Serbs and Croats deigned to offer them. Little wonder therefore that Radovan Karadžić insisted on Belgrade radio, 'The unification of the Serbian people . . . will take place . . . We stand much better than our adversaries and have enough reasons to give the negotiating efforts of the EC and the international community a chance.'[53] He went on to explain that 'we will be very fair and cooperative and will give a chance to the international community and our adversaries . . . to agree on everything politically, sign this [ultimatum] and have it ratified *by the international community.*' This would speed up international recognition.

Karadžić was treated as an awkward but obligatory feature of the peace process by the mediators. Despite treating him (and the Croat Mate Boban) on the same level as President Izetbegović, the Western negotiators had eyes for only one partner. Lord Owen was not alone in putting his hopes for peace in the hands of Slobodan Milošević. The Washington meeting produced a fresh flood of testimonials to Slobo the Peacemaker. Andrei Kozyrev told a group of US senators, 'We have to count on Milošević to handle the Serbian part of this problem for us.'[54] The French foreign minister, Alain Juppé, went even further in his assessment of the Serb leader's change of heart: 'We can take him at his word.'[55]

Milošević made a few high profile gestures of support for the Washington Deal. Serb border guards appeared before the television cameras at selected crossings of the Drina between Bosnia and Serbia and 'enforced' the blockade on supplies to their brothers in Bosnia. But this stopped once Western television stations had enough evidence of enforcement and had withdrawn their camera crews. Meanwhile the vivisection of Bosnia went on, usually justified by detailed reference to the Vance-Owen map of the cantonised republic.

Back in November 1992, Lord Owen and Cy Vance had ruled out any acceptance of the division of Bosnia-Hercegovina into three ethnically or religiously based confederal states. They saw clearly what the effort to bring about such a shallow confederation would mean:

> Such a plan could achieve homogeneity and coherent boundaries only by . . . forced expulsion of populations . . . The International Conference . . . condemns [these] totally . . . and calls for the reversal of those which [have] already taken place . . . A confederation formed of three such states would be inherently unstable, for at least two would surely forge immediate and stronger connections with neighbouring states of the former Yugoslavia.[56]

By July 1993, Lord Owen's spokesman was bullying the Muslims and their Christian allies to accept precisely that proposal. With that unruffled self-confidence which defied all previous failures by the peacemongers, John Mills told the world's press on behalf of Lord Owen and Mr Stoltenberg, 'The message to the Muslims is *negotiate or perish* . . . If they want to be practical they can secure a solid future.'[57] Several times, Lord Owen expressed his irritation with the Muslims' unwillingness to throw themselves on the mercy of their enemies. Perhaps his pique at Izetbegović's dawdling to his doom reflected Lord Owen's sense of shame at his role in events. If so, he resolutely resisted showing it in public.

The shaky central government for the confederal Bosnia planned at the Geneva talks had as a central element an ombudsman. Thorvald Stoltenberg may have been overshadowed by his British co-chairman but the absurdity of the idea that an ombudsman was the key to the architecture of peace was purely Scandinavian in its surrealism. No doubt an ombudsman would have done a great deal for conditions in Auschwitz too.

If nothing else, the Geneva meeting on 16–17 June marked the point at which even the principal protagonist of the Vance-Owen Plan had to admit its complete and utter failure. Lord Owen's comments to the BBC interviewer were revealing, as much for what they didn't say. They may stand as the epitaph to peacemaking:

> I am not sure that partition is the right word. But it's certainly a far more ethnic division of Bosnia-Hercegovina than I would ever have wished to see, but there we are, that's the reality. This is what the three peoples who have fought each other particularly ferociously over the last two months *have brought on themselves* (emphasis added).

Is this the endgame? Whatever noble ambitions had motivated him at the start of his mission, Lord Owen was now wearily ready to accept peace at any price. In February 1993, Lord Owen admitted that he 'was shattered to arrive in the United States at the end of January to discover that informed opinion, even among many good friends, believed that Vance and I were somehow rewarding cleansing and aggression'.[58] Five months later, when asked if the apparent Serb-Croat deal to partition Bosnia, leaving the Muslims with their own reservation, marked the 'endgame' of the war, Owen replied:

> I hope so. I think it is such a miserable ghastly war if we can bring it to an end, far better to get a settlement . . . We won't get back to what we originally talked about . . . It is ridiculous to pretend that there is a great deal of honour in it . . . I find it a bitter pill to swallow . . . I think it is a triumph for far too many of the forces of evil than I would like to see. There is much too much territorial gain from aggression. There is still the bitter legacy of ethnic cleansing.

However, despite his references to 'evil' and 'ethnic cleansing' and even the need for a war crimes tribunal – 'which I hope is not given up'! (presumably not to try the peace-promoting Mr Milošević) – Lord Owen was able to finish with the doxology of all true peacemakers in the Balkan conflict: 'There are faults on all sides.' Blessed are the peacemakers, for they have homes to go to away from the war zone.[59]

'Slick Willie' was not to be left out of the charade, but fresh from bombarding the defenceless Somalis even his cynicism was breath-taking. The American President was prepared to accept the dismemberment of Bosnia, 'If the parties themselves agree, genuinely and honestly agree'.[60] Why they should have been fighting for so long, if they could 'genuinely and honestly agree', President Clinton chose not to elucidate.

Douglas Hurd admitted the futility of the reliance on negotiations if they were not pursued in good faith: 'The only way of making absolutely sure that there is peace, that the Bosnian Serbs withdraw, is to send an army to make them do so.' But 'no one' had suggested that. It was hardly a conclusion likely to encourage negotiation in good faith. Nor was the Foreign Secretary willing to encourage a discussion about the merits of intervention once it became irrevocably clear that mediation had only provided time and excuse for more mayhem.[61]

The debate about intervention brought together strange bedfellows. Western conservatives stood shoulder to shoulder with old fellow travellers and anti-NATO peaceniks in their determination that no military aid should pass to Bosnia. Crusty Tories, convinced by Milošević's nationalist rhetoric that he was really one of them, resisted intervention alongside veteran opponents of any active anti-Western policy anywhere like Tony Benn and Bruce Kent. While, on the other side of the barricades, Lady Thatcher was the most trenchant voice decrying the moral and political bankruptcy of the West's crocodile tears, but in the unusual company of Senator Joseph Biden (best known to the British public for plagiarising the speeches of Neil Kinnock, Labour's long-suffering Punch to Margaret Thatcher's unconquerable Judy). Although the Labour front bench shadowed every error of the Major team over Bosnia as in so much else, radicals like Ken Livingstone had criticised the official line of blind support for the EC line of non-recognition from the start. Tony Banks was heard to utter the unprecedented words from the opposition benches, 'Margaret Thatcher articulated the deep anguish of many people', and he supported the ex-Prime Minister's call for air strikes to halt Serb advances.

Sir Edward Heath and Lord Healey, the two elder statesmen whose willingness to provide soundbites at the drop of a hat had made them darlings of the broadcast media, were both stern anti-interventionists. Sir Edward's contempt for small countries took in his own and other EC states so it was hardly surprising that he opposed any intervention on behalf of Bosnia. The fact that Margaret Thatcher took the opposite view may for once have been irrelevant in Heath's calculation of his own stance, but petty domestic obsession with the Iron Lady's over-arching stature seems to have led Denis Healey to make the extraordinary charge that Lady Thatcher was 'as responsible as anyone for the mess' in Yugoslavia![62] Healey had spent much of the previous decade issuing blood-curdling warnings of the likely cost of intervention from the Falklands to the Gulf, but despite achieving maximum points for the inaccuracy of his prophecies, Channel 4 News and BBC's Newsnight could not hear enough of him.

It is however worth recalling some of Healey's nonsense about the Gulf in order to understand the mentality of the British establishment. Labour and Tory alike were drenched with unshakeable ignorance and self-confidence in equal degree. Healey had warned in 1990 that a war in the Gulf would mean 'the price of oil [up] to $65 a barrel . . . the collapse of the US banking system . . . a great slump worse than the 1930s . . . a holy war uniting the whole of the Muslim world from Morocco to Indonesia . . . this nation sleepwalking to disaster with its eyes open and its mind closed.'[63] Of course, it was Lord Healey who was on auto-pilot, where he has remained since.

In addition to warning of another Vietnam, Healey revealed that he had the old warrior's deep-seated prejudice against Germans and Croats. As he admitted, 'I was involved with Yugoslavia in the last war' and had in 1945 assured the Labour Conference of his support for Stalin and Tito's measures against those whom they decreed to be 'fascists'. So great was his animus that it liberated him from the tyranny of chronology. Healey, like most of the embittered anti-interventionists, turned the course of events upside down to justify blaming Germany for the war. In April 1993, he told radio listeners that 'The central problem is that the moment Britain had given in to German pressure by recognising Croatia and Slovenia unconditionally over a year ago, they really then set loose the dogs of war.'[64] The inhabitants of Vukovar and Dubrovnik were clearly under an illusion when they claimed that the hounds of Mars had been howling around their doors months earlier. But Healey's contempt for the facts of history led him even to predate Carrington's resignation by eight months: 'Lord

Carrington was very strongly opposed to the mistakes to which I referred – the unconditional recognition of Croatia, which incidentally was simply a reward to the Germans for supporting John Major at Maastricht and it is not surprising that shortly after that he [Carrington] gave up his role.' Healey's anti-German dogmatism reached a peak in a television debate with a survivor of the Holocaust, Rabbi Hugo Gryn, who supported intervention in Bosnia, but whom Healey constantly interrupted and hectored. Having berated people who knew nothing of the situation, Healey went on to insist that Germany was acting as she did 'because Germany had been Croatia's ally during the Second World War' and 'during that period the Croats killed up to a million Serbs', which showed that however fragile his knowledge of history, Healey was well up with the most exaggerated Serb propaganda. Ignoring Serb atrocities, Healey insisted, 'Don't forget that the Croat forces who are killing Muslims and Serbs . . . are wearing swastikas on their helmets, some of them are wearing SS uniforms and they give the Nazi salute.'[65] In practice, this line of non-intervention demonised the Croats and if anything justified intervention against them.

Healey, like Hurd, repeated the establishment's mantra that arming the underdog or victim would simply lead to more killing. Hurd called it supporting a 'level killing field'. By implication these statesmen preferred an uneven killing field. What they seemed to want was for the Serbs to go in for a quick kill and get this embarrassing issue over and done with. The 'Great and Good' in Britain were united on this approach. They would neither intervene nor lift the arms embargo on the weaker side.

The British press took a more diverse approach. The *Guardian* and *Independent* took up the hawkish line as did the *New York Times*, while the *Daily Telegraph* lapsed into Little Englander contempt for concern about human suffering and ignored the strategic consequences of the shift in the balance of power and the decline in respect for the West. Although *The Times* carried editorials which criticised government policy, its regular columnist and former editor, Simon Jenkins, struggled manfully to sound the government line. Like many proponents of inaction, Jenkins liked to criticise the armchair advocates of intervention, almost as if his entire career had been spent campaigning like

Caesar rather than sitting at a keyboard tapping out opinions, albeit from a hard seat rather than a comfortably upholstered convenience.

As a long-term doubter of the efficacy and justice of using British military power from the Falklands to Bosnia, Jenkins deployed all his skill to argue the futility of intervention. Any and every serviceable historical example was pressed into service. Some ended up backfiring: Jenkins seemed not to know that while America failed to pacify Lebanon by force, Syria had done just that (which was why Lebanon had ceased to disturb armchair strategists). Instead he insisted from the vantage point of his command centre in Wapping that 'peace arrived when Lebanon's factions exhausted themselves'. When David Pryce-Jones – far from an Arabophile – pointed out that 'peace was imposed by a massive and purposeful intervention from Syria' and that '*Pax syriana* exposed the weak will and token gestures of the West', Jenkins simply shifted his line in a subsequent radio debate, dropped his argument that civil wars had to be left to burn themselves out and argued instead that the West would not be prepared to use the same level of violence deployed by Assad of Syria to stop the war in Bosnia. This shift of line showed a tactical dexterity worthy of a great commander (and a better cause) but suggested that the motives for his opposition to intervention were more deep-rooted than Jenkins' smooth reasoning admitted.[66]

One of the little ironies of the Yugoslav war was that throughout Western Europe, but especially in Britain, it was those politicians and journalists who had prided themselves on their liberal, progressive and European credentials who showed themselves most dead-set against intervention and were determined to keep refugees out of their own countries. Liberal Tories like Ken Clarke and Baroness Chalker backed Douglas Hurd in his hard line towards the defenceless. Chalker's insistence on keeping people 'close to their homes' for their own good would be ranked among the most cynical utterances of a twentieth-century British politician if the Minister for Overseas Development could be held responsible for her own statements. Of course, forty-five years earlier, the 'We don't want them here' school in the British establishment had done for scores of thousands of would-be refugees from Yugoslavia. Their heirs and successors in the 1990s showed that in that regard at least Mr Major's much-vaunted return to traditional values was bearing fruit.

Although the British government avoided publicly breaking ranks with its more reluctant allies and openly siding with Belgrade, backbench Tory MPs, like Harold Elletson (who also had consorted with extreme Russian nationalists like Zhirinovsky) never tired of justifying the Serbs or denouncing interventionists like Margaret Thatcher. Despite widespread evidence that the Belgrade authorities were reneging on their promises to cut military and economic aid to the Bosnian Serbs, Derek Prag, the Conservative MEP for Hertfordshire, assured Tanjug, the official Yugoslav news agency on 22 May 1993, 'that sanctions against the Federal Republic of Yugoslavia, if the Yugoslav government *continued its current policies with determination* [!] should be abolished within a few weeks.'[67] (Emphasis added.) Then the way would be open for a further step towards the restoration of Yugoslavia. The indefatigable Mr Prag wrote to the *Independent* a few days after his Tanjug interview on the need for 'exchanges of population and property' (as if they were not already under way in General Mladić's inimitable way) because 'our [i.e. the EC's] aim must be . . . far-reaching economic cooperation *at the very least* [emphasis added] possibly in a customs union [between Bosnia] with Croatia and Serbia.'[68]

Against the background of those sort of comments, it is hardly surprising that so many people in ex-Yugoslavia presumed that a hidden agenda was being pursued by the West to support Milošević and his programme for reasons which lay beyond the understanding of the human beings on the receiving end in the Balkans. Opposition-minded Serbs, in particular, long interpreted every step by the EC governments and the Bush administration as evidence of *support* for Belgrade. They argued that the West European governments (and the Bush administration) never wanted the Serbs to be defeated. Apart from the evident failure of the Western Alliance to bring its power to bear to back its anti-Milošević rhetoric and the clearly counter-productive nature of the sanctions and the arms embargo, there were hints that the Serb opposition's interpretation of the West's real purposes were not without foundation, as Eagleburger's comments to CNN suggested.

Respectable opinion in the West scoffs at Balkan conspiracy theorists. Certainly their all-embracing theories which explain every twist and turn in events as part of a puppet-show are not convincing, but nonetheless some evidence does exist to back up their interpretation of events. As the *New York Times* reported in July 1992: 'Western officials say the embargo's main accomplishment may have been to prevent the breakaway republics of Croatia and Bosnia from buying the types of heavy weapons that could turn the tide on the battlefield.'[69] In other words, the embargo aided the Serbs to achieve an hegemony in the region which otherwise they could not have gained. The West preferred an *Ordnungsmacht* to dominate the Balkans, and Serbia fitted the bill. If that was the case, it is a damning conclusion.

It is a grim reality that nothing concrete can be adduced to disprove this interpretation. The only powerful argument against the cynical view of Western policy is the still more damning argument that no Western government let alone the EC or NATO together was capable of pursuing a coherent policy. In short, their very public flounderings were the reality. The plausible alternative to the Machiavellian interpretation of the inefficacy of Western policy is that crass stupidity not cynical *Realpolitik* dictated its course throughout the crisis. In other words, in its response to the Yugoslav crisis, the West was not waving, but drowning.

In midsummer 1993, both Croats and Muslims believed they had evidence that the British in particular had used their influence to help set the two communities at each others' throats.[70] It was a mark of the collapse of British prestige in the region that allegations were made that the British secret service had wanted to promote a split between Croat and Muslim so that HM Government's softly-softly approach to the Serbs could be justified. If Douglas Hurd's long-predicted Lebanonisation of Bosnia could be demonstrated in front of the TV cameras then pressure for intervention against the Serbs would wane.

Not only local journalists but even senior officials of the Croatian government were convinced that several violent incidents between Croats and Muslims had been provoked by the SIS and military intelligence officers. The constant harping by British ministers and spokesmen on the Croat-Muslim tensions was seen in the Balkans as evidence that the hidden hand of Whitehall was pursuing its own agenda at the expense of the Yugoslavs. The long history of intelligence cooperation between the British and Yugoslav communist secret services did little to calm these suspicions.

Naturally, the evidence of squabbling among even the European allies argues against the conspiracy theory. The West Europeans were squabbling among themselves as well as with the Americans. President Mitterrand's foreign minister, Roland Dumas, let it be known that 'the responsibility of Germany and the Vatican for the acceleration of the crisis [was] brutally evident.'[71] Of course, the evident brutality was not German but that of France's old ally, Serbia, but Dumas let that point pass.

The British government helped to orchestrate a campaign against air strikes at the beginning of August 1993. However half-baked the US administration's idea, and however much it would no doubt have gone off at half-cock *à la* Somalia, it was very different from the obstructionist British attitude. Once again, John Major's government was in a position to play its trump card: British troops on the ground. Whitehall argued again and again, using 'authentic' statements from 'our boys in Bosnia' to back up its claim that air strikes would do no good and put the boys at risk. Malcolm Rifkind's hostages were doing their bit. Saddam Hussein must have envied their efficacy in stalling military action. He had made the mistake of placing innocent civilians – women and children – in front-line locations as his 'human shield', but the British government had provided General Mladić with a 'military shield'.

Needless to say, it was typical of the Foreign Office that having fought tooth and nail to stymie action against the Serbs, it then claimed it was in the front line of those issuing ultimatums to General Mladić. Heights of Newspeak and Doublethink were reached in the official propaganda. Old hands from King Charles Street, like the Tory MP and *Daily Telegraph* columnist, George Walden, were moved to inform their readers, 'When there is any question of stepping up military pressure on the Serbs, it is the British Foreign Secretary who feels obliged to issue a *disguised* [! – emphasis added] ultimatum that, should any harm come to UN personnel *defending the Muslims* [!], the RAF is waiting in the Adriatic, poised to strike.'[72]

How could anyone, least of all the Conservative MP for Buckingham, have overlooked all the statements making clear that British troops might just be allowed to defend themselves *in extremis* but certainly not anyone else? Mr Walden might have noticed the television pictures of weeping people denied shelter in the British bases at the height of the fighting on the grounds that the rules of engagement forbade anything so one-sided.

Sanctions on commercial trade with Serbia and Montenegro disguised the West's real policy of turning the screw on Bosnia via the arms embargo until the Bosnians were so weak that they gave in of their own accord to Serbian demands. By midsummer 1993, even Milošević had dropped his repetitive lies about the war in Bosnia being an entirely Bosnian affair conducted without aid from Serbia. On the contrary, he told Serb television viewers, 'Every citizen is well aware of the burden borne by Serbia in its assistance and solidarity with our people outside Serbia. It turned out that all that we have had to go through in these past few years was worth it.'[73] Few Serbs (or Croats and Muslims for that matter) needed reminding that it was Milošević's policies which had placed that burden on the population of Yugoslavia. Those in the West who did not want to attribute a burden of guilt to him would not listen to confessions from his own mouth. However, already in April 1991, Milošević had emphasised the importance of force in the politics of partitioning Yugoslavia. He told the press that 'Questions of borders are essential questions of state. And borders, as you know, are always dictated by the strong, *never by the weak*. Accordingly it is essential that we be strong.'[74] Serbia was still strong two and half years later while Bosnia was growing weaker. Milošević had judged the situation aright. The West wanted the Bosnians to capitulate to their hopelessness.

As Sir Edward Heath, a close supporter of the Major/Hurd line put it so succinctly: 'So long as you hold out any hopes to the Bosnians . . . then you abolish any hopes of peace.'[75] The aim of the West was to reduce the Bosnians to helplessness and despair and then proclaim peace.

PART FOUR

Grim Futures – Some Conclusions

By the middle of 1993, those who foretold the Lebanonisation of Yugoslavia could take a grim satisfaction in their foresight. Many of them, particularly the leaders of the international community, were witnessing the consequences of their own handiwork. If the break-up of Yugoslavia was bound to be traumatic that should not have meant that it had to be as catastrophic as events turned out. The bloody death of Yugoslavia bequeathed a pattern of instability and not only among the bleeding successor states in the Balkans. So much Western prestige had been put on the line and found wanting that the influence and reliability of the USA and of NATO were sorely degraded. The Russian military learnt the lesson as much as Somali warlords. Vladimir Zhirinovsky's emergence as the leader of the most popular party in Russia may have taken Western leaders by surprise but his rhetoric made sense to many Russians because of their failures. Far from being a local tragedy the slow death of Bosnia was the sinister herald of a new world of dangerous temptations and unconvincing restraints. The writing is on the wall for Western post-Cold War complacency, but does the West have leaders able to understand the message of the manner of Yugoslavia's death?

14

The Outlook for the post-Yugoslav Balkans

A region far from our central strategic concerns.

Warren Christopher

More than two years after the outside world was forced to take notice of the disintegration of Yugoslavia when fighting broke out at Slovenia's border crossings with Italy and Austria, the prospects for the successor-states and their peoples are bleaker than ever. Even if a halt to the fighting could be achieved, it is likely to be merely an armistice before a Croatian or Muslim war of *revanche* broke out or before Serbian expansionism moved on to another target. Furthermore, the physical destruction along with other economic as well as human costs of war are likely to undermine any attempt to establish stable social orders, let alone pluralist democracy. A state of emergency will persist de facto in Croatia, Serbia and whatever becomes of Bosnia-Hercegovina. It will probably spread where it has not already.

Lord Owen tried to justify his about-turn on the Vance-Owen Plan and his sudden willingness to act as the go-between for a Serb-Croat carve-up of Bosnia in June 1993, by arguing that the economic and agricultural basis for life was being threatened by the continued dislocation of farming and the distribution of foodstuffs. However, his anxiety to invoke understanding for his volte-face seemed directed as much to his domestic audience in Britain and around the European Community as to the Bosnians themselves.

> I beg people to realise that *we* [emphasis added] can't go through another winter with fighting in Bosnia-Hercegovina without the most appalling misery . . . Nowhere near as much agricultural land is going to be utilised [this year]. The extent

> to which the housing stock is vulnerable to winter weather is far greater than it was last year.[1]

The defenders of preserving the arms embargo even at the cost of inflicting defeat on Bosnia repeatedly argued that it was the only way to make the provision of humanitarian aid acceptable to the Serb forces. Without Serb consent – which only came so long as the UNHCR and Red Cross among other aid agencies provided a goodly proportion of the assistance to General Mladić's supporters – it was claimed that it would have been impossible to send thousands of tons of food and medicines to the desperate population of areas still loyal to the Bosnian government, Muslim, Serb and Croat alike.[2]

However by midsummer 1993, as the military position of the Bosnian government forces reached it deepest crisis point, suddenly 'compassion-fatigue' seemed to hit the statesmen who had doggedly defended the withholding of arms from the Bosnians so at least they could be fed. With the collapse of the Vance-Owen Plan, Douglas Hurd and Boutros-Boutros Ghali began to hint that unless the warring parties came to a quick settlement, then there would be little point in continuing the expensive and exposed UNPROFOR operation in Croatia and Bosnia. However, they were the very people who had consistently argued that UNPROFOR's non-interventionist role of riding shotgun for the civilian aid convoys was an essential if difficult humanitarian duty which those calling for military intervention on the side of Bosnia or a lifting of the arms embargo were callously prepared to put at risk.

With both Serb and Croat governments engaged in a complex game of sabre-rattling over their own disputes and mutual intrigue to the disadvantage of the Muslims and other Sarajevo loyalists, midsummer 1993 offered the prospect of the 'international community' ditching the Yugoslav problem and washing its hands of the humanitarian crisis because it had all got too much.[3] Naturally, there was no hint that any of the international statesmen felt any responsibility for letting Bosnia slip into the condition of the Lebanon. Even if Western leaders and the UN bureaucrats seemed heartily sick of the Bosnians' unwillingness to buckle under to its enemies – and some old UN hands must have remembered that it took three years to stifle Biafra – given their past record of indecisiveness it was unlikely that they would summon the energy and political courage to abandon their half-hearted role in Bosnia. More likely was a continuation of UNPROFOR's standing on the sidelines picking up the pieces of ethnic cleansing.

Some Western leaders even seemed optimistic that with Bosnia partitioned or sunk into a military stalemate, then peace would return to the region. Serbia would be satiated and calm down. Everyone would turn to the urgent tasks of reconstruction and set about trying to restore their shattered economies. Throughout the crisis this naive faith in the attractive power of what faceless and uncharismatic Western politicians regarded as normality had dogged US and EC understanding of the roots of the conflict. Normality is of little interest to Balkan bandits and their leaders. Or, to put it in local terms, the sort of normal way of life which they seek is a continuation of tribal warfare and plunder. The rule of law and title-deeds to property are not half so attractive to the men who have torn Yugoslav society apart as arbitrary possession based on power.

Lord Owen once remarked that he could imagine Milošević stepping aside and taking up a lucrative position in the world of international finance. It was a comment which suggested the peacemaker's imagination ran ahead of his understanding of what motivates a cannibalistic politician like Milošević. Equally naively, Douglas Hurd told George Soros in January 1993 that sanctions would soon force Milošević from power. Subsequently, Lawrence Eagleburger let the cynical cat out of the bag when he admitted that the US government and its allies knew that sanctions would strengthen Milošević's hand in domestic Serbian politics.[4]

However devious his route, the persistently successful pursuit of power has marked out Slobodan Milošević from his local rivals. Has anyone ever met a Serb who expected Milošević to renounce power before his death? Most expect him to die violently: some even killed by a fellow Serb, a few that that Serb will be himself. For all of his iron self-control, it is not only the pattern of suicide in his family past which points to this end for Milošević. Having embarked on his course, fate itself seems to draw him towards self-destruction by rewarding each audacious defiance of the world with success. Step by step, Milošević is drawn on to further triumphs, burning more bridges behind him as he advances.

Despite the fact that the logic of his policies and position seem to push him towards some final act of self-destructive violence, it would be foolish to underrate Milošević's capacity for survival in the medium term. Like so many of the twentieth century's extremists, he has shown a striking capacity to play the moderate or the man holding the 'real hardliners' in check. Certainly, even after the events of 1991–93, many Western leaders seemed to suffer from a psychological need to have Milošević as their partner for peace.

It was striking that when Dobrica Ćosić was dropped as Federal President at the beginning of June 1993, even the *Guardian*, which had been the most consistently sceptical media voice in Britain about Milošević's alleged virtues as a pragmatist, could still print without demur the interpretation of an anonymous but clearly pro-Milošević 'Serbian analyst' to the effect that 'Mr Ćosić was one of the intellectual authors of the vision of a "greater Serbia".' The disinforming conclusion was that, 'This could be a signal . . . that greater Serbia is dead.'[5] There can be little doubt that this was the signal Milošević wanted to send to the West. It was just another confirmation of his role as the mediator between the warring parties rather than the ringmaster who had set the dogs of war at each others' throats. As with so much of Milošević's propaganda, it found willing ears in the West.

In Serbia itself and other parts of ex-Yugoslavia, the fall of Ćosić was understood differently. It marked the end of any pretence that the Socialists and their radical Serbian nationalist allies saw the constitution as anything other than a useful façade. This was confirmed a few days later by the violent scenes in and outside the Belgrade Parliament which culminated in the arrest and beating-up of Vuk Drasković.

The savage mistreatment of Drasković was clearly calculated to test both domestic reaction to Milošević's triumph in the war and also to see whether Western prattle about human rights would disqualify him as the favoured interlocutor between UN and EC mediators on the one hand and the victims of his war inside Yugoslavia on the other. As ever, Milošević had calculated correctly that he was more valuable to the would-be Metternichs in London and Paris than any bearded oppositionist. President Mitterrand intervened to obtain the release of Vuk and his wife and this was trumpeted as yet another triumph for French diplomacy and pressure. On the contrary, it showed once again Milošević's contempt for the West: seeing Drasković was no longer a threat, he let him go – to France, well out of his way.

Drasković's supporters held only timid and poorly attended demonstrations on his behalf after his arrest. This brought out how weak the democratic opposition was. Vuk's subsequent statements indicating a shift back to a hard line on Kosovo and against a 'Muslim state' in Bosnia suggest that in so far as he retained political ambitions, he recognised that only a nationalist line could rally support against Milošević. If the West believed that Drasković would prove the steel in the feeble reed of Serbian pluralism, it turned out to be a mistake. To be fair to Drasković, he had taken the risk of back-peddling on his original Serb nationalist programme from 1991 and it had done him no good. He learned the lesson and after his return to Serbia, Drasković reverted to his old nationalist rhetoric, reminding Serbs that Kosovo was their Jerusalem and denouncing the threat of an Islamic 'fundamentalist state' in the heart of Europe.[6]

If Drasković learned the lesson that the West's values carried little weight with those forces who determined Serb politics, Milošević never doubted it. He knew that the only plausible threat to his position came from the dark forces which his regime fostered and unleashed. Men like Šešelj and 'Arkan' or even Ratko Mladić are more likely to be prepared to conceive and carry through the bold and ruthless measures which would be required to topple Milošević. But even they probably lack the political and military basis for a successful coup. Assassination remains a danger to Milošević, but any rational plotter would have to be confident that he had the supporters available not only to kill Slobodan Milošević but to neutralise his regime.

One of Milošević's strengths is the relative unpopularity of the hardmen of Serb nationalism. It is true that Šešelj's Radical Party garnered more votes than any other party apart from the Socialists in the general election in December 1992, but many ordinary Serbs, including the *apparatchiks* forming Milošević's power-base, resent the criminal and thuggish behaviour of Serbia's self-proclaimed 'war heroes'. As the war went on so the disruptive and menacing behaviour of Šešelj's supporters in Serbia itself turned voters against him. This was made clear in the elections on 19 December 1993, which followed Milošević's split with Šešelj in October. The Serbian Socialists gained an absolute majority despite hyper-inflation adding zeroes to prices at a breath-taking rate and without more than the usual electoral malpractice.

The paramilitary extremists have not entirely disappeared. Šešelj survives, albeit battered, while Arkan sided with Milošević, his paymaster. The Socialist Party's comfortable *nomenklatura* is not at ease with the simmering potential for violence which the militias represent. The *apparatchiks* want a quiet life to enjoy their privileges. The hardmen have no desire to settle down yet. In many ways the tension between the Socialist establishment and the nationalist militias resembles the situation in Nazi Germany in the first eighteen months after Hitler came to power in January 1933. Then the authoritarian right in the German establishment, which had done so much to bring Hitler to power, were worried and disgusted by the behaviour of Röhm's Brownshirts, whose disorderly and corrupt brutality alienated a lot of ordinary Germans too. Hitler, of course, resolved the tension by acting ruthlessly to kill Röhm and scores of SA leaders in the Night of the Long Knives on 30 June 1934.

Milošević may yet decide to do something similar to the local warlords who served his purpose so well in the past. He could be confident of earning further Western approval for exterminating the likes of Šešelj or Arkan. The applause in London and Paris may already be ringing in his ears. Perhaps he anticipates that Washington too would be pleased with him. However, moving against the radicals has far more risk than stifling Belgrade's ineffective intellectual opposition. It may be that the official Serbian forces of order could strike down the radicals but only at a cost which might include a severe risk to Milošević himself. In all probability, he will continue apparently to cosy up to the radicals while preparing their elimination. Of course, Šešelj will be trying to do much the same.

So far Milošević has succeeded in playing off one warlord against another in much the same way as he undercut his rivals in the other republics. When Šešelj turned against him in autumn

1993, Milošević could still rely on Arkan's backing in the general election in December. This gave to the lacklustre campaign of Milošević's Socialist Party the glamour of a war criminal's support. It also helped to split the psychotic vote – not a negligible factor in Serbian elections.

The effect of a dirty war in which plunder has been as much a motive as patriotism can only be the destabilising of Serbian society. Young men have become accustomed to using arbitrary violence and to treating the norms of civil society with contempt. The incipient breakdown of law and order inside Serbia herself was always inherent in the use and glorification of the freebooter.

The Hercegovinan Croat mafia represents a similar possible challenge to the establishment of a law-abiding Croatian state. The combination of the indifference to legality inherited from communism combined with the effects of two years of a war economy which encouraged black-marketeering and embargo-breaking makes matters bad enough for those wanting to establish a Western-style society in Croatia, but the influence of the unscrupulous Hercegovinan Croat political connection could seriously undermine Croatian democracy and commitment to civil rights.

Already prominent Croats like the Speaker of the Sabor, Stipe Mesić, and Cardinal Kuharić have criticised the influence of Hercegovinan Croats in Zagreb or the role of Mate Boban himself. The unintended effect of the war has been to create similar social phenomena in all warring states: the freebooter will be a figure of importance for some time to come. Mesić also implicitly criticised President Tudjman's media policy when he urged the political parties to keep out of the press. Criticism of the pro-Hercegovinan faction around Tudjman may herald a split within the HDZ into liberal and conservative factions, which would also be geographically based.[7]

Many Dalmatian and Istrian Croats especially feel that their Hercegovinan brothers' involvement in the Bosnian war has damaged the standing of Croatia in the world. Any revival of the tourism so vital to the regional economy depends upon a variety of factors, but certainly collusion between the Hercegovinan Croats and the Bosnian Serbs to liquidate the Muslims would have a catastrophic impact on Croatia's reputation. Given the tense stand-off with the Serbs in Krajina and the economic and infrastructure problems resulting from the war, it is difficult enough to attract tourists back in any case. But dreams of achieving a Greater Croatia out of the ruins of Bosnia do not assist recovery.

Whatever the grim economic, social and political prognostications which could be made about Serbia and Croatia as the war entered its third year, it was Bosnia's Muslims who faced the most bitter prospects. Despite occasional victories on the battlefield against the Croats, the Bosnian state was in a strategically unviable position. In fact, even successful local actions against HVO forces in Bosnia or Hercegovina simply worsened the Bosnian Army's overall position because they helped to cement the de facto alliance between Serbia and the Croats. Given Mladić's overwhelming firepower, the Bosnian Army always faced sudden catastrophe if the Serb Army chose to act wholeheartedly to relieve pressure on the Croats. Of course, nothing could please the Serbs more than to see their two enemies at each other's throats.

Unlike both Croatia and Serbia, Bosnia lacked the economic and agricultural resources to survive even at a subsistence level without foreign humanitarian aid. By midsummer 1993, UN and other relief agencies were warning more and more urgently that they could no longer sustain the effort. Already deliveries of food and medicines were falling off sharply by the end of June. This was the product of the increasing physical obstacles to aid convoys across ever more complicated and violent battlefields, but also because of the compassion-fatigue of the aid donors. Some of the aid donors also saw bringing about a food crisis among the supporters of the Sarajevo government as the best way of bringing the war to a rapid end. If Serb artillery had failed to force a Bosnian capitulation, then starvation would surely complete the destruction of the Bosnians' will to resist.

Even if international aid agencies were to continue food supplies, or to resume them after an interval, it is difficult to avoid the conclusion that destitution will be the fate of the bulk of the people who remained loyal to the Sarajevo government. After a year of fighting, hundreds of thousands of people had become accustomed to being refugees in their own land; it would take little to push them across borders to become outcasts in a foreign land.

Having abandoned Bosnia to its fate, it is difficult to see how Western governments can avoid accepting refugees from the carnage. Certainly so long as the hope existed that a viable Bosnian state might result from the Vance-Owen Plan, then the conscience of the West European public could be calmed when refugees were turned back and callously urged to stay 'close to their homes'. But if it finally became clear that the 'international community', and especially the rich and powerful countries to the west of Yugoslavia, had abandoned any pretence of expecting a peace to arrive other than that of the grave, then Western public opinion might yet shame the governments in London and Paris and their allies into providing sanctuary to the survivors. After all, even Daladier's France did not send back refugees from Franco in 1939 to face his firing squads. (Of course, it has to be admitted that the British government can call into account the precedent of 1945 if it prefers to adopt the 'We don't want them here' policy which Kenneth Clarke and Baroness Chalker seemed to echo in 1992.)[8]

Having listened with more than half an ear to the Serbophile propaganda about the danger of establishing an 'Islamic fundamentalist state' in Europe, the Major/Mitterrand camp may yet achieve the creation of Europe's own Palestinian problem. The sense of betrayal by the EC states, especially Britain and France, among Bosnian loyalists became bitterly palpable. Vice-President Eup Ganić gave voice to it when he warned of the danger of anti-Western terrorism after the abandonment of any semblance of continued support for the Vance-Owen Plan.

Worse still from the point of view of the security of Western Europe is the fact that the EC countries were repeatedly seen to shy away from confrontation with the Serbs because of their threats of retaliation against UN forces or even through terrorism against Western civilian populations. Desperate and embittered Bosnian Muslims may provide a breeding ground for extremist groups who argue that only terror will oblige the West Europeans and the USA to take measures on behalf of the Muslim cause as inevitably the Bosnian cause will become as much a religious as a national one.[9]

Already the small number of Islamic fundamentalists in Bosnia have seen their case strengthened by Western inaction despite a thousand condemnations of Serb advances and a hundred 'last warnings'. The radicalisation of young Muslims in refugee camps at home or abroad will be very difficult to defuse. It is after all very difficult to argue against a mullah who says that if Bosnia had had oil and a corrupt dynasty like the Al-Sabbahs of Kuwait, then the West would have come hurrying to its aid. Instead it had a democratically elected government – even Dr Karadžić's only complaint was that being in the minority, he would have to kill his way to establishing a state in which his supporters were the majority.

The Serbs will probably prove successful in radicalising the surviving Muslims and then they and their hangers-on in the West will be able to crow: 'We told you so.' In itself, it should be little comfort for anyone, even the Serbs, since they are most likely to be the objects of any terrorist campaign. The West will probably turn a blind eye to the continuation of ethnic cleansing under the euphemism of anti-guerrilla warfare – it may even provide expert aid (so that Sandhurst or West Point-style discipline prevents any excesses) – but abroad among the milling refugees and their disappointed Muslim sympathisers living in Western Europe, who themselves will have been alienated by their governments' hypocrisy, any Islamic fundamentalist struggle may find the necessary few supporters.

The other states of the Balkans will find themselves caught in this permanent round of tension. Greece and Albania most of all will find it hard to return to any kind of normality so long as war and the threat of war combined with terrorism flourishes to their north. It is easy to imagine that Kosovo sooner rather than later will explode in hopeless rebellion, or will be the scene of increasing guerrilla penetration from across the Albanian border. Either way, a Serb-Albanian war cannot be ruled out.

If Serbia invaded Albania Greece would be sorely tempted to join in, just as in the event of a Macedonian breakdown, which might well result from such a war given the large Albanian minority in Macedonia. Already Greece has been massing troops along its borders with both Macedonia and Albania. At present, the hysterical tone of Greek propaganda about Macedonia is still nominally defensive – claiming that Macedonia has designs on Greek territory.[10] But already the line towards Albania has become more aggressive with the electoral victory of PASOK in Greece. Needless to say, Macedonia has felt renewed pressure as a result of PASOK's return to power on an even more radically anti-Skopje platform than the ousted Mitsotakis government.

The presence of a Greek population in southern Albania (Northern Epirus, to Greek irredentists) is a ground for concern in Athens. Greeks there are entitled to full civil rights like everyone else, but there is growing evidence of Greek efforts to stimulate demands for *Enosis* among the Albanian Greeks as well as to undermine the parlous Albanian economy. The EC may yet face the embarrassing problem of a Balkan war caused by an EC member.

To people throughout the Balkans, the West Europeans are seen as increasingly irrelevant. Despite their wealth and nominal military power, the Twelve have proved a paper tiger. In addition to their unwillingness to resort to force to uphold their 'civilised principles' in Bosnia, the region has come to see that the EC's economic self-interest means that it will do little to promote prosperity there. On the contrary, high tariffs, particularly on foodstuffs, hit the Balkan countries' efforts to become free market economies badly.

With the threat of war hanging over them and the loss of hope in Westernisation, the Balkan states are being forced back into the 1930s path of pursuing economic autarky as the route to military security and economic well-being. Then it proved an illusion, as it will tomorrow. But the West in general, and the European Community in particular, has left the Balkans with little choice. The countries in South-Eastern Europe are condemned to live with suspicion, insecurity and poverty for the foreseeable future. Their tragedy has not gone unnoticed elsewhere. Throughout the rest of the ex-communist world, the lessons of the Balkan crisis are being studied closely and already acted on.

15

From the Balkans to the Baltics: Learning dangerous lessons

> What experience and history teach is this – that people and governments never have learnt anything from history.
>
> Hegel

What went wrong is the immediate question which springs to mind after contemplating the disastrous failure of European and international mediation in Yugoslavia since June 1991, but it is much more important to consider what could go wrong in the future and not only in the Balkans. The world is slowly learning the lessons of the Balkan crisis even if Western leaders remain doggedly determined to ignore them and to turn a blind eye to its consequences. Beyond Bosnia lies a world which is not so smug and complacent as Washington, London and Paris would like to think. The decomposition of the international order established after the Second World War and in the wake of decolonisation, which transferred old colonial entities to new indigenous masters, is going on apace. The West is only slowly waking up to the fact that the Cold War certainties did not only end for the 'losing side', but for the West too.

Anti-interventionists constantly used the argument that the world was filled with other Yugoslavias to justify the West's failure to intervene on its doorstep. Any quick survey of separatism around the world will soon turn into a lengthy exercise as one insurrection succeeds another *intifada* from the generally peaceful decay of states like Canada or Belgium through to the bloodshed in parts of India's vast multi-cultural chaos or Sri Lanka's paradisical killing fields. But it was the spectre of Soviet collapse and then continuing fission within the post-Soviet republics which haunted the imaginations of Western statesmen. They had sent the wrong signals in 1991 in the hope of cajoling troublesome races back into the cosy Soviet corral. They are still haunted by nostalgia for yesterday's world.

Just as the implosion of Yugoslavia revealed the absence of Western contingency planning so the collapse of the Soviet Union seemed to take the West by surprise when it actually happened. It was most unwelcome. The disintegration of the Soviet Union was among other things an implicit rebuke to those West European politicians who had glibly signed treaties guaranteeing its continued existence. The ink on all the treaties guaranteeing its existence had hardly dried. President Bush's warnings against 'suicidal nationalism' were still echoing, but still the peoples of the Soviet Union insisted on going their own way.

Even after December 1991, the West and its key aid institutions preferred to ignore the emergence of independent republics in what had been the Soviet Union. Jacques Attali's European Bank for Reconstruction and Development (the BERD) insisted that republics hoping for its assistance remain in the trouble zone! It was a kind of post-Soviet ERM in which monetary control was not in the hands of the fiscal puritans at the Bundesbank, but the profligate Viktor Geraschenko, who was restored to office as head of the former Soviet State Bank at the insistence of Western institutions! Chancellor Kohl made the preservation of unity a condition for economic aid in September 1991. This sort of misguided obsession with rescuing what could be preserved of Soviet bogus federalism rather than building a genuinely post-Soviet set of economies had the effect of limiting the republics' sovereignty and therefore their capacity to carry through real economic reforms even if Russia chose not to. Because Russia continued to bear a huge burden of defence spending and bureaucratic growth, inflation was continually exacerbated after 1991 and exported to the other republics. Late in the day, M. Attali's BERD changed tack but only after a great deal of economic damage had been done.[1]

In Russia, influential figures like Yeltsin's long-term adviser, Gennadi Burbulis, reckoned in the spring of 1992, less than three months after the red flag had been hauled down for the last time from the Kremlin, 'There is a logic that will bring [the republics] back again to our way. *Europe will not take them as they are.*'[2] In the confused situation in the post-Soviet republics, it is easy to concentrate on the high-profile and dramatic areas of structural breakdown, from hyper-inflation to local wars, and to ignore the tendencies towards restoration of an imperial model.

For the moment, the disintegrating features are most obvious. This leads to the disquieting thought that as the former Soviet republics reform their economies so the resemblance between them and Yugoslavia on the eve of its breakdown grows rather than diminishes. Economic change from a command economy to a modified free market produces the social conditions for radicalism. The mafias which operated extensively underground come to the surface and flourish in circumstances of *nomenklatura* privatisation and accompanying inflation which further weakens police and other officials' probity. The mafiosi and 'businessmen' usurp the role of the old party bosses and become local patrons, often dressing up their financial and physical power with rhetoric about local or national interests. They are often compared to the medieval robber barons by those who take the 'long view' and see them as setting normality on its feet, but those who actually live under such conditions find the 'short term' uncomfortable and are less imbued with optimism.

The similarities between Russia's position and Serbia's role in Yugoslavia should not be exaggerated, but the existence of Russian minorities in every other republic created conditions for Krajina-like rebellions. Twenty-six million Russians live outside the Russian Federation in other former Soviet republics and frequently their economic conditions have worsened and they are the victims of anti-Russian sentiments, long suppressed and now given more or less free rein. After decades of exporting people to the other republics Russia is experiencing a significant inward migration. Combined with the uncertainties endemic to change and the widespread yearnings for a clear pattern of life again, this disquieting return of the Russian diaspora is damaging to Russian self-esteem.

At first it was the opponents of Yeltsin who took to waving the Russian tricolour and demanding protection for the Russians in the 'near abroad'. It was the Soviet nostalgics' talk about

Russia's right to a zone of special interest, including the ex-Union republics, which the Russian Foreign Minister, Andrei Kozyrev, claimed that he was satirising when he delivered a forty-minute hardline harangue to his colleagues at the Stockholm CSCE Summit in December 1992. Soon that 'joke' turned sour as the tenets of the ultra-conservative camp became the foreign policy doctrine of the new Russia.

On 30 December 1992, Russian television broadcast President Yeltsin's message to his people. In it he reminded them that

> We have much in common with the states of the CIS, the Baltic republics and Georgia, and we shall inevitably be cooperating closely. However, we shall remember the fact that millions, tens of millions of our compatriots reside in these states. It is the right and duty of Russia and Russia's leadership to protect their interests. Who knows maybe at some time our peoples will wish to establish even closer bonds.

A shudder must have gone through Yeltsin's audience in the CIS republics (which also receive Russian television) at those words, and his reassurance moments later – 'The imperial period in Russia's history has ended' – will have cut little ice.[3]

By June 1993, Yeltsin made fewer bones about demanding a *droit de regard* for Russia in her relations with the former Soviet republics. This applied particularly to the Baltic states. Both Estonia and Latvia had felt swamped by the Soviet policy of deliberately importing hundreds of thousands of outsiders, mainly Russians, into their territories after the Second World War. If Stalin and his successors had intended to dilute Estonian and Latvian identity beyond the point of no return, they failed. However, they left the newly independent republics with a thorny problem: almost half the population of Latvia by 1992 was made up of people who had moved into the Republic since 1944 or their descendants. The position of ethnic Estonians was better in their Republic, but still they shared their territory with a non-Estonian minority population approaching a third of the total. It was natural that the indigenous peoples of Latvia and Estonia should have wanted to protect their language and culture through political measures, but some of the laws adopted by the independent republics offered a handle to be grabbed by interfering Russians from Moscow, whose concern for minority rights was outweighed by their anxiety to destabilise states whose independence they could not accept.

Unlike the internal borders in Yugoslavia, the Russian Federation's borders have little historical basis and were established by various administrative *fiats* issued arbitrarily by the Soviet leadership, Khrushchev's allocation of the Crimea to the Ukraine in 1954 being the most notorious of these land-grants (or thefts, depending on your standpoint). No previous Russian state had been delimited in the west or south in the same way. Now, for instance, the Moscow Military District no longer lies at the heart of a military system but is a border district, which the Russian Defence Minister, Pavel Grachev, finds 'mind-boggling'.[4]

Clearly, it is reasonable for Russians in all walks of life in the Russian Federation to take an interest in the well-being of their fellow Russians in other states, but it is hard for those states to feel politically and militarily secure when they hear some of the official rhetoric about conditions inside their territory and when they see from whom it comes. For instance, when it is made a part of official Russian military thinking that part of the task of the Russian Army is not only to defend the rights and interests of Russians in the territory of the former USSR, but also of 'those identifying ethnically and culturally with Russia', then the smaller and weaker states bordering Russia may be forgiven for sounding alarm bells. Of course, they have generally refrained from doing so because it would be a futile gesture, probably a provocative one. The West has made it clear that its deaf ear would be firmly facing the direction of any tocsin.[5]

Meanwhile geopolitics dominates Russian military thinking about the country's position in the vast Eurasian land mass. One military paper, *Voennaya mysl*, published the following argument:

> Like any living organism, the Heartland lives as long as it breathes. Its 'lungs' are the seas connecting it with the outside world. One 'lung' consists of Far Eastern coastal waters . . . ; the second one consists of the Baltic, Northern and Black Seas, which give access to the Atlantic and Mediterranean. Take

> away one of them and Russia will begin to suffocate; take away both and it will perish.[6]

At the turn of the century the Oxford geographer, Halford Mackinder's geopolitical theorising attracted a great deal of attention – largely outside Britain. Then his views carried more weight in Germany than at home; today a Russian 'Eurasianist' tradition is being reborn on the principles of geopolitical strategy derived from Mackinder. These theories reinforce the historical arguments which say it is wrong and dishonourable for Russia to renounce the conquests of Peter the Great and Catherine the Great in the West, ranging as they do from the Baltic coasts to the Crimea.

On 29 October 1992, Yeltsin halted 'temporarily' the withdrawal of Russian troops from the Baltic states. At the same time, fuel supplies were interrupted. Russia's inheritance of a highly centralised energy system from the Soviet Union has given the Kremlin a powerful weapon in any political struggle with the other republics. (It may not have been by chance, as *Pravda* used to say, that President Elchibey of Azerbaijan was toppled after he supported plans for an oil pipeline to take his republic's only source of wealth to the West through Turkey rather than Russian territory.)

Just as the Serbs were able to persuade or bamboozle Westerners into accepting their claim to de facto control over large areas of Croatia and Bosnia-Hercegovina, in which they did not even constitute a majority, so Western governments and media have completely accepted the Russian arguments about persecuted minorities in Moldova, for instance, as well as the Baltic states. These so-called Russian separatists often come from very mixed backgrounds. Already in 1990, pro-Soviet separatist forces made their appearance on the left bank of the Dniestr River which divides Moldova. At the time of the hardline putsch in Moscow in August 1991, these groups effectively seized control of the left bank and refused to recognise Moldovan independence, proclaiming their own revealingly named, 'Moldovan Autonomous *Soviet Socialist Republic*', complete with hammer and sickle emblem on its flag. Like their counterparts in Krajina, the Transnistrian separatists set up barricades to block roads and rail links and though they claimed to be the victims of the chauvinist oppression of the Romanian-speaking majority in Moldova, their militia was far better equipped and quickly curtailed the activities of the police still loyal to the Moldovan authorities.

It has been commonplace for Western diplomats and media to talk about 'Russophone separatists' in Moldova, but the ethnic argument turns out to be shallow if not bogus. It is not just that Romanian-speakers make up the largest group in the Transnistrian population (about 40 per cent), but also that among the leadership of the misnamed Russian nationalists are also many Romanian-speakers, like the Chairman of their Soviet, Maracutsa. Far from being a clear-cut inter-ethnic dispute, the Moldovan-Transnistrian dispute is in fact in essence a struggle between Soviet nostalgics and supporters of local independence. With the collapse of the USSR, the Transnistrian authorities based in Tiraspol, the seat of the former Soviet now Russian 14th Army, simply transferred their loyalties to the next biggest political unit available, Russia. In this they were supported by the commander of the 14th Army, Alexander Lebed, whose willingness to back the separatists was the source of their military superiority over the lightly armed police force of the Moldovan Republic.

Just as events in Krajina a few years ago seemed local squabbles of no consequence to the rich West, so it is easy to dismiss straws in the wind like the Transnistrian dispute as unpleasant exotica without significance. As other ex-Soviet enclaves with real or alleged minority problems are activated to destabilise other newly independent republics, the significance of the Transnistrian dispute becomes more apparent. Just as people at the centre of Serbia were flying a kite to see how far they could go by promoting Krajina's dissatisfactions, so what has happened on the left bank of the Dniestr provides a model of how to destabilise a republic which has proved unwilling to go along with the new Commonwealth of Independent States, set up to take over so many Soviet functions, albeit unsuccessfully.

The orchestrator of Russian involvement in Transnistria, General Alexander Lebed, is not a marginal 'hardliner', operating beyond the reach of central control. On the contrary, he was a high-flyer close to the centre of new military thinking. Lebed is a paratrooper, like his patron, the Russian Defence Minister Pavel

Grachev, and furthermore was a key figure in the defence of Boris Yeltsin's headquarters, the Moscow White House, during the August coup in 1991. Westerners talk glibly about democrats and hardliners – as once they did in Yugoslavia – but a Russian democrat can be very hardline towards non-Russians or on the issue of Russian rights in the 'near aboard'. As disillusionment with the West's willingness to fulfil its promises of generous economic aid has combined with growing contempt for the West's impotence to use its potential power effectively in the Balkans, so the whole Russian political spectrum has tilted towards the nationalist position and even the sweet-talking Kozyrevs and Churkins occasionally slip into the rhetoric of Russian national-power.[7]

The second battle for the Moscow White House on 3–4 October 1993 was a bloody affair, unlike the first, but its consequences for Russia's fellow former Soviet republics were the opposite of 1991's. Instead of marking the decisive defeat of the reintegrating tendency of Soviet nostalgics, the bombardment of Khasbulatov, Rutskoy, et al. in the White House by Yeltsin's troops marked a change in his government's rhetoric towards the other republics. Far from using his triumph over the openly pro-Soviet nostalgics to break any links with the imperialist past, Yeltsin let his foreign minister, Kozyrev, use blunt and intimidating language towards Russia's immediate neighbours, while the Russian Army extended its zone of intervention by deploying troops in Georgia to protect the Shevardnadze regime there from his predecessor, Zviad Gamsakhurdia, who had been overthrown in a coup in 1992.

At the same time Russia acted to protect the Abkhazian separatists in Georgia. Until the fall of the White House, it had been commonplace to argue that evidence of support from Moscow for pro-communist hardliners in the other CIS republics was the work of Vice-President Rutskoy's camp, but with his fall the support continued. Even the Transnistrian separatists who had sent volunteers to Moscow to help Rutskoy faced no consequences after 4 October. Instead both the Russian Foreign Ministry and the Army made clear their opposition to the Moldovan government's desire to restore its authority.

In the aftermath of the strong showing of Vladimir Zhirinovsky's Liberal Democrats in the Russian elections on 12 December

1993, many Western politicians and opinion makers hurried to explain the new Russian belligerence towards its neighbours as being a necessary response by the 'democrats' to the surge in support for the hardliners; but chronology does not support this view. It was precisely at a time when the 'hardliners' seemed shattered and intimidated by their defeat on 4 October, and when both opinion polls and State Security alike were reporting a misleadingly large pro-Yeltsin vote in December that Russia began to throw her weight around in the former Soviet Union more obviously than ever.

In addition to extending the deployment of Russian troops in combat roles, the Kremlin also pressured states like Georgia and Azerbaijan into the CIS. Away from the 'near abroad', Kozyrev voiced the Russian military-industrial complex's demand for a veto on NATO enlargement in Central Europe. In many ways, the electoral triumph of Zhirinovsky and his rabid and aggressive rhetoric afterwards simply facilitated Russia's new 'forward' policy by providing a convenient bogeyman with whom to frighten the West into agreeing to concessions to Russian policy.

In effect, it is the Russian Army, the former Red Army, which is the determinant of Russian policy towards its immediate neighbours in the CIS, and *not* the Foreign Ministry. The 14th Army in Moldova is only the most extreme case. Despite his popularity, Yeltsin's core power-base remains an alliance between military and security officials who despised Gorbachev's ineffective reforms and liberal economists, who can nonetheless talk tough on Russian rights. The December election results showed how shallow the popular base of reform is in Russia and emphasised the 'democrats' ' dependence on the so-called power ministries.

All Yeltsin's advisers are aware that effective reform, whether of the economy or to restore Russian military power, is threatened by the disintegration of the state. They recognise that the separatist tendencies which led to the break-up of the Soviet Union extend inside Russia too. Even as it tries to restore Russian influence abroad, the Kremlin struggles against fissiparous pressures at home. As John Lough has remarked, 'Just as the disintegration of the USSR did not stop at the borders of the Russian Federation, it is highly unlikely that attempts to preserve and reunite the Russian Federation would not extend into parts of the "near abroad" as well.'[8]

For Serbia to throw her weight around may be one thing, but if Russia chose to imitate her then the consequences would be very different. Western Europe has been able to put up dykes to hold back the flood of would-be refugees from Yugoslavia, but the ripples from any similar crisis inside the former Soviet Union would swamp our border defences, even if only by propelling ten refugees for every asylum-seeker from Bosnia.

At the same time as Russian spokesmen called for the acceptance of de facto autonomy for Krajina, they were also pressuring their neighbours in the 'near abroad' to accept much the same for Russian-speakers there. For instance, as Bosnia entered her death throes in midsummer 1993, the volume of Russian complaint about the maltreatment of her 'pieds noires' in the Baltic states became a crescendo. Day by day, Yeltsin's government stepped up its pressure on the Estonians and Latvians. Already troop withdrawals had been halted. Now fuel supplies were stopped with the ultimatum that the parliaments of both republics had failed to provide full civil rights to their resident Slavs. At the same time, in the Estonian town of Narva with its huge Russian majority (96 per cent), preparations were under way for a Krajina-style referendum on local autonomy. This was supported by the Mayor of St Petersburg, Anatoly Sobchak, another reformer turned nationalist, who had uttered dismissive abuse of the Estonians before and engaged in the psychologically significant step of ordering the blanking out of foreign language, especially English, signs in St Petersburg. Revulsion at the sight of Latin letters was as common among Russian nationalists as their Serbian counterparts.

Down in distant Tadjikistan, Russian troops and ex-KGB men were propping up the ex-communist regime on the pretext that they were taking 'necessary steps to protect Russia's national interest'. Military action was required in order to 'defend the national and geopolitical interests of Russia and its allies'.[9] The regime in Tadjikistan denounced its opponents as Muslim fundamentalists, conscious that this would alarm public opinion in Russia itself and tap the knee-jerk reaction of 'enlightened' opinion in the West.

Little media attention was given to the savage war of restoration going on in the foothills of the Hindu Kush which probably cost more lives than Bosnia but less video film. The state-controlled Russian media gave the official view of what was happening in this out of the way part of the 'near abroad'. Russian military and security police activities there were portrayed as protection of the Russian-speakers in Tadjikistan, whatever their citizenship. Viktor Barannikov, the Russian Security Minister, told Radio Moscow's World Service that Russia's 'immediate sphere of . . . interest [was] the security of our fellow countrymen and their protection'. In order to achieve this the Tadjik-Afghan border had to be 'secured'.[10] After sending in reinforcements in mid-July 1993, Defence Minister Grachev himself went to Tadjikistan to assert Russia's determination to control the border with Afghanistan and to teach the rebels a lesson which no one would forget. Grachev told Russian television, 'This is an undeclared war against Russia. My aim and my duty . . . [is] to restrain the enemy and *inflict such destruction on him that nobody will dare lift up their hand against Russian people again.*'[11] Tadjikistan is a faraway country of which genuinely few people know anything and certainly far from the centres of EC or US interest – much further than Bosnia. If you pity poor Bosnia, think of Tadjikistan, still further from Allah and closer to Russia.

In the Caucasus, other savage post-Soviet wars raged on. The fate of Georgia aroused much attention because of the return to his home republic of Eduard Shevardnadze. The role of the apostle of perestroika in international relations overshadowed the realities of politics in Georgia and distracted attention from the nature of political conflict there. Shevardnadze's democratically elected predecessor, Zviad Gamsakhurdia, was ousted from power in a coup at Christmas 1991. A speechifying nationalist, Gamsakhurdia was not the sort of figure whom James Baker and Hans-Dietrich Genscher warmed to. They were delighted by the restoration to power in Georgia of their old friend, Shevardnadze. They did not look too closely at the savage and brutal means used to restore him who had been after all the republic's KGB boss and then Communist Party leader. Had they done so, Baker and Genscher would have been less happy to visit Georgia and ignore the shooting and beating of protesters while shaking hands with the organiser of repression, Shevardnadze's number two Jabba Ioseliani.

Like Arkan and Jurkka in Yugoslavia, Ioseliani is a former criminal turned politician. The mafioso may become 'Deputy-Chairman of the State Council', but remains a hoodlum for all that. Despite his revival of a pseudo-medieval cult of Georgian chivalry under the guise of the *Mhkedrioni* (the Horsemen), Ioseliani remains the chief black-marketeer and drug-pusher in the Caucasus – no mean position. It is not only in the Caucasian ex-Soviet republics that the Yugoslav model of the interpenetration of old secret police, Party and mafiosi has become the norm. The mafiaisation of the former communist bloc is a widely acknowledged phenomenon – east of the old Iron Curtain. To the West, all that matters is that the racketeers have official titles, wear suits and know how to do business.

Elsewhere in the Caucasus the war between Armenia and Azerbaijan drags on. The dispute about the Armenian-inhabited enclave of Nagorny-Karabakh started in 1988 and like events in Yugoslavia had all sorts of genuine and spontaneous causes, but the prolongation and embitterment of the war also serve political purposes. The role of the Russian military and arms suppliers has been equivocal here, at least in the sense that they have backed one side, then the other. However, a strategic goal has been to weaken both sides and to emphasise their dependence on Russia. By shifting arms and logistical supplies from Armenia to Azerbaijan and then back again, the Russian military establishment helped to discredit independence among ordinary people. War-weariness calls out for a return to stability. Of course, it is one thing to shatter a society and quite another to rebuild it. The return to power in Baku of the old communist boss, Geidar Aliev, with the aid of a local 'businessman' turned militia leader, followed the recipe pioneered by Shevardnadze in neighbouring Georgia. Again the West has breathed a sigh of relief as a familiar face is restored to the group photograph of heads of ex-Soviet republics.[12]

Some commentators and officials even openly propose that the West through the UN endorse a Russian military role in restabilising the republics. Already Russian 'peacekeepers' control the situation in Moldova and play a role on both sides of the Caucasus as well as in Central Asia. The argument goes that since the Russian military is going to act anyway, the UN should try to exercise influence by dressing up the Russian Army in blue helmets. What difference this will make on the ground is not clear, but just as the West and UN were happy to accept that Ratko Mladić underwent a metamorphosis when he changed from wearing a JNA general's hat to a Bosnian Serb Army cap, so a blue helmet and cravat for Alexander Lebed of the 14th Army will no doubt wish away any political role which he might have played in Moldova, for instance.

Leaving aside the ominous developments inside the former Soviet Union, the West's failure in the Balkans has revived Russian influence throughout the former Soviet bloc. This could only increase tension. However, once it became clear that NATO was not going to spread its protective umbrella eastwards across the old Cold War dividing line through Europe, the small states of the region faced an ugly choice: either they could try to reinvent the Little Entente which had proved so feeble before 1939 or they could look for protection from the old imperial power.

Serbia's neighbours faced the clearest choice. When Elizabeth II visited Hungary in the spring of 1993, the Foreign Office put high-flown words about how the European Community acted as a promoter of peace into her regal mouth, but when the Hungarians asked Britain for anti-aircraft weapons to help protect their airspace from Serb incursions, they were turned down. It would be too provocative for Douglas Hurd. The Foreign Office seemed to think that the Serb regime was gentlemanly: Mr Milošević would never attack a defenceless neighbour, but might be tempted by a fair contest.

Hungary could not afford to indulge in such fantasies. If the West would not supply the means of self-defence, then Budapest would have to look elsewhere. The West is strong on words and declarations about what is unacceptable but in a crunch situation what sort of small country would wish to rely on Washington or London? Douglas Hogg's sneering comments to the Bosnians about not waiting for the cavalry will have been heard around the world. Needless to say, after Hurd's snub of the Hungarians' right to self-defence, Budapest was not too choosy about finding a defence supplier. Russia was only too happy to step in. After all, with the collapse of the Comecon trading system, Russia had inherited the Soviet Union's large debt to Hungary. Russia's economic plight meant that any exports were to be promoted, so Andrei Kozyrev offered the Hungarians equipment from Moscow's Cold War cornucopia to provide for Hungary's rearmament. Instead of anti-aircraft missiles, the Kremlin offered its most modern jet-fighters, the Mig–29. Unlike Western defensive weapons, the Russian supplies could have a dual role. Certainly, Mig–29s might deter any Serbian adventure over the Hungarian border, but such a powerful weapons system threatened the whole regional military balance.

The destabilisation of the fragile military balance between Hungary, Slovakia and Romania may well have been in the back of Kozyrev's mind. In the capitals of Hungary's three ex-communist neighbours, Bratislava, Bucharest and Belgrade, suspicion of Hungary's attitude to their territorial integrity was bound to exist. The Serb regime routinely accused others of taking the same predatory view of neighbours' territories containing minorities as Belgrade had done. But in addition to the Hungarians of the Vojvodina, twenty per cent of the Slovak population was Magyar and about two million Hungarians lived in Romania. Slovakia and Romania were naturally alarmed by Hungary's acquisition of high-grade Soviet weaponry.

Bratislava and Bucharest recognised that the West would do little for them so they too began to look east for help in rebuilding their armed forces. Slovakia has its own tank industry (making the T–72 under licence), but it too looked to the Kremlin for aircraft to match the Hungarians'. Hungary may be able to get US$800 million, but even poor little Slovakia is set to acquire 180 million dollars' worth. Romania opened military talks with Moscow but also looked to China and Israel for assistance, especially in rebuilding its air force.[13]

The significance of these arms deals will not be short-lived. Sophisticated aircraft systems have a long shelf-life. Poor states in Central and Eastern Europe will not replace their investment quickly. Orders for Mig–29s lock them into a fifteen- or twenty-year-long relationship with their Russian suppliers. Training, repairs and re-equipment will mean constant dependence on Russia. The irony of the West's unwillingness to help the new democracies to defend themselves, if only against each other, is that they are being pushed back under the tutelage of Moscow. Only those who don't read the newspapers can think that the new Russia has irrevocably renounced all the old ambitions and is immune to the temptations of power and hegemony.

The West's terror of trouble has led it to foster the arms race elsewhere too. It is not only in the ex-Warsaw Pact countries that a massive rearmament is under way. At the other end of the Balkans, NATO's two least friendly allies, Greece and Turkey, are in the process of a massive arms build-up. This has been fed by their other European and US allies. No doubt if the worst case arises and these weapons are used against each other, the other NATO allies will impose an arms embargo after the event and send in bandages instead.

By acting as though war in Europe's backyard was only a humanitarian issue (and one grudgingly acknowledged even as that), the West revealed its strategic blindness. Purblind 'realists' unable to see further than their number-crunching, and brass-hats unwilling to risk tarnishing their laurels won so cheaply in the Gulf confirmed the complacency of politicians who were anxious to bask in the end of history and their outstanding role in bringing it about. The revenge of history is still marching on. The impact of revolutionary events in Eastern Europe and the Soviet Union has still failed to provoke a revitalisation, let alone a change of Western elites. Yesterday's men, hidebound by the corrosive certainties of the Cold War, are steering us blindly into the future, hoping that the trouble in the Balkans does not lead to anything worse during their watch. Afterwards, as elder statesmen, if further disorder breaks out on the vulnerable shrinking perimeter of civilisation, they will be ready to take action – as peacemakers and mediators of course. But so long as they are in office, they remain powerless to act and so condemn us to a repetition of the lessons which they never learned.

Postscript

'Nobody but a fool wants air strikes'

Lord Owen[1]

At lunchtime on Saturday, 5 February, 1994, a single mortar-bomb landed in the market at Sarajevo and killed sixty-eight people. Immediately, the disinformation machine went into operation. In defiance of all common sense, the Serbs[1] claims that this murderous shell was not fired by them were retailed by Western pundits as plausible. UNPROFOR as ever preferred the deconstructionist approach, saying that it was impossible to tell who had fired the shell. Presumably, for UNPROFOR it was even open to doubt whether the Serb forces were besieging the city at all, let alone had spent the previous two years firing every kind of ordnance into the place. The sceptics were supported by well-known figures who had long cast doubt on larger massacres. The market massacre was 'staged' according to the French National Front leader, Jean-Marie Le Pen, in order to discredit the gallant Serbs. In *The Times*, Simon Jenkins added his sceptical voice to those doubting the guilt of the obvious culprit.[2] But gruesome television pictures of the carnage set off a chain reaction around NATO capitals and it was impossible for Western governments and even the UN hierarchy to refuse to do 'something'. Tragically, the next few weeks were to show that the 'world community' was still led by gesture-politicians determined to silence public disquiet at home in the short term rather than resolve the Yugoslav crisis.

Of course, the Western elite had long since written off the Bosnians and left them to their fate. Lord Owen told BBC television news on 28 January, 1994, that there was nothing that the 'international community' could do to promote peace, warning the Muslim-led government that things were going to get 'worse down the track'. The obdurate refusal of the Bosnian government to capitulate and salve the tawdry consciences of peacemakers and presidents alike, whose declarations of principle about never accepting the fruits of aggression had long since been silently interred, continued to rankle and the Western media was increasingly briefed that the victims of the war were to blame for lengthening it. However, hardly a week after Lord Owen's counsel of despair the massacre in Sarajevo market set in train a sudden assertion of Western power which led to a volte-face on all sides.

After the slaughter even John Major and Douglas Hurd were forced by public opinion into their most cynical U-turn. They joined the rest of NATO (apart from Serbia's loyal ally, Greece) in threatening air-strikes under UN authority against the Serb positions around Sarajevo. The guns fell silent. After some hesitation, they were moved outside the twenty-kilometre exclusion zone. Naturally, Lord Owen's pessimism about the prospects of peace and the value of air power evaporated as his previous convictions and he was among the first to step forward and claim the credit for setting up the prospects of peace starting 'last August'.[3]

Not only did the heavy artillery fall silent. Even the Serb snipers – so long described as beyond the control of Karadzić and Mladić – stopped their random slaughter too. Naturally, the do-nothings could not admit that the clear threat of force had brought Karadzić to his senses. On the contrary, it was soon discovered that the good doctor had been about to do the very same all along and the NATO ultimatum was mere coincidence. The fact that Karadzić had broken many more promises even than there had been cease-fires in Bosnia was forgotten in the haste of those whose words had helped condemn scores of thousands to death to avoid admitting culpability.

Sceptics about Western resolve had less to explain away. It is true that the cease-fires and withdrawals of heavy weapons arranged first around Sarajevo, then Tuzla, brought welcome relief from bombardment to the citizens and refugees in those cities, but soon enough it was clear that the Serb weaponry had been relocated to bring misery to other besieged towns. Each of the new targets of Mladić's fury was a UN 'safe haven', but to the battered inhabitants of Bihać or Gorazde that status meant only a badge of scorn.

While the Serbs understood the NATO ultimatium to mean that they should concentrate their fire out of range of CNN's cameras (and were probably encouraged to understand it that way), the United States made serious efforts to calm the Muslim-Croat fighting in Hercegovina. On 1 March the Americans achieved a genuine cease-fire by a mixture of bribes, threats and strategic reasoning. On 18 March Tudjman and Izetbegović were present in Washington to give their blessing to a federal Bosnia-Hercegovina and to the prospects of a confederal Croatia and Bosnia. The agreement to halt the fighting in Mostar and Hercegovina between Croats and Muslims was a blow to the Serbs. Milosević's strategy of divide and rule had been thwarted, but the basic causes of tension remained between the Serb forces and their Muslim-Croat opponents.

However, the Serbs were emboldened by several factors. First of all, the European Union countries had only agreed to the NATO ultimatum provided it was supported by Russia. Both John Major and the French Defence Minister, Léotard, went to Moscow immediately before the decision and gained Russian agreement. The British, especially, were anxious to have Russian help to forestall any decisive American action. Even though the new UNPROFOR commander in Sarajevo was the SAS General, Sir Michael Rose, any idea that John Major had chosen to adopt an 'action man' approach to the Bosnian tragedy was soon shown to be illusory.

When the Serbs intensified their onslaught on Bihać and Gorazde at the end of March 1994 nothing happened, and UNPROFOR spokesmen cast doubt on the strength of the offensive. Even when the Serbs treated Rose with contempt by denying him access to Gorazde and offering him the umpteenth 'general cease-fire' instead, their scorn was treated as yet another step forward in the 'peace process'. Only the direct threat of a rapid and pulverising Serb advance to UN personnel in Gorazde led the Secretary-General's authority to be invoked to launch a two-plane air strike on 10 April (repeated the next day). The 'peace processors' hurried forward to insist that this action was taken to protect UNPROFOR and other UN personnel in the town and not the beleaguered population of the 'safe area'. In other words, the UN was not taking sides even against those threatening its own representatives!

Briefly, the Bosnian government side was jubilant about the sudden display of firmness, but disillusion soon set in. As ever, it was simply the backdrop to renewed efforts to make the government in Sarajevo fall in with the partition of the country. Even the Serbs' continuing advances were explained as their contribution to the 'peace process': far from wanting more land, they were simply conquering more territory to provide additional bargaining counters on top of the seventy per cent of Bosnia-Hercegovina already under their control.

What the brief NATO air strikes could not blot out was the catalogue of recent UN and US peace-keeping blunders. President Clinton's first year in office had managed to produce one fiasco after another, first of all in Somalia, then in Haiti. Each time, the United States retreated in the face of local rabbles when they showed any contumely towards its forces. If the Haiti fiasco in the autumn of 1993 was primarily an American débâcle, the Rwanda massacres after 6 April 1994, the second anniversary of the international recognition of Bosnia's independence, had horrifying echoes of Sarajevo. Just as the French UN forces had signally failed to protect the Bosnian deputy-premier, Turajlić, in 1992, so the Rwandan Prime Minister Agathé Uwillingimana, was murdered (in this case along with eleven Belgian Blue Helmets incapable of protecting themselves, let alone her). The UN's first response was to retreat: 'We all think of Somalia and worry about a similar occurrence elsewhere.'[4]

While NATO oscillated between getting tough and trying to wheedle all sides back into the murderous peace process, it ignored the growing crisis in the south. The West had long since agreed to leave Kosovo to stew, but in mid-February the Greek government decided to match the NATO ultimatum to the Serbs over the bombardment of Sarajevo with its own *démarche*: it announced the closure of the frontier with Macedonia.

Greece's decision to blockade her border with Macedonia exposed the European Union's common foreign policy yet again as an exercise in rhetoric masking compliance by the Eleven with the most vindictive policies of the Twelfth. Macedonians must have realised how ineffectual the Eleven would be in their publicly-proclaimed determination to thwart the strangulation of the new republic when a hero of the 1991 *troika*, Hans van den Broek, was despatched to make Athens comply![5]

By April it was clear that US involvement still meant pressuring the Bosnian government into making concessions and ignoring growing threats to peace. The NATO ultimatum in February was declared a one-off response by US Defence Secretary, Perry.[6] The sudden flurry of activity on 10–11 April was just the prelude to renewed negotiations. The reason was obvious: Russia had no further interest in cooperating with a Western agenda.

Vitaly Churkin, the Russian mediator, suggested that instead of getting tough with the Serbs for defying UN resolutions, sanctions should be lifted! President Yeltsin predicted 'war without end' if NATO renewed its air strikes. Already, in February, the Kremlin had seized the initiative, much to the relief of the West Europeans, and sent its own troops into Sarajevo to police the cease-fire and gain the strategic high-ground in every sense.

Russian history shows repeatedly how a backward country can still achieve international success through shrewd policies and clear-eyed assessments of the illusions and follies of the objectively stronger.[7] Having steeled themselves to threaten action, NATO leaders proved incapable of following through on success. Instead of sending their own troops to reinforce the cease-fire they dithered and left open a gap into which the strategic grandmasters in the Kremlin quickly moved pawns of their own.

Instead of understanding the strategic own-goal that they had scored by refusing to deploy their own forces at the moment of triumph when the threat of air strikes had forced the Serbs to back down, the Western leaders joined the Bosnian Serbs in cheering the arrival of Russian troops in Sarajevo. The Russian paratroops gave the two-fingered Serb salute as they entered Serb-controlled areas and passed through rejoicing crowds. Even some Western statesmen seemed a little alarmed by signs of lack of neutrality, but the peace-processors took heart.

Whatever the flaws of Disraeli's Balkan policy, a century earlier he had shown clear-sight when Russian troops threatened to wash their boots in the warm waters of the Mediterranean. John

Major's cabinet took as long to decide whether to redeploy *two* companies of Coldstream Guards inside Bosnia as Disraeli's colleagues had needed to send the fleet to the Dardanelles in 1878. For politicians allegedly haunted by the Sarajevo complex of 1914, it was an extraordinary achievement to create the conditions for a new East-West confrontation there eighty years on.

Any survey of the charlatanry of a 'peace process',[8] which seemed bent on turning every chance of stopping the fighting and reversing aggression into fresh fiasco, must come to an angry and contemptuous conclusion. Aristotle insisted that there are occasions when indignation is the only appropriate response and indifference is a sign of folly. Looking back on tens of thousands of needless deaths, the murder of a culture and the vandalisation of its monuments accompanied by the prattle of peacemakers, Louis MacNeice's contemptuous verdict in 1938 on the illusions of appeasement returns to haunt us as the epitaph of continuing low, dishonest and doomed diplomacy:

> Conferences, adjournments, ultimatums.
> Flights in the air, castles in the air.
> The autopsy of treaties, dynamite under bridges.

Notes

Introduction

1. Metternich's attempt to stifle his sovereign Franz I's concern for the fate of the rebellious Greeks at the hands of the Ottoman Turks in the 1820s is quoted in Alan Sked (ed.), *Europe's Balance of Power, 1815–1848* (Macmillan: London, 1979), p. 7. In September 1876, Sir Henry Elliot wrote to the Foreign Secretary, Derby, 'We may and must feel indignant at the needless and monstrous severity with which the Bulgarian insurrection was put down, but the necessity which exists for England to prevent changes from occurring here which would be most detrimental to ourselves, is *not affected* by the question whether it was 10,000 or 20,000 persons who perished.' Quoted in M. D. Stojanović, *The Great Powers and the Balkans, 1875–1878* (CUP: Cambridge, 1939; 2nd edition, 1968), pp. 106–107.

2. Throughout I have used the term 'Yugoslav' as a political rather than a strictly ethnic one, meaning the inhabitants of the territory which broadly constituted the Yugoslav state after 1918. Of course, Albanians and others might object to this since they are not 'Slavs' of any kind, even southern ones, but if the term is accepted as a geographical one which also implied citizenship of a common state (from 1918 until 1991) without any other qualitative implications I hope it proves as useful to the reader as I feel it was necessary to the author. Needless to add, this use of 'Yugoslav' excludes other South Slavs (Bulgarians or the Slavic inhabitants of northern Greece) who belong to communities which were never part of the Yugoslav state.

3. See R. T. Shannon, *Gladstone and the Bulgarian Agitation, 1876*

(The Harvester Press: Brighton, 1975) pp. 37–8, also p. 202; and chapter 4 below.
4. See Paul Garde, *Vie et Mort de la Yougoslavie* (Fayard: Paris, 1992), p. 383.
5. Quoted in *Frankfurter Allgemeine Zeitung* (29 Nov 1991). For Mitterrand's Foreign Minister's attribution of blame to a Germano-Vatican alliance, see chapter 13 below.
6. Quoted in Elie Kedourie, 'On Not Getting a Ph.D. The Manuscript that failed' in *Encounter* 406 (Jun 1988), p. 64. For a full discussion of modern Metternichianism, see chapter 2 below.

I: Outbreak of War

1. Emphasis in the original, quoted in Roman Rosdolsky, *Engels and the 'Non-historic' Peoples* (Critique Books: Glasgow, 1986), pp. 77–78.
2. See *Koreni* (Belgrade, 1955), p. 141.
3. For the wartime events, see chapter 6 below.
4. See Mladen Mutić, 'Neither dead nor at rest' from *YU Panorama* (1 Nov 1991), quoted in Ljubo Boban, 'Still More Balance on Jasenovac and the Manipulation of History' in *East European Politics and Societies* 6 (Spring, 1992), p. 214. For this theme, see Robert M. Hayden, 'Recounting the Dead: The Rediscovery and Redefinition of Wartime Massacres in Late and Post-Communist Yugoslavia' in Rubie S. Watson (ed.), *Memory and Opposition under State Socialism* (School of American Research: Sante Fe, 1993). For the Balkan folklore about the unquiet dead, see Paul Barber, *Vampires, Burial and Death: Folklore and Reality* (Yale UP: New Haven, 1988).
5. See Grmek, Gjidara & Simac (eds), *Le nettoyage ethnique* (Fayard: Paris, 1993), p. 287, and Paul Garde, *Vie et Mort de la Yougoslavie*, p. 351.
6. For the myth of Kosovo, see chapter 8 below. For the official sponsorship of the cult of *dead* Serb rulers, see Sabrina Ramet, *Balkan Babel* (Westview: Boulder, Colorado, 1992), pp. 30–31.
7. See Vladimir Zerjavić, *Opsesije i megalomanije oko Jasenovac i Bleiburga* (Globus: Zagreb, 1992). Franjo Tudjman set himself up as the target of Serbian propaganda, as so often, when he published a dense and poorly argued book, *Bespuća povijesne zbiljnosti: Rasprava o povijesti i filozofii zlosilija* (*Wilderness of Historical Reality. A Treatise on the History and Philosophy of Evil Brutality*) (Zagreb, 1990), about, among many other things, the horrors of the Second World War in Yugoslavia. It was easy to take quotations out of context

and peddle them as Tudjman's actual thoughts, but the Croatian President's rambling musings on genocide left him open to precisely that sort of attack and a wiser statesman would have expressed himself more clearly or probably avoided the issue altogether. For English-speaking readers, the *TLS* carried an extensive correspondence about Tudjman's book and its relation to the war in Yugoslavia running from 1991. For analysis of Tudjman's book and the propaganda debate, see Anto Knezević, *An Analysis of Serbian Propaganda: the Misrepresentation of the Writings of the Historian, Franjo Tudjman in the Light of the Serbian-Croatian War* translated by Sibelan E. S. Forrester and the author (Domovina TT: Zagreb, 1992).

8. For the Bleiburg massacre and the controversy surrounding it, see works by Nikolai Tolstoy, Christopher Booker, et al.

9. For the re-emergence of nationalism after Tito, see chapter 8 below.

10. For the Kosovo crisis, see chapter 9 below.

11. The failure of reform communism took many Western academics, diplomats and statesmen by surprise. The figures with whom they had consorted turned out to be universally despised and often more corrupt and incompetent than the 'hardliners'. Fascinating newsreel footage survives of Milošević's behaviour in Kosovo Polje.

12. For the downfall of Milošević's rivals in the Communist leadership, see Ramet, *Nationalism and Federalism* (Indiana UP: Bloomington, Indiana, 1992), pp. 225ff.

13. For evidence of the infiltration of weapons and training among so-called Chetniks in Bosnia well before the Muslims led by Alija Izetbegović could be accused of 'seizing' power and therefore frightening the Serbs, see Ramet, *Nationalism and Federalism*, p. 259.

14. See Alexander Singer, *NIN* (4 Oct 1987), quoted in Branka Magaš, *The Destruction of Yugoslavia* (Verso: London, 1993), pp. 111–112.

15. For Agrokomerc, see Harold Lydall, *Yugoslavia in Crisis*, (Clarendon Press: Oxford, 1989) pp. 168–71.

16. For Milošević as a 'Balkan Lincoln' and the notion that among Serbs 'a not wholly dishonourable longing for revenge still burns', see Andrew Roberts' editorial page article in the *Sunday Telegraph* (15 Sep 1991). I am assured that, on nearer acquaintance with Balkan realities, Mr Roberts changed his mind. However, the endorsement of Serb policies in the 1990s by such influential journals as the *Church of England Newspaper* which published as late as 22 May 1992 a front-page story 'Serbia: Memories of a Holocaust fuel civil war' liberally quoting pro-Serb propagandists, denying current Serb and JNA atrocities while playing up Croat crimes from fifty years earlier, have gone by without the Church hierarchy

distancing themselves from them. The role of Evangelical and Christian fundamentalist groups in supporting supposedly Orthodox Serb anti-Catholic and still more anti-Muslim positions has been one of the less discussed but politically significant aspects of the struggle for international influence by Great Serbian ex-communists as among their Russian counterparts anxious to stifle the independence of the Central Asian republics. Such groups have their spokespeople in Parliament as well as the religious press.

17. See interviews in *Le Monde* (12 Jul 1989) and *Libération* (19 Oct 1990).

18. See James Gow, *Legitimacy and the Military: Yugoslavia in Crisis* (Pinter Publishers: London, 1992), pp. 136–139.

19. Quoted in John Newhouse, 'The Diplomatic Round', in *The New Yorker* (24 Aug 1992), p. 60.

20. See *Libération* (19 Oct 1990).

21. See Ramet, *Nationalism and Federalism*, p. 254. Plans for the partition of Bosnia-Hercegovina were not only thought up by the Republic's neighbours, but became the stuff of so-called 'mediation' after fighting spread there in the spring of 1992. The Vance-Owen partition plans and Lord Owen's subsequent advocacy of 'realism', i.e. that the men with guns should get enough of what they wanted to calm them down, is discussed in chapter 13 below.

22. See Nora Beloff, 'Message to the People of Slovenia' in *The South Slav Journal* 13 (47–48 Spring-Summer, 1990 but in fact published on 21 Sep 1991), p. 142.

23. Drasković's political programme went through several remarkable shifts in the two years after the war began in Yugoslavia. He went from extreme nationalist to model democrat (when talking to Western leaders and journalists) and back to an outspoken opponent of a Muslim state in Europe, for which see chapter 14 below.

24. Quoted in Mark Thompson, *A Paper House* (Hutchinson Radius: London, 1992), p. 205.

25. Many post-communist nationalists have adopted the notion that the nation which they have decided to use as their new vehicle to power is the peculiar victim of Western racism. Russian national-bolsheviks like to invoke the idea of 'Russophobia' to rally people to their cause and discredit their critics as 'cosmopolitans' or foreign agents. These slogans of 'Serbophobia' or 'Russophobia' are simply demogogic developments of Edward Said's claim that much Western criticism of Third World tyranny is motivated by 'Orientalism'.

26. Quoted in Misha Glenny, *The Fall of Yugoslavia* (Penguin edition: Harmondsworth, 1993), p. 60.

27. See the *Financial Times* (8 May 1991) for advocacy of the 'military solution'; and Sabrina Ramet, *Balkan Babel*, p. 50, for Adzić's comment.
28. See Ivo Banac, 'Post-Communism as Post-Yugoslavism' in *Eastern Europe in Revolution* (Cornell UP: Ithaca, NY, 1992, pp. 183–84; see also chapter 2 below for the Soviet-Yugoslav exchanges in 1991.
29. For the relations between the JNA and Slovenia as well as Jansa of *Mladina*, see especially James Gow, *Legitimacy and the Military*, (Pinter Publishers: London, 1992), pp. 78ff.
30. See Bogdan Denitch, *Limits and Possibilities*, pp. 76–77 and p. 141 note 4.
31. Ramet has written extensively on the counter-cultures of waning Yugoslavia, see the relevant essays in *Balkan Babel*. I cannot say that I am grateful to Rupert Katritzky for inflicting the music of Laibach on me during a journey in his *Kubelwagen*.
32. Of course, in practice, Slovenes exaggerated the ease of transition to the West and not merely because of EC obstruction. Slovenia's high standard owed much to her capacity to export goods to other parts of Yugoslavia. Serbian trade boycotts before the declaration of independence were only a foretaste of the disruption of normal patterns of intra-Yugoslav trade brought on by the wars in Croatia, then Bosnia.
33. Quoted in J. F. Brown, *Nationalism, Democracy and Security in the Balkans* (RAND: Santa Monica, 1992), p. 150.

2: Countdown: The West and the Yugoslav Crisis

1. Quoted in E. H. Carr, *The Twenty Years' Crisis, 1919–1939*, (3rd edition, Macmillan: London 1981), p. 208.
2. As reported by John Cole on the Six O'Clock News, BBC 1 John Major was still optimistic in the House of Commons on 1 July 1991, when he assured MPs that the EC *troika* had helped to 'defuse' the Yugoslav crisis!
3. 'News at Ten', ITV (27 Jun 1991).
4. Channel 4 News, 7pm (27 Jun 1991).
5. See *Independent on Sunday* (30 Jun 1991).
6. Channel 4 News, 7pm (27 Jun 1991).
7. For the role of Poos, see Peter Hort, '*Gewissensfragen an Luxemburg*' in *Frankfurter Allgemeine Zeitung* (*FAZ*) (3 Jul 1991), which also reports his more praiseworthy role during the Gulf War when he supported the Allied coalition against Saddam, though even then Poos could not avoid a hint of the Ruritanian ridiculous when he

denied the President of the European Parliament, Baron Crespo, access to military briefings on the grounds that such matters were beyond his competence. Jacques Poos seems to have an endless flow of such grandiose and fatuous *obiter dicta*: the most revealing of his pint-sized totalitarian ambition was 'Our Community is not just a Common Market. It is a Community where the life has to be harmonised.' Interview for 'Newsnight', BBC 2 (13 Nov 1991).

8. For the views of the restorationist Habsburg Foreign Ministry, see Vladimir Dedijer, *The Road to Sarajevo* (Macgibbon & Kee: London, 1966), p. 73.

9. Quoted in Elie Kedourie, 'On Not Getting a Ph.D. The Manuscript that Failed' in *Encounter* 406 (Jun 1988), p. 64.

10. For Gorbachev's threats, see Don Oberdorfer, *The Turn: How the Cold War came to an end*, pp. 397–404.

11. For Bush's speech in Kiev, see Paula Franklin Lytle, 'US Policy Toward the Demise of Yugoslavia: the Virus of Nationalism' in *East European Politics and Societies* 6 (Fall 1992), pp. 310–11.

12. For the Bush-Yeltsin declaration and Elchibey's reaction, see the reports in the BBC's *SWB* in January 1993. Elchibey was overthrown in June 1993 in a coup led by Suret Husseinov, a typical post-communist warlord-'businessman' whose troops then installed the old KGB and Party leader, Aliev, back in power. The 'international community' accepted this coup without demur and sent out CSCE observers who nonchalantly endorsed the validity of the 99.8% endorsement of Aliev's comeback at so-called presidential elections on 3 October 1993, but my own impression of their legitimacy was less favourable not just because of blatant multiple voting, but also because I myself was able, or rather obliged, to vote for Mr Aliev by enthusiastic officials anxious to show he had the support of the 'whole world'!

13. I owe the 'Bush Doctrine' to Richard Wagner of the Smithsonian Institute in Washington, DC.

14. Quoted in Lawrence Freedman & Efraim Karsh, *The Gulf Conflict, 1990–1991* (Faber & Faber: London, 1993), p. 413.

15. *International Herald Tribune* (28 Mar 1991).

16. Kissinger's pessimism is quoted in Walter Isaacson, *Kissinger: A Biography* (Faber & Faber: London, 1992), p. 504.

17. For Heath's comments, see 'The knight of Easter Island' in the *Guardian* (19 Jun 1993). Douglas Hurd, Heath's former private secretary as well as current Foreign Secretary, was anxious to restore central institutions *immediately after* the failed Soviet coup, in this he echoed his mentor and must have given comfort to federalists

everywhere, and not only in bunkers in Belgrade and Moscow: 'I don't myself think that it's going to be sensible from their point of view *or ours* [emphasis added] to have fifteen separate foreign policies, fifteen separate defence policies, fifteen separate applications to the West for help.' (*Evening Standard*, 27 Aug 1991).

18. In addition to Kissinger's *A World Restored: the Politics of Conservatism in a Revolutionary Era* (First edition, 1957. Victor Gollancz: London, 1977), see Walter Isaacson, *Kissinger: A Biography*, pp. 74–77.

19. See Predrag Simić, 'Civil War in Yugoslavia' in Clesse & Kortunov (eds), *The Political and Strategic Implications of the State Crisis in Central and Eastern Europe* (Institute for European and International Studies: Luxembourg, 1993), pp. 232–233.

20. See ibid., p. 216.

21. See *Financial Times* (8 May 1991). This editorial echoed, presumably unconsciously, a speech by Slobodan Milošević three weeks earlier: 'The army has the constitutional authority and constitutional obligation to defend the constitutional order . . . What kind of coup is it, if tomorrow the army exercised its constitutional authority and proceeds to disarm those [Croatian] units . . .? This isn't some kind of coup. The army must disarm paramilitary formations in the interests of defending the constitutional order . . . to defend peace in the country and its territorial integrity.' Quoted in Lenard J. Cohen, *Broken Bonds* (Westview: Boulder, Colorado, 1993), p. 203. For a British Foreign Office Minister's endorsement of this line, see below (& note 22).

22. In answer to a question from Sir David Steel whose most significant contribution to Anglo-Yugoslav relations had been to fly to Yugoslavia for Tito's funeral 'wearing a bright red tie which I thought entirely appropriate for a Socialist country'. See *Against Goliath: David Steel's Story*, p. 246.

23. See Hansard col. 1137 (27 Jun 1991).

24. See *Le Monde* (26–27 May 1991).

25. See Hugh Poulton, *The Balkans* (Minority Rights Group: London, 1991), p. 100. Another long-term observer of the Balkans, J. F. Brown, *Eastern Europe and Communist Rule* (Duke UP: Durham, 1988), pp. 361–6 analysed the JNA's position as the last genuinely Yugoslav body but decided it was 'difficult to see the Yugoslav army being used'.

26. Quoted in John Pinder, *The European Community and Eastern Europe* (RIIA/Pinter Publishers: London, 1991), p. 75.

27. See chapter 1 above and Simić, 'Civil War in Yugoslavia', p. 231.

28. For di Michelis, see Viktor Meier, *Zuviel nach Belgrad geschaut: die Europäische Gemeinschaft und Jugoslawiens Realitäten* in *FAZ* (15 Apr 1991). Since then his golden days as Italy's Foreign Minister have come to an end and di Michelis can be heard defending himself against corruption charges by arguing that he stole like the others in Italian politics. He also faces charges of sexual harassment at the time of writing. See also Laslo Sekelj, *Yugoslavia: the process of Disintegration* translated by Vera Vukelić (Atlantic Research Publications: New York, 1993), pp. 245–55.
29. When Andreotti asked the fateful Rome Summit in October 1990 to 'guarantee' the Soviet Union, presumably against its own peoples, only Mrs Thatcher and the Danes objected, not least because their countries had never accepted Stalin's incorporation of the Baltic states, unlike Nazi Germany, Fascist Italy, Vichy France and Franco's Spain – all of whose impeccably democratic successors were happy to continue to do so.
30. See col. 324 Hansard (23 Jun 1993).
31. See Newhouse, 'The Diplomatic Round', p. 61.
32. Quoted in Roger Boyes, 'America gets tough with Serbs in policy switch' in *The Times* (23 Apr 1992).
33. See Newhouse, 'The Diplomatic Round', p. 61.
34. Quoted in Paula Franklin Lytle, 'US Policy Toward the Demise of Yugoslavia' in *East European Politics and Societies* 6, pp. 309–10.
35. See Patrick Glynn, 'Yugoblunder' in *The New Republic* (24 Feb 1992), p. 16.
36. See Lytle, 'US Policy Toward the Demise of Yugoslavia', p. 309.
37. Mr Hogg was interviewed on 'Today', BBC Radio 4 (3 Sep 1991). If stupidity is making the same mistake twice or more times, history's judgement on Hogg's intelligence will not be generous. See his comments in Sarajevo on the international community's unwillingness to come to the aid of a state whose independence it had recognised, quoted in chapter 11 below.
38. Chancellor Kohl signed the Soviet-German Treaty on Good Neighbourliness, Partnership and Cooperation on 9 November, a year to the day since the opening of the Berlin Wall, but also exactly fifty years since Hitler had met Molotov in Berlin to discuss the division of the world into spheres of influence, upon which they failed to agree.
39. Andreotti was quoted in the *FAZ* (23 Jan 1991).
40. See Viktor Meier, '*Stabilisierung der Konfusion*' in ibid.
41. Quoted in François Fejtö, *A History of the People's Democracies:*

Eastern Europe since Stalin translated by Daniel Weissbort (Penguin: Harmondsworth, 1974), p. 532 note 1.

42. See his article in *Le Monde* (25 Apr 1991).

43. See 'EG: *Abkommen nur mit Gesamtstaat Jugoslawien*' in *FAZ* (14 May 1991).

44. See '*Europa-Parlament wünscht den Erhalt Jugoslawiens als Ganze*' in *FAZ* (17 May 1991).

45. See *Le Monde* (25 Jun 1991).

46. See Ramet, *Nationalism and Federalism in Yugoslavia*, p. 253. Baker is quoted in Daniel Patrick Moynihan, *Pandemonium: Ethnicity in International Politics* (OUP: Oxford, 1993), p. 166.

47. See Anand Menon et al., 'A Common European Defence?' in *Survival* 34 (Autumn, 1992), p. 108.

48. See Julij Kwizinskij (German transliteration), '*Von deutschen Torschützen und sowjetischen Querpässen*' in *FAZ* (25 Mar 1993). See also his memoirs, *Vor dem Sturm. Erinnerungen eines Diplomaten* (Siedler: Berlin, 1993).

49. For instance, Sir Fitzroy Maclean told 'Newsnight', BBC 2 (17 Dec 1991) that the Serbs had been 'understandably . . . very conscious of the German danger' and he accepted the characterisation of modern Germany as 'the Fourth Reich'.

50. See 'Kohl links aid to stable union' in the *Guardian* (5 Sep 1991).

51. See Roger Boyes, 'America gets tough with the Serbs in policy switch' in *The Times* (23 Apr 1993). Zimmermann later resigned from the State Department in January 1994, after several other officials had done so expressing their disagreement with Bush's then Clinton's policy of tough words followed by inaction in Yugoslavia, but it transpired that Mr Zimmermann was about to become a victim of the Clinton White House's affirmative action programme and be asked to make way for 'a woman or a non-white male' at the top of the State Department's refugee affairs department. See Edwin M. Yoder Jr., 'A Good Man Who Shouldn't Be Lost' in *International Herald Tribune* (19 Jan 1994).

52. See Philip Zelikow, 'The new Concert of Europe' in *Survival* 34 (Summer, 1992), p. 29.

53. See Wynaendts, *L'Engrenage*, p. 58.

54. See '3 July, 1991' in Hansard (1–12 Jul 1991), col. 332. Mr Hurd used almost the same words in an interview for BBC 1's 'On the Record' (30 Jun 1991) in which he also foresaw 'ethnic cleansing'. Hurd's expectations of atrocities did not conclude that intervention was the appropriate response. In this at least he was the natural successor to Castlereagh as Henry Kissinger noted (*A World Restored*,

p. 295) 'Castlereagh did not deny that the atrocities committed by the Turks "made humanity shudder". But, like Metternich, he insisted that humanitarian considerations were subordinate to maintaining the "consecrated structure" of Europe.'

3: The Road to Sarajevo: The Balkans, 1804–1914

1. See Mackenzie's speech to the Royal United Services Institute (9 Dec 1992) reprinted in the RUSI Journal.
2. For the history of the Balkans before 1800, see Georges Castellan, *Histoire des Balkans xive-xxe siècle* (Fayard: Paris, 1991).
3. For the international background to the decay of the Ottoman Empire, see M. S. Anderson, *The Eastern Question, 1774–1923* (Macmillan: London, 1966). For a sympathetic portrait of the Ottoman Empire, see the two volumes by Stanford J. Shaw & Ezel Kural Shaw, *History of the Ottoman Empire and Modern Turkey* (CUP: Cambridge, 1976).
4. For the *devshirme* and related matters, see Stanford J. Shaw & Ezel Kural Shaw, *History of the Ottoman Empire* I, pp. 122–31.
5. For the internecine bloodletting among Christians in Serbia and other parts of Ottoman Europe, see Andreas von Razumovsky, *Ein Kampf um Belgrad* (Ullstein Verlag: Berlin, 1980), pp. 9–56. See also Charles & Barbara Jelavich, *The Establishment of the Balkan National States, 1804–1920* (University of Washington Press: Seattle, 1977), pp. 34–37, and Fred Singleton, *A Short History of the Yugoslav Peoples*, chapter 5.
6. According to the *Blue Guide*, the pyramid had 56 rows and a total of 952 skulls. Cf. J.-M. Domenach, *Yougoslavie* (Editions Seuil: Paris, 1960), p. 78.
7. For the deep penetration of Ottoman influence on their Balkan subjects, see Djilas, *Land Without Justice* and the discussion in Andreas Razumovsky, op. cit., pp. 57ff. Russia suffered a similar psycho-political trauma under Mongol domination which was sublimated under Tsarist autocracy. See Tibor Szamuely, *The Russian Tradition* paperback edition (Fontana: London, 1988) and Karl A. Wittfogel, *Die Orientalische Despotie. Eine vergleichende Untersuchung totaler Macht* (Ullstein: Berlin, 1977). This is also one of the themes of Ivo Andrić's, *Bridge over the Drina*. For a self-conscious argument that Serbs should imitate their Turkish masters, see Čubrilović, quoted below.
8. For the origins of the Karadjordjević-Obrenović feud, see Razumovsky, op. cit., pp. 88–90.

9. For the Philhellene crusaders, see William St Clair, *That Greece Might Still be Free* (London, 1972).
10. C. M. Woodhouse commented, 'The neutrality of the French and British fleets was Olympian not only in its aloofness, but also in its unpredictability: Greeks and Turks alike never knew which side they would be neutral on next.' See *The Greek War of Independence. Its Historical Setting* (Hutchinson: London, 1952), p. 111. The French Admiral de Rigny foreshadowed certain elements in UNPROFOR when he argued, for instance, that, far from being taken as slaves, the Greeks whom the Ottoman commander Ibrahim Pasha had taken aboard his fleet went willingly!
11. For the Russians' contemptuous treatment of the Serbs and their presumptuous aspiration to brotherhood, see Razumovsky, op. cit., p. 53.
12. For Vuk Karadžić, see Duncan Wilson, *The Life and Times of Vuk Stefanović Karadžić, 1787–1864: Literature, Literacy and National Independence in Serbia* (OUP: Oxford, 1970).
13. See Rosdolsky, *Engels and the 'Nonhistoric' Peoples* (Critique Books: Glasgow, 1987), p. 102. For a modern Croat work popularising a myth favourable to Jellaćić, see Andelko Mijatović, *Ban Jelaćić* (Mladost: Zagreb, 1990). The restoration of a horseback statue of Jellaćić to central Zagreb in 1989 was clear evidence of the decay of communism.
14. See Engels, 'The Magyar Struggle' in David Fernbach (ed.), *Karl Marx: The Revolutions of 1848. Political Writings* volume I (Penguin: Harmondsworth, 1973), pp. 221–222, and Rosdolsky, *Engels and the 'Nonhistoric' Peoples*, pp. 85–86.
15. Quoted in Rosdolsky, op. cit., p. 186 note.
16. In addition to Rosdolsky, anyone interested in the themes of race, nationalism and Marxism should consult Walker Connor, *The National Question in Marxist-Leninist Theory and Strategy* (Princeton UP: Princeton, 1984) and Ian Cummins, *Marx, Engels and National Movements* (St Martin's Press: New York, 1980), especially chapter two. Engels would be glad to know that even if much of his teaching has been abandoned in recent years, at least his teaching on the reactionary peoples lives on. Even the otherwise impeccably anti-racialist *Guardian* allowed the notion of the blood guilt of the Croats to be repeated in its pages. Edward Pearce repeatedly characterised Croats *en bloc* as savage murderers: for instance, 'Indeed so much has the slashing of neck arteries been the historic way of the Croats that one wonders if our version of the native name should not be pronounced with a dipthong to rhyme with throat.' (*Guardian*, 31 Aug 1993). Such language leaves the reader with little alternative but

to conclude that genocide is the logical response to such inherently barbaric and reactionary people as the Croats.

17. See Rosdolsky, op. cit., p. 51.

18. See David Lloyd George, *Memoirs of the Peace Conference* (Yale UP: New Haven, 1939), II, p. 514.

19. Quoted by Fred Singleton, *A Short History*, p. 101.

20. Quoted in Ivo Banac, *The National Question in Yugoslavia*, p. 109.

21. For Russia's calculation of her own interests in the Balkans, see above and chapter 4 below.

22. See Philip Cohen's paper, 'Desecrating the Holocaust', on anti-Semitism in later nineteenth-century Serbia as well as the use of alleged inherent Croat anti-Semitism to justify contemporary Serb actions against Croat and Muslim. Of course, it is the current Serbian campaign to identify the Croats and Muslims as inherently fascist which draws attention to the flaws in Serbia's past, which the cult of Serbia as a plucky ally of the Western democracies after 1914 obscured.

23. On the cult of the martyr assassin in Serbia, see Vladimir Dedijer, *The Road to Sarajevo*. The Russian counterparts are analysed in Anna Geifman, *Thou Shalt Kill: Revolutionary Terrorism in Russia, 1894–1917* (Princeton University Press: Princeton, 1993).

24. See Banac, *The National Question in Yugoslavia*, p. 108.

25. For Apis, see David Mackenzie, *Apis: the Congenial Conspirator* (Westview; Boulder, Colorado, 1989). Russian opinion, too, was shocked by the 'tsar killers' in Belgrade, see Dedijer, *The Road to Sarajevo*, p. 512, though, in its short-sighted way, Nicholas II's government judged it a beneficial move since it damaged Serb-Habsburg relations. In the end such myopia was to cost the Tsar (and his family) their lives in almost as savage circumstances.

26. For the fate of brother Djordje, see Razumovsky, *Ein Kampf um Belgrad*, pp. 103–04. After living in strict detention until 1941, Djordje survived the Second World War to live out a privileged old age in his own house in Dedinje under Tito's protection rather like a Balkan Henry Pu-Yi in Peking. Like Mao, Tito wanted to show how merciful he was to the representatives of the old order – after exterminating countless thousands of their potential supporters. Like Pu-Yi, Djordje published carefully edited memoirs (in 1968). Such was his rehabilitation that Prince Djordje was supposed to attend a reception for Queen Elizabeth and his cousin, Prince Philip, on their visit to Tito, the social summit of the Marshal's career, in October 1972. Sadly, on the eve of his reintroduction into court circles, Djordje died.

27. For the formation of the Balkan League, see A. J. P. Taylor, *The Struggle for Mastery in Europe*, pp. 483ff.
28. See Fritz Fischer, *Krieg der Illusionen: Die deutsche Politik von 1911 bis 1914* (Droste Verlag: Düsseldorf, 1969), p. 219.
29. The role of Apis, et al., is discussed in David Mackenzie, *Apis: the Congenial Conspirator, passim*, as well as in Razumovsky, *Ein Kampf um Belgrad*, pp. 47–50 & pp. 102–25.
30. A contemporary observer, Lev Trotsky, emphasised the antagonisms festering among the anti-Turkish allies. See his *The Balkan Wars* (Pathfinder Books: New York, 1991).
31. One recently reprinted example of the international indignation at the atrocities committed against Turkish prisoners and 'cleansed' Muslim civilians was the report issued by the Carnegie Endowment for International Peace. See *The Other Balkan Wars. A 1913 Carnegie Endowment Inquiry in Retrospect with a New Introduction and Reflections on the Present Conflict by George Kennan* (Carnegie: Washington, DC, 1993). I am grateful to Andrew Pierce for kindly sending me a copy of this important book, which still provides the best introduction to the cause and consequences of the Balkan Wars, 1912–13. For the apprehension of the Jewish majority in Salonika at the prospect of incorporation into Greece, see Gilles Veinstein (ed.), *Salonique, 1850–1918: La 'ville des Juifs' et le réveil des Balkans* (Éditions Autrement: Paris, 1992), pp. 251ff.
32. See Taylor, *Struggle for Mastery*, p. 520.
33. See ibid., p. 485.
34. For the history of Bosnia-Hercegovina under Habsburg rule, as well as before and since, see Noel Malcolm's *Bosnia: A Short History* (Macmillan: London, 1994) forthcoming.
35. See Taylor, *Struggle for Mastery*, p. 490.
36. See Istvan Déak, *Beyond Nationalism*, p. 191. In fact, nationals of enemy powers remained at liberty in the Dual Monarchy until 1917 – little wonder it lost!
37. Quoted in Taylor, *Struggle for Mastery*, p. 494.
38. See Samuel R. Williamson, *Austria-Hungary and the Origins of the First World War* (Macmillan: London, 1991), p. 163.
39. See ibid., p. 173.
40. Italian intrigues were as disastrously corrupt and shallow before 1914 as they were in the run-up to 1991. See Richard Bosworth, *Italy and the Approach of the First World War* (Macmillan: London, 1983), pp. 116–17. However, at least the Italians relished the absurdity of the Great Powers joining together to threaten naval action against Montenegro if King Nikola refused to give up his ambitions

to incorporate the Albanian town of Scutari (Shköder) despite the town's position thirty miles *from* the sea!

41. For Hartwig, see Dominic Lieven, *Russia and the Origins of the First World War*, pp. 41–42. Sazonov's shrewd insight into Hartwig's exaggerated Slavism is quoted in G. P. Gooch, *Before the War. Studies in Diplomacy* (Longman: London, 1938), II, p. 332.

42. Published in the German attempt after 1918 to attribute war-guilt to everyone else except Kaiser Wilhelm II's government, *Deutsches Weissbuch über die Verantwortlichkeit der Urheber des Krieges* (Berlin, 1919), p. 99, but there is little reason to doubt this instruction's authenticity since Sazonov was clearly looking to the middle distance *not* the immediate future as the Germans implied.

43. For Poincaré's alarm in 1912, see Samuel R. Williamson, Jr, *Austria-Hungary and the Origins of the First World War*, p. 117, and Lieven, *Russia and the Origins of the First World War*, p. 48.

44. See Dedijer, *The Road to Sarajevo*, for the conspirators. Also Razumovsky, *Ein Kampf um Belgrad*.

45. For Vaso Čubrilović's future activities, including his advocacy in 1937 of the expulsion of the Albanians in Kosovo ('*Iseljavanje Arnauta*'), see chapters 5 & 8 below.

4: 1876 and all that

1. Quoted in Michael Bentley, *Politics without Democracy, 1815–1914* (Collins/Fontana: London, 1984), p. 225.

2. For a succinct but thorough account of the Greek insurrection, see Richard Clogg, *A Concise History of Greece* (CUP: Cambridge, 1992), pp. 7–46.

3. See Shannon, *Gladstone and the Bulgarian Agitation*, p. 40.

4. Quoted from the *Manchester Guardian* (9 Mar 1877) in R. W. Seton-Watson, *Disraeli, Gladstone and the Eastern Question* (Macmillan: London, 1935), p. 214.

5. See Shannon, *Gladstone and the Bulgarian Agitation*, p. 33.

6. Quoted in Seton-Watson, *Disraeli, Gladstone and the Eastern Question*, p. 214.

7. See ibid., p. 58.

8. See Shannon, *Gladstone and the Bulgarian Agitation*, pp. 153–55.

9. For 'Essex Man', see Andrew Gimson's article in the *Sunday Telegraph* (18 Apr 1993).

10. Quoted in Shannon, *Gladstone and the Bulgarian Agitation*, p. 154.

11. See R. T. Shanon, *The Crisis of Imperialism* (Granada: St Albans, 1976), p. 127.

12. Quoted in Shannon, *Gladstone and the Bulgarian Agitation*, p. 121.
13. Cobden is quoted in Daniel Pick, *War Machine: the Rationalisation of Slaughter in the Modern Age* (Yale UP: New Haven, 1993), p. 22.
14. Quoted in Seton-Watson, *Disraeli, Gladstone, and the Eastern Question*, p. 75.
15. See ibid., p. 77.
16. Quoted in ibid, pp. 88–89.
17. Alan Clark took part in a 'Panorama' debate on intervention on BBC1 (19 Apr 1993) when he claimed that 'Muslim' forces killed their own people as a way of obtaining sympathy. For the recurring myth of the victims' provocation or self-infliction of genocide, see Robert F. Melson, *Revolution and Genocide: On the Origins of the Armenian Genocide and the Holocaust* (Chicago University Press: Chicago & London, 1992), esp. pp. 10–12 & pp. 152–154 and literature cited in note 14 on p. 289.
18. Quoted in Seton-Watson, *Disraeli, Gladstone and the Eastern Question*, pp. 282–83.
19. See ibid., p. 282.
20. See ibid., p. 552–53.
21. For the bitterness of divisions in public opinion in Britain, see ibid., pp. 559.
22. Ibid., pp. 532–33.
23. Ibid., pp. 491–92.
24. Quoted in ibid., pp. 492–93. Disraeli's 'rational basis' for the restoration of the Ottoman Empire was the same sort of fanciful wishful thinking that had Hans-Dietrich Genscher proposing to restore the Soviet Union and Yugoslavia as parts of an 'all-European confederation based on the values of the Charter of Paris'! Quoted in the *FAZ* (5 Aug 1991).
25. Salisbury is quoted in Seton-Watson, p. 500.
26. Quoted in ibid., p. 496, but only a decade later, Salisbury privately admited that he thought Disraeli 'had acquired an exaggerated view of Turkish vitality and power . . .' ibid., p. 559.
27. Ibid., p. 503.
28. Quoted in M. S. Anderson, *The Eastern Question, 1774–1923: A Study in International Relations* (Macmillan: London, 1966), p. 178.
29. Quoted in Shannon, *Gladstone and the Bulgarian Agitation*, p. 155 & pp. 278–79. It was the same argument already pronounced by Metternich himself.
30. See Shannon, *Gladstone and the Bulgarian Agitation*, p. 30. The Northern Irish problem lurked in the back of the minds of British statesmen dealing with Bosnia in the 1990s too. It was the pro-Major

journalist, Simon Jenkins, writing in *The Spectator* (1 Jan 1994) who went so far as to argue that 'as in the former Yugoslavia, . . . the essence of political reform in Ulster is to acknowledge segregation – *and even the fact of ethnic cleansing* [emphasis added] – and try to construct *tolerant* [!] self-governing communities across the divide.'

31. For the brothers Aksakov, see Andrzej Walicki, *The Slavophile Controversy: History of a Conservative Utopia in Nineteenth Century Russian Thought* translated by Hilda Andrews-Rusiecka (OUP: Oxford, 1975), pp. 496–97.

32. See Dietrich Geyer, *Russian Imperialism: 1860–1914* (Berg: Leamington Spa, 1987), pp. 58–59.

33. See Walicki, *The Slavophile Controversy*, p. 499.

34. See Dietrich Geyer, *Russian Imperialism* (Berg: Leamington Spa, 1987), pp. 59–60.

35. *Russia's* 'first democratic war' and perhaps its last. See Geyer, *Russian Imperialism*, p. 71.

36. See David Saunders, *Russia in the Age of Reaction and Reform: 1801–1881* (Longman: London, 1992), p. 280 & p. 305.

37. See Leo Tolstoy, *Anna Karenina* translated by Louise & Aylmer Maude with an introduction by John Bayley (OUP: Oxford, 1980), pp. 799–800.

38. See F. M. Dostoevsky, *The Diary of a Writer* translated and annotated by Boris Brasol (Ianmead: Haslemere, 1984), p. 426.

39. For an account of Russian nationalism linking nineteenth-century themes with the emergent strands of post-Soviet Russian nationalism, see Stephen K. Carter, *Russian Nationalism: Yesterday, Today, Tomorrow*, (Pinter: London, 1990)

40. Quoted in Barbara Jelavich, *Russia's Balkan Entanglements, 1806–1914* (CUP: Cambridge, 1991), p. 272.

41. Quoted in Dietrich Geyer, *Russian Imperialism*, p. 69 & p. 67.

42. Quoted in David Saunders, *Russia in the Age of Reaction and Reform, 1801–1881*, p. 280.

43. See Hans Kohn, *Panslavism: Its History and Ideology* (University of Notre Dame Press: Notre Dame, Indiana, 1953), p. 170.

44. See Barbara Jelavich, *Russia's Balkan Entanglements*, p. 172.

45. See David Mackenzie, 'Panslavism in Action: Chernaiev in Serbia (1876)' in *The Journal of Modern History* 36 (1964), p. 279–97.

46. See Barbara Jelavich, *Russia's Balkan Entanglements, 1806–1914*, p. 170.

47. See Charles Jelavich, *Tsarist Russia and Balkan Nationalism: Russian Influence on the Internal Affairs of Bulgaria and Serbia,*

1879–1886 (Los Angeles, 1958), p. 12; cf. M. S. Anderson, *The Eastern Question*, p. 227 note 1.

5: From one World War to the Next 1914–1941

1. Quoted in Joachim Remak, *Sarajevo: The Story of a Political Murder* (Criterion Books: New York, 1959), p. 110.
2. See Banac, *The National Question in Yugoslavia*, p. 116.
3. For the Salonika operation, see Alan Palmer, *The Gardeners of Salonika* (London, 1965).
4. Quoted in Klaus Hildebrand, *The Foreign Policy of the Third Reich* translated Anthony Fothergill (Batsford: London, 1973), p. 154.
5. For the trial at Salonika and differing interpretations, see Razumovsky, *Ein Kampf um Belgrad* and David Mackenzie, *Apis: the Congenial Conspirator.*
6. Trumbić quoted in Alex N. Dragnich, *The First Yugoslavia*, p. 8.
7. For D'Annunzio's seizure of Fiume (Rijeka) in 1919, see Michael A. Ledeen, *The First Duce: D'Annunzio at Fiume* (Johns Hopkins UP: Baltimore, 1977).
8. See census figures for 1921 in Georges Castellan, *Histoire des Balkans*, p. 410.
9. See Banac, *The National Question in Yugoslavia*, p. 156.
10. See ibid., p. 154.
11. For the diverse peoples of Yugoslavia, see Joseph Rothschild, *East-Central Europe between the Two World Wars* (University of Washington Press: Seattle, 2nd edition, 1977), pp. 202–04.
12. See chapter 9 below, for the Albanians' discontents.
13. See George D. Jackson Jr., *Comintern and Peasant in East Europe, 1919–1930* (Columbia University Press: New York, 1966), pp. 7–14.
14. Quoted in E. H. Carr, *The Twenty Years' Crisis: 1919–1939*, p. 58.
15. See Aleksa Djilas, *The Contested Country* (Harvard UP: Cambridge, Mass., 1991), pp. 49ff.
16. For the young Tito, see Razumovsky, *Ein Kampf um Belgrad*, pp. 232 ff.
17. For the background to Tito's appointment as General-Secretary, see Djilas, *The Contested Country* p. 92, and Razumovsky, *Ein Kampf um Belgrad.* Tito was a beneficiary of the great purge with which Stalin shattered the émigré communists in Moscow but whose tentacles also reached out throughout the international Communist movement.
18. See Alex N. Dragnich, *The First Yugoslavia*, p. 80. Sir Nevile was convinced that Alexander 'regarded a dictatorship as temporarily in

the best interests of Yugoslavia . . . No greater or truer patriot ever existed.' Cf. Sir Nevile Henderson *Water under Bridges* (Hodder & Stoughton: London, 1945), p. 181. See also R. W. Seton-Watson, *The South Slav Question and the Habsburg Empire* (Constable: London, 1911), pp. 336–337 and *Water under Bridges* and his use as a respectable source by Alex N. Dragnich, 'The Anatomy of a Myth: Serbian Hegemony' in *Slavic Review* 50 (Fall, 1991), pp. 659–662.

19. See Ramet, *Nationalism and Federalism*, p. 49.

20. Many people took Stalin's espousal of an anti-Fascist Popular Front at face value and reviled the British and French for appeasing Hitler at Munich. The revulsion at appeasement was right but it was naive to expect Stalin to have acted if the Western democracies were willing to embroil themselves in war with Hitler in 1938 any more than in 1939. The veteran and sympathetic observer of Soviet foreign policy, Louis Fischer commented, 'As long as the Allies followed a policy of appeasement and surrender to the fascist aggressors, the Bolsheviks were pro-Ally. And the moment the Allies took a firm stand against a fascist aggressor [in 1939], the Bolsheviks made a pact with him. That is what is called dialectics.' Quoted in William L. O'Neill, *A Better World. The Great Schism: Stalinism and the American Intellectuals* (Simon & Schuster: New York, 1982), p. 16.

21. See Banac, 'Post-Communism as Post-Yugoslavism', p. 171.

22. See statistics in Joseph Rothschild, *East-Central Europe between the Two World Wars*, pp. 278–79. Already during the First World War, deserters from the Habsburg Army who joined the Volunteer Corps set up in Odessa by Serbia were soon disillusioned to find themselves treated as merely parts of the Serbian Army rather than as the embryo of a 'Yugoslav Army' and put under Serbian commanders. See Banac, *The National Question in Yugoslavia*, pp. 121–123.

23. See Banac, *The National Question in Yugoslavia*, p. 220. For a more favourable view, see Dragnich, *The First Yugoslavia*, but even Professor Dragnich concludes that the Kingdom was unsatisfactory for all concerned.

24. For instance, Alexander I shifted to a more compromising position with regard to his Catholic subjects after the dictatorship. He set about negotiating a concordat with the Vatican. It was ratified by the Skupstina after his murder in 1935. The Orthodox Church promptly excommunicated the Serb deputies who voted for it. See Castellan, op. cit., p. 414.

25. For Alexander's provision of sanctuary to Austrian Nazis after the failure of the 1934 putsch, see Razumovsky, p. 114.

[26] For a sympathetic account of Paul, see Cecil Parrott, *The Tightrope* (Faber & Faber: London, 1975).
[27] For the *Sporazum*, see Djilas, *The Contested Country*, pp. 128–135.
[28] Quoted in Stephen Clissold (ed.), *Yugoslavia and the Soviet Union, 1939–1973: A Documentary Survey* (RIIA/OUP: London, 1973), p. 6.
[29] For the Soviet-Yugoslav Pact, see Clissold, *Yugoslavia and the Soviet Union*, pp. 122–124. After the war *everyone* insisted that they had been against the Pact. Djilas recounts an amusing anecdote about Ivo Andrić, later an official author of Tito's regime, member of the Communist Party and Nobel Prize winner, but also Yugoslav representative in Berlin in 1941: 'In 1951, the army arranged an exhibit of the 1941 uprising on the Kalmagdan terrace, with models, sketches and blown-up photographs. One of these huge photographs showed Yugoslavia signing the Tripartite Pact. [The Foreign Minister] Cvetković and Ribbentrop were seen affixing their signatures, while Andrić – then royal envoy and minister plenipotentiary to Berlin – was standing in the background straight and tall in full dress, in all his majesty . . .' The great writer and equally great opportunist scurried to the still powerful Djilas, 'You know that exhibit on the Kalmegdan? I'm in one of the pictures. People will recognise me. They'll begin to wonder, they won't understand.' The picture was removed. (See Milovan Djilas, *Rise and Fall* (Macmillan: London, 1985), pp. 54–55.)
[30] The rapidity of the Yugoslav Army took almost everybody by surprise. A few people like Edmund Glaise von Horstenau, the future German military adviser to the Pavelić regime in Zagreb, were tipped the wink by the Yugoslav military attaché in Berlin not to expect much resistance, but most observers, especially in Allied circles, took it for granted that the Army would do as well as the Serbs in 1914 having had the chance to learn from the Polish and French experience of *Blitzkrieg*. In fact, the disastrous British expedition to the Balkans showed how low on the learning curve they were eighteen months after the start of the war. See Edmund Glaise von Horstenau, *Ein General im Zwielicht* (Böhlau Verlag: Vienna, 1988), pp. 79ff.

6: Wartime, 1941–44

[1] See Tito's speech to the Pan-Slav Congress in Belgrade, 8 December 1946, quoted in Hans Kohn, *Pan-Slavism* (University of Notre Dame Press: Notre Dame, Indiana, 1953), p. 236.

2. See Martin Van Creveld, *Hitler's Strategy, 1940–41: the Balkan Clue* (London, 1973).
3. For the Ustasha regime, see Ladislaus Hory & Martin Broszat, *Der kroatische Ustasche Staat, 1941–1945* (*Vierteljahresheft für Zeitgeschichte*: Stuttgart, 1964). Drasković is quoted in Wolfgang Libal, 'Das Messer ist unser Zeichen' in *Die Zeit* (19 Feb 1993), p. 3.
4. See the *Independent* (26 May 1993).
5. Quoted in *Vreme* (19 Aug 1991); cf. Robert M. Hayden, 'Balancing Discussion of Jasenovac and the Manipulation of History' in *East European Politics and Societies* 6 (Spring, 1992), p. 212.
6. For the atrocities in the Second World War, see Jonathan Steinberg, *All or Nothing: The Axis and the Holocaust, 1941–43* (Routledge: London, 1990) which focuses on Yugoslavia. Although Pavelić's NDH would never have come into existence without the German conquest of Royal Yugoslavia, critics of Croats' passive as well as active acceptance of the Ustasha regime should remember that even some of its allegedly bitterest opponents at first tried to collaborate with it. For instance, some local communists tried to set up a Communist Party of the NDH. It was only Pavelić's intolerance and the sudden outbreak of the German-Soviet war which scuppered Yugoslav communists' opportunistic attempts to take advantage of German conquest just as their comrades in France, for instance, tried to play off the German occupiers against Vichy with some success. See Viktor Meier, 'Yugoslavia's National Question', pp. 103–104. The politics of occupation, civil war and revolution are never as neat as their apologists suppose.
7. See Singleton, *Yugoslav Peoples*, p. 178.
8. For the number of Ustasha activists, see ibid., p. 181.
9. See Djilas, *Contested Country*, pp. 125–127 & note pp. 212–213.
10. For the composition of the Partisans and their elite, see Djilas, *Wartime* (Secker & Warburg: London, 1977).
11. See Djilas, *Land without Justice*, p. 39.
12. See 'Christ and the Commissar' in George Urban (ed), *Stalinism: Its Impact on Russia and the World*, pp. 242–44.
13. For Churchill's cynical question, see Fitzroy Maclean, *Eastern Approaches* (Penguin: Harmondsworth, 1991), pp. 402–403.
14. For the role of locally recruited SS troops and other mountain troops in Yugoslavia, see James Lucas, *Hitler's Mountain Troops* (Arms and Armour Press: London, 1992), pp. 68–72, pp. 144–63 & p. 204. For the gross exaggerations of the casualties inflicted by the understrength Muslim SS division 'Handschar', which was in action

only from January until September 1944, see Mervyn Hisket, 'Islam and Bosnia' in *The Salisbury Review* (Jun 1993), p. 6.

15. For the Chetniks' relations with the Axis, see Roberts, *Tito, Mihailović and the Allies* (Duke UP: Durham, NC, 1987), esp. pp. 55–75 & pp. 120–25.

16. See Pavlovitch, *The Improbable Survivor* (Hurst: London, 1988), pp. 140–42.

17. The Partisans of course relied on Stalin's advice when it came to deciding such a momentous issue as their attitude towards an Allied landing in Dalmatia. See Walter R. Roberts, *Tito, Mihailović and the Allies*, p. 102 & p. 108; also Djilas, *Wartime*, pp. 281–82.

18. For Stalin's disgust at the failure of the Partisans to disguise their communist credentials effectively, see Djilas, *Conversations with Stalin*, p. 76. For once Stalin was not cynical enough: Western liaison officers were usually indifferent to the Partisans' ideology when they did not actually share it. (So-called Chetniks fighting after 1991 continued to wear the red stars on their helmets with pride into 1994, when there should have been plenty of time to repaint them with a quaint old Serbian sign.)

19. For the Croat fascists' evasion of justice, see Mark Aarons & John Loftus, *Ratlines: How the Vatican's Nazi Networks Betrayed Western Intelligence to the Soviets* (Mandarin: London, 1991). *Ratlines* is a much more interesting and differentiated book than the Channel 4 documentary of the same title, broadcast at the height of the onslaught on Vukovar.

20. For Macmillan's diary entries see Alistair Horne, *Macmillan, 1894–1956* (Macmillan: London, 1988), pp. 271–272 and p. 258. At the same time, Macmillan referred to 'about 40,000 Cossacks and White Russians, *with their wives and children* . . . To hand them over is condemning them to slavery, torture and probably death . . . We have decided to hand them over.' Ibid., p. 259. There can be no doubt that the Western politicians and military responsible for the forced deportations knew they were handing over innocents as well as quislings. None of Macmillan's bogus Scottish romantic waffle about Highland parallels – 'It's rather as if you had been fighting alone for four years with the Campbells as your ally – then they ask you to hand over the MacFarlanes and MacTaggarts to them.' Ibid., p. 276 – can disguise the fact that he was lucky to be on the winning side: others were executed for handing over anti-Nazi refugees to the Gestapo, or the Clan Hitler as Laval might have argued in his defence.

21. See Peter Lord Carrington, *Reflect on Things Past: The Memoirs*

of Lord Carrington (Collins/Fontana: paperback edition London, 1989), pp. 64–65. Professor Sir Michael Howard recently wrote revealingly in the *London Review of Books* (27 Jan 1994), p. 9, of his post-war experiences in 'liberated' Slovenia: 'My own landlord, a gentle Italian doctor, was dragged from his bed in the middle of the night by a Partisan patrol commanded by a pleasant-faced boy even younger than I was, who told me when I protested that the doctor was on the list of notorious war-criminals. For all I know he was. In any case, when I rang my commanding officer to ask for instructions, that admirable man told me to go straight back to bed unless I wanted to start the Third World War.' Frank Chapple's memoirs, *Sparks Fly! A Trade Union Life* (Michael Joseph: London, 1984) p. 40, record the experience of a then communist in the lower ranks, 'There were Russian and Yugoslav prisoners-of-war in a camp near us and it was difficult for me to understand their reluctance to be repatriated to their communist homelands . . . Many of the Yugoslavs in the refugee camp near us were so determined not to be sent home that they went on a violent rampage.'

22. See Nikolai Tolstoy, *Victims of Yalta* (Hodder & Stoughton: London, 1977; paperback edition, 1978) and Nicholas Bethell, *The Last Secret: Forcible Repatriation to Russia, 1944–47* introduced by Hugh Trevor-Roper (André Deutsch: London, 1974).

23. See Carrington, *Reflect on Things Past*, p. 65.

24. Carrington's comments to Tudjman are reported in Wynaendts, *L'Engrenage*, pp. 142–143.

25. Evelyn Waugh's *Unconditional Surrender* remains the most vivid account of the absurdities of Western pro-Stalinist/Titoite propaganda.

26. See John Alcock, 'Yugoslavia's Defence Preparedness in the Context of Yugoslav Society', in Milivojeć (ed.), Allcock & Maurer, *Yugoslavia's Security Dilemmas*, p. 294. UN humanitarian aid filled the gaps in local supplies, particularly for the Bosnian Serb and JNA forces, without which post-war agricultural and economic changes would have made prolonged large-scale warfare in the 1990s impossible.

27. The myth of Tito's enormous military strength was constantly invoked by pro-Serb and anti-interventionists to argue against UN or Western action to halt the fighting after 1991, and no amount of academic demolition of the inflated figures given for the German Army had any effect on those who wanted to believe in Serb invincibility. Just as no consideration of technological change was permitted to influence perceptions of the options for ending the war.

For the absence of the *Luftwaffe* and the role of Allied air superiority in making partisan warfare viable, see Wing-Commander Tony Le Hardie, 'Wartime Lessons on air supremacy' in the *Independant* (12 Feb 1994), who notes that 'the major German offensive . . . in May 1944, was brought to standstill *solely by air strikes* [emphasis in original].' Wing-Commander Le Hardie should know since he was commander of the Forward Fighter Sector on the island of Vis as well as liaison officer at Tito's HQ (January-August, 1944).

28. See Djilas, *Conversations with Stalin*, p. 87.

7: Tito, 1944–80

1. See *The Prince*, chapter 8.
2. See Paul Garde, *Vie et Mort de la Yougoslavie*, p. 82.
3. See Djilas, *Wartime*, pp. 384–85.
4. For the suspicions of the Albanian Stalinist, Enver Hoxha, about Tito's aims, see Jon Halliday (ed.), *The Artful Albanian: the Memoirs of Enver Hoxha* (Chatto & Windus, London, 1986), pp. 88ff, and Gavriel D. Ra'anan, *International Policy Formation in the USSR: Factional 'Debates' during the Zhdanovschina* (Archon Books: Hamden, Connecticut, 1983), pp. 46–47.
5. See Djilas, *Conversations with Stalin*, pp. 140–41.
6. For the Macedonian question in postwar Greek politics, see Peter J. Stavrakis, *Moscow and Greek Communism. 1944–49* (Cornell UP: Ithaca, 1989); for general background see Richard Clogg, *A Concise History of Greece* (CUP: Cambridge, 1992). Since the outbreak of war in Yugoslavia, Greek hysteria about the prospect and alleged threat of Macedonian independence has assumed extraordinary proportions. See also Svetozar Vukmanović, *How and Why the People's Liberation Struggle of Greece met with Defeat* (Merlin Press: London, 1985).
7. For the cautious approach of the Partisans towards the retreating Germans, see Nora Beloff, *Tito's Flawed Legacy: Yugoslavia & the West: 1939 to 1984* (Gollancz: London, 1985), p. 58.
8. For Mihailović's trial and execution, see Beloff, *Tito's Flawed Legacy*, p. 81 & p. 116.
9. Quoted in Sirc, *The Yugoslav Economy under Self-Management*, p. 13.
10. For the Cominformist crisis, see Ivo Banac, *With Stalin Against Tito: Cominformist Splits in Yugoslav Communism* (Cornell UP: Ithaca, New York, 1988).
11. See Djilas, *Tito*, p. 125.

12. Wolfgang Leonhard, *Die Revolution entlässt ihre Kinder* (Europäische Bildungsgemeinschaft: Stuttgart, 1980), p. 489.
13. See Djilas, *Rise and Fall*, pp. 237–245.
14. See Sirc, *The Yugoslav Economy*, p. 37.
15. For Yugoslav State Security Service (SDS) attacks in Britain, see Milivojević, *Descent into Chaos*, p. 13.
16. Quoted in Vladimir Tismaneanu, *Reinventing Politics: Eastern Europe from Stalin to Havel* (The Free Press: New York, 1992), p. 50.
17. See Fedor Burlatsky, *Khrushchev and the First Russian Spring: the Era of Khrushchev through the Eyes of his adviser* translated by Daphne Skillen (Weidenfeld & Nicolson: London, 1991), p. 91.
18. For Tito's revealing speech, see Marko Milivojević, *Descent into Chaos: Yugoslavia's Worsening Crisis* (Institute for European Defence & Strategic Studies: London, 1989), p. 23.
19. See *Borba* (23 Dec 1971).
20. Quoted in Marko Milivojević, 'The Political Role of the People's Army', p. 22.
21. See Brown, *Surge to Freedom* (Adamantine Press, Twickenham, 1991), p. 223.
22. For the annual celebration of youth, see Razumovsky, *Ein Kampf um Belgrad*, p. 8 and Valentin Pelosse, 'Yougoslavie: la mémoriale de Josip Broz Tito' in Alain Brossat (ed.), *À l'Est la Mémoire retrouvée* (La Découverte: Paris, 1990), pp. 229–245.
23. For Tito's Soviet uniform, see Beloff, *Tito's Flawed Legacy*, p. 109.
24. See Djilas, *Tito* (Viena, 1980) p. 122; cf. Koene, p. 210.
25. See Maclean, *Disputed Barricade*, p. 460.
26. See Pavlovitch, *Improbable Survivor*, especially p. 44 for perceptive comments on the cult of Tito abroad.
27. See Pavlovitch, *Tito*, p. 13.
28. See Sava Bosnitch, 'The Cult of Tito's Personality, 1943-?', p. 73 note 56; Pavlovitch, *Tito*, p. 91, and Valentin Pelosse, 'Le mémorial de Josip Broz Tito' in *À l'Est la Mémoire retrouvée*, pp. 229–245.
29. See Pavlovitch, *Tito*, pp. 80–81.
30. See Burlatsky, *Krushchev*, p. 118. On another occasion the uncouth Khrushchev squirted orange juice all over the white admiral's uniform that Tito wore to host his guest aboard his yacht off Brioni. See Burlatsky, p. 122.
31. See Cal McCrystal, 'Dropping in for plots and plum brandy' in the *Independent* (16 Aug 1992).
32. For the Yugoslav security services, see Marko Milivojević, 'The

Role of the Yugoslav Intelligence and Security Community' in John B. Allcock (ed.) et al., *Yugoslavia in Transition*, pp. 199–237.

33. Quoted in Lenard Cohen, *Broken Bonds*, p. 29.

34. See Sirc, 'In the light of Yugoslav experience' in A. Clayre (ed.), *The Political Economy of Cooperation and Participation* (OUP: Oxford, 1980), p. 162.

35. See Sirc, *The Yugoslav Economy*, p. 250.

36. Quoted in James Sherr, *Soviet Power: the Continuing Challenge* (RUSI/Macmillan: London, 1987), p. 22.

37. Jimmy Carter's Deputy-Secretary of State, Warren Christopher, paid tribute to Tito with typical lack of foresight: 'The *vitality* of the country which he served so long and faithfully is his *enduring* legacy. The people of Yugoslavia have our deep sympathy at this tragic moment of loss.' Quoted by Reuters ('Keyword; Tito-Carter', 4 May 1980 – Sunday AM cycle).

8: After Tito: The Breakdown of Yugoslavia

1. Like all the most unstable and flawed constitutions, the 1974 Yugoslav model was immensely long-winded and, if not precise, it sought to regulate almost every aspect of life in its 406 articles covering more than 300 closely printed pages. By contrast, the most stable constitution in the world which also regulates a multi-ethnic society, the US Constitution contains only 24 articles covering a dozen pages. The Treaty on European Union has favoured Titoite wordiness in preference to American precision. It is easy to see why Maastricht distracted the European Community from the war in its backyard up to (and after) December 1991, since it contains no fewer than 238 articles (taking in the Treaty of Rome's provisions as well) plus protocols some of which in their turn have more than 50 articles!

2. Keith Miles was very perceptive and funny about the way the EC walked with its eyes open but unwitting into the Yugoslav trap at Maastricht despite events earlier in 1991. Pity it was the Slovene government rather than the British which chose to rely on his advice!

3. For the Feni project, see Dimitrije Djordjević, 'The Yugoslav Phenomenon' in Joseph Held (ed.), *The Columbia History of Eastern Europe in the Twentieth Century* (Columbia UP: New York, 1992), p. 338. The scandal surrounding the lavish appointments of Jacques Attali's European Bank for Reconstruction and Development in 1993 illustrated the illusions of the Western *apparatchiki* about the east. One of his senior officials defended the EBRD's Carrara marble by

arguing that such splendour would give East European supplicants something to aspire to. He obviously did not realise that throughout the former communist world, people had marbled halls but lacked the profits to sustain them, let alone any rational use for them.

4. For the development statistics, see Ramet, *Nationalism and Federalism*, pp. 136–176. See also Lydall, *Yugoslavia in Crisis*, pp. 188–89. Even allowing for the higher cost of living in Slovenia, the gap in terms of social product between that republic and Kosova was still 5:1, and the gulf in standard of living even higher without the transfer payments from Slovenia which reduced her income without apparently enriching the poor. (This seems to be a universal problem with international or interregional aid. See the work of Peter Bauer on the reasons why.)

For the comparative population figures, see the table below:

	Surface sq/ km	Population (1985)	% growth (1961–81)	household size
Bosnia	51,129	4,314,000	126	4
Slovenia	20,251	1,927,000	119	3.2
Croatia	56,538	4,655,000	111	3.2
Montenegro	13,812	613,000	124	4.1
Macedonia	25,713	2,017,000	136	4.4
Serbia	55,968	5,787,000	118	3.4
Vojvodina	21,506	2,084,000	110	3
Kosovo	10,887	1,762,000	164	6.9
Total	255,804	23,159,000	121	3.6

Source: Bogomil Ferfila, 'Confederation or Disintegration?' in *Problems of Communism* (July-August, 1991), esp. p. 19.

5. For a comparison between the collapse of the Soviet Union and Yugoslavia, see Veljko Vujačić & Victor Zavlasky, 'The Causes of Disintegration in the USSR and Yugoslavia' in *Telos* 88 (Summer, 1991), pp. 120–140.

6. The survival and indeed the adaptability of the smart communists in the post-communist world is one of themes of a perceptive series of essays edited by Georges Mink & Jean-Charles Szurek, *Cet Étrange Post-Communisme: Rupture et transitions en Europe centrale et orientale* (Presses du CNRS/La Découverte: Paris, 1992).

7. For the death of Ranković, see Libal, *Das Ende Jugoslawiens: Chronik einer Selbstzerstörung* (Europaverlag: Vienna, 1991), pp. 115ff.

8. No adequate biography of Milošević exists, but the basic facts of his career are well-known. Despite their similar ends his parents were very different in their approach to life. His mother left his father in 1948, the year of Tito's split with Stalin and of her own brother's

suicide (apparently as a result of his Cominformism, though she was a devout Titoite communist). If every man marries his mother, then it is hardly surprising that Slobodan Milošević chose the ideological hawk, Mirjana Marković. She has often been compared with Elena Ceauşescu for her Marxist dogmatism and her own political role. (The Miloševićs had good comradely relations with the Ceauşescus across the Danube until their unfortunate end in 1989.) Unlike Slobo, Mirjana Milošević remains publicly loyal to Marxism-Leninism and a critic of bourgeois nationalism, which has led Lord Owen to see her as a force for reason in Belgrade.

9. For Kosovo, see chapter 9 below.

10. I was once present during a television studio discussion about Bosnia when one British-Serb screeched at someone who identified himself as a Muslim: 'You are a Serb who was forcibly converted!'

11. For Ćosić's refusal to accept the Muslims as a 'nation', see Ramet, *Nationalism and Federalism*, pp. 189ff.

12. See Viktor Meier, 'Yugoslavia's National Question' in Lyman H. Letgers (ed.), *Eastern Europe: Transformation and Revolution, 1945–1991* (Heath: Lexington, Mass., 1992), pp. 109–110.

13. For Saudi and other Muslim countries' subsidy of Islam in Yugoslavia as part of Tito's offensive to gain legitimacy in the Third World, see Ramet, *Balkan Babel*, pp. 165–174.

14. For Abdić, see chapters 1 and 12.

15. See Ramet, *Balkan Babel*, p. 124.

16. For the political changes in Slovenia and Croatia at the end of the 1980s, see also Ramet, *Nationalism and Federalism* and Mark Thompson, *A Paper House*.

17. Quoted in Ivo Banac, 'Political Change and National Diversity' in Stephen R. Graubard (ed.), *Eastern Europe . . . , Central Europe . . . , Europe* (Westview: Boulder, Colorado, 1991), p. 161.

18. Quoted in *Politika* (26 Jun 1990).

19. Although Tudjman aspired to match the Machiavellian gifts of Milošević, he was always out-smarted – but came back for more. See chapter 10 below.

20. For Tudjman's moderation, see chapter 1 above.

21. See Cohen, *Broken Bonds*, p. 195, quoting Milošević (15 Jan 1991); 'In our opinion, any division [of Yugoslavia] into several states that would separate parts of the Serbian people and put them within separate sovereign states cannot be acceptable.' But he added to scotch any moderate reform: 'In our opinion a confederation is not a state.'

22. For Rupel's concern, see Ramet, *Nationalism and Federalism*, pp. 219–220.
23. See Sekelj, *Yugoslavia*, pp. 222–226 for the disparate and shaky anti-Milošević alliance among other party hierarchs around Yugoslavia in the late 1980s; and Cohen, *Broken Bonds*, pp. 197ff.

9: Kosovo : Myth in the Service of Aggression

1. The Serbian sage was quoted by the Twenty-One Serbian Theologians and Monks in their 'appeal for the Defence of the Serbian People and their Sanctuaries in Kosovo and Metohija', published on Good Friday 1982. See Anne Yelen, *Kossovo, 1389–1989: Bataille pour les Droits de l'Âme* (L'Âge d'Homme: Lausanne, 1989), p. 133.
2. It has not only been the Serbs who have tried to rewrite and, if necessary, invent an anachronistic account of Kosovo's history for modern nationalistic purposes. Even the assassin of the Sultan Murad, Milos Obilić was 'Albanianised' by some Albanian nationalist historians anxious to hit the Serbs in their most sensitive historical spot. See Arshi Pipa, 'Serbian Apologetics: Marković on Kosovo' in *Telos* (1991), p. 168.
3. For the cult of Obilić among the assassins of Franz Ferdinand, see Dedjier, *The Road to Sarajevo*, pp. 235ff.
4. For the reconquest and the nationalist enthusiasm and expansionism encouraged by victory in 1912–13, see Banac, *The National Question in Yugoslavia*, pp. 103ff.
5. See the reprint of the Carnegie Endowment's report (Washington, DC, 1993).
6. See Banac, *The National Question in Yugoslavia*, pp. 298–99, and Ramet, *Social Currents in Eastern Europe*, p. 175.
7. The full text of *Iseljavanje Arnauta* is not available in English (but it has been translated into French), see Grmek, Gjidara & Simac (eds), *L'nettoyage ethnique*, pp. 161–185. Cf. Philip Cohen, 'Desecrating the Holocaust', p 30.
8. Ibid.
9. Quoted in *Newsweek* (31 Aug 1992).
10. This point has been missed by many EC diplomats and mediators. I attended a conference in Luxembourg in July 1993, at which a senior Dutch official regretted that the EC had not anticipated the 'ethnic cleansing' and therefore provided 'humane means of transport' to evacuate its victims as if they would have left their homes unless intimidated by brutality and the imminent fear of death!

11. See Banac, 'Political Change' in Banac (ed.), *Eastern Europe in Revolution*, p. 160.
12. Cf. Ramet, 'War in the Balkans' in *Foreign Affairs* 71 (Fall, 1992), p. 83.
13. See *FAZ* (11 Jul 1986).
14. See *FAZ* (29 Jun 1993).
15. Quoted in Banac 'Post Communism as Post-Yugoslavism' in Banac (ed.), *Eastern Europe in Revolution*, p. 174.
16. See Banac, *The National Question in Yugoslavia*, pp. 293–94.
17. See ibid., p. 295.
18. See Ramet, *Federalism and Nationalism*, p. 260.
19. Quoted in the *Guardian* (2 Aug 1993).
20. See Banac, *The National Question in Yugoslavia*, p. 295.
21. See Grmek (ed.) et al., *Le nettoyage ethnique*, p. 151.
22. See Robin Alison Remmington, 'Yugoslavia' in Teresa Rakowska-Harmstone (ed.), *Communism in Eastern Europe* 2nd edition (Manchester UP: Manchester, 1984), p. 279.
23. See Ramet, *Social Currents in Eastern Europe*, p. 174.
24. See Bogdan Denitch, *Limits and Possibilities*, p. 90.
25. This illuminating speech was published in Milošević's *Godine Raspleta* (Belgrade, 1989), pp. 147–48; cf. John B. Allcock, 'Rhetorics of Nationalism in Yugoslav Politics' in John B. Allcock (ed), et al., *Yugoslavia in Transition*, p. 293.
26. See Cornelia Sorabji, 'Crimes against Gender or Nation?' in *WARREPORT* 18 (Feb-Mar, 1993), p. 16.
27. See the *Guardian* (2 Aug 1992).
28. See Christopher Cviić, 'A Culture of Humiliation' in *The National Interest* 32 (Summer, 1993), pp. 79–82; see also the text of the 'Memorandum' in Grmek (ed.), et al., *Le nettoyage ethnique*, p. 252.
29. See Bogdan Denitch, *Limits and Possibilities*, p. 142 note 10.
30. See the statistics in James Gow, *Legitimacy and the Military*, pp. 64–72.
31. See Denitch, *Limits and Possibilities*, pp. 82–83.
32. See Daniel S. Schiffer, *Le Temps du Réveil. Entretien avec Dobrtsa Tchossitch* (Éditions L'Âge d'Homme/Institut serbe: Lausanne, 1992), p. 30. Alain Finkielkraut has remarked that in this late twentieth-century Holocaust it is the Nazis who take themselves for, or at least pose as, the Jews. See *Comment peut-on être croat?* (Gallimard: Paris, 1992).
33. See Hugh Poulton, *The Balkans*, p. 61.
34. See Ćosić, *La Yougoslavie et la Question serbe* (L'Âge d'Homme/Institut serbe: Lausanne, 1992), p. 19–20.

35. For Macedonia's difficulties, see Robert Austin, 'Albanian-Macedonian Relations: Confrontation or Cooperation?' in *RFE/RL Research Report* 2 (22 Oct 1993), pp. 21–25, and Duncan M. Perry, 'Macedonia: From Independence to Recognition' in *RFE/RL Research Report* 3 (7 Jan 1994) pp. 118–121.
36. For Vojvodina, see Stan Markotich, 'Vojvodina: A Potential Powder Keg' in *RFE/RL Research Report* 2 (19 Nov 1993), pp. 13–18, and Edith Oltay, 'Hungarians under Political Pressure in Vojvodina' in *RFE/RL Research Report* 2 (3 Dec 1993), pp. 43–48.

10: The War in Croatia, 1991–92

1. Quoted in the *Washington Post* (18 Oct 1988), cf. Ramet, *Nationalism and Federalism*, p. 321.
2. Norman Cigar, 'The Serbo-Croatian War, 1991: Political and Military Dimensions' in *Journal of Strategic Studies* 16 (1993), p. 311, mentions as many as 200,000 rifles, plus 2400 mortars and artillery pieces. For the JNA on the eve of the war, see Anton Bebler, 'Staat im Staate: Zur Rolle des Militärs' in Furkes & Schlarp, (eds), *Jugoslawien: Ein Staat zerfällt* (Rowohlt Verlag: Reinbek bei Hamburg, 1991), pp. 106–133.
3. For the Spegelj Affair, see Cohen, *Broken Bonds*, p. 191, and Ramet, *Nationalism and Federalism*, p. 250.
4. For an unduly sympathetic portrait of the Krajina Serbs and their anxieties about a revived Ustasha-German alliance, see Misha Glenny, *The Fall of Yugoslavia*, pp. 24ff. Whether the new Croat constitution was so unjust to them must be doubted as the Serbian constitution carried very similar provisions with regard to the relationship between Serb nation and the rest – and of course the actual treatment of Albanians in Kosovo was far worse than anything that was even alleged against the new Croatian authorities.
5. For the events in Borovo Selo, see Russell, *Prejudice and Plum Brandy*, pp. 214–15
6. For Paraga, see Cohen, *Broken Bonds*, p. 240. For his arrest, see *The Times* (23 Nov 1991).
7. For Milošević's role, see Cigar and the transcript of the tape, *Independent* (30 Sep 1991).
8. The combined wars in Croatia and Bosnia took more journalists' lives than any previous conflict. At least forty were killed in the fighting. Serb suspicion and dislike of criticism was generally responsible.
9. See chapter 13 below.
10. The close links between organisations like the International

Institute for Strategic Studies in London and governments may have helped spread the view of how impossibly difficult and dangerous intervention might be. The IISS insists on its autonomy – 'It is independent of governments and is not an advocate of any particular interest – but it published John Zametica, *The Yugoslav Conflict* (IISS/Brassey's Adelphi Paper 270: London, 1992), an author who subsequently expanded his propagandistic activity to include formal political status as the grandly entitled 'deputy-foreign minister of the Bosnian Serb Republic'. Publishing authors like the renamed 'Jovan Zemetica' suggests that while the IISS may be independent of the British government, its links with the Bosnian Serb Republic are less clear cut. (It should be noted that Zemetica's research was also supported by the Pew Charitable Trust and the Smith Richardson Foundation in case other would-be Balkan propagandists are looking for funding.)

11. For the fighting at Vukovar and its sinister aftermath, see Glenny, *Fall of Yugoslavia*, pp. 123–4.

12. For the reticence of the International Committee of the Red Cross to reveal its knowledge about Nazi atrocities during the Second World War, see Jean-Claude Favez, *Une Mission Impossible? Le CICR, les déportations et les camps de concentrations nazis* (Lausanne, 1988). For the general problem and precedents for Western indifference to well-documented cases of genocide, see Robert Melson, *Revolution and Genocide: On the Origins of the Armenian Genocide and the Holocaust* (Chicago UP: Chicago, 1992). For the dubious Russian role in peacekeeping and keeping the secrets of the mass graves, see Keith Dovkants, 'The Colonel who betrayed the UN' in the *Evening Standard* (21 Apr 1993).

13. For the London press's concern for cultural artefacts rather than people, see Alec Russell, *Prejudice and Plum Brandy: Tales of a Balkan Stringer* (Michael Joseph: London, 1993), p. 222: 'The editor of *The Times* was said to ask daily about the state of Titian's *Assumption*.' For an editor of *The Times* and his views, see chapter 13 below. Zeljko Sikić, president of Dubrovnik Council, was amazed by the Western intelligentsia's indifference to human suffering and obsessive concern for 'heritage': 'Just because the medieval quarter still stands, are the Serbian attacks acceptable? I suppose if the centre of London was flattened you would say, "Oh, that doesn't matter, just as long as the Tower is in one piece." ' Ibid., p. 219.

14. For the attack, see Edgar O'Ballance, *Civil War in Yugoslavia*, p. 86.

15. For the internal politics of Croatia and privatisation, see Ivo

Bicanic, 'Croatia's Economic Stabilisation Program' in *RFE/RL Research Report* (21 Jan 1994) pp. 36–42.

16. For the flare-up of the Maslenica Bridge issue in January, 1993, see *SWB* Jan 1993.

17. For the disastrous Croatian intervention in Hercegovina, see chapter 12 below.

11: The Peacemakers

1. Speech to the Institute of International Politics and Economics, Belgrade (11 Mar 1992), quoted by Predarg Simić in Clesse & Kortunov (eds), *The Political and Strategic Implications of the State Crises in Central and Eastern Europe*, p. 197. Douglas Hurd told Channel 4 viewers as late as 2 August 1993 'I think we Europeans have done the things that we could do and we've done them well.'

2. 'Newsnight', BBC 2 (28 Jun 1991).

3. Douglas Hurd never indulged in the hubris of a Poos: 'It is the hour of Europe. If anyone can achieve it, it is the European Community.' BBC Radio 4 News (27 Jun 1991) or 'If there is one problem which the Europeans can solve, it is the Yugoslav problem . . . It's not up to the Americans.' Channel 4 News (27 Jun 1991).

4. Two years later, Douglas Hurd made clear his distaste for the break-up of Yugoslavia and the pace of recognition of Slovenia and Croatia in an interview on 'Newsnight', BBC2 (14 Jul 1993).

5. Interview with Jonathon Dimbleby, 'On the Record', BBC1 (30 Jun 1991).

6. See 'President must restore America's role as world leader' in *The Times* (12 Jul 1993).

7. Interview on 'The World at One', BBC Radio 4 (5 Jul 1991).

8. Quoted in the *FAZ* (7 Jun 1991).

9. Lord Carrington set out the credo of international passivity in an interview on Channel 4 News (11 May 1992) long after he had passed on the peace-maker's baton to Lord Owen. Douglas Hurd made the sentiment that peace would come about only by negotiation an inevitable chant during any interview or public statement.

10. The EC's inimitable mixture of pomposity and blindness is quoted in Wynaendts, *L'Engrenage*, p. 63.

11. For the Yugoslavs' 'lead' on the arms embargo at the UN on 25 Sep 1991, see Nigel S. Rodley, 'Collective Intervention to protect human rights' in Rodley (ed.), *To Loose the Bands of Wickedness*, p. 15.

12. Quoted in the programme, 'Diplomacy and Deceit' on Channel 4 (2 Aug 1993).
13. See *The Times* (26 Oct 1991).
14. Joao da Silva on 6pm News, BBC1 (7 Jan 1992). In fact the attack was witnessed by another white-pointed EC helicopter flying with the victims to Varazdin and which was also damaged. In other words, there could be no doubt that the monitors' aircraft were deliberately attacked. Hurd and the Serbian Deputy-Foreign Minister, Dobrasov Veizović, were quoted on Channel 4 News (7 Jan 1992).
15. Denials of responsibility became commonplace. As a sign of the influence of de-constructionism on the international community, it became normal for commonsense to be denied whenever an outrage took place. UN officials would seriously debate whether Serbs or Muslims had fired shells which killed civilians in bread queues or markets in besieged Sarajevo, as though the thousands of Serb shells which failed to make headlines by killing just one or two people were of no relevance to deciding the origin of those which splattered their way into the news bulletins! (See Robert Block in the *Independent* (8 Feb 1994).
16. Quoted by Brian Hanrahan on 6pm News, BBC1 (7 Jan 1992). On the same programme, Martin Bell reported that, 'The Federal side are inclined to trust the United Nations as an impartial peacekeeping force.' Of course, what this meant was that the Serbs thought the UN would be even more malleable than the EC. The failure of supposedly NATO-trained forces to show any understanding of psychological intimidation and disorientation techniques was not the least extraordinary aspect of the peacemakers' poor performance in the Balkans. When it came to 'psy-ops', the Serbs knocked NATO into a cocked hat. One aspect of this was clearly the presumption of retired international statesmen like Carrington, Vance and Owen that they could flatter the Serb leaders (jumped-up psychiatrists like Karadžić) into malleability by admission into their distinguished company. Of course, the Serbs felt they were doing the international has-beens a favour by letting them have a renewed whiff of the oxygen of publicity which their moribund careers lacked.
17. For Greece's recent human rights' record, see the annual Amnesty International reports.
18. See the *Independent* (16 Aug 1992).
19. See *The Times* (23 and 24 Apr 1992).
20. Full diplomatic relations were taken up with Macedonia only in February 1994, but solely because the USA did not wish to offend its

NATO ally, Greece, by exchanging ambassadors with a state which Greece was bent on throttling at birth.

21. For the mini-televisions at the Lisbon Summit, see *The Times* (27 Jun 1992).

22. See *The Times* (20 Jul 1992).

23. Hogg's inflammatory comments were broadcast by all British television and radio channels as well as inside ex-Yugoslavia.

24. Mr Hurd was interviewed on Channel 4 News (15 Jul 1992).

25. As reported on 6 o'clock News on BBC1 (17 Jul 1992).

26. See chapter 13 below.

27. Quoted on 6pm News, BBC 1 (20 Jul 1992).

28. Interview with Channel 4 News (20 Jul 1992).

29. The fantastic venue of the Carrington/Karadžić talks was shown on Channel 4 News (15 Jul 1992).

30. Quoted in *Financial Times* (15 Aug 1992).

31. Cheney was quoted on Channel 4 News (28 May 1992).

32. Lewis Mackenzie's sudden devotion to the study of history was as unconvincing as the rest of his pronouncements. In effect, whatever his personal intentions, the Canadian UNPROFOR commander became a conduit for exactly what the Serb commanders wanted the West to hear. Later on, after resigning from UNPROFOR, Mackenzie made a lecture tour in North America funded by a Serb-American lobby group. The astuteness of this first of Bosnia's great media generals may be judged from the comment: 'I had no idea that it was a Serb pressure group who were paying.' See the *Guardian* (5 Feb 1994). It is odd to have to report that UN generals proved more malleable than journalists. Perhaps that is why the casualty rate among reporters (at least 40 dead) was so much higher.

33. See *Newsweek* (5 Jul 1992).

34. See Herbert Kremp, 'Die Erfahrungen der Wehrmacht sind tabu' in *Die Welt* (29 Aug 1992).

35. As a way of understanding any pressure that Britain, or any alliance to which it belonged, might bring to bear, the Major cabinet's repeated chorus about the horrors of Ulster (3000 dead in twenty-five years) must have rung as sweet music in the ears of Bosnian Serb generals killing at a weekly rate of Ulster's total death-toll.

36. Bush's resentment of the burden of office did not prevent him running again for the Presidency. After the failure of Appeasement, Halifax too made the revealing comment, 'The criticism excited by Munich never caused me the least surprise. I should very possibly have been among the critics myself, *if I had not happened to be in a position of responsibility.*' (Quoted in Andrew Roberts, *The Holy Fox*,

p119.) Of course, what both Bush and Halifax meant was the opposite: the splendours of high office made them *irresponsible* and should have silenced their impudent critics. Douglas Hurd certainly took this view in his speech to the Travellers Club (9 Sep 1993) widely quoted in the media.

37. As broadcast by Channel 4 News (1 Jul 1992).

38. Quoted in the *Financial Times* (15 Aug 1992).

39. See the *Financial Times* (29 Aug 1992).

40. See *Le Figaro* (18 Mar 1992); Ms Tutwiler was quoted in the *Guardian* (23 Jun 1992).

41. See *Le Figaro* (18 Mar 1992).

42. M. Cot was interviewed by 'The World This Week', Channel 4 (21 Sep 1991).

43. For 'Yugoslavia: everyone's a loser', see *Financial Times* (26 Aug 1992); for Vance's comment, see *International Herald Tribune* (16 Apr 1992). However, Mr Vance's enthusiasm for peace led him into dubious paths: for instance, he tried to prevent Lawrence Eagleburger or other high officials in Washington from talking to representatives of the Bosnian government so that they would feel no encouragement for their cause. See the *Wall Street Journal* (14 Jan 1993).

44. Quoted in Malcolm Muggeridge, *The Thirties: 1930–1940 in Great Britain* (Hamish Hamilton: 2nd edition, London, 1967), p. 212.

45. See my 'The Lion it was that died' in *The Spectator* (5 Dec 1992), p. 20, for the full list of initials! As with all his most disastrous measures (e.g. blind adherence to the Exchange Rate Mechanism, about to end in tears), Mr Major's opponents in the Official Opposition were distinguished by their full support for his errors and their urging of him to go further down the path of disaster. The heirs of MacDonald did not neglect the idea of the conference as panacea merely wanting the jamboree brought forward. Labour's Defence Spokesman, Dr David Clark: 'I think there is a new urgency . . . and the government ought to bring forward the date of that peace [London] conference which is nearly three weeks away because in those three weeks thousands of people are likely to die and millions of people could be displaced. It literally is a matter of life and death. They should be bending every sinew to bring forward that conference.' Interview with 'Newsnight', BBC 2 (7 Aug 1992).

46. See *Sunday Telegraph* (27 Sep 1992). Whatever he said about Panić's prospects in the autumn of 1992, in February 1993, Lord Owen blithely contradicted himself, explaining that Milošević had been the man to deal with all along. See chapter 13 below.

47. If every man has the face he deserves, then the lining and wearying of Lord Owen's features from his glad confident start as mediator through to his tortured role as messenger-boy for the perpetrators of genocide eighteen months later would seem to confirm that dictum. By February 1994, Lord Owen was telling the media, 'Only a fool would support air strikes' (8 Feb 1994). Douglas Hurd was quoted on the 6pm News, BBC Radio 4 (25 Jul 1992).
48. Ibid.
49. The scene was captured by the cameras of various news organisations.
50. Interview with Channel 4 News (28 Aug 1992). Mr Major's personal horror of being shut out of international meetings came out strongly when he listed the sanctions which recalcitrant parties would face. 'Do you wish to be considered as part of Europe? . . . If we do not cooperate the pressure will inexorably increase – condemnation. . . . even tougher sanctions . . . no trade . . . no international recognition or role . . . diplomatic isolation.' Channel 4 News (26 Aug 1992). Mr Major appears to travel abroad twice as often as Mrs Thatcher. See 'No Contest' in the *Daily Telegraph* (27 Jan 1994).

12: The War in Bosnia, 1992–93

1. From *The Art of War*, quoted in Michael Walzer, *Just and Unjust Wars: A Moral Argument with Historical Examples* (2nd edition. Basic Books: New York, 1992), p. 164.
2. Whatever the immediate occasion of the fighting, there is no doubt that the Serb forces, as promoted by Federal agencies like the JNA and KOS, had long been preparing for this eventuality.
3. See Mark Mazower, *The War in Bosnia: an Analysis* (Action for Bosnia: London, 1992), p 11. For detailed evidence of 'ethnic cleansing', see Helsinki Watch, *War Crimes in Bosnia-Hercegovina* (Helsinki Watch: New York, 1992).
4. See ibid.; also James Gow, 'One Year of War in Bosnia-Hercegovina' in *RFE/RL Research Report* 2 (4 Jun 1993), pp 1–13.
5. For Izetbegović's moderate approach and its rebuff by the EC, see Wynaendts, *L'Engrenage*, p. 63, and Cohen, *Broken Bonds*, pp. 237–38. It is typical of the inversion of truth in the diplomatic and media battles surrounding the Bosnian catastrophe that the myth is so widely disseminated that it was Muslim or Croat intransigence and determination on independence which produced the war rather

than Serbian contempt for others' rights and the 'international community's' false game of blaming the victim as equally at fault.

6. See *Vreme* (19 Apr 1992), quoted in James Gow, 'One Year of War in Bosnia and Hercegovina', p. 8.

7. Quoted in Ramet, *Federalism and Nationalism*, p. 260.

8. See the *Guardian* (10 Aug 1993).

9. The UN's anti-genocide convention was honoured in the breach as much by Western states – who debated whether the term was appropriate as scores of thousands were liquidated – as by their predominantly Serbian murderers. For academic studies, see Anthony Clark Arend & Robert J. Beck, *International Law & the Use of Force: Beyond the UN Charter Paradigm* (Routledge: London, 1993) and Nigel Rodley (ed.), *To Loose the Bands of Wickedness: International Intervention in Defence of Human Rights* (Brassey's: London, 1992).

10. See Andrić's *A Letter from 1920*.

11. Mladić had of course earned his spurs in the Croatian war as commander of the JNA forces based at Knin.

12. For the war crimes, see the Helsinki Watch report (op. cit.) and *Le Nouvel Observateur Le Livre noir de l'ex-Yougoslavie: Purification ethnique* preface de Paul Bouchet (Arléa: Paris, 1993).

13. It was striking that both Croats and Muslims did better in the winter fighting when the Serbs' shortage of manpower told more because they could not deploy their firepower and armour nearly as effectively.

14. See the pictures on Channel 4 News (12 May 1992). Norman Stone hit the right note when he instinctively marked the occasion by singing the theme tune of Dad's Army, 'Run rabbit, run rabbit, run, run, run . . .'

15. For more on Mackenzie, see chapter 13 below. For all his braggadocio, after leaving Bosnia Canada's hero was soon on television pleading for the appeasement of the Serbs – from whom by-the-by it transpired he had received fees for a speaking engagement. See Mackenzie's plea – 'Force has been rewarded for the last twenty centuries, that's the reality . . . Stop the killing by appeasing. It's distasteful in the extreme but stop the killing' – on 'Newsnight', BBC2 (24 May 1993).

16 Mitterrand's policy fluctuations during the war in Bosnia became increasingly erratic, suggesting a senile desperation to court publicity and if possible public approval, regardless of the inconsequence of his actions. For the Lisbon Summit in 1993, see chapter 13 below.

17. See e.g. Channel 4 News (1 Jul 1992). It would be distasteful to recount the number of false dawns since then.

18. By the summer of 1993, the Serbs had established the following tariff:
UNHCR was to pay a toll of US$350 for each aid truck passing Serb lines. The Serb contempt for the UNPROFOR troops was evident in the heavier tolls for military vehicles whose crews were in no position to argue unlike the unarmed civilian drivers of aid trucks: wheeled military vehicles were to pay US$500 each while tracked military vehicles (e.g. tanks) were to fork out US$850. It was not uncommon for the Serbs also to pilfer military equipment like flak jackets. See the report on 'The World at One' BBC Radio 4 (2 Jul 1993).

19. As the people of Sarajevo hoped for NATO air strikes to put some fear into their tormentors on the surrounding hills, the shabby argument was often used by Western statesmen that such bombing raids might injure the civilians in the city. Fifty years after the Holocaust, the same callous unwillingness to use air power to give at least a psychological boost to the underdog was evident in Whitehall and Washington as it had been in 1942. The Majors, Hurds and Hoggs should reflect on the memoirs of a survivor of Auschwitz who recalled the only air raid made on that factory of death: 'We ceased to work, and the German soldiers and civilians ran to shelters. Most of us didn't . . . We had nothing to lose, only expected to enjoy the destruction . . . This happy feeling did not change also after the Americans indeed began to bomb, and *obviously we had casualties too* – wounded and dead. How beautiful it was to see squadron after squadron burst from the sky, drop bombs, destroy buildings, and kill also members of the *Herrenvolk*. Those bombardments elevated our morale . . .' Quoted in Martin Gilbert, *Auschwitz and the Allies* (Mandarin edition: London, 1991), p. 316.

20. Channel 4 News (22 May 1992).

21. The reluctance of the professional humanitarians (as distinct from volunteers) to raise awkward issues of deliberate human rights abuse has a long history. During the Second World War, the Red Cross preferred to remain silent about its knowledge of Hitler's death camps because publicity might have hindered its work distributing aid to those who were *not* going to be gassed. See Jean-Claude Favez, *Une Mission Impossible? Le CICR, les déportations et les camps de concentration nazis* (Lausanne, 1988).

22. Interview, Channel 4 News (1 Jul 1992).

23. For how far the Pale debate was playacting, see below.

[24] See *Politika* (10 May 1993). Also *Le Figaro* (12 May 1993).
[25] Naturally, neither UN nor national governments wanted to see any exposure of corruption or partiality in UNPROFOR, but like UN operations elsewhere, e.g. Cambodia, it was riddled with corruption and journalists in Sarajevo drew attention to the free availability of UNPROFOR rations on the black market. For a good analysis of where corruption and political partiality meet, see Keith Dovkants, 'The colonel who betrayed the UN' in the *Evening Standard* (21 Apr 1993). The Austrian General, Greindl, produced a rather innocuous report about the allegations, playing down their seriousness.
[26] See the *Independent* (17 Sep 1992).
[27] See *SWB*/1630 A1/2 (6 Mar 1993).
[28] For Lord Owen and Stoltenberg's support for Abdić in his challenge to Izetbegović, see Laura Silber, 'Canny survivor ready for carve-up deal' in the *Financial Times* (25 Jun 1993).
[29] Croats in Croatia proper were far from united in support of the HVO's increasing interference in Hercegovina, see chapter 14 below.
[30] Figures from 'Midnight News', BBC Radio 4 (19 Apr 1993).
[31] A piquant feature of the phantasmagoric nature of the UN was the Secretary-General's appointment of a 'Yugoslav' diplomat to be one of his mediators in the conflict between Georgians and Abkhaz in the Caucasus! At the same time defunct Yugoslavia continued to provide eight UN monitors for UNAVEM (the United Nations Angola Verification Mission) in strife-torn Angola, where conditions must have seemed like home from home. See *SIPRI Yearbook 1993* (Stockholm International Peace Research Institute OUP: Oxford, 1993), p 64.

13: Last Chances for Peace

[1] Interview with 'Newsnight', BBC2 (2 Sep 1992).
[2] Quoted on 6pm News, BBC1 (28 Aug 1992).
[3] Lord Owen's boasts were carried on Channel 4 News (3 Nov 1992).
[4] Even when he had to renege on all the London Principles of Civilised Conduct after the rejection of the Vance-Owen Plan, David Owen continued his lonely work appearing on half a dozen breakfast news programmes each day, day after day. Owen's willingness to carry on 'mediating' after his frequently proclaimed principles had been breached recalls another British peer's mediation in 1938. A. J. P. Taylor commented on Lord Runciman's mission to the Sudetenland at the height of the crisis: 'Runciman's report was

bogus. As first drafted, it outlined arrangements by which Germans could be satisfied within Czechoslovakia. He then rewrote the report when told that Hitler wanted self-determination and had been promised it.' See *English History, 1914–1945* (OUP: Oxford, 1965), p. 426.

5. Quoted in the *International Herald Tribune* (12 Mar 1993).

6. For Panić's use as a smokescreen, see Owen's interview in *Foreign Affairs* 72 No. 2 (Spring, 1993), p. 9.

7. Eagleburger was quoted from CNN's *Crossfire* (23 Feb 1993) in Cohen, *Broken Bonds*, p. 261.

8. Quoted in *Newsweek* (5 Apr 1993).

9. Quoted in Wohlstetter, 'Bosnia as Future', p. 4. Note that it would be Mr Milošević whom other Europeans would have to welcome back into the family fold as leader of the Serbs.

10. Quoted in Lawrence Freedman & Efraim Karsh, *The Gulf Conflict, 1990–1991* (Faber & Faber: London, 1993), p. 414.

11. For Douglas Hurd's search for a still more distinguished person than the previous peace-mediators, see the *Guardian* (17 Apr 1993). The thought does not seem to have passed the minds of Western statesmen that by dignifying the likes of Radovan Karadžić or Mate Boban with the opportunity to hob-nob with 'distinguished persons', they gave them less incentive to make peace. Of course, the retired mediators relished their return to the international stage too and were never far from a microphone to announce the progress of their holy work to an increasingly incredulous world.

12. For the imported luxuries in the Belgrade Hyatt, despite the UN sanctions, see Wynaendts, *L'Engrenage*, p. 50: 'Even during the strongest sanctions, this hotel remained an astonishing haven of luxury.'

13. Quoted in *Le Monde* (2 Apr 1993).

14. Quoted in the *Daily Telegraph* (2 Apr 1993).

15. See *The Times* (21 Aug 1992).

16. See the *Daily Telegraph* (20 Feb 1993). Needless to say, a year later, the UN forces still lacked common communications equipment to enable the most basic of joint operations to be conducted between the disparate contingents of Blue Helmets.

17. The British government's irresponsibility in both placing troops and aid workers in the position of potential hostages and then openly to describe them as such can be found repeatedly, but see John Major's comments broadcast on the 9pm News BBC1 (29 Jun 1992).

18. Quoted in the *Financial Times* (11 Feb 1993).

19. Quoted in the *Independent* (13 Aug 1993).

20. See the President's statement as broadcast on the 9pm News, BBC 1 (14 May 1993).

21. As quoted on 'The World at One', BBC Radio 4 (30 Apr 1993). President Clinton himself later claimed that 'John Major told me he wasn't sure he could sustain his government . . . The British . . . felt it was more important to avoid lifting the arms embargo than to save the country.' Quoted in the *Daily Telegraph* (18 Oct 1993). If Major was shabby enough to cling to office on the votes of the half-dozen hard core of pro-Serb Tory MPs (including members of the government) plus their more numerous 'It's nothing to do with us' allies in his party, rather than do another U-turn to save lives, then Clinton was not the man to play judge since his own officials admitted to the Holocaust survivor, Elie Wiesel, who had come to plead for US intervention to save lives, that 'the moral stakes in Bosnia were high, *but* [emphasis added] . . . there were even higher *moral* [sic] stakes at play: "the survival of the fragile liberal coalition represented by this president." '! Quoted in the *International Herald Tribune* (5–6 Feb 1994) without any State Department dementi.

22. For the paper tiger of Islamic fundamentalism, see 'All we get is Talk' in *Time* (31 May 1993), p. 5. Rafsanjani's Iran continued to supply oil to Serbia throughout the conflict and may have been partly paid with Serb-manufactured weapons surplus to requirements. The Muslim countries provided only 30 of the 1747 planeloads of supplies to Sarajevo in 1992. For Third World sympathy for Serbo-Yugoslavism, see the *International Herald Tribune* (16 Sep 1992).

23. See *SWB/Former USSR* SU/1691 A1/1 (18 May 1993).

24. For Rifkind's confusion of the gunmen with the people of Bosnia, see BBC News (13 Mar 1993).

25. See the *Financial Times* (26 Oct 1992).

26. See *The Times* (20 May 1993).

27. Lord Owen's somewhat tortured logic was broadcast by Channel 4 News (3 Nov 1992).

28. See the *Guardian* (24 Apr 1993).

29. Interview, 'Today', BBC Radio 4 (24 Apr 1993).

30. Mr Hurd's invitation to continue the massacre was broadcast on 'Today', BBC Radio 4 (11 Feb 1993).

31. Lord Owen's slightly bleary observations (after a long night of negotiations) were broadcast on 'The World This Weekend', BBC Radio 4 (2 May 1993). Dr Karadžić's unkempt and distressed appearance in Athens may have been due less to a verbal drubbing from Milošević than because it was the morning after a very heavy night before. According to the anti-interventionist Tory MP, Harold

Elletson, a dinner given by the good doctor for a visiting gang of British MPs went on until 3am leaving little time for sleep before his early morning flight to Athens. See 'Bangers, brandy and a night on the peace' in the *Daily Telegraph* (6 May 1993).

32. See Channel 4 News (5 May 1993).

33. See *Time to Declare* (Penguin Books: Harmondsworth, 1992), p. 9 & pp. 43–44.

34. Quoted in the *Sunday Times* (30 May 1993).

35. See his interview in *Foreign Affairs* 72 (Spring, 1993), p. 2. Members of the 'great and good' like Vance and Owen, who took for granted the purity of their own motives and bridled at the suggestion of appeasement, should remember A. J. P. Taylor's sardonic remark that the Munich agreement 'was a triumph for all that was best and most enlightened in British life'.

36. For Mackenzie's lecture tour, see 'Serbs bankroll Speeches by ex-UN Commander' in *Newsday* (22 Jun 1993). Mackenzie defended himself in a letter, in which he admitted, 'I could see only 300 meters in any direction in Sarajevo. I am not qualified to comment on what was going on in the rest of Bosnia and have said so many times.' See *Newsday* (12 Jul 1993). Unfortunately it was precisely his role as UNPROFOR commander in Bosnia which gave the impression that he was qualified to put journalists into the big picture.

37. Lord Owen's lack of insight into his employers' approach to the crisis is quoted in the *International Herald Tribune* (18 May 1993), and compounded by his naive faith in Russian promises: 'The Russian Federation is very clear that they wish the plan to be implemented . . . [The Russians] will send in border monitors in, I think, very large numbers. And I think they will also be prepared . . . to put forces in to help the safe areas policy.' No doubt had Russian promises been sincere – which they were not – the Russian troops would have proved as helpful as in the UN areas of Croatia; helpful, that is, to the Serbs.

38. See *SWB/Former USSR* SU/1691 A1/1 (18 May 1993). The British government welcomed Russia's assistance in thwarting any intervention and preserving the one-sided arms embargo. A leaked Foreign Office memorandum, obviously and pretentiously modelled on George Kennan's famous, 'Long Telegram' from Moscow at the start of the Cold War, notes, 'The most useful Russian contribution of all . . . has been its firm resistance to US pressure for lifting the arms embargo against the Muslims and carrying out air strikes against the Serbs. The UK has consistently opposed this *lunatic idea* [emphasis added], but our style has been cramped by the need to

tend the "special relationship" . . . It has been *reassuring to know that when the crunch came* (as it did on 29 June), *the Russian veto would be forthcoming* . . .' Of course, Kennan advocated 'containment' whereas the British 'X' proposed to bring Russian forces to the shores of the Adriatic. Truly a diplomatic revolution.

39. Shaposhnikov was quoted in *SWB/Former USSR* SU/1691 A1/1 (18 May 1993).

40. See 'Hurd rules out use of troops in Bosnian conflict' in *The Times* (30 Apr 1993).

41. Hurd quoted in *The Times* (23 May 1993). For Garel-Jones, see Hansard (6 May 1993), col. 291.

42. See *SWB/Former Soviet Union* SU 1700 i (28 May 1993).

43. See the *Guardian* (5 Aug 1993).

44. Quoted in the *Daily Telegraph* (27 May 1993).

45. See my 'Doing business with war criminals' in *The Spectator* (15 May 1993).

46. Interview, 'The World This Weekend', BBC Radio 4 (23 May 1993).

47. Lord Clarendon quoted in Paul Kennedy, *The Realities Behind Diplomacy: Background Influences on British External Policy, 1865–1980* (Collins/Fontana: London, 1981), pp. 75–76.

48. President Clinton's interview was broadcast on 'News at Ten', ITV (2 Jul 1993).

49. Interview, Channel 4 News (21 Jun 1993).

50. Interview, 'Newsnight', BBC 2 (21 Jun 1993).

51. See 'Newsnight', BBC2 (21 Jun 1993) and the *International Herald Tribune* (19 Jun 1993).

52. The news of this belated – and, needless to add, meaningless – change of mood among the Twelve was reported by a breathless James Cox on 'Newsnight', BBC2 (21 Jun 1993).

53. See *SWB/Eastern Europe* 1726 C1/2 (28 Jun 1993).

54. See the *Guardian* (21 May 1993).

55. See *Le Figaro* (24 May 1993).

56. Quoted by Albert Wohlstetter in his paper, 'Bosnia as Future' (30 Jul 1993).

57. Quoted in *The Times* (28 Jul 1993).

58. Stoltenberg's surrealistic proposal was quoted in the *Guardian* (7 Aug 1993). For Lord Owen's blaming everyone except the mediators for contributing to the partition of Bosnia on the lines unanimously condemned at the London Conference, see Owen's interview with 'Today', BBC Radio 4, 18 June 1993. See also *Foreign Affairs* 72 (Spring, 1993), p. 3.

59. Interview, 'Today', BBC Radio 4 (18 Jun, 1993).
60. Quoted in the *International Herald Tribune* (19–20 Jun, 1993).
61. Having admitted that truth, Mr Hurd did not draw the obvious conclusion but insisted that the farce of mediation must go on.
62. See the *Independent* (15 Apr 1993).
63. For the false prophets of doom in the Gulf, see the *Sunday Times* (3 Mar 1991).
64. Lord Healey spoke on 'The World This Weekend', BBC Radio 4 (18 Apr 1993). As a young ex-communist turned Labour Party candidate, in the immediate postwar years Denis Healey was an apologist for the new 'socialist' [sic] order 'already firmly established in many countries in eastern and southern Europe'. He told the Labour Party Conference in 1945, 'If the labour movement [sic] finds it necessary to introduce a *greater degree of police supervision and more immediate and drastic punishment for their opponents* than we in this country would be prepared to tolerate, we must be prepared to *understand their point of view*.' [Emphasis added.] See 'What did Mr Healey really think in 1945?' in the *Sunday Telegraph* (19 Nov 1989) as well as Healey's somewhat lame reply emphasising his later role as an anti-communist after 1948.
65. Interview, 'Newsnight', BBC2 (28 Apr, 1993).
66. For Jenkins' views, see various columns in *The Times*. Mr Jenkins often seems more concerned by putative future 'Muslim' revenge and atrocities than by past Serb acts: for instance, ending the arms embargo would mean that 'Britain and the West would be associated with any anti-Serb atrocities – *of which there would be plenty* [emphasis added]' (17 Apr, 1993) or establishing safe havens would create 'hotbeds of Muslim revanchism' (8 May 1993) or 'UN safe havens [would be] safe for what? For Muslim militias to . . . seek bloody revenge on Serbs and Croats' (9 Jun 1993). For Jenkins' unwitting – or witless – endorsement of the Syrian solution, see 'They die so we feel better' in *The Times* (17 Apr 1993) and for David Pryce-Jones' use of knowledge and reason to demolish it, see his letter in *The Times* (21 Apr 1993) describing the brutal reality of *pax syriana*.
67. Quoted in *SWB/Eastern Europe* EE/1700 C1/13.
68. See his letter to the *Independent* (26 May 1993).
69. Quoted in Sabrina Ramet, 'War in the Balkans' in *Foreign Affairs* 71 (Fall, 1992), p. 94.
70. See 'Britanski obavjestajci z Hrvate i Muslimane' in *Vjesnik* (19 Jul 1993).
71. Quoted in *Le Monde diplomatique* (Sep 1993).
72. See George Walden, 'Our troops should not have to be the Gurkhas

of Europe' in the *Daily Telegraph* (5 Aug 1993). With the significant exception of its columnist, Noel Malcolm (a most formidable expert on the Balkans), and correspondents in the field like Alec Russell, the *Daily Telegraph* more and more took over the *Financial Times* role as the voice of official British thinking.

73. For Milošević's speech, see Cigar, op. cit.

74. See ibid.

75. Sir Edward Heath was interviewed on 'Today', BBC Radio 4 (3 Sep 1993). His contempt for small countries knows few bounds. Even the little member states of his beloved European Community are dismissed when they step out of line: 'We are a nation of 50 million. Why should we take notice of 21,000 people [in Denmark]? In politics there is a terrible tendency to listen to the minority, just because they bellyache . . . I wouldn't pay too much attention to the Irish . . .' See Peter Conrad 'Anatomy of a Knight' in the *Observer Magazine* (13 Sep 1992), p. 23. See also Heath's 'Bosnia is not worth the risk' in *The Times* (8 Feb 1994).

14: The Outlook for the post-Yugoslav Balkans

1. Warren Christopher was quoted in the *New York Times* (18 Jul 1993). Could the US Secretary of State be truly without any sense of the Chamberlain-esque resonance of his policy U-turn? For Lord Owen's comments, see 'Owen castigates international intrigue that killed peace plan' in *The Times* (24 Jun 1993).

2. Lord Owen admitted at Christmas, 1993, that as much as 40 per cent of aid went in pay-offs and 'tolls'.

3. The indignation of a group of Swedish Blue Helmets at an attempt by some two hundred desperate Croats to rescue themselves by sheltering under the cover of the Blue Flag in November 1993, reflected the do-gooders' firm belief that they decide who is a humanitarian case. In this instance, the survival of the humanitarians took precedence.

4. Owen to author, September, 1992. See George Soros' contribution to the Channel 4 Season of programmes, 'Bloody Bosnia' (9 Aug 1993).

5. See the *Guardian* (2 Jun 1993).

6. See, for instance, Drasković's article, *'Confrontation avec la verité'* from 1987 which contains the standard charges against the Albanians (re-published in '*Nationalismes. La Tragédie Yougoslave*' in *Le Monde diplomatique: Manières de voir* No. 17 (Feb 1993), pp. 84–85. For his more recent return to the rhetoric of 'greater Serbia', see his

comments, 'Kosovo is the Serbian Jerusalem. Kosovo is the capital of the Serbian nation. Kosovo must remain part of Serbia' in *The Times* (24 Sep 1993); also 'Drasković back in the fray for "greater Serbia" ' in the *Independent* (24 Sep 1993).

7. See *FAZ* (14 Jun 1993) and *RFE/RL News Brief* (14–18 Jun 1993).

8. For an informative study of the postwar refugee problem, see M. J. Proudfoot, *European Refugees, 1939–52: A Study in Forced Population Movement* (Faber & Faber: London, 1957). For the classic study of how Britain pressed the Soviet Union to take back Displaced Persons regardless of their fate, see Nikolai Tolstoy, *Victims of Yalta* (Hodder & Stoughton: London, 1978, revised paperback edition, 1979). See note 22 to chapter 6.

9. For Ganić's comments on the threat of terrorism, see BBC Radio news (21 Sep 1993). Since any internationally brokered settlement is likely to be on the basis of a truncated Muslim-Bosnia at the mercy of its neighbours and poorly protected, if at all, by UN observers, the potential for radicalisation is likely to remain strong.

10. For Greece and Albania and Macedonia, see Noel Malcolm, 'The new bully in the Balkans' in *The Spectator* (15 Aug 1992).

15: From the Balkans to the Baltics: Learning dangerous lessons

1. For the Western banks' support for Geratschenko, see *The European* (12 Sep 1991). For Chancellor Kohl's statement, see the *Guardian* (5 Sep 1991). Geratschenko subsequently became the *bête noire* of the pro-reform lobby, but survived his Western-orientated colleagues' downfall after the hardline-nationalist victory in the December 1993 elections in Russia, and remained as the money-printing chairman of the State Bank and therefore a key obstacle to any Western-style market reform. Geratschenko may lack the political ambition of a Milošević but he fits the bill of the sort of communist banker whom the West found congenial until it was too late.

2. Burbulis is quoted in John Lough 'The Place of the "Near Abroad" in Russian Foreign Policy', in *RFE/RL Research Report* 2 (12 Mar, 1993), p. 25.

3. See *SWB/Former Soviet Union* SU/1576 C1/1 (1 Jan 1993).

4. For this, and much else, see Lough, op. cit. ' "Near Abroad"in Russian Foreign Policy', p. 22 & p. 27.

5. For Russia's military doctrine, see Lough, op. cit.

6. Quoted in Lough, op. cit. p. 27.

7. For the tradition of 'geo-politics' in Russia following on the

Mackinder school, see Milan Hauner, *What is Asia to us? Russia's Asian Heartland, Yesterday and Today* (Unwin Hyman: London, 1992). I have been a frequent visitor to Moldova and Transnistria since 1991. For Lebed's role in August 1991, see Ruslan Khasbulatov, *The Struggle for Russia: Power and Change in the Democratic Revolution* edited by Richard Sakwa (Routledge: London, 1993), pp. 188–89.

8. See Lough, op. cit. p. 29. For a perceptive account of the Janus-faced nature of Russian foreign policy, charming to the West and bullying to its near neighbours (the so-called 'dinner jacket/flak jacket' approach), see Suzanne Crow, 'Russia Asserts Its Strategic Agenda' in *RFE/RL Research Report* 2 (17 Dec, 1993), pp. 1–8.

9. See *SWB* SU/174li (16 Jul 1993).

10. See *SWB* SU/1747 C1/3 (22 Jul 1993). It is striking that the fall of the 'hardliner' Barannikov, who was arrested after the violence in Moscow in October 1993, had no effect on Russia's approach to Tadjikistan or the rest of the 'near abroad'. If anything, pressure on Russia's neighbours has been stepped up.

11. Quoted in *SWB* SSU/1744 C2/1 (19 Jul 1993).

12. I have visited Georgia and Azerbaijan (as well as other ex-Soviet republics) on behalf of the British Helsinki Human Rights Group.

13. For the booming arms trade in the regions around Serbia, see '*Millionengeschäft mit MIGs*' in *Die Welt* (19 Jul 1993). See 'Hungary to get Mig–29 fighters from Russia as debt-payment' in *SWB/Eastern Europe* EE/1710 A2/3 (9 Jun 1993) as well as '*Aufrüstung an der Donau*' in *Der Spiegel* (2 Aug 1993). Also '*Millionengeschäft mit MIGs*' in *Die Welt* (19 Jul 1993). The cult of stability regardless of the price runs through British policy towards the whole ex-communist world and bogeys of Islamic fundamentalism or nuclear proliferation are rattled to scare off thought. On 27 January 1993, in a speech at Chatham House entitled 'The New Disorder', the Foreign Secretary, Douglas Hurd, painted a picture of continuing insecurity because 'Russia still bristles with nuclear weapons, a deadly inheritance from the communists. The authorities there and in Ukraine, Belarus and Kazakhstan are committed by treaty to dismantling most of this arsenal. But the risks of proliferation abound when there is disorder.' Ukraine refused to ratify the START treaty and tried to avoid returning the nuclear missiles which it inherited from the Soviet Union to Russia, the only threat to her independence. Ukraine's lack of allies now as NATO has shunned her and the failure of the UN to uphold Security Council resolutions in Bosnia are hardly reassuring, particularly when British diplomats write the following in

policy documents: 'Russia will not accept the loss of Ukraine any more than the English think of Ireland as a totally foreign country.' The first part is truer than the second in that sentence, since most English people regard even Northern Ireland as profoundly alien and Mr Major's government seems bent on finding a way of dumping the Ulster problem through much the same means as it has tackled the Bosnian issue. See 'X', point 25.

Postscript

1. Speaking in Belgrade, as broadcast by the One O'Clock News, BBC1 (7 Feb 1994). On ITN's lunchtime news, Lord Owen damned NATO's bemedalled heroes of forty-five years of peace when he insisted, 'I know of no military leader who believes that this [threat of air strikes] will do anything but exacerbate the situation' (7 Feb 1994).
2. See *Le Monde* (16 Mar 1994) and *The Times* (13 Apr 1994).
3. See his interview on the One O'Clock News, BBC1 (28 Jan 1994). John Major's visit to Sarajevo on 18 March to bask in the glory of a successful intervention which he had striven with might and main for three years to thwart was distasteful gesture politics even by his standards.
4. Fred Eckehard of the UN as interviewed on Channel 4 News (8 Apr 1994).
5. For the Macedonian issue, see C.Sr. 'Mazedoniens Kampf gegen Athens Embargo' in *Neue Züricher Zeitung* (8 Sept 1994), 7.
6. On Easter Sunday, Defence Secetary Perry egged-on Mladić's onslaught against Gorazde: 'We will not enter the war to stop that from happening.' See *International Herald Tribune* (4 Apr 1994).
7. See Suzanne Crow, 'Russia Asserts Its Strategic Agenda' in *RFE/RL Research Report* vol. 2, no. 50 (17 Dec 1993), pp. 1–8.
8. The contagious nature of the Bosnian 'peace process' was confirmed when it was announced that Lord Carrington had been appointed to mediate between the supporters of Inkatha and the ANC in South Africa – a triumph of hope over experience if ever there was one! See the *Independent* (12 Apr 1994).

Bibliography

This bibliography is intended for the Western reader, especially an English-speaking reader. The best English-language sources for keeping abreast of developments in Yugoslavia and throughout the ex-Soviet bloc are the BBC's *Summary of World Broadcasts* Eastern Europe and former Soviet Union sections (abbreviated as *SWB*) and the *Radio Free Europe/Radio Liberty Research Reports* (abbreviated as *RFE/RL Research Reports*). *Balkan War Report* (incorporating *Yugofax*, issued by the Institute for War and Peace Reporting) is also a valuable source of information.

Alexander, Stella, *Church and State in Yugoslavia since 1945* (CUP: Cambridge, 1979)

Almond, Mark, *Blundering in the Balkans: The European Community and the Yugoslav Crisis* (School of European Studies: London & Oxford, 1991)

Arend, Anthony Clark & Beck, Robert J., *International Law and the Use of Force: Beyond the UN Charter Paradigm* (Routledge: London, 1993)

Banac, Ivo, *The National Question in Yugoslavia: Origins, History, Politics* (Cornell UP: Ithaca, NY, 1984)

Banac, Ivo, *With Stalin Against Tito: Cominformist Splits in Yugoslav Communism* (Cornell UP: Ithaca, NY, 1988)

Beloff, Nora, *Tito's Flawed Legacy: Yugoslavia and the West, 1939–1984* (Gollancz: London, 1985)

Bouchet, Paul (preface), *Le Livre Noir de l'ex-Yougoslavie: Purification ethnique et crimes de guerre* (Documents rassemblés par *Le Nouvel Observateur* et *Reporters san frontières*) (Arléa: Paris, 1993)

Brown, J.F., *Eastern Europe and Communist Rule* (Duke UP: Durham, North Carolina, 1988)

Brown, J.F., *Surge to Freedom: the End of Communist Rule in Eastern Europe* (Adamantine Press: Twickenham, 1991)

Brown, J.F., *Nationalism, Democracy and Security in the Balkans* (RAND: Santa Monica, 1992)

Carlton, David & Schaerf, Carlo (editors), *South-eastern Europe after Tito: A powder-keg for the 1980s?* (London, 1983)

Castellan, Georges, *Histoire des Balkans (xive-xxe siècle)* (Fayard: Paris, 1991)

Clesse, Armand & Kortunov, Andrei, (editors) *The Political and Strategic Implications of the State Crises in Central and Eastern Europe* (Institute for European and International Studies: Luxembourg, 1993)

Clogg, Richard, *A Concise History of Greece* (Cambridge University Press: Cambridge, 1992)

Cohen, Lenard, *Broken Bonds: The Disintegration of Yugoslavia* (Westview: Boulder, Colorado, 1993)

Cohen, Philip J., *Desecrating the Holocaust: Serbia's Exploitation of the Holocaust as Propaganda* (Distributed by the author: an earlier excerpt was published in *Midstream* 38 No. 8 [November 1992], pp. 18–20.)

Connor, Walker, *The National Question in Marxist-Leninist Strategy* (Princeton UP: Princeton, NJ, 1984)

Cornwall, Mark (editor), *The Last Years of Austria-Hungary* (University of Exeter Press: Exeter, 1990)

Cviič, Christopher, *Remaking the Balkans* (RIIA/Pinter Publishers: London, 1991)

Dedijer, Vladimir, *The Road to Sarajevo* (Macgibbon & Kee: London, 1966)

Dedijer, Vladimir, *The Battle Stalin Lost: Memoirs of Yugoslavia: 1948–1953* (Grosset & Dunlap: New York, 1972)

Djilas, Aleksa, *The Contested Country: Yugoslav Unity and Communist Revolution, 1919–1953* (Harvard UP: Cambridge, Mass., 1991)

Djilas, Milovan, *Wartime: With Tito and the Partisans* translated by Michael B. Petrovich (Secker & Warburg: London, 1977)

Djilas, Milovan, *Rise and Fall* (Macmillan: London, 1985)

Donia, R.J., *Islam under the Double Eagle: The Muslims of Bosnia and Hercegovina, 1878–1914* (Westview: Boulder, Colorado, 1981)

Drakulić, Slavenka, *Sterben in Kroatien: Vom Krieg mitten in Europa* (Rowohlt Verlag: Reinbek bei Hamburg, 1992)

Dunn, John F., *Europe's Troubled Corner: How to Overcome Instability and Tensions in the Balkans* (Wilton Park Paper 66, HMSO: London, 1992)

Emmert, T.A. & Vucinich, Wayne, *Kosovo: Legacy of a Medieval Battle* (Minneapolis, 1989)

Finkielkraut, Alain, *Comment peut-on être croate?* (Gallimard: Paris, 1992)

Furkes, Josip, & Schlarp, Karl-Heinz (editors), *Jugoslawien: Ein Staat zerfällt* (Rowohlt Verlag: Reinbek bei Hamburg, 1991)

Garde, Paul, *Vie et Mort de la Yougoslavie* (Fayard: Paris, 1992)

Gellhard, Susanne, *Ab heute ist Krieg: Der blutige Konflikt im ehemaligen Jugoslawien* (Fischer Verlag: Frankfurt-am-Main, 1992)
Geyer, Dietrich, *Russian Imperialism: The Interaction of Domestic and Foreign Policy, 1860–1914* translated by Bruce Little (Berg: Lemington Spa, 1987)
Glaise von Horstenau, Edmund, *Ein General im Zwielicht: Die Erinnerungen Edmund Glaise von Horstenau* volume 3 *Deutscher Bevollmächtigter General in Kroatien und Zeuge des Unterganges des, 'Tausendjährigen Reiches'* edited with an introduction by Peter Broucek (Böhlau Verlag: Vienna, 1988)
Glenny, Misha, *The Fall of Yugoslavia: the Third Balkan War* (Penguin edition: Harmondsworth, 1993)
Gow, James, *Legitimacy and the Military: the Yugoslav Crisis* (Pinter Publishers: London, 1992)
Griffiths, Stephen Iwan, *Nationalism and Ethnic Conflict: Threats to European Security* (SIPRI/OUP: Oxford, 1993)
Grmek, Mirko, Gjidara, Marc, & Simac, Neven (editors), *Le nettoyage ethnique: Documents historiques sur une idéologie serbe* collected, translated and annotated by the editors (Fayard: Paris, 1993)
Gutman, Roy, *Witness to Genocide: the First Inside Account of the Horrors of 'Ethnic Cleansing' in Bosnia* (Element: Shaftesbury, Dorset, 1993)
Jackson Jr, George D., *Comintern and Peasant in Eastern Europe, 1919–1930* (Columbia University Press: New York, 1961)
Jelavich, Barbara, *Russia's Balkan Entanglements, 1806–1914* (CUP: Cambridge, 1991)
Jelavich, Charles & Barbara, *The Establishment of the Balkan National States, 1804–1920* (Washington UP: Seattle, 1977)
Koenen, Gerd, *Die grossen Gesänge: Lenin, Stalin, Mao Tse-tung Führerkulte und Heldenmythen des 20. Jahrhunderts* (Eichborn Verlag: Frankfurt-am-Main, 1991)
Kohn, Hans, *Pan-Slavism: Its History and Ideology* (University of Notre Dame Press: Notre Dame, Indiana, 1953)
Laffan, R.G.D., *The Serbs: The Guardians at the Gate* (Original edition, Oxford, 1918: reprinted Dorset Press: New York, 1989)
Lendvai, Paul, *Eagles in Cobwebs: Nationalism and Communism in the Balkans* (Doubleday: Garden City, NY, 1969)
Libal, Wolfgang, *Das Ende Jugoslawiens: Chronik einer Selbstzerstörung* (Europa Verlag: Vienna, 1991)
Lydall, Harold, *Yugoslavia in Crisis* (Clarendon Press: Oxford, 1989)
Mackenzie, David, *Apis: The Congenial Conspirator* (Westview: Boulder, Colorado, 1989)
Mackenzie, David, 'Panslavism in action: Chernaiev in Serbia, 1876' in *Journal of Modern History* 36 (1964), pp. 279–297
McLynn, Frank, *Fitzroy Maclean* (John Murray: London, 1992)

Magaš, Branka, *The Destruction of Yugoslavia: Tracking the Break-Up, 1980–92* (Verso: London, 1993)
Malcolm, Noel, *Bosnia: A Short History* (Macmillan: London, 1994)
Milivojević, Marko, *Descent into Chaos: Yugoslavia's Worsening Crisis* (Institute for European Defence and Strategic Studies: London, 1989)
Norris, H.T., *Islam in the Balkans: Religion and Society between Europe and the Arab World* (Hurst: London, 1993)
Parlement européen, *La Crise dans l'Ex-Yougoslavie* (CECA-CEE-CEEA: Luxembourg, 1993)
Parrott, Cecil, *The Tightrope* (Faber & Faber: London, 1975)
Pavlovitch, Stevan K., *The Improbable Survivor: Yugoslavia and its Problems, 1918–1988* (Hurst: London, 1988)
Pavlovitch, Stevan K., *Tito: Yugoslavia's Great Dictator* (Hurst: London, 1992)
Poulton, Hugh, *The Balkans: Minorities and States in Conflict* foreword by Milovan Djilas (Minority Rights Group: London, 1991)
Proudfoot, Malcolm J., *European Refugees: A Study in Forced Population Movement* (Faber & Faber: London, 1957)
Ramet, Sabrina P., *Social Currents in Eastern Europe: the Sources and Meaning of the Great Transformation* (Duke UP: Durham, NC, 1991)
Ramet, Sabrina P., *Nationalism and Federalism in Yugoslavia, 1962–1991* Second edition (Indiana UP: Bloomington, Indiana, 1992)
Ramet, Sabrina P., *Balkan Babel: Politics, Culture and Religion in Yugoslavia* (Westview: Boulder, Colorado, 1992)
Rathfelder, Erich (editor), *Krieg auf dem Balkan: Die europäische Verantwortung* (Rowohlt Verlag: Reinbek bei Hamburg, 1992)
Razumovsky, Andreas Graf, *Ein Kampf um Belgrad: Tito und die jugoslawische Wirklichkeit* (Ullstein Verlag: Berlin, 1980)
Roberts, Walter R., *Tito, Mihailović and the Allies, 1941–1945* second edition with a new foreword by the author (Duke UP: Durham, NC, 1987)
Rosdolsky Roman, *Engels and the 'Nonhistoric' Peoples: The National Question in the Revolution of 1848* translated and edited by John-Paul Himka (Critique Books: Glasgow, 1987)
Rothschild, Joseph, *East-Central Europe between the Two World Wars* (Washington UP: Seattle, 1974)
Rusinow, Denison I., *The Yugoslav Experiment, 1948–1974* (University of California Press: Berkeley, 1977)
R.W. Seton-Watson, *Disraeli, Gladstone and the Eastern Question: A Study in Diplomacy and Party Politics* (Macmillan: London, 1935)
Shannon, Richard, *Gladstone and the Bulgarian Agitation, 1876* (Harvester Press: Hassocks, 1975)
Shannon, Richard, *The Crisis of Imperialism, 1865–1915* paperback edition (Granada: St Albans, 1976)

Simms, Brendan, *Yugoslavia: The Case for Intervention* (Bow Group: London, 1993)

SIPRI, *SIPRI Yearbook 1993: World Armaments and Disarmament* (Stockholm International Peace Research Institute/OUP: Oxford, 1993)

Sirc, Ljubo, *Between Hitler & Tito: Nazi Occupation and Communist Oppression* (André Deutsch: London, 1989)

Stefan, Ljubica, *From Fairy Tale to Holocaust: Serbia: Quisling Collaboration with the Occupier during the Period of the Third Reich* with reference to Genocide against the Jewish People (Zagreb, 1993)

Steinberg, Jonathan, *All or Nothing: The Axis and the Holocaust, 1941–43* (Routledge; London, 1990)

Sunjić, Melita H., *Woher der Hass? Kroaten und Slowenen kämpfen um Selbstbestimmung* (Amalthea Verlag: Vienna, 1992)

Thompson, Mark, *A Paper House: The Ending of Yugoslavia* (Hutchinson Radius: London, 1992)

Tomasevich, Jozo, *War and Revolution in Yugoslavia, 1941–1945: The Chetniks* (Stanford, Calif., 1975)

Veinstein, Gilles (editor), *Salonique, 1850–1918: La 'ville des Juifs' et le réveil des Balkans* (Éditions Autrement: Paris, 1992)

Williamson Jr, Samuel R., *Austria-Hungary and the Origins of the First World War* (Macmillan: London, 1991)

Wilson, Duncan, *The Life and Times of Vuk Stefanović Karadžić, 1787–1864: Literacy, Literature and National Independence in Serbia* (OUP: Oxford, 1970)

Wimmer, Michaela, Braun, Stefan, & Spiering, Joachim, *Brennpunkt Jugoslawien: Der Vielvölkerstaat in der Krise – Hintergründe, Geschichte, Analysen* (Wilhelm Heyne Verlag: Munich, 1991)

Winkler, Willi (editor), *Europa im Krieg: Die Debatte um den Krieg im ehemaligen Jugoslawien* (Suhrkamp: Frankfurt-am-Main, 1992)

Yelen, Anne, *Kossovo, 1389–1989: Bataille pour les droits de l'âme* (L'Âge d'Homme: Lausanne, 1989)

Zametica, John, *The Yugoslav Conflict* (IISS/Brassey: London, 1992)

Articles

Anderson, Scott, ' "With friends like these . . ." The OSS and the British in Yugoslavia' in *Intelligence and National Security* 8 (April 1993), pp. 140–171

Banac, Ivo, 'Political Change and National Diversity' in Stephen R. Graubard (editor), *Eastern Europe . . . Central Europe . . . Europe* (Westview: Boulder, Colorado, 1991), pp. 145–164

Banac, Ivo, 'Post-Communism as Post-Yugoslavism: The Yugoslav Non-

Revolutions of 1989–1990' in Ivo Banac (editor), *Eastern Europe in Revolution* (Cornell UP: Ithaca, NY, 1992), pp. 168–187

Bombelles, Joseph T., 'Federal Aid to the Less Developed Areas of Yugoslavia' in *East European Politics and Societies* 5 (Fall 1991), pp. 439–465

Bosnitch, Sava D., 'The Cult of Tito's Personality, 1943–?' in *South Slav Journal* volume 13 nos 47–48 (Spring-Summer 1991), pp. 20–38

Clissold, Stephen, 'Murder in Marseilles' in *South Slav Journal* volume 7 nos 23–24 (Spring-Summer 1984), pp. 18–26

Ferfila, Bogomil, 'Yugoslavia: Confederation or Disintegration?' in *Problems of Communism* 40 (July-August 1991), pp. 18–30

Gagnon Jr, V.P., 'Yugoslavia: Prospects for Stability' in *Foreign Affairs* 70 (Summer 1991), pp. 17–36

Gati, Charles, 'From Sarajevo to Sarajevo' in *Foreign Affairs* 71 (Fall 1992), pp. 64–78

Golubović, Zagorka, 'Yugoslav Society and "Socialism": The Present-Day Crisis of the Yugoslav System and the Possibilities for Evolution' in Ferenc Fehér & Andrew Arato (editors), *Crisis and Reform in Eastern Europe* (Transaction Publishers: New Brunswick, NJ, 1991), pp. 393–454

Glynn, Patrick, 'Yugoblunder' in *The New Republic* (24 February 1992), pp. 15–17

Gow, James, 'One Year of War in Bosnia and Hercegovina' in *RFE/RL Research Report* 2^{23} (4 June 1993), pp. 1–13.

Heppell, Muriel, 'Dobrica Ćosić and the "Yugoslav Idea" ' in *South Slav Journal* volume 7 nos. 23–24 (Spring-Summer 1984), pp. 2–12

Irvine, Jill A., 'Tito, Hebrang, and the Croat Question, 1943–1944' in *East European Politics and Societies* volume 5 (Spring 1991), pp. 306–340

Joffe, Josef, 'Collective Security and the Future of Europe: Failed Dreams and Dead Ends' in *Survival* 34 (Spring 1992), pp. 36–50

Kraft, Evan 'Yugoslavia 1986–1988: Transition to Crisis' in Ferenc Fehér & Andrew Arato (editors), *Crisis and Reform in Eastern Europe* (Transaction Publishers: New Brunswick, NJ, 1991), pp. 455–480

Krakhmal'nikova, Zoya, 'Russophobia, Antisemitism and Christianity: Some Remarks on an Anti-Russian Idea' in *Religion, State and Society* 20 (1992), pp. 7–28

Larrabee, F. Stephen, 'Instability and Change in the Balkans' in *Survival* 34 (Summer 1992), pp. 31–49

Lough, John, 'The Place of the "Near Abroad" in Russian Foreign Policy' in *REF/RL Research Report* 2 (March 1993), pp. 21–29

Lytle, Paula Franklin, 'U.S. Policy Toward the Demise of Yugoslavia: The "Virus of Nationalism" ' in *East European Politics and Societies* 6 (Fall 1993), pp. 303–318

Mackenzie, David, 'Panslavism in Practice: Chernaiev in Serbia (1876)' in *Journal of Modern History* 36 (1964), pp. 279–297
Markus, Ustina, 'Ukraine and the Yugoslav Conflict' in *RFE/RL Research Report* 2 (23 July 1993)
Meier, Viktor, 'Yugoslavia's National Question' in Lyman H. Letgers (editor), *Eastern Europe: Transformation and Revolution, 1945–1991* (D.C. Heath: Lexington, Ma., 1992), pp. 102–114
Newhouse, John, 'The Diplomatic Round. Dodging the Problem' in *The New Yorker* (24 August 1992), pp. 60–71
Pelosse, Valentin, 'La mémoriale de Josip Broz Tito' in Alain Brossat, Sonia Combe, Jean-Yves Potel & Jean-Charles Szurek (editors), *À l'Est la Mémoire retrouvée* (La Découverte: Paris, 1990), pp. 229–245
Pipa, Arshi, 'Serbian Apologetics: Marković on Kosovo' in *Telos* (1991) pp. 168–176
Ramet, Sabrina P., 'Primordial Ethnicity or Modern Nationalism: The Case of Yugoslavia's Muslims, reconsidered' in *South Slav Journal* volume 13 nos 47–48 (Spring-Summer 1991), pp. 1–20
Ramet, Sabrina P., 'War in the Balkans' in *Foreign Affairs* 71 (Fall 1992), pp. 79–98
Remington, Robin Alison, 'The Military as an Interest Group in Yugoslav Politics' in Dale R. Herspring & Ivan Volgyes (editors), *Civil–Military Relations in Communist Systems* (Westview: Boulder, Colorado, 1978), pp. 181–199
Rogel, Carola, 'Slovenia's Independence: A Reversal of History' in *Problems of Communism* 40 (July-August 1991), pp. 31–40
Ströhm, Carl Gustaf, 'Blauhelme verdienen am Leid des Krieges' in *Die Welt* (23 November 1992)
Trotsky, Leon, *The Balkan Wars, 1912–13* translated by Brian Pearce, edited by George Weissman & Duncan Williams (Pathfinder Press: New York, 1981)
Wohlstetter, Albert, 'Bosnia as Future', unpublished paper (July 1993)
Wrede, Hans-Heinrich, ' "Friendly Concern" – Europe's Decision-making on the Recognition of Slovenia and Croatia' in *The Oxford International Review* iv (Spring 1993), pp. 30–32
'X' (a Foreign Office memorandum, summer 1993)
Zelikow, Philip, 'The new Concert of Europe' in *Survival* 34 (Summer 1992), pp. 12–30

Acknowledgements

Many people have encouraged me, discussed particular issues or given help during the preparation of this book. Although they are in no way responsible for the result, I would like to thank: Anne Applebaum, Bojan Bujić, Edward Cowan, Chris Cviić, Meya Freundlich, Nile Gardiner, Branka Magas, Noel Malcolm, Zeljko Mandić, Keith and Slava Miles, Faris and Senad Nandić, Lord Owen, Ognen Pribićević, Peter Robinson, Sir Michael Rose, Chandler Rosenberger, Drago Stambouk, Johnathan Sunley and Albert Wohlstetter.

Gerry Frost (now the Centre for Policy Studies) and Andrew MacHallam of the Institute for European Defence & Strategic Studies were encouraging and kindly arranged the Research Fellowship from the Bradley Foundation which helped to fund some of the research.

Richard Addis of the *Daily Mail*, Dominic Lawson of the *Spectator*, Charles Moore then at the *Daily Telegraph* and Martha Brandt of the *Wall Street Journal* permitted me to write about the war at various moments and therefore encouraged the production of this book after a fashion, even if Sarah Hannigan, then still at Heinemann, might have preferred her frustrating author to concentrate solely on the text, but she was kind enough to treat him with remarkable good grace.

Norman and Christine Stone put up with more than anyone else but as ever helped more too. My special thanks to them.

Index

AUSTRIA
HUNG
R Drava
SLAVONIA
Osijek
Zagreb
SLOVENIA
CROATIA
Vakovar
R Sava
BOSNIA-
BANJA LUKA
MAGLAJ
BIHAC
HERCEGOVINA
KRAJINA
Zenica
VITEZ
Kiseljak
Maslenica
Knin
Gornji Vakuf
SPLIT
MOSTAR
R Neretva
Metkovic
Dubrovnik
UN Safe Areas from Spring 1993
TERRITORY HELD BY
Serbs in Bosnia and Croatia
Bosnian Croats
Bosnian Muslims
ADRIATIC SEA
ITALY